Takeshi Obata

ART

Tsugumi Ohba

STORY

Platinum End

PLATINVM END

5

CHARACTERS

Mirai Kakehashi

First-year high school student. His parents and brother died in an accident when he was seven. After a painful life with his abusive relatives, he attempted to commit suicide and survived through Nasse's help.

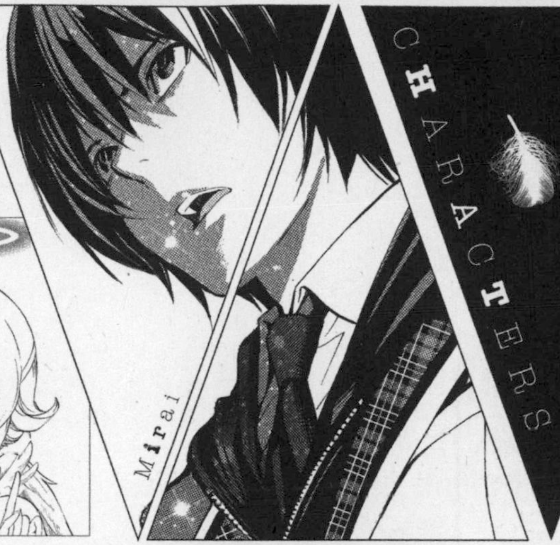
Mirai

Nasse

A special-rank .ngel who wants bring happiness to Mirai's life. ight and bubbly.

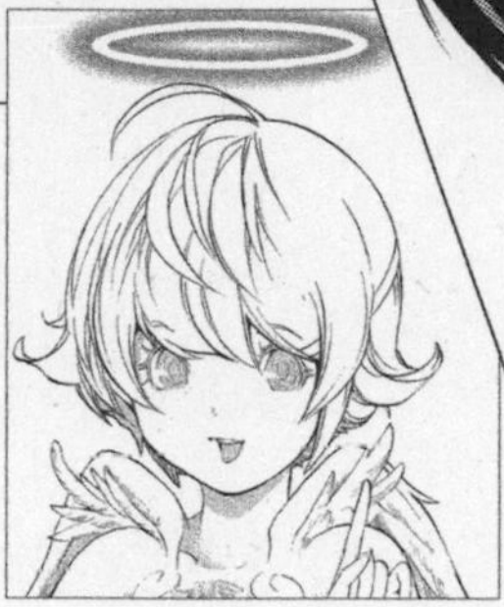

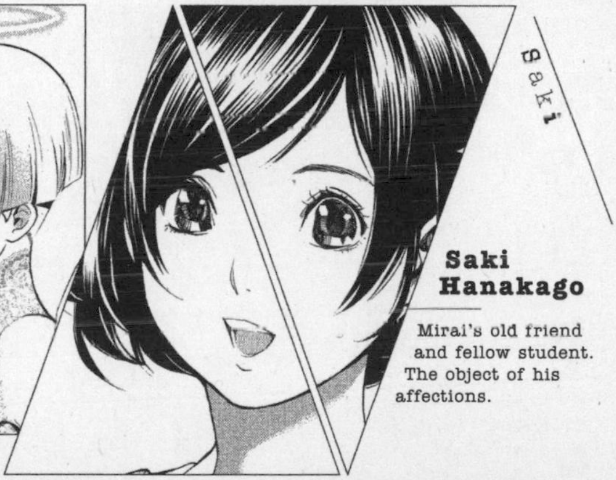
Saki

Saki Hanakago

Mirai's old friend and fellow student. The object of his affections.

Revel

A second-rank .gel who chose .aki as his god candidate.

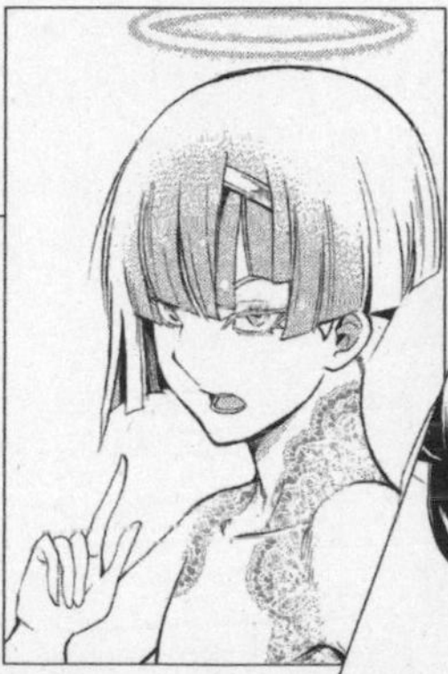

Story

"My time has come.
I leave the seat of god to the next human.
To a younger, fresher power.

The next god shall be selected from
the 13 humans chosen by you 13 angels.

When the chosen human is made the next god,
your angelic duty is finished, and you may live
beside that god in peace.

You have 999 days remaining..."

CHARACTERS

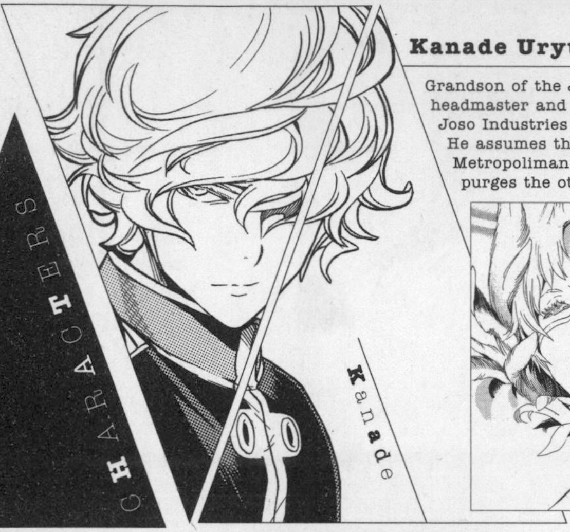
Kanade

Kanade Uryu

Grandson of the Joso Academy headmaster and son of the Joso Industries president. He assumes the form of the Metropoliman character and purges the other god candidates.

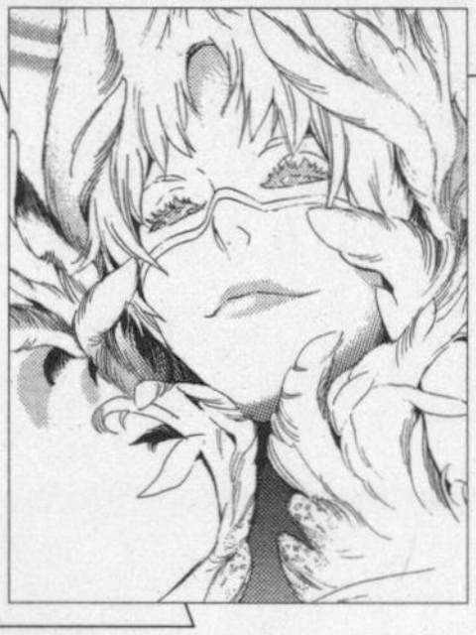

Meyza

The special-rank angel who chose Kanade. For unknown reason she was elevated from rankless to the top special rank.

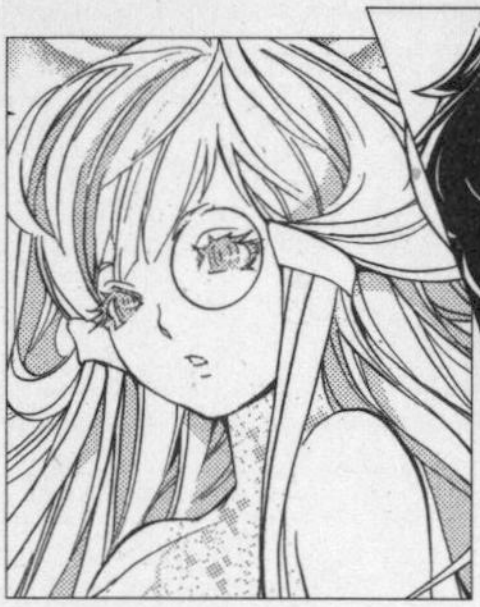

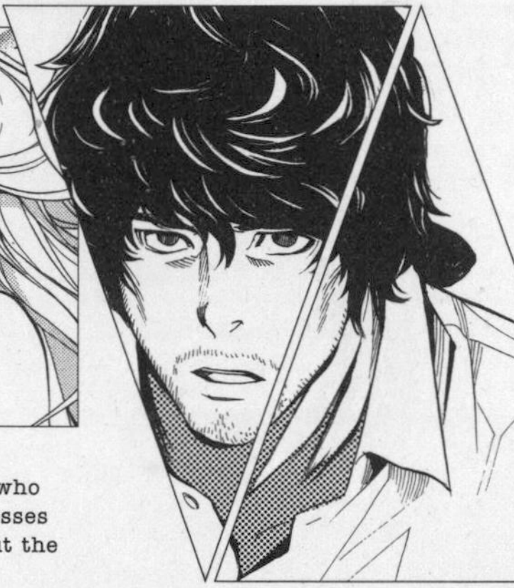
Nanato

Nanato Mukaido

An apparel company employee who leaves work due to late-stage cancer. A family man with a wife and kid.

Baret

The first-rank angel who chose Mukaido. Possesses great knowledge about the celestial world.

Story

PROMISE

Mirai accepts her feelings and tells her they should work together like they did as children.

HER CONFESSION

Saki reveals that she joined her classmates in bullying Mirai. She chose death out of her guilt.

CLASH

Mirai joins Mukaido in the fight against Metropoliman, and witnesses the face behind the mask.

CONTENTS

5

#13 Face of Determination

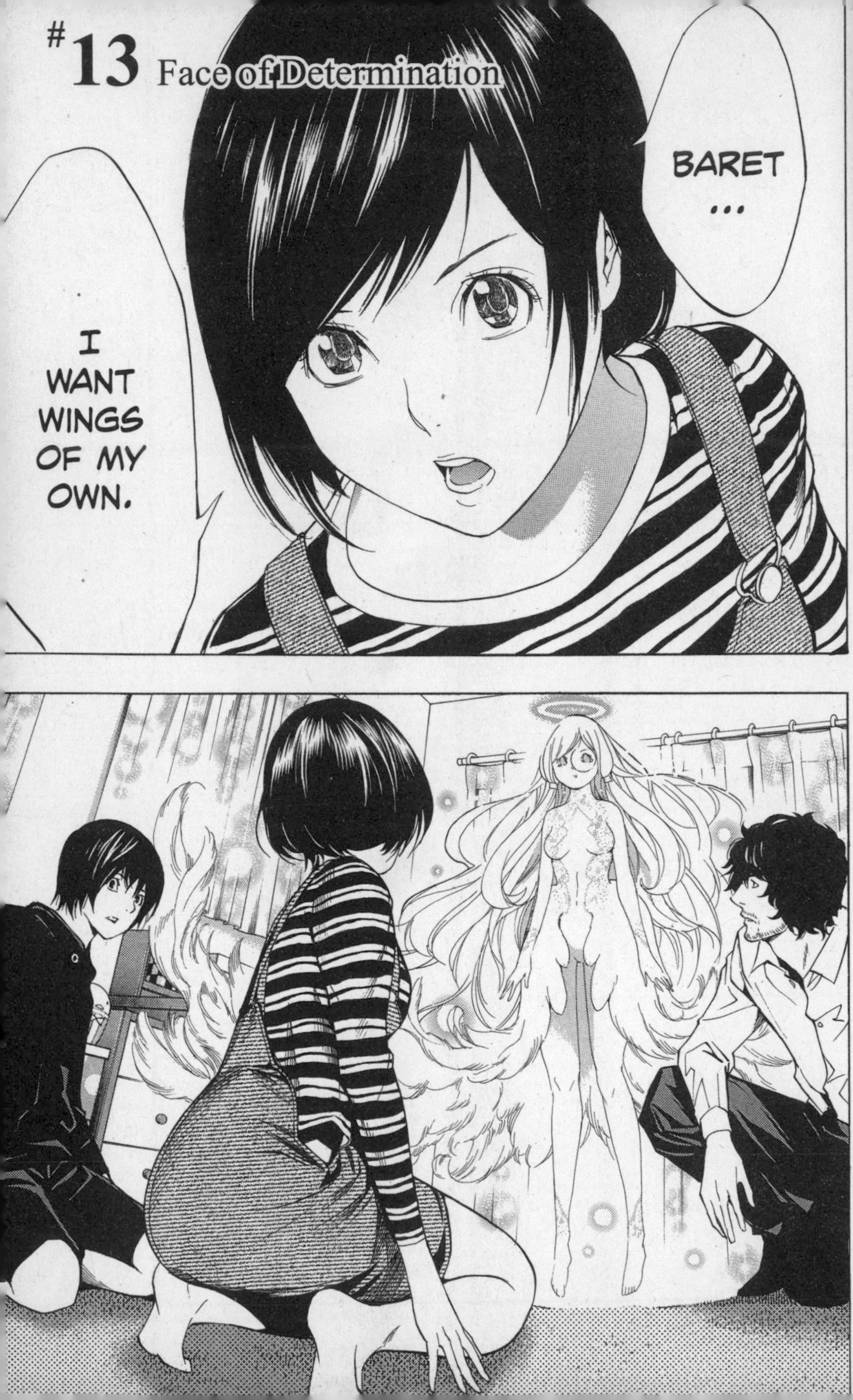
BARET ...
I WANT WINGS OF MY OWN.

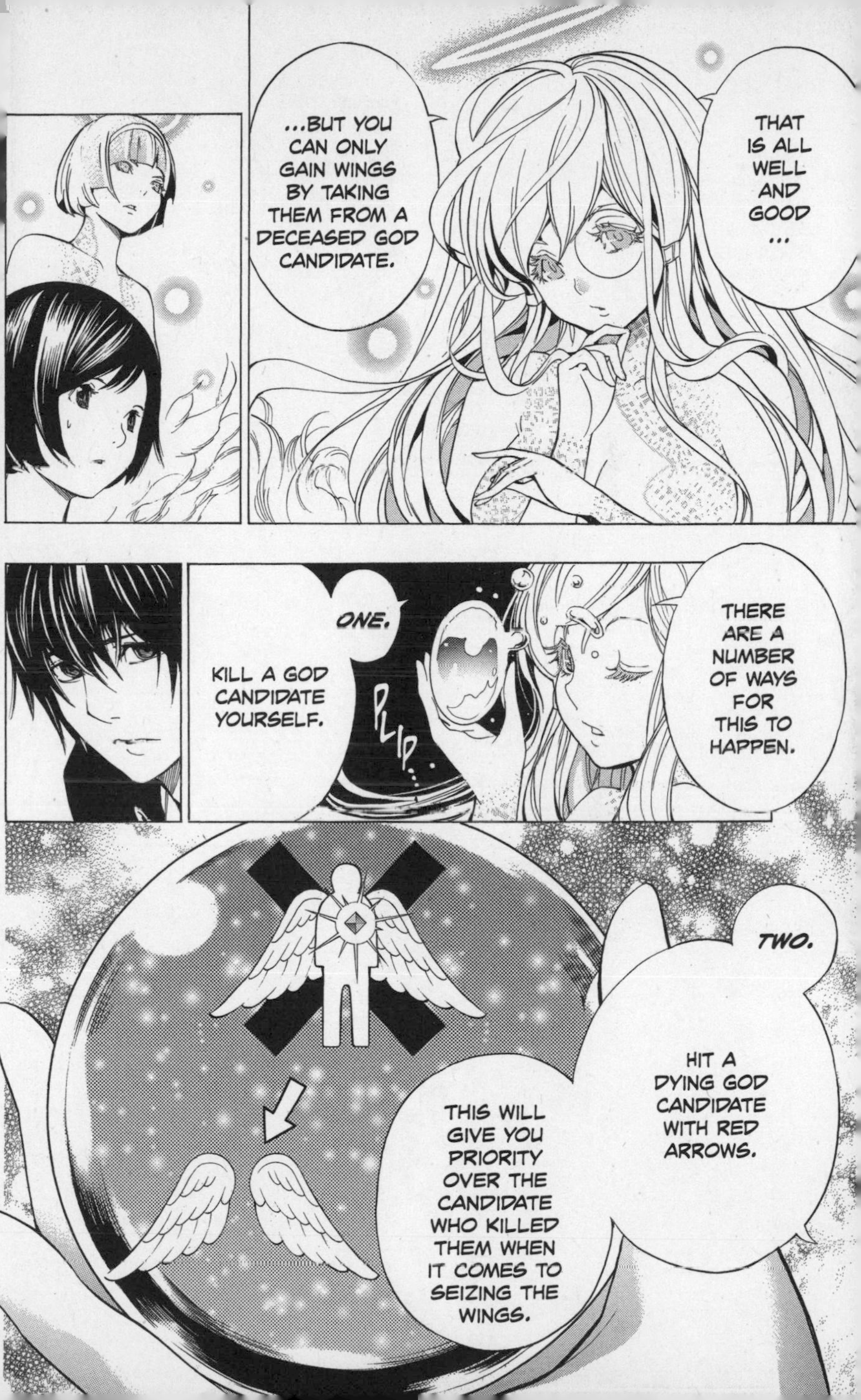
THAT IS ALL WELL AND GOOD ...
...BUT YOU CAN ONLY GAIN WINGS BY TAKING THEM FROM A DECEASED GOD CANDIDATE.
THERE ARE A NUMBER OF WAYS FOR THIS TO HAPPEN.
PLIP...
ONE.
KILL A GOD CANDIDATE YOURSELF.
TWO.
HIT A DYING GOD CANDIDATE WITH RED ARROWS.
THIS WILL GIVE YOU PRIORITY OVER THE CANDIDATE WHO KILLED THEM WHEN IT COMES TO SEIZING THE WINGS.

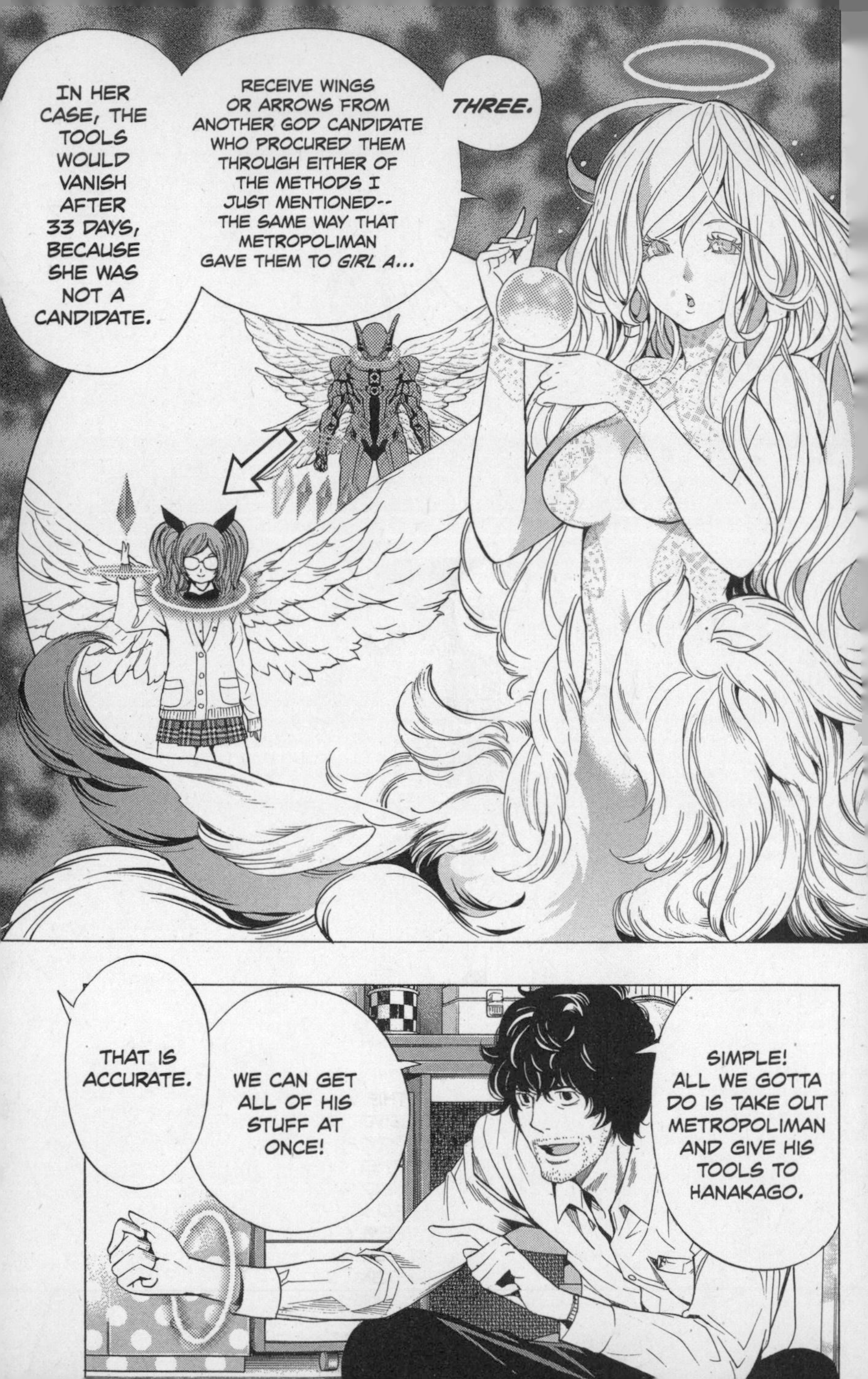
THREE.
RECEIVE WINGS OR ARROWS FROM ANOTHER GOD CANDIDATE WHO PROCURED THEM THROUGH EITHER OF THE METHODS I JUST MENTIONED-- THE SAME WAY THAT METROPOLIMAN GAVE THEM TO GIRL A...
IN HER CASE, THE TOOLS WOULD VANISH AFTER 33 DAYS, BECAUSE SHE WAS NOT A CANDIDATE.
SIMPLE! ALL WE GOTTA DO IS TAKE OUT METROPOLIMAN AND GIVE HIS TOOLS TO HANAKAGO.
WE CAN GET ALL OF HIS STUFF AT ONCE!
THAT IS ACCURATE.

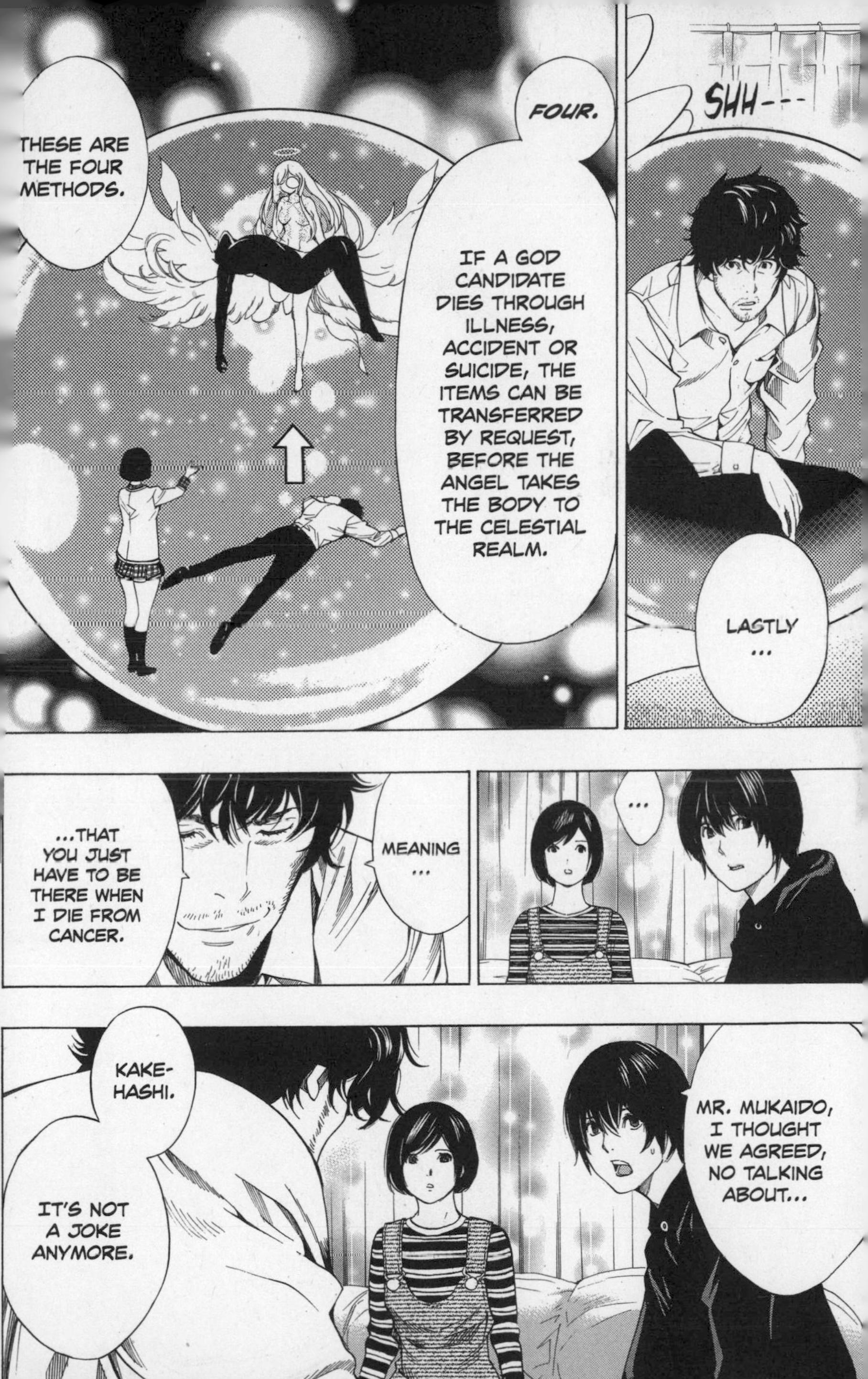
SHH---
LASTLY ...
FOUR.
IF A GOD CANDIDATE DIES THROUGH ILLNESS, ACCIDENT OR SUICIDE, THE ITEMS CAN BE TRANSFERRED BY REQUEST, BEFORE THE ANGEL TAKES THE BODY TO THE CELESTIAL REALM.
THESE ARE THE FOUR METHODS.
...
MEANING ...
...THAT YOU JUST HAVE TO BE THERE WHEN I DIE FROM CANCER.
MR. MUKAIDO, I THOUGHT WE AGREED, NO TALKING ABOUT...
KAKE-HASHI.
IT'S NOT A JOKE ANYMORE.

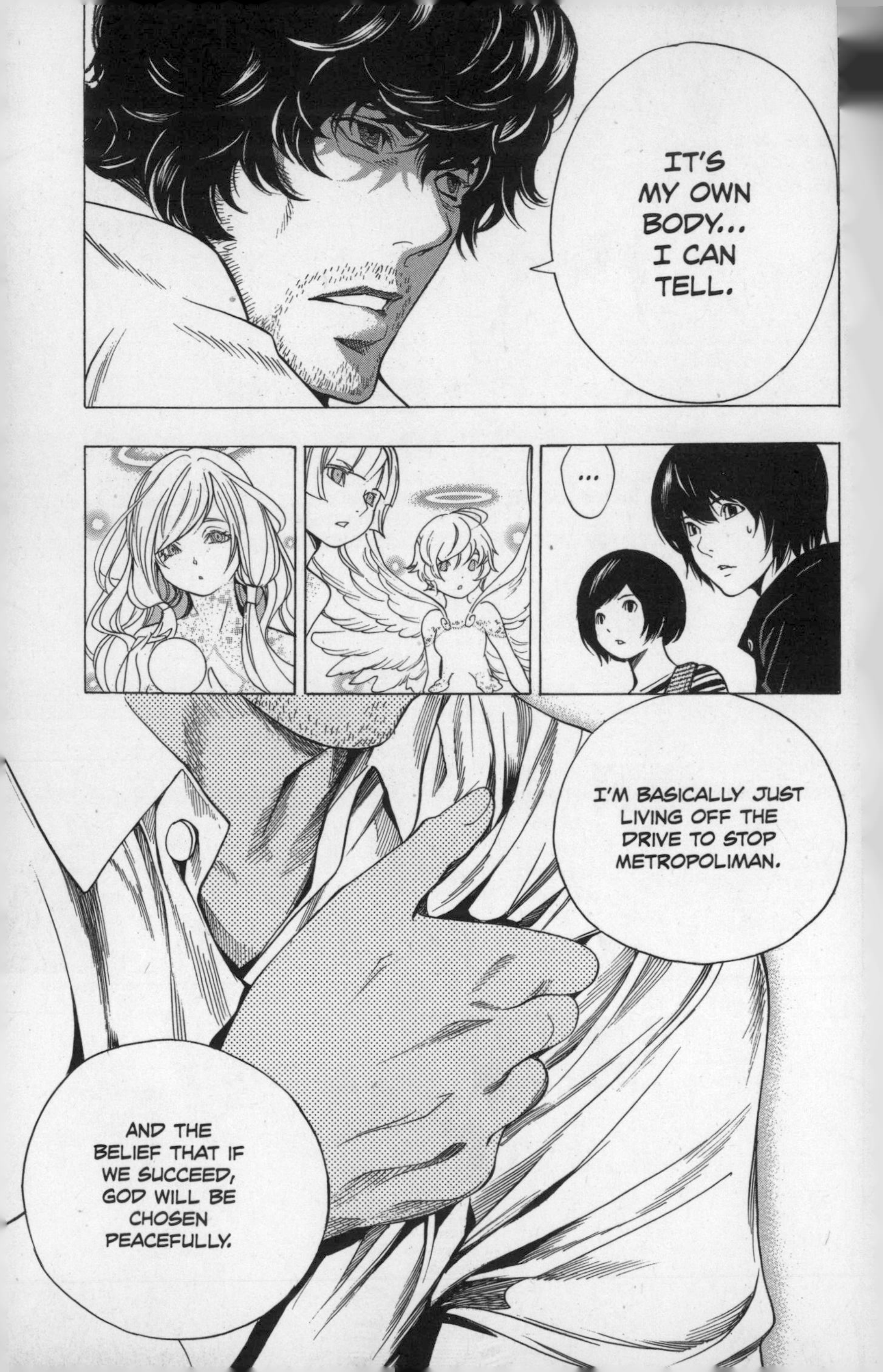
IT'S MY OWN BODY... I CAN TELL.
...
I'M BASICALLY JUST LIVING OFF THE DRIVE TO STOP METROPOLIMAN.
AND THE BELIEF THAT IF WE SUCCEED, GOD WILL BE CHOSEN PEACEFULLY.

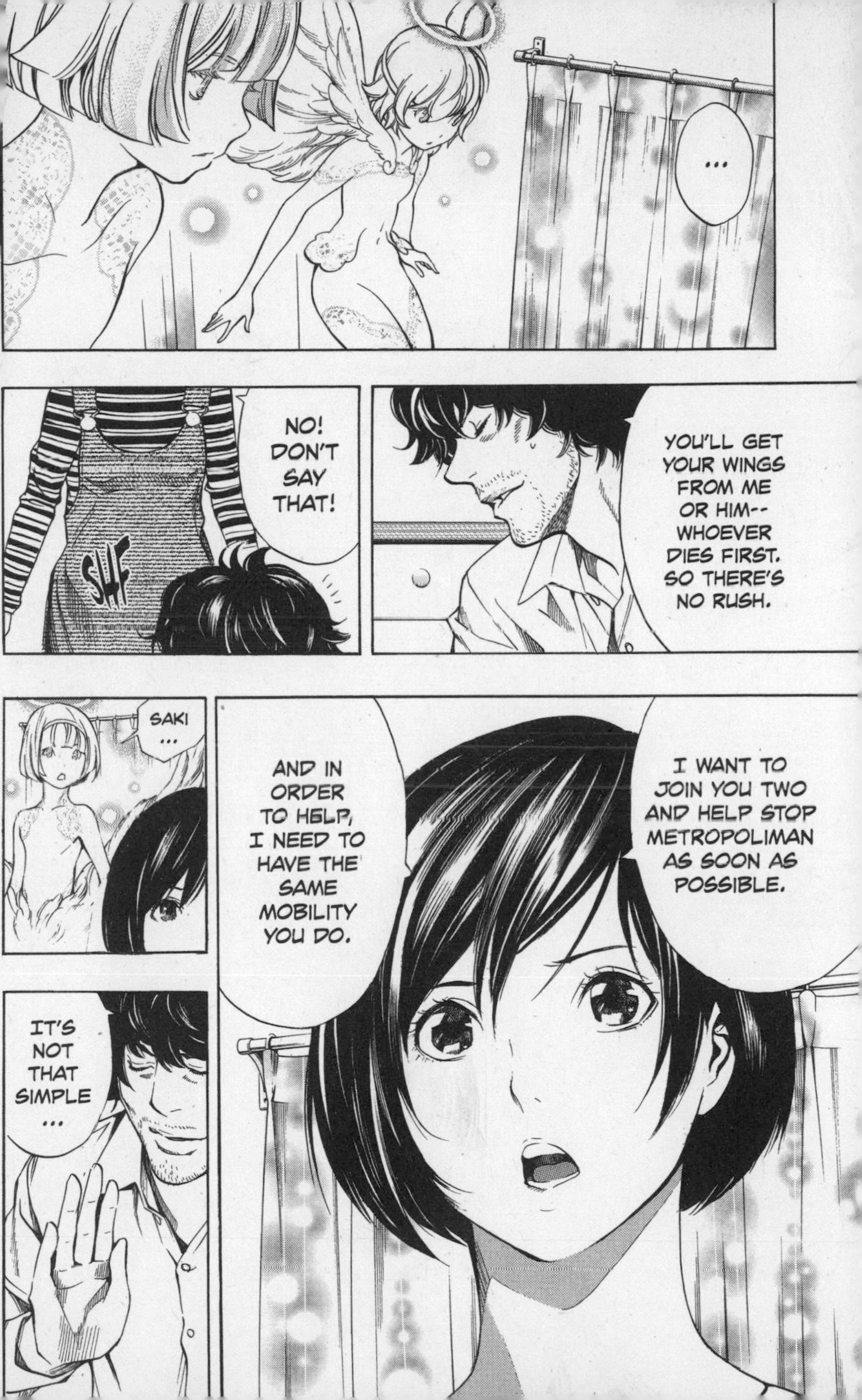
...
YOU'LL GET YOUR WINGS FROM ME OR HIM-- WHOEVER DIES FIRST. SO THERE'S NO RUSH.
NO! DON'T SAY THAT!
I WANT TO JOIN YOU TWO AND HELP STOP METROPOLIMAN AS SOON AS POSSIBLE.
AND IN ORDER TO HELP, I NEED TO HAVE THE SAME MOBILITY YOU DO.
SAKI ...
IT'S NOT THAT SIMPLE ...

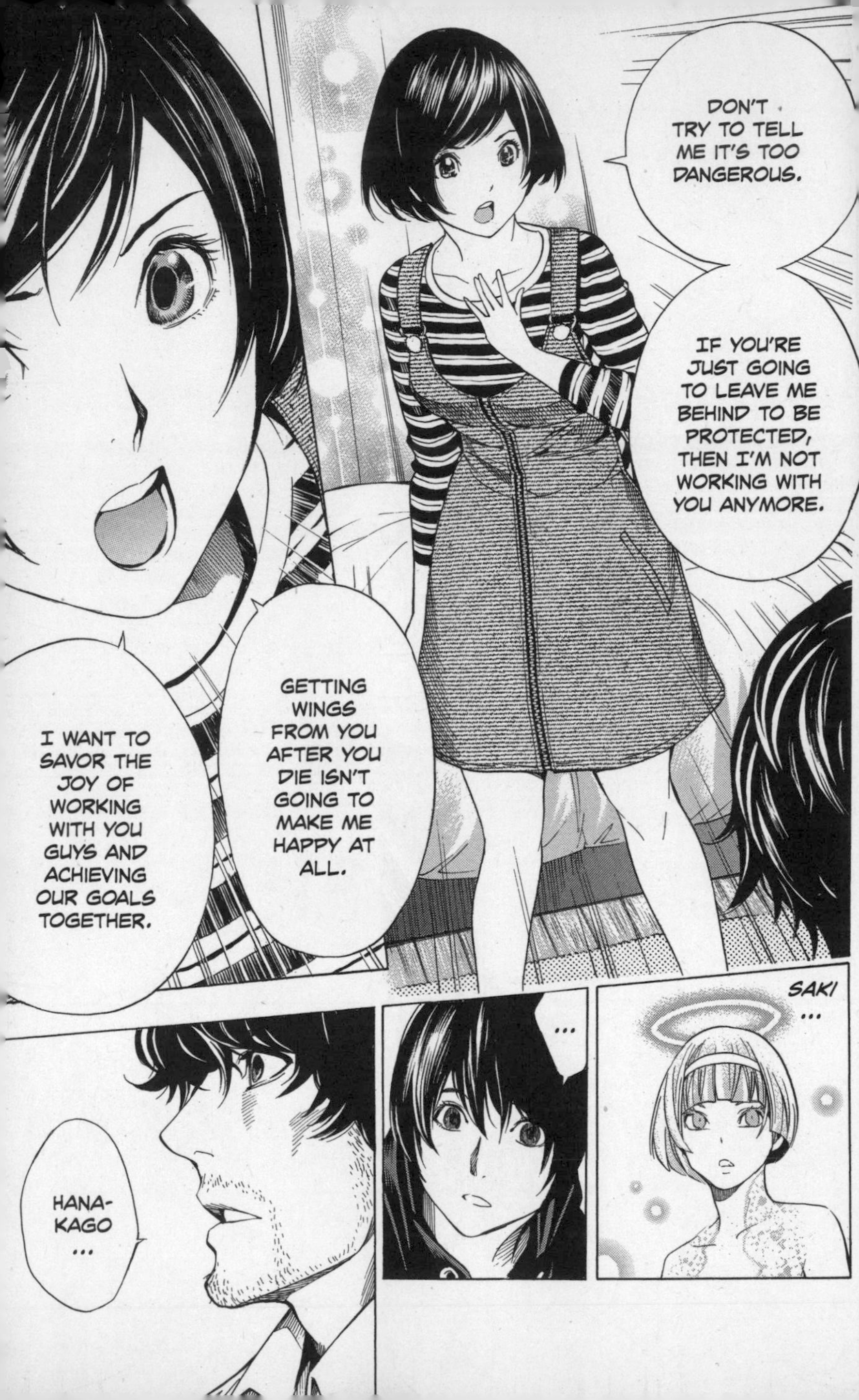
DON'T TRY TO TELL ME IT'S TOO DANGEROUS.
IF YOU'RE JUST GOING TO LEAVE ME BEHIND TO BE PROTECTED, THEN I'M NOT WORKING WITH YOU ANYMORE.
GETTING WINGS FROM YOU AFTER YOU DIE ISN'T GOING TO MAKE ME HAPPY AT ALL.
I WANT TO SAVOR THE JOY OF WORKING WITH YOU GUYS AND ACHIEVING OUR GOALS TOGETHER.
SAKI ...
...
HANA-KAGO ...

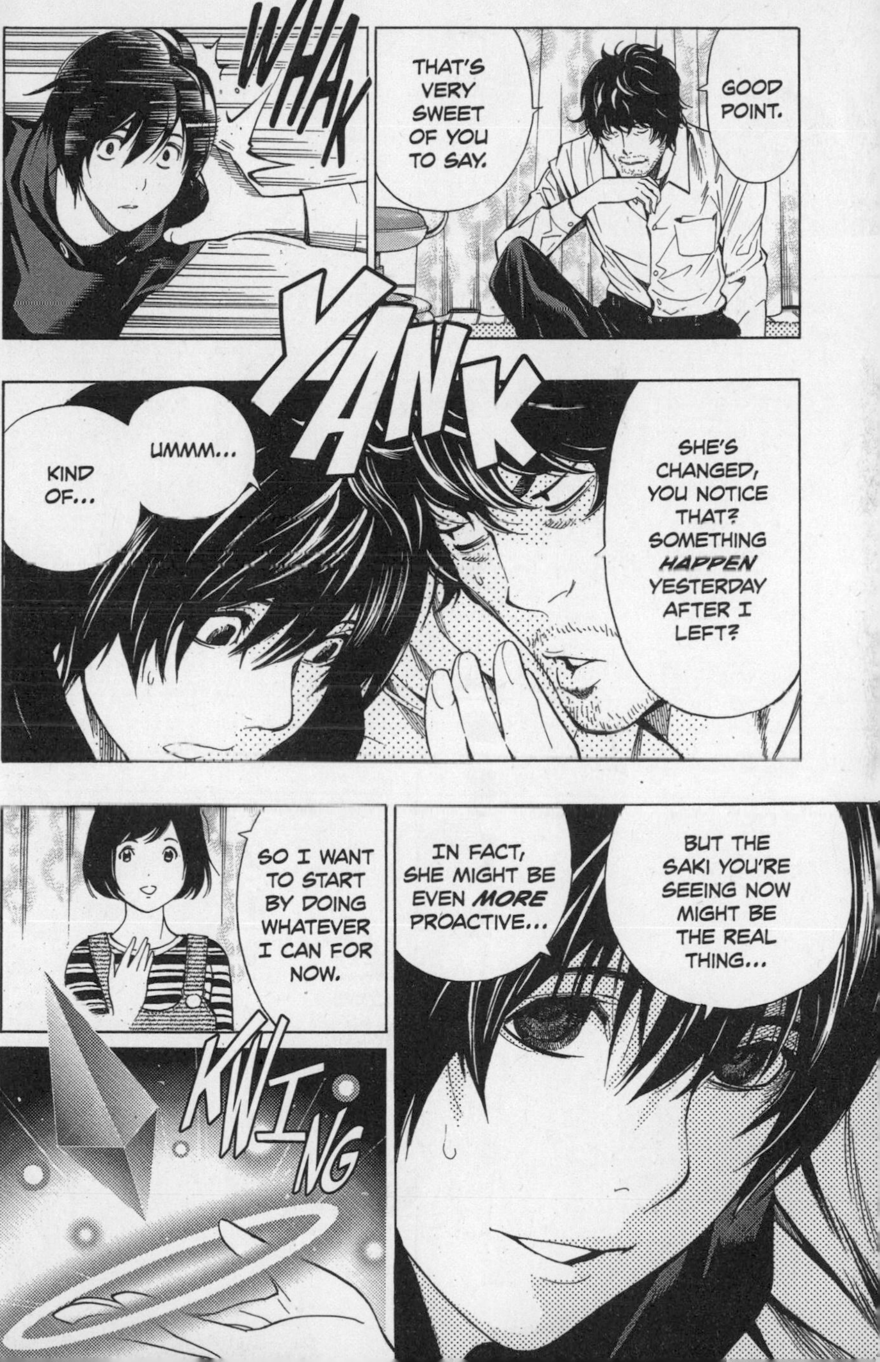
GOOD POINT.
THAT'S VERY SWEET OF YOU TO SAY.
WHAK
YANK
SHE'S CHANGED, YOU NOTICE THAT? SOMETHING *HAPPEN* YESTERDAY AFTER I LEFT?
UMMM...
KIND OF...
BUT THE SAKI YOU'RE SEEING NOW MIGHT BE THE REAL THING...
IN FACT, SHE MIGHT BE EVEN *MORE* PROACTIVE...
SO I WANT TO START BY DOING WHATEVER I CAN FOR NOW.
KWING

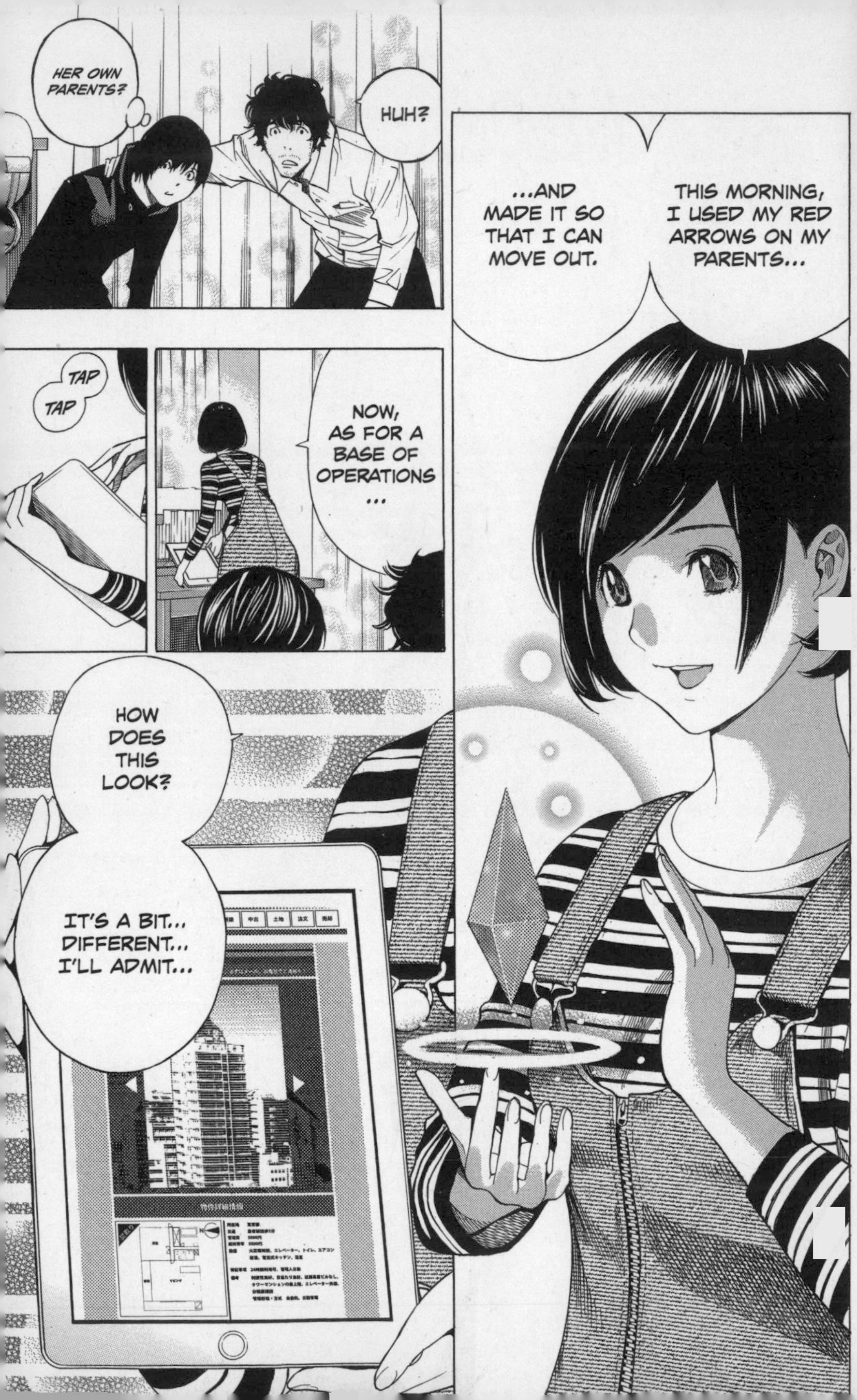
THIS MORNING, I USED MY RED ARROWS ON MY PARENTS...
...AND MADE IT SO THAT I CAN MOVE OUT.
HUH?
HER OWN PARENTS?
NOW, AS FOR A BASE OF OPERATIONS ...
TAP TAP
HOW DOES THIS LOOK?
IT'S A BIT... DIFFERENT... I'LL ADMIT...

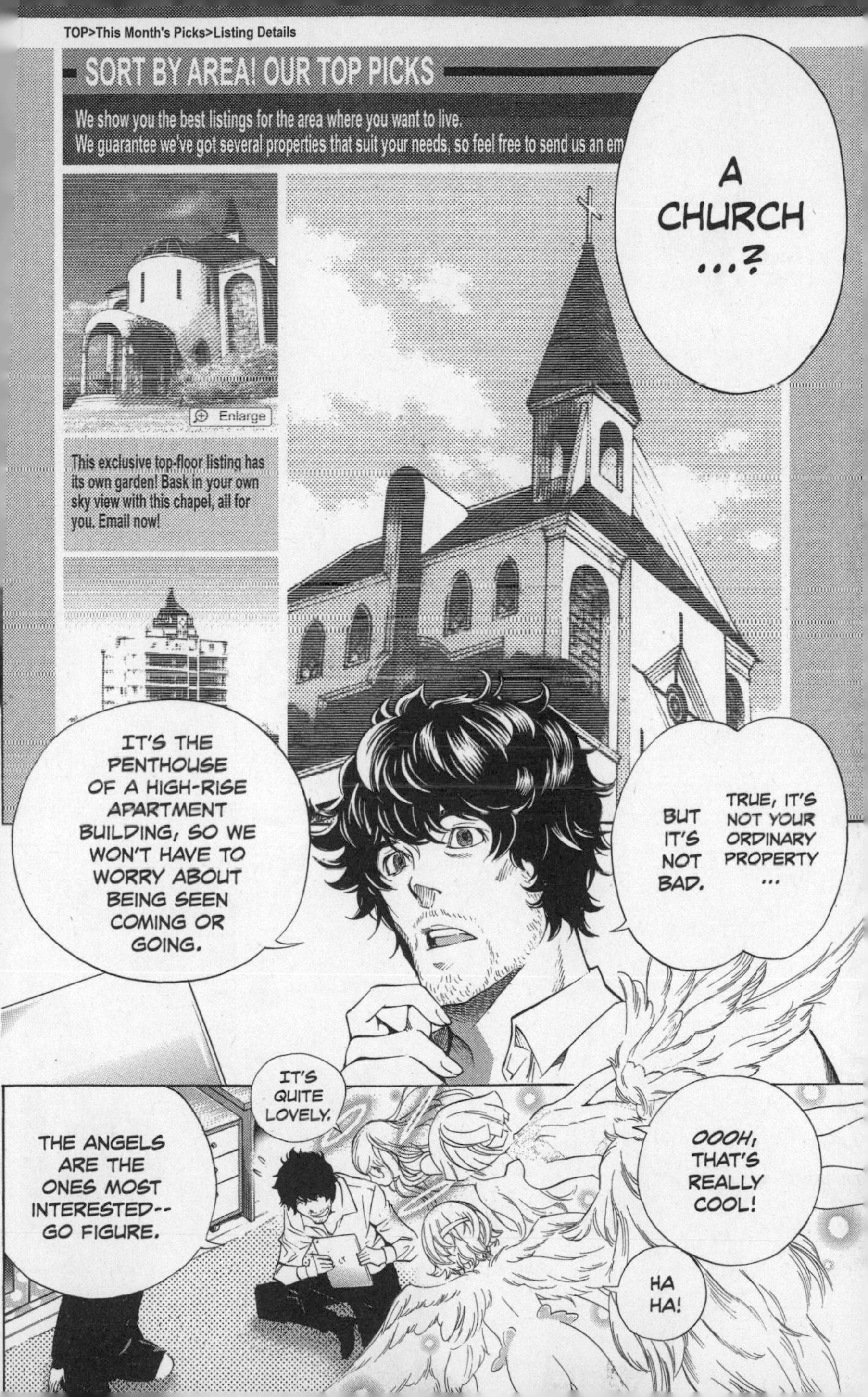
TOP>This Month's Picks>Listing Details
SORT BY AREA! OUR TOP PICKS
We show you the best listings for the area where you want to live.
We guarantee we've got several properties that suit your needs, so feel free to send us an em
Enlarge
This exclusive top-floor listing has its own garden! Bask in your own sky view with this chapel, all for you. Email now!
A CHURCH ...?
TRUE, IT'S NOT YOUR ORDINARY PROPERTY...
BUT IT'S NOT BAD.
IT'S THE PENTHOUSE OF A HIGH-RISE APARTMENT BUILDING, SO WE WON'T HAVE TO WORRY ABOUT BEING SEEN COMING OR GOING.
OOOH, THAT'S REALLY COOL!
HA HA!
IT'S QUITE LOVELY.
THE ANGELS ARE THE ONES MOST INTERESTED-- GO FIGURE.

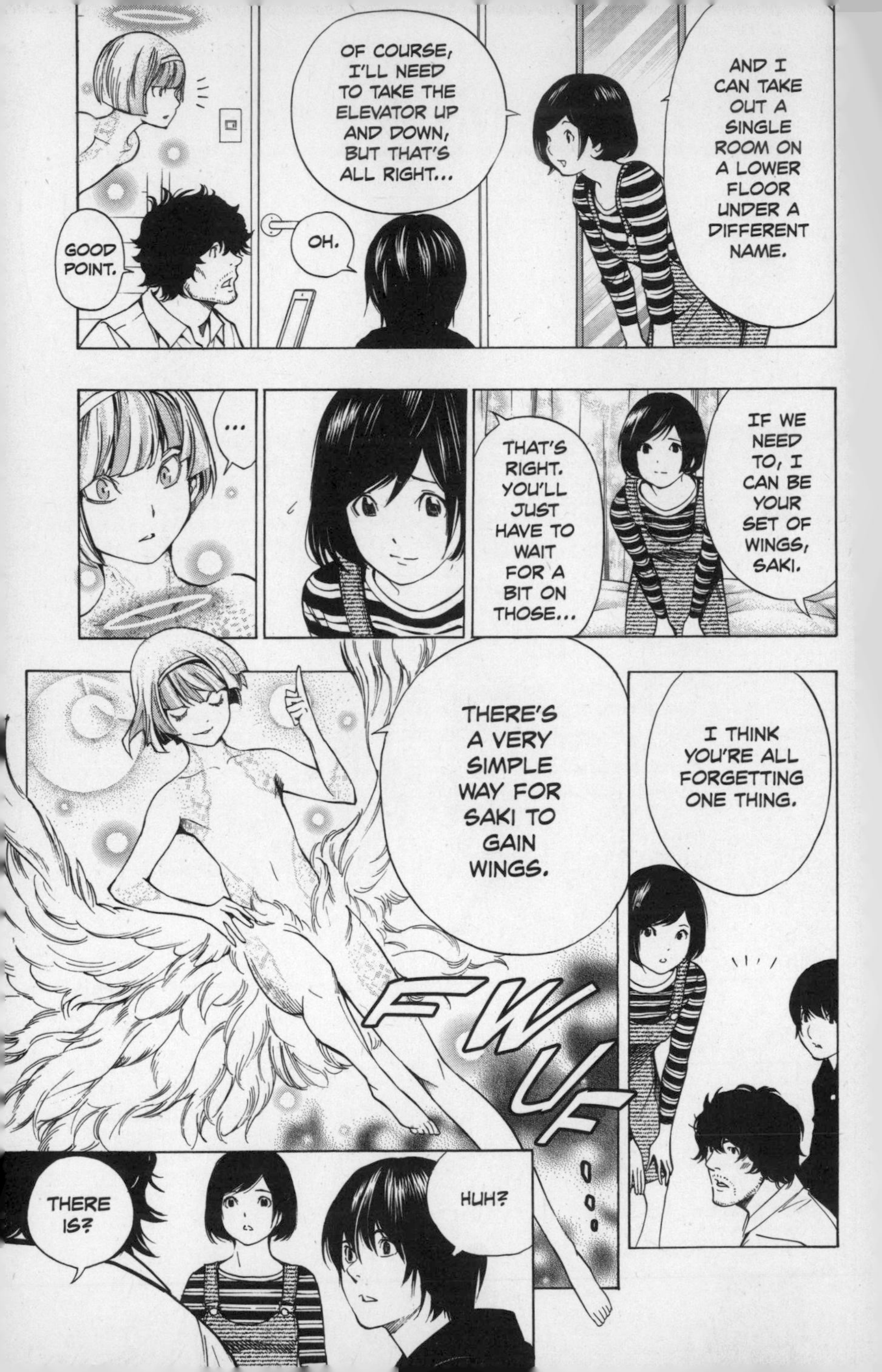
AND I CAN TAKE OUT A SINGLE ROOM ON A LOWER FLOOR UNDER A DIFFERENT NAME.
OF COURSE, I'LL NEED TO TAKE THE ELEVATOR UP AND DOWN, BUT THAT'S ALL RIGHT...
OH.
GOOD POINT.
IF WE NEED TO, I CAN BE YOUR SET OF WINGS, SAKI.
THAT'S RIGHT. YOU'LL JUST HAVE TO WAIT FOR A BIT ON THOSE...
...
I THINK YOU'RE ALL FORGETTING ONE THING.
THERE'S A VERY SIMPLE WAY FOR SAKI TO GAIN WINGS.
FWUF
HUH?
THERE IS?

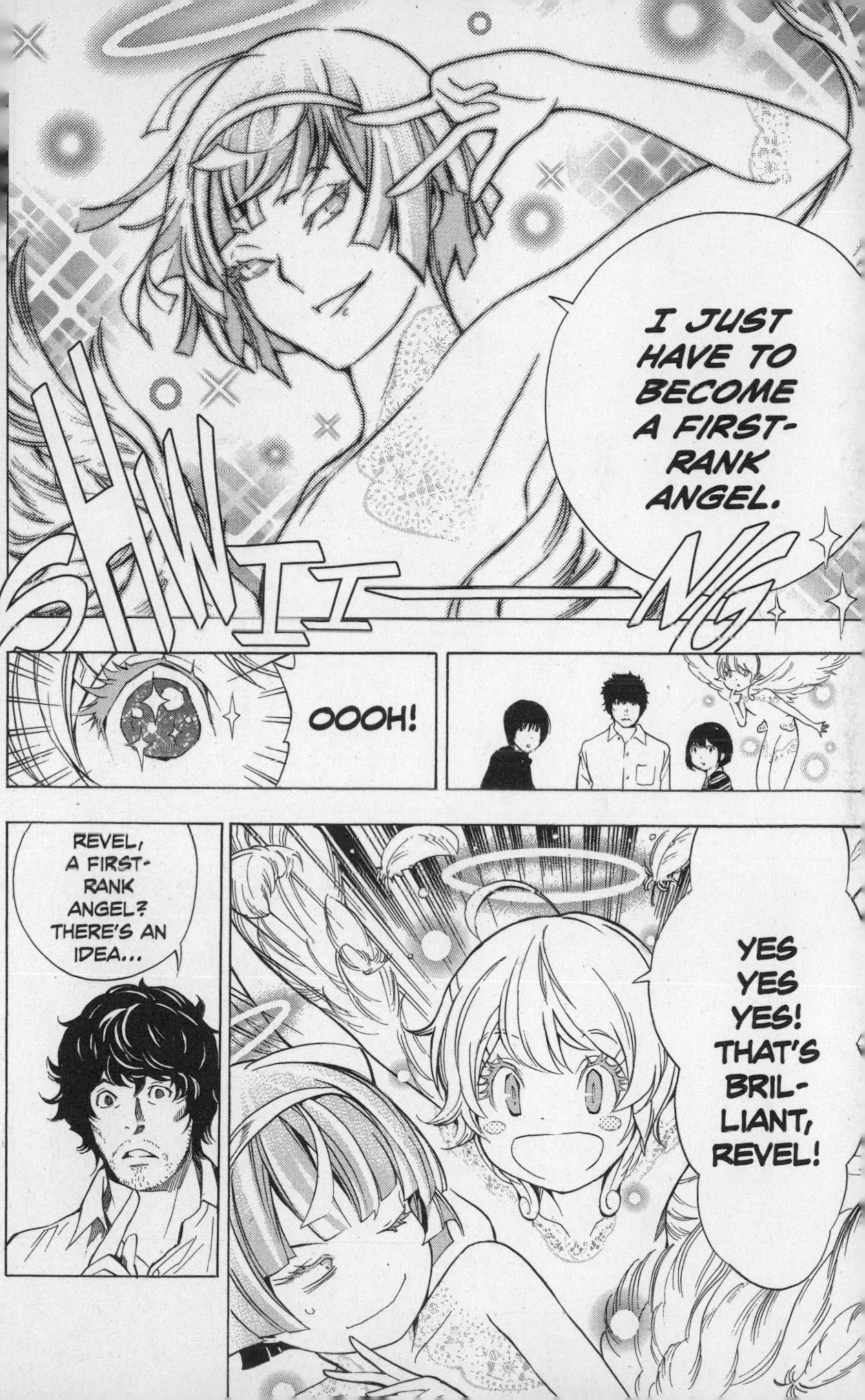
I JUST HAVE TO BECOME A FIRST-RANK ANGEL.
SHWII—NG
OOOH!
YES YES YES! THAT'S BRIL-LIANT, REVEL!
REVEL, A FIRST-RANK ANGEL? THERE'S AN IDEA...

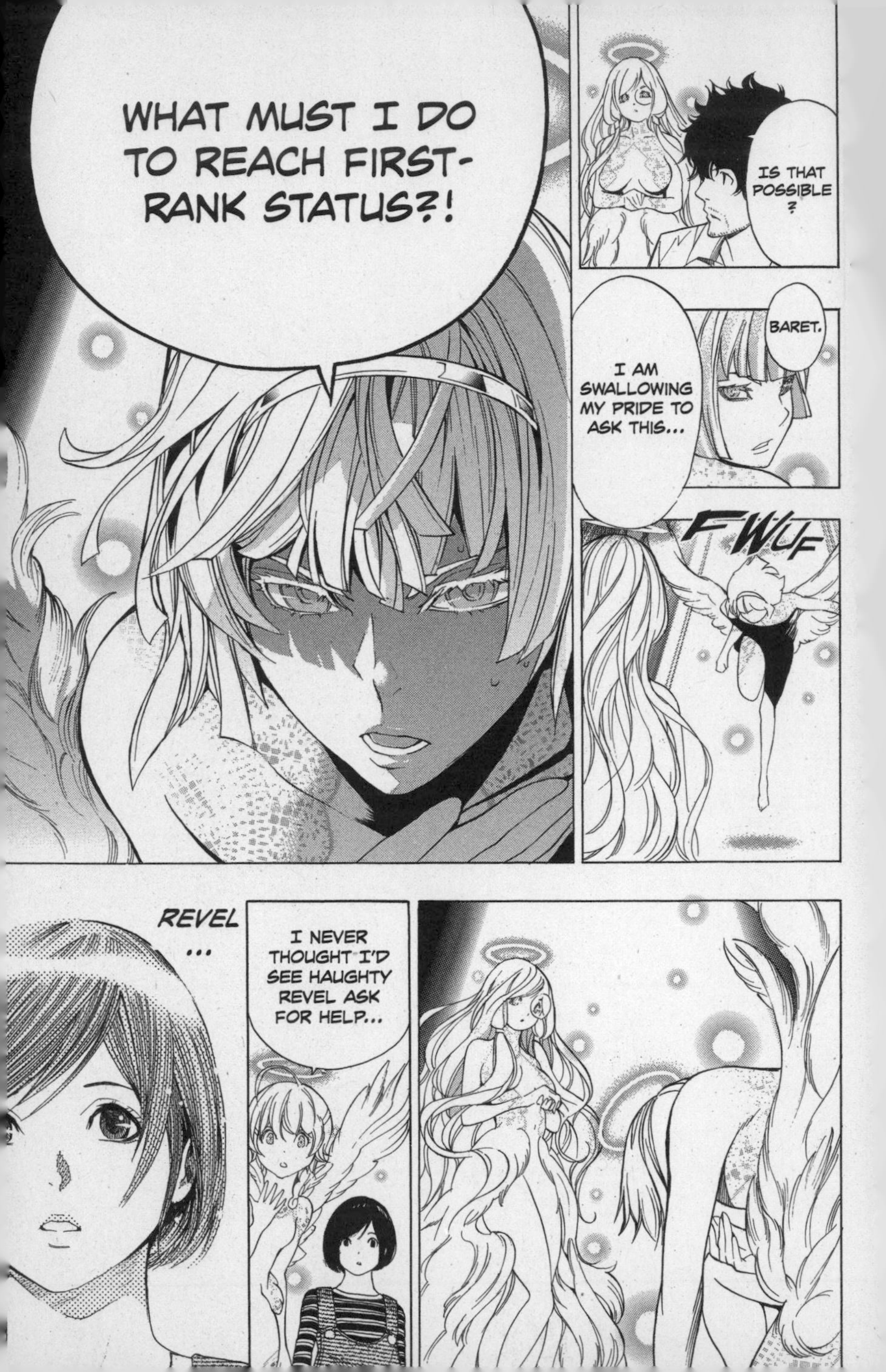

IS THAT POSSIBLE?
BARET.
I AM SWALLOWING MY PRIDE TO ASK THIS...
FWUF
WHAT MUST I DO TO REACH FIRST-RANK STATUS?!
I NEVER THOUGHT I'D SEE HAUGHTY REVEL ASK FOR HELP...
REVEL...

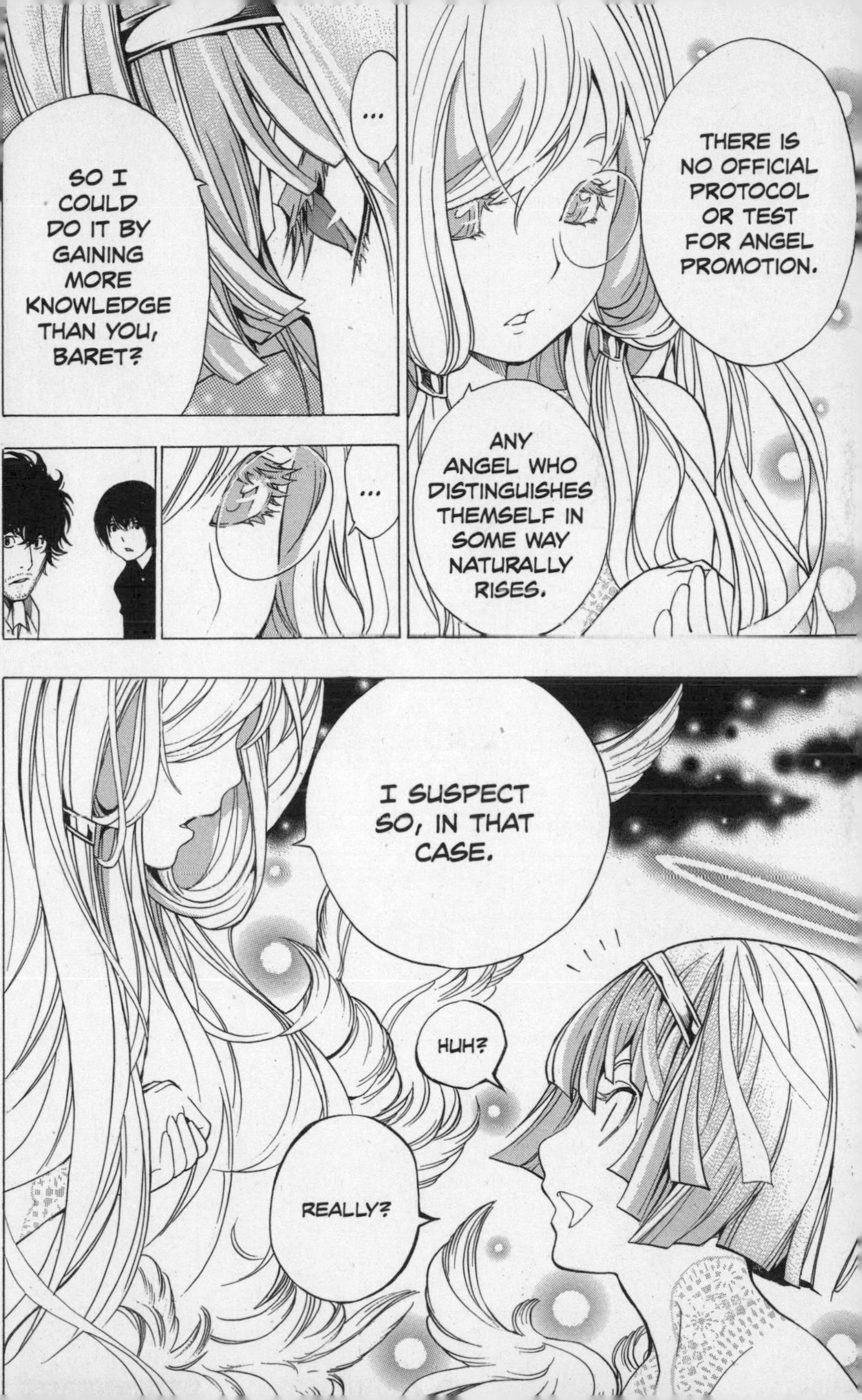
THERE IS NO OFFICIAL PROTOCOL OR TEST FOR ANGEL PROMOTION.
ANY ANGEL WHO DISTINGUISHES THEMSELF IN SOME WAY NATURALLY RISES.
...
SO I COULD DO IT BY GAINING MORE KNOWLEDGE THAN YOU, BARET?
...
I SUSPECT SO, IN THAT CASE.
HUH?
REALLY?

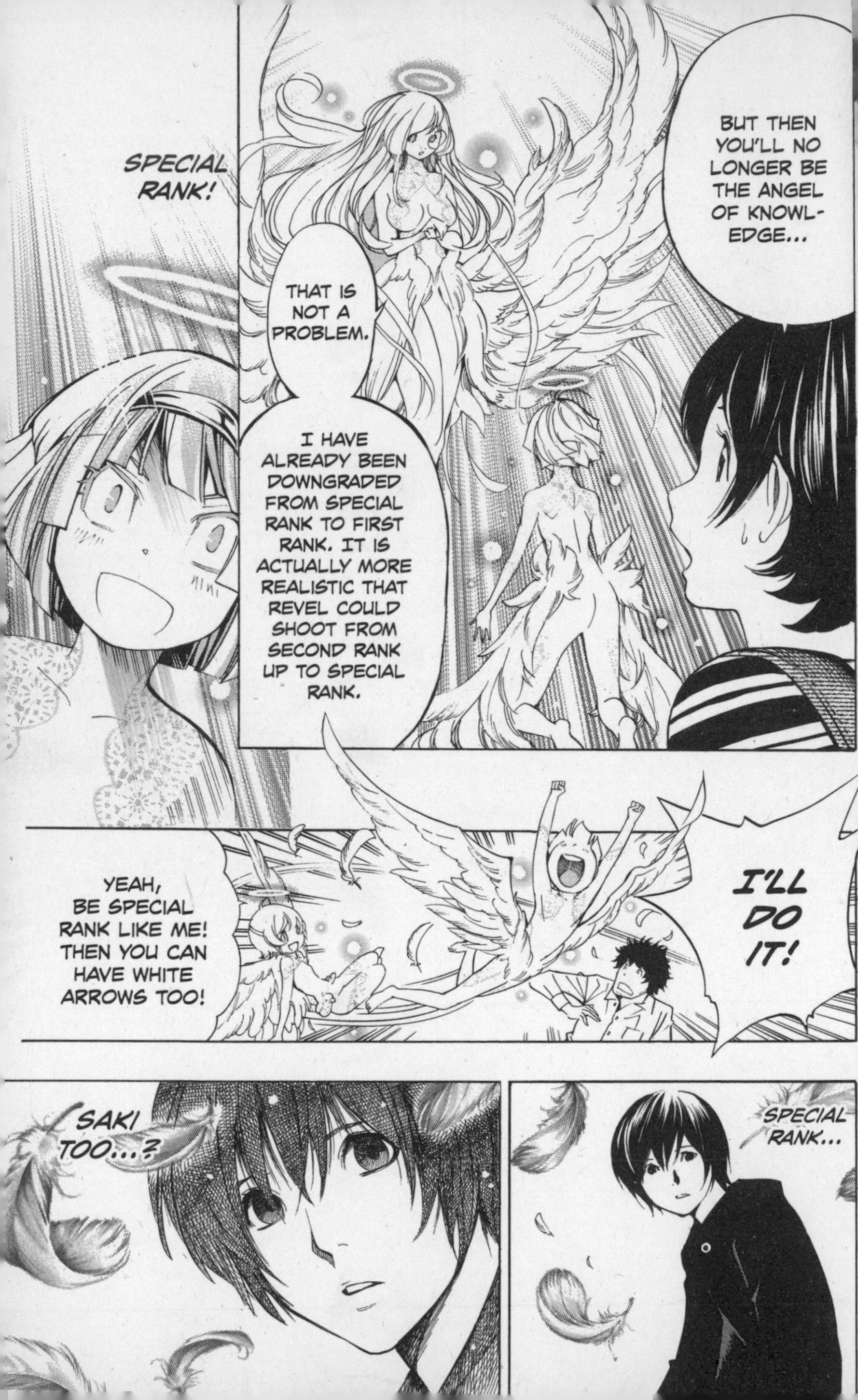
BUT THEN YOU'LL NO LONGER BE THE ANGEL OF KNOWL-EDGE...
THAT IS NOT A PROBLEM.
I HAVE ALREADY BEEN DOWNGRADED FROM SPECIAL RANK TO FIRST RANK. IT IS ACTUALLY MORE REALISTIC THAT REVEL COULD SHOOT FROM SECOND RANK UP TO SPECIAL RANK.
SPECIAL RANK!
I'LL DO IT!
YEAH, BE SPECIAL RANK LIKE ME! THEN YOU CAN HAVE WHITE ARROWS TOO!
SPECIAL RANK...
SAKI TOO...?

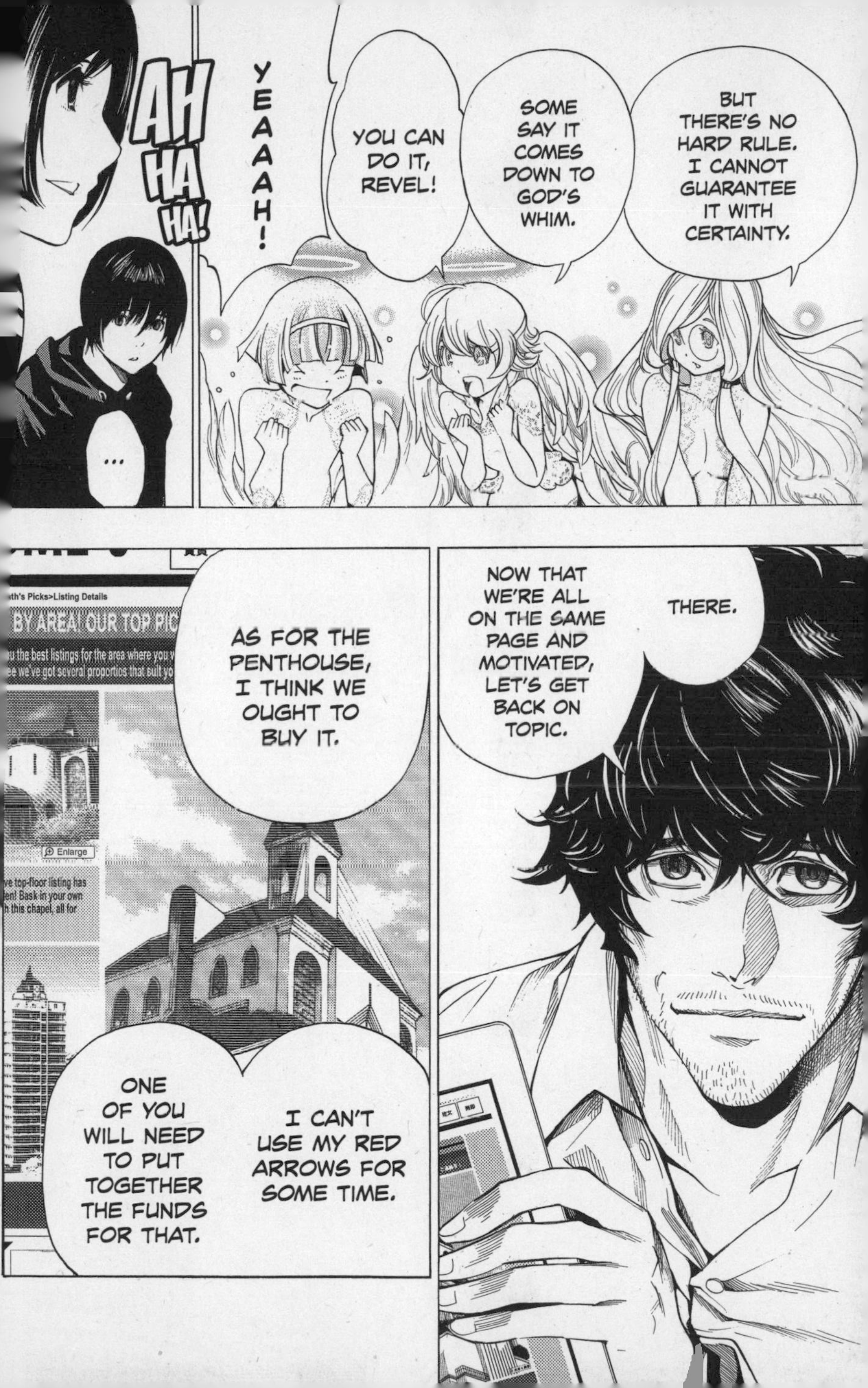
BUT THERE'S NO HARD RULE. I CANNOT GUARANTEE IT WITH CERTAINTY.
SOME SAY IT COMES DOWN TO GOD'S WHIM.
YOU CAN DO IT, REVEL!
YEAAAAH!
AH HA HA HA!
...
THERE.
NOW THAT WE'RE ALL ON THE SAME PAGE AND MOTIVATED, LET'S GET BACK ON TOPIC.
AS FOR THE PENTHOUSE, I THINK WE OUGHT TO BUY IT.
th's Picks>Listing Details
BY AREA! OUR TOP PIC
Enlarge
I CAN'T USE MY RED ARROWS FOR SOME TIME.
ONE OF YOU WILL NEED TO PUT TOGETHER THE FUNDS FOR THAT.

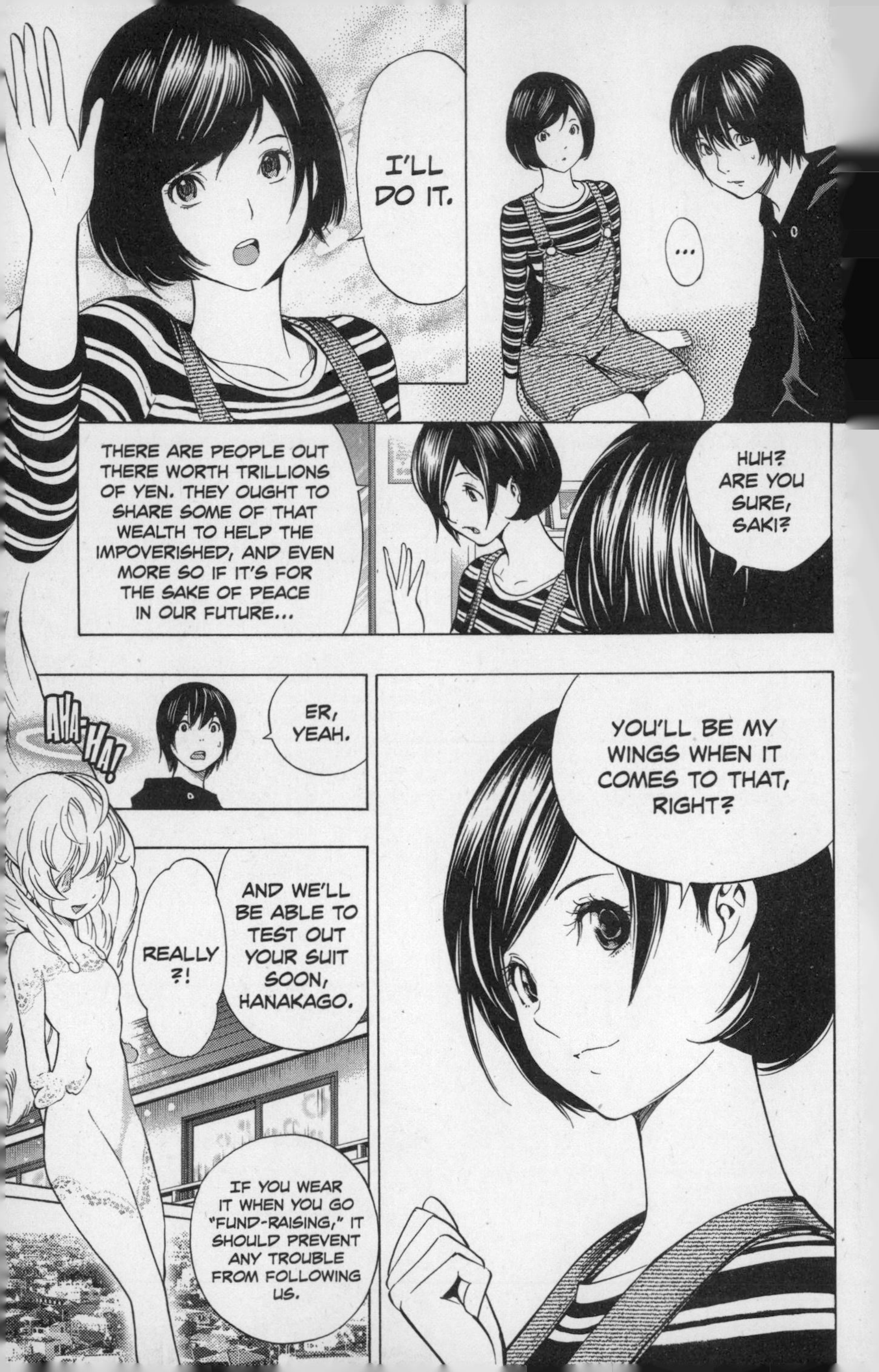
…
I'LL DO IT.
HUH? ARE YOU SURE, SAKI?
THERE ARE PEOPLE OUT THERE WORTH TRILLIONS OF YEN. THEY OUGHT TO SHARE SOME OF THAT WEALTH TO HELP THE IMPOVERISHED, AND EVEN MORE SO IF IT'S FOR THE SAKE OF PEACE IN OUR FUTURE...
YOU'LL BE MY WINGS WHEN IT COMES TO THAT, RIGHT?
ER, YEAH.
AHA-HA!
AND WE'LL BE ABLE TO TEST OUT YOUR SUIT SOON, HANAKAGO.
REALLY?!
IF YOU WEAR IT WHEN YOU GO "FUND-RAISING," IT SHOULD PREVENT ANY TROUBLE FROM FOLLOWING US.

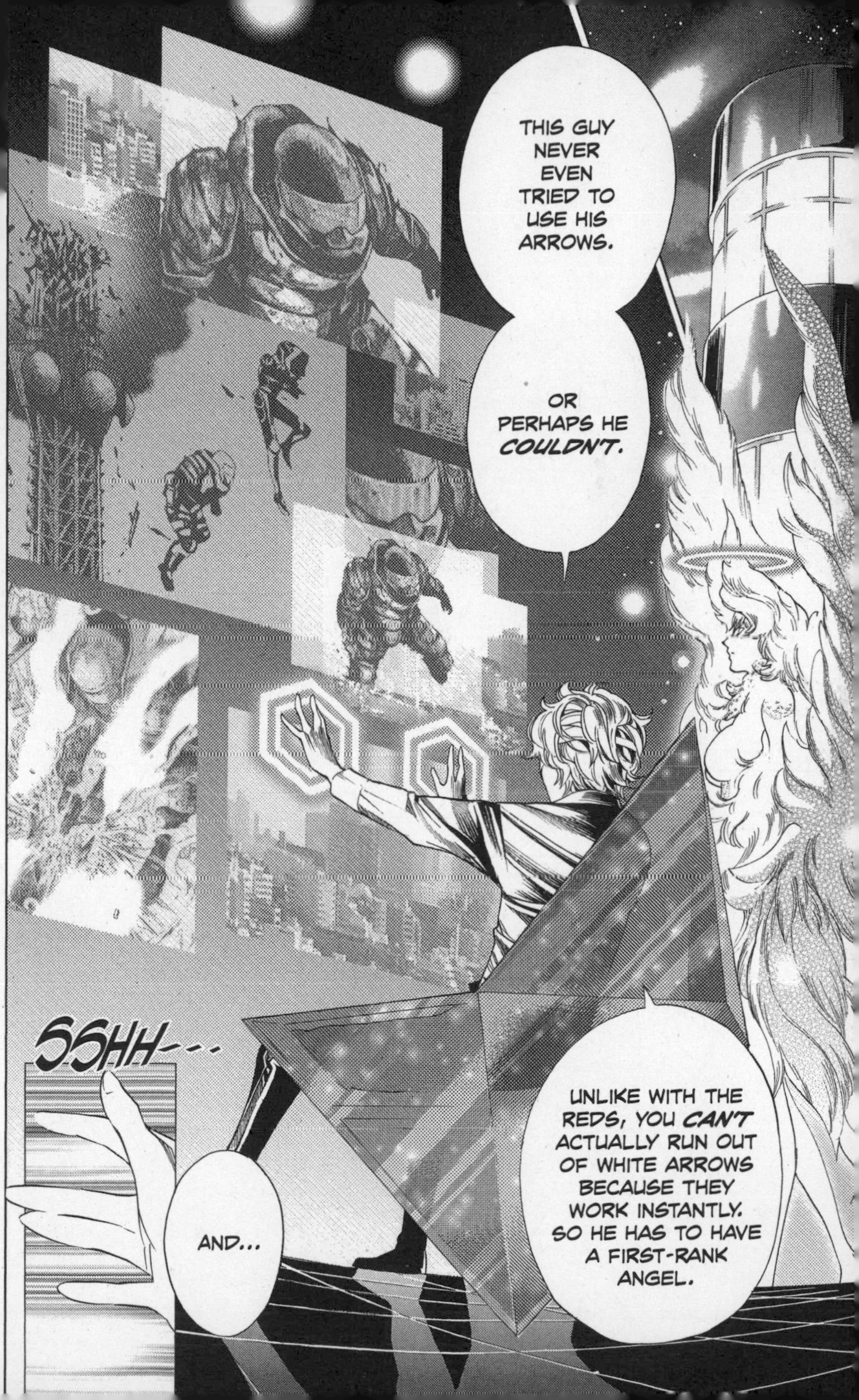
THIS GUY NEVER EVEN TRIED TO USE HIS ARROWS.
OR PERHAPS HE *COULDN'T*.
UNLIKE WITH THE REDS, YOU *CAN'T* ACTUALLY RUN OUT OF WHITE ARROWS BECAUSE THEY WORK INSTANTLY. SO HE HAS TO HAVE A FIRST-RANK ANGEL.
SSHH---
AND...

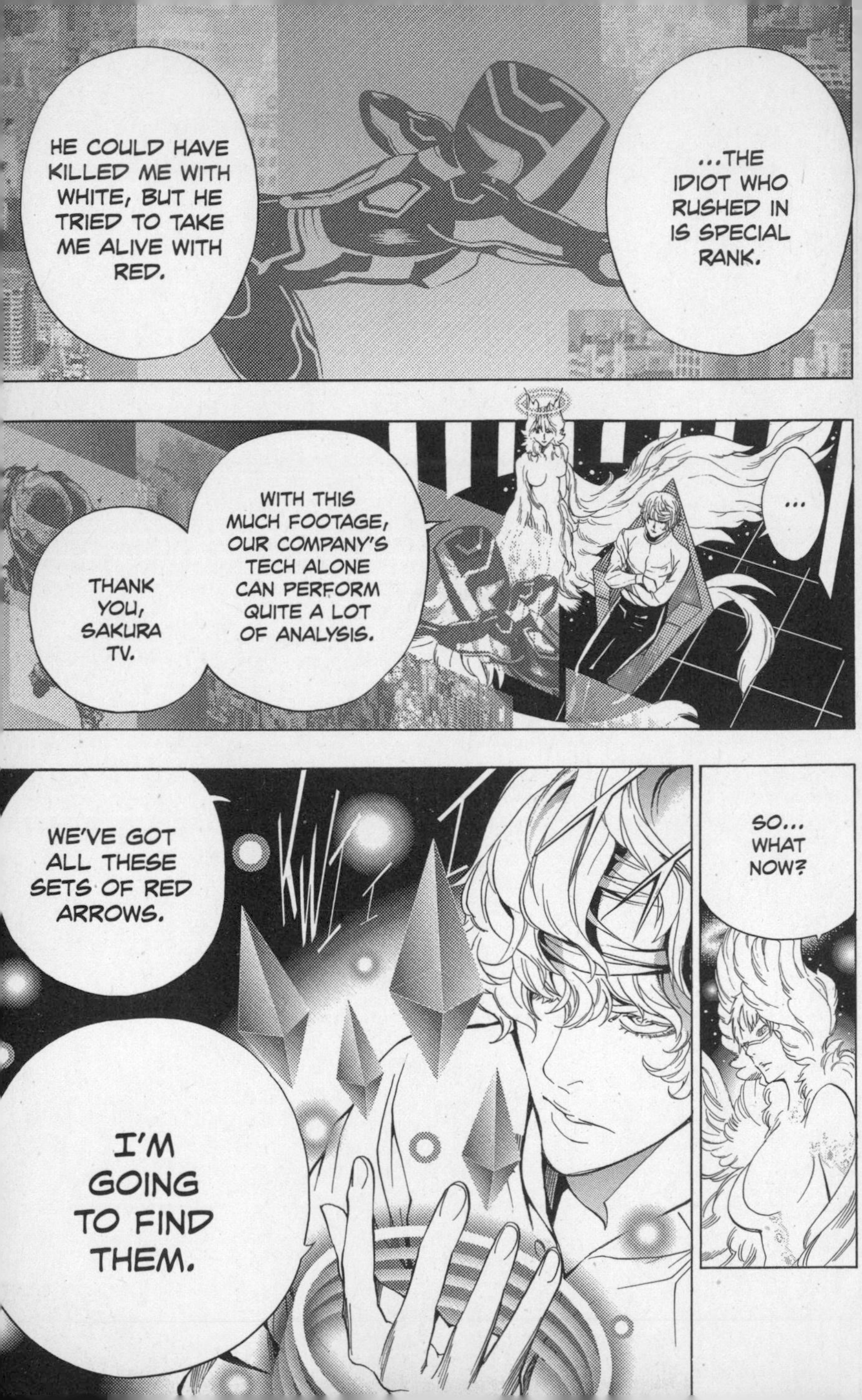
...THE IDIOT WHO RUSHED IN IS SPECIAL RANK.
HE COULD HAVE KILLED ME WITH WHITE, BUT HE TRIED TO TAKE ME ALIVE WITH RED.
...
WITH THIS MUCH FOOTAGE, OUR COMPANY'S TECH ALONE CAN PERFORM QUITE A LOT OF ANALYSIS.
THANK YOU, SAKURA TV.
SO... WHAT NOW?
WE'VE GOT ALL THESE SETS OF RED ARROWS.
I'M GOING TO FIND THEM.

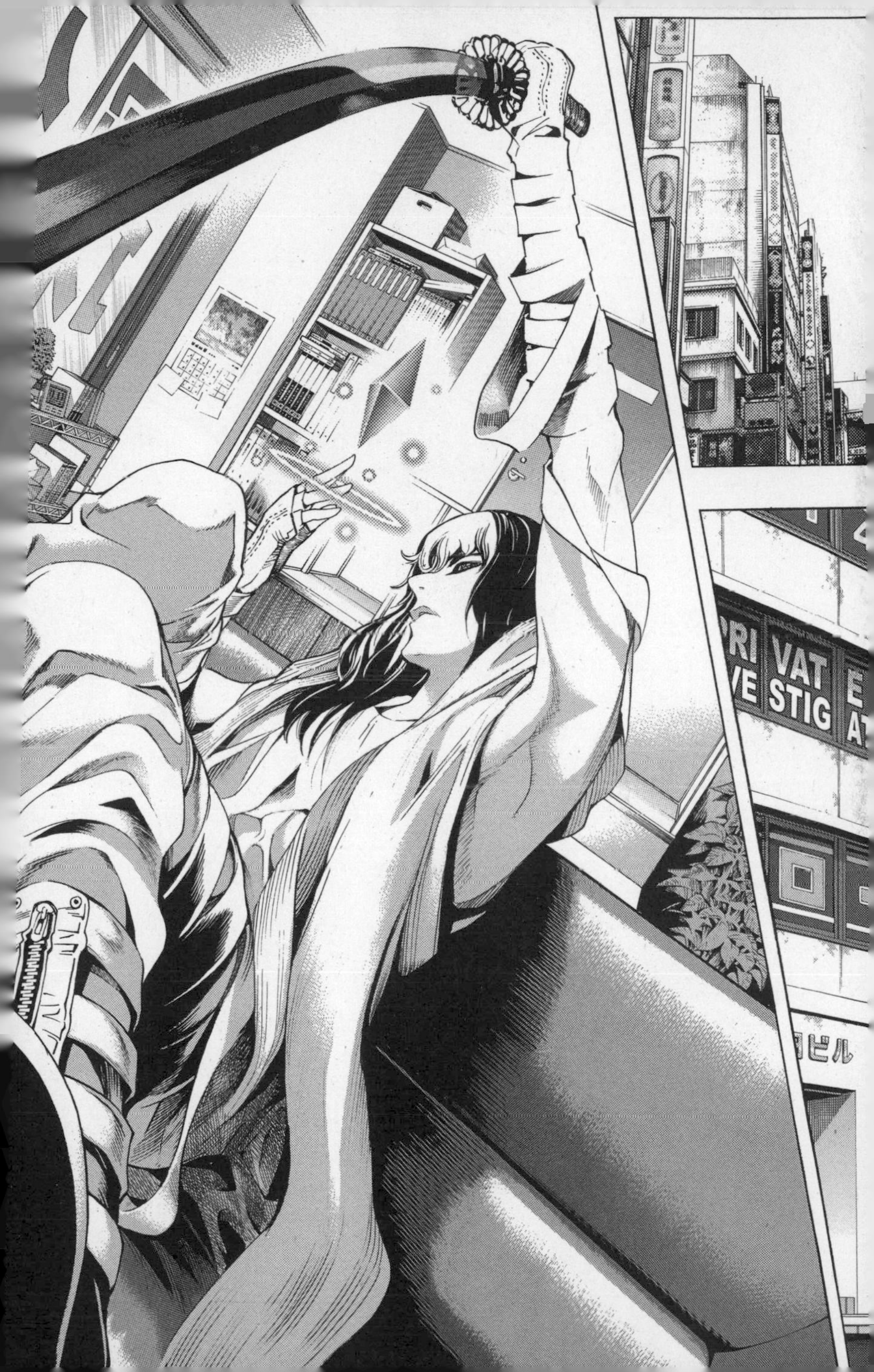
PRI VAT E
VE STIG AT

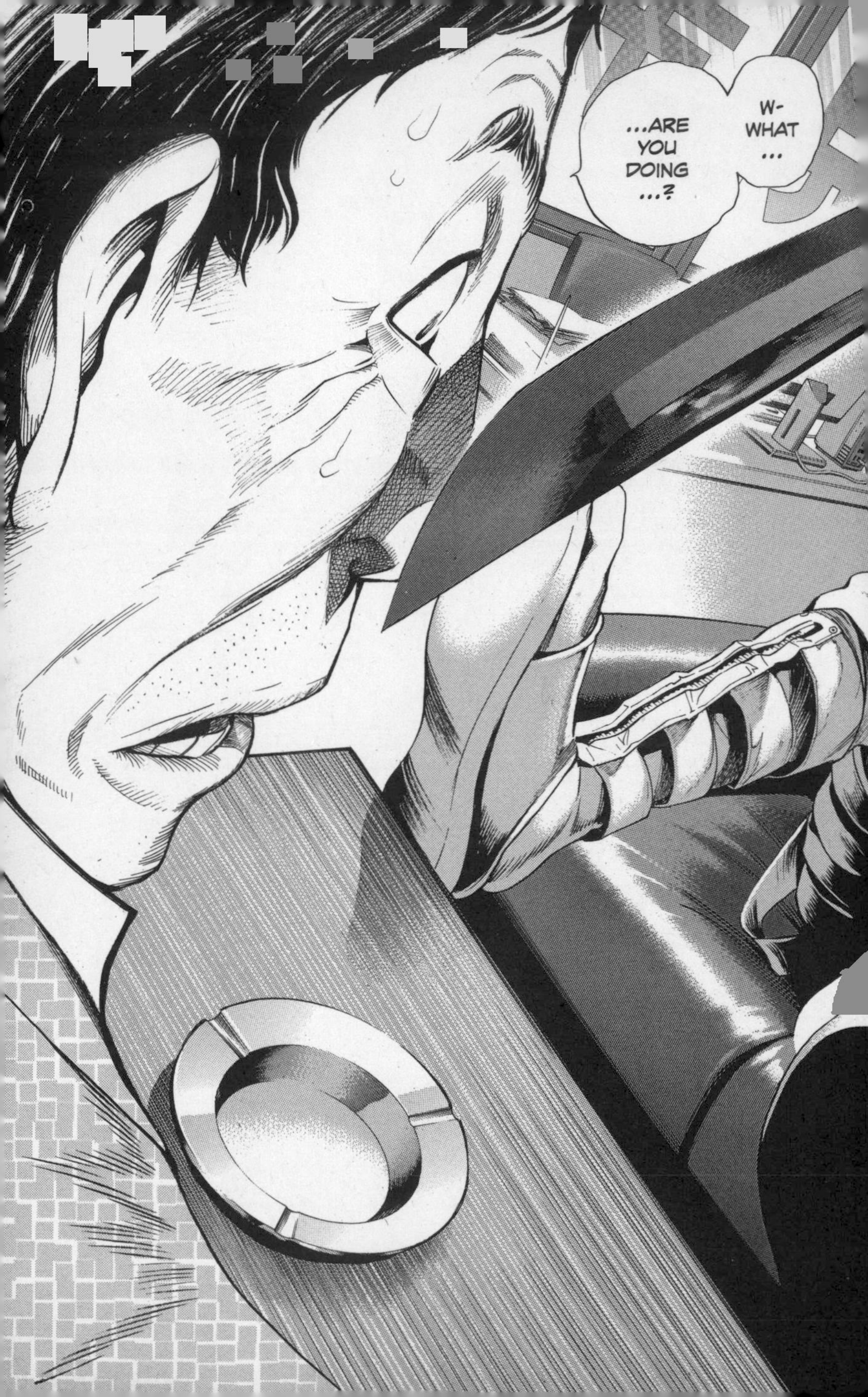
W-WHAT ...
...ARE YOU DOING ...?

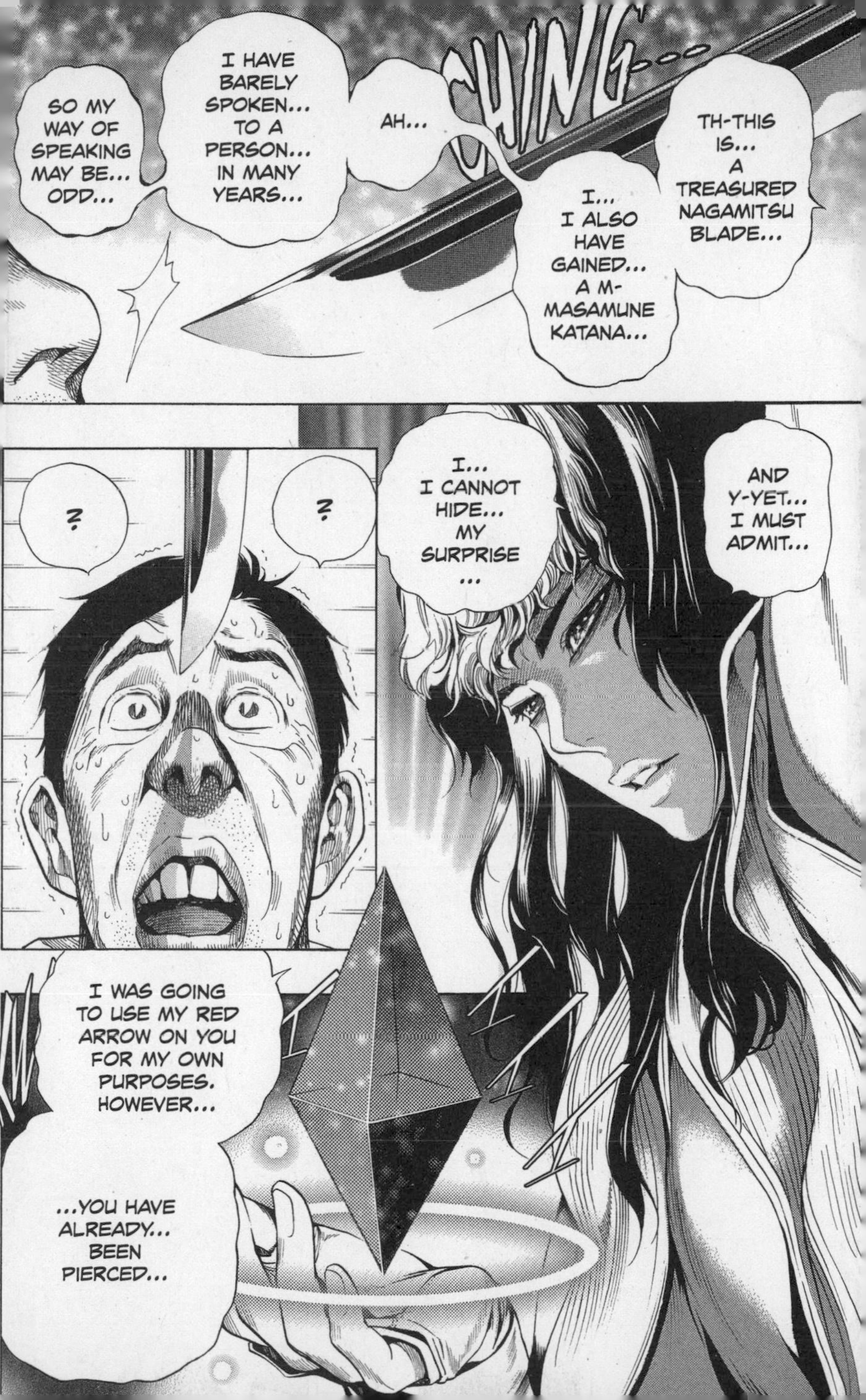
TH-THIS IS... A TREASURED NAGAMITSU BLADE...
I... I ALSO HAVE GAINED... A M-MASAMUNE KATANA...
SHING...
AH...
I HAVE BARELY SPOKEN... TO A PERSON... IN MANY YEARS...
SO MY WAY OF SPEAKING MAY BE... ODD...
AND Y-YET... I MUST ADMIT...
I... I CANNOT HIDE... MY SURPRISE ...
?
?
I WAS GOING TO USE MY RED ARROW ON YOU FOR MY OWN PURPOSES. HOWEVER...
...YOU HAVE ALREADY... BEEN PIERCED...

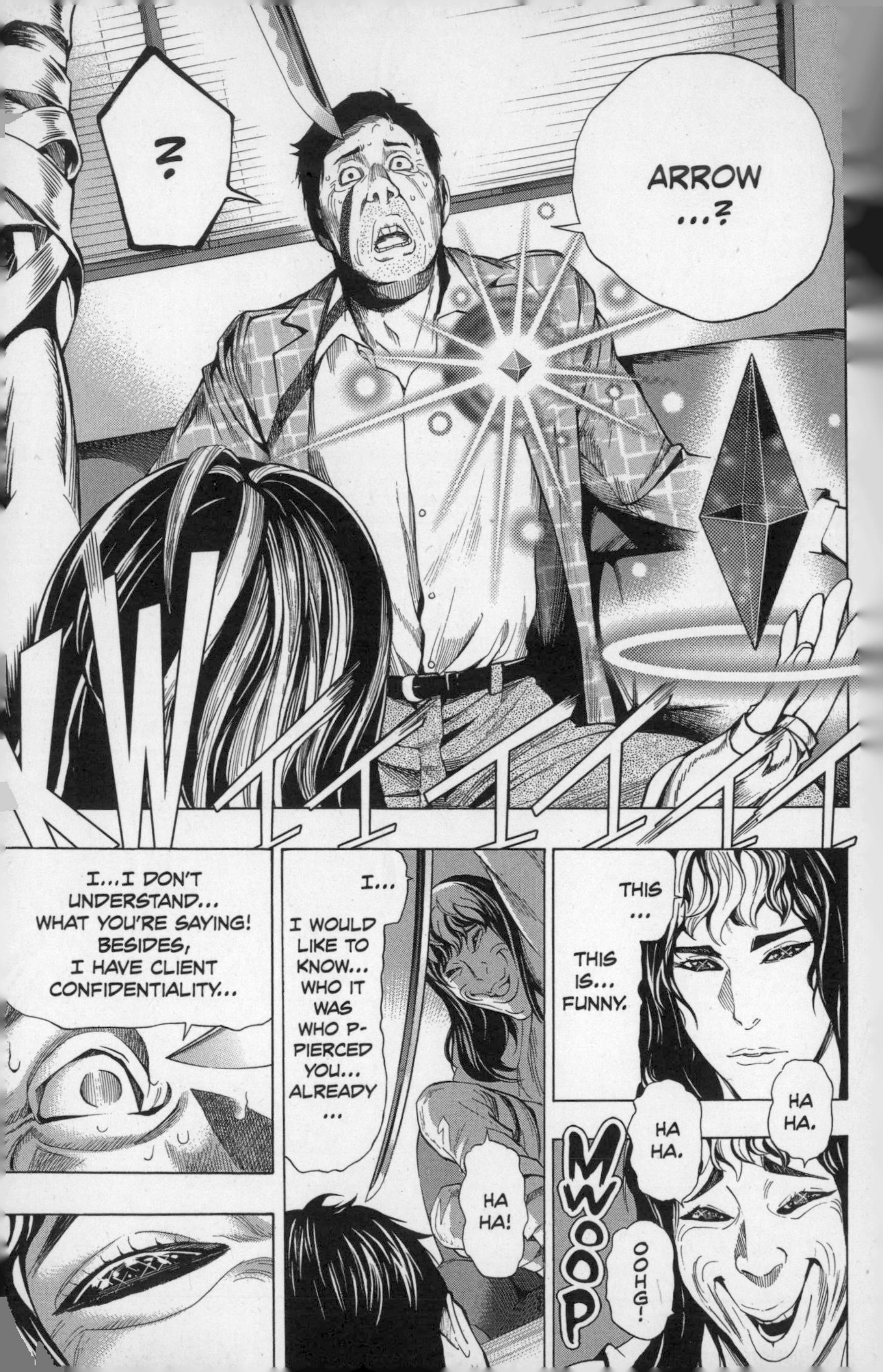
ARROW ...?
?
THIS ...
THIS IS... FUNNY.
HA HA.
HA HA.
MWOOP
OOHG!
I...
I WOULD LIKE TO KNOW... WHO IT WAS WHO P-PIERCED YOU... ALREADY ...
HA HA!
I...I DON'T UNDERSTAND... WHAT YOU'RE SAYING! BESIDES, I HAVE CLIENT CONFIDENTIALITY...

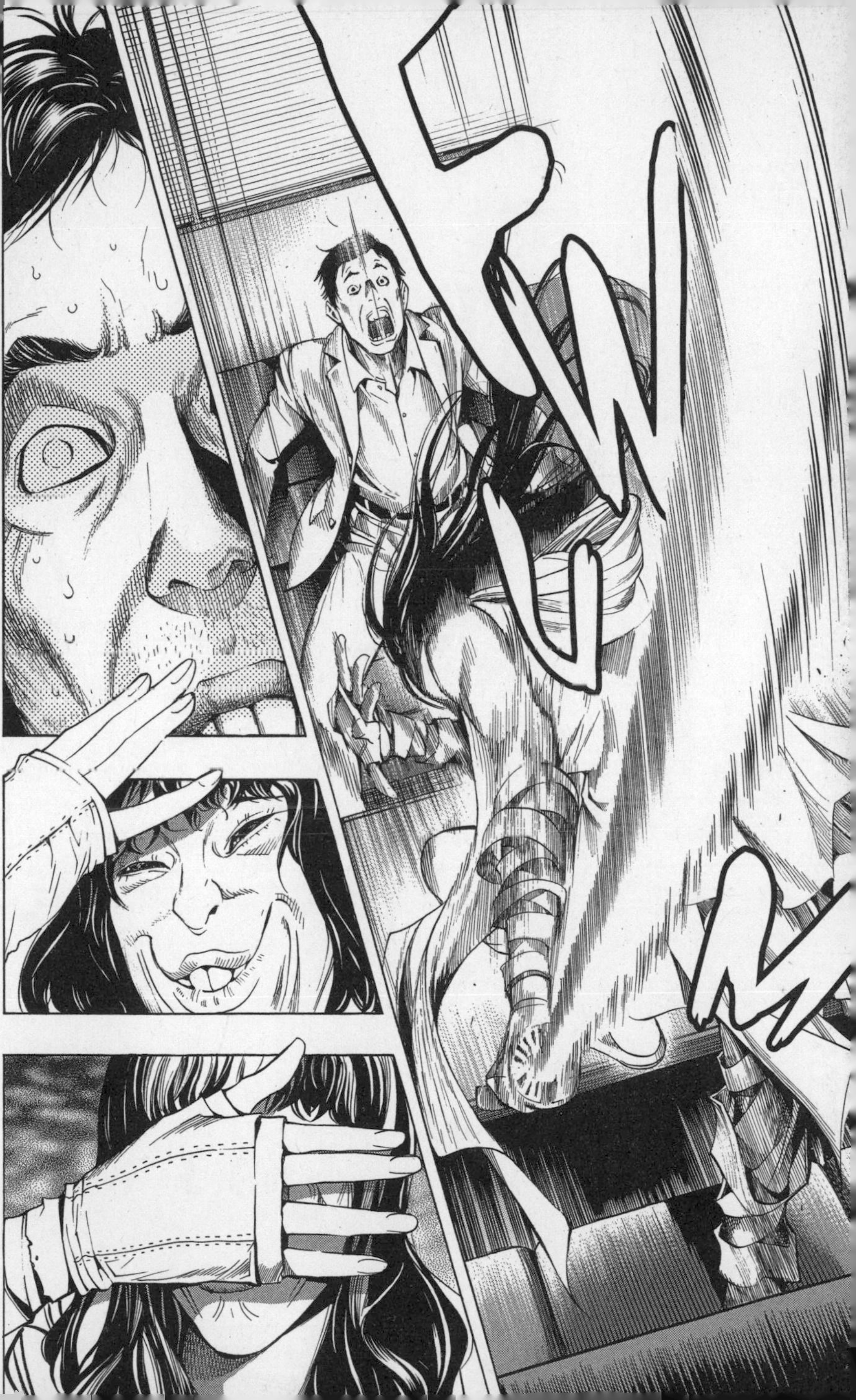

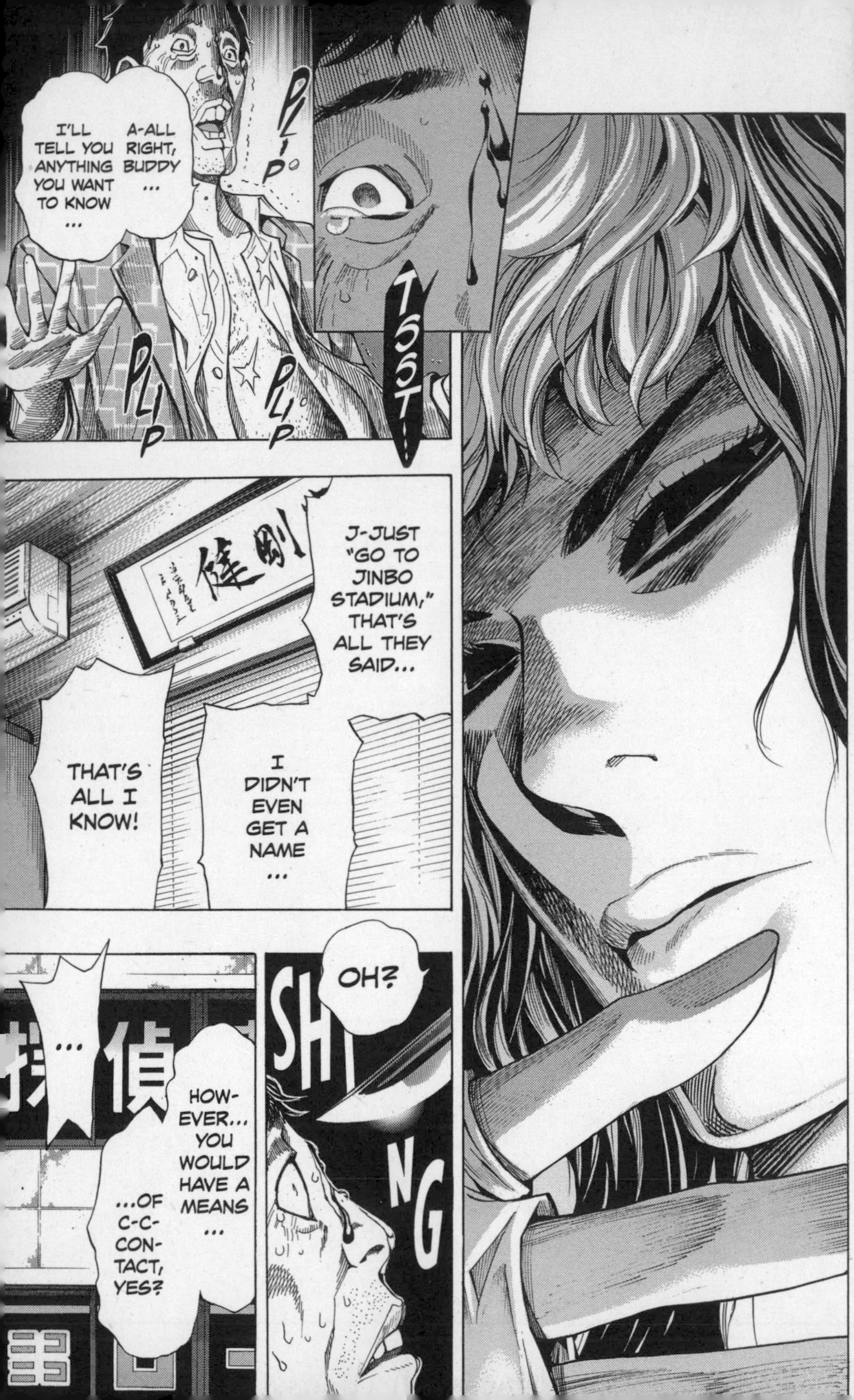

PLIP
TSSST...
A-ALL RIGHT, BUDDY...
I'LL TELL YOU ANYTHING YOU WANT TO KNOW...
PLIP
PLIP
J-JUST "GO TO JINBO STADIUM," THAT'S ALL THEY SAID...
I DIDN'T EVEN GET A NAME...
THAT'S ALL I KNOW!
OH?
SHING
...
HOW-EVER... YOU WOULD HAVE A MEANS...
...OF C-C-CONTACT, YES?

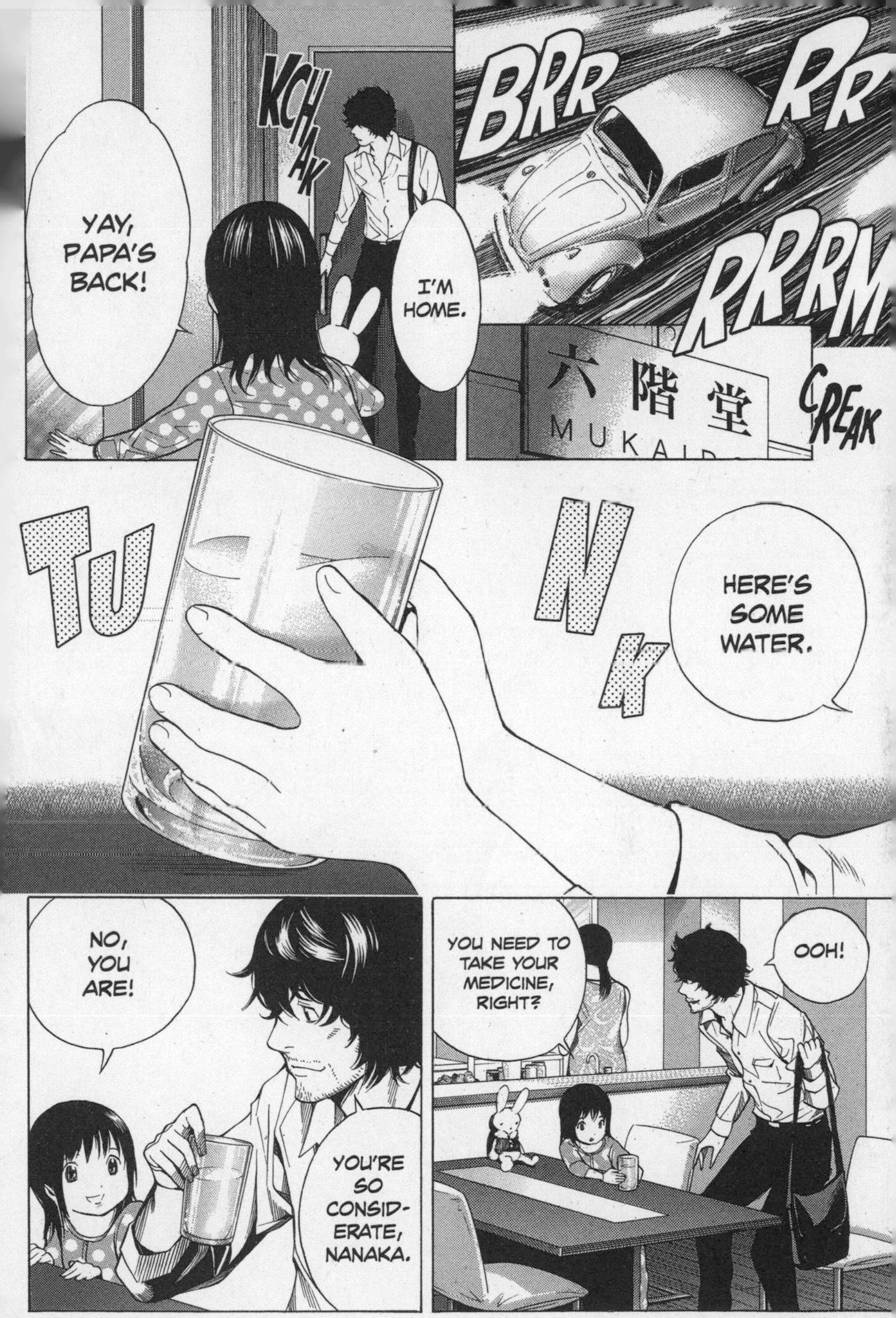
BRRR
RRRRM
六階堂
CREAK
KCHAK
I'M HOME.
YAY, PAPA'S BACK!
TUNK
HERE'S SOME WATER.
OOH!
YOU NEED TO TAKE YOUR MEDICINE, RIGHT?
YOU'RE SO CONSID-ERATE, NANAKA.
NO, YOU ARE!

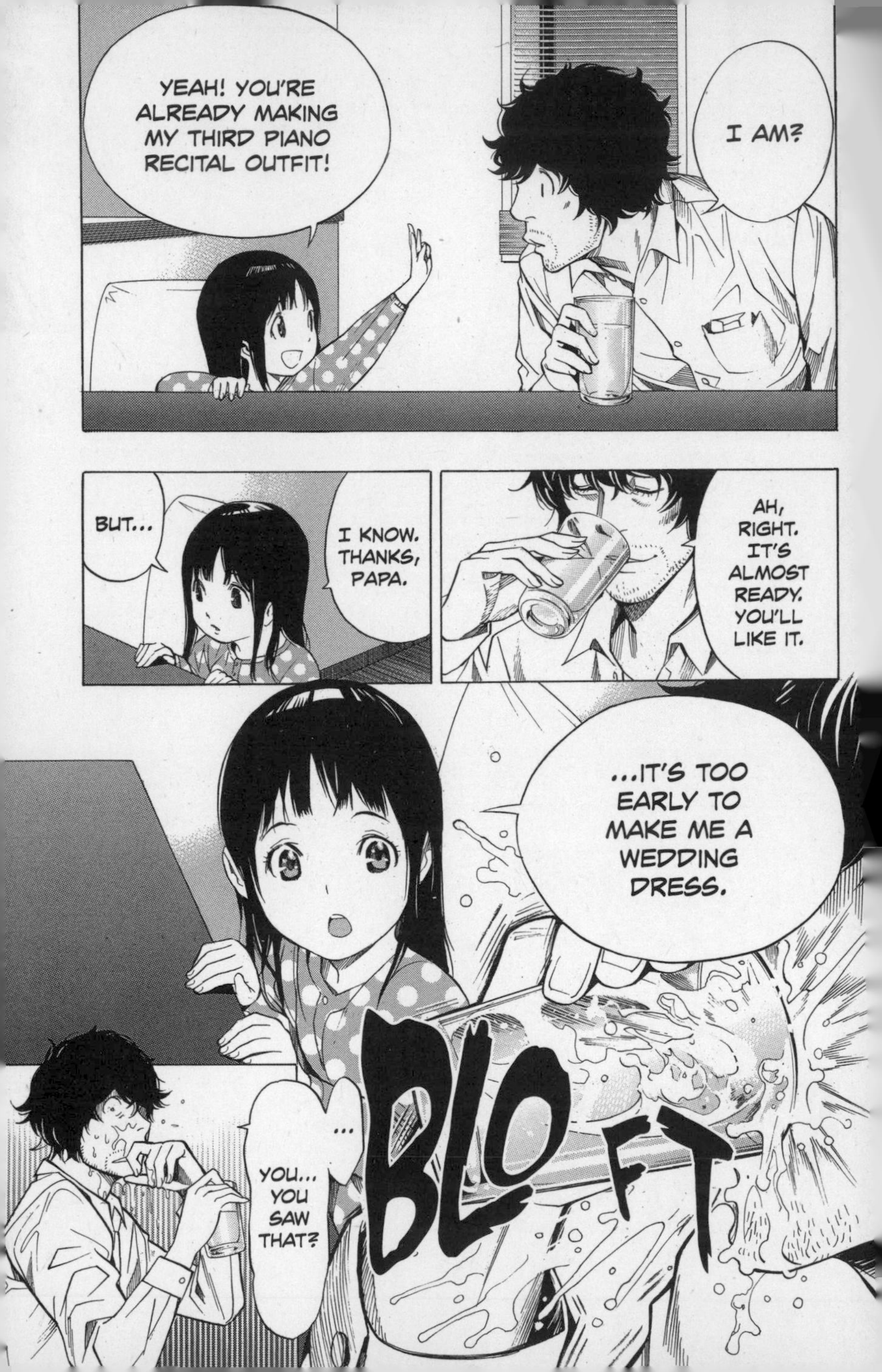
I AM?
YEAH! YOU'RE ALREADY MAKING MY THIRD PIANO RECITAL OUTFIT!
AH, RIGHT. IT'S ALMOST READY. YOU'LL LIKE IT.
I KNOW. THANKS, PAPA.
BUT...
...IT'S TOO EARLY TO MAKE ME A WEDDING DRESS.
BLOFT
...
YOU... YOU SAW THAT?

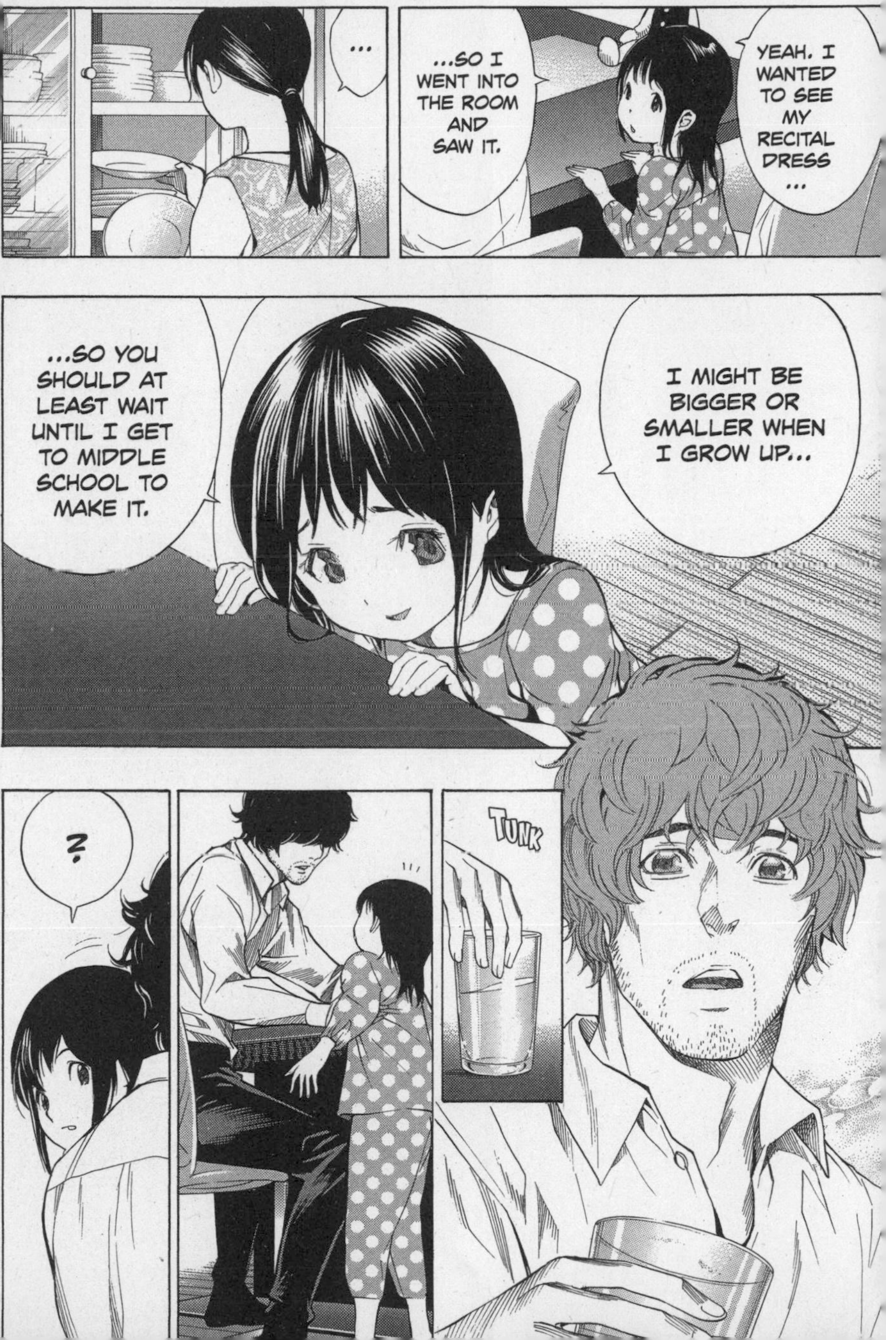
YEAH. I WANTED TO SEE MY RECITAL DRESS ...
...SO I WENT INTO THE ROOM AND SAW IT.
...
I MIGHT BE BIGGER OR SMALLER WHEN I GROW UP...
...SO YOU SHOULD AT LEAST WAIT UNTIL I GET TO MIDDLE SCHOOL TO MAKE IT.
TUNK
?

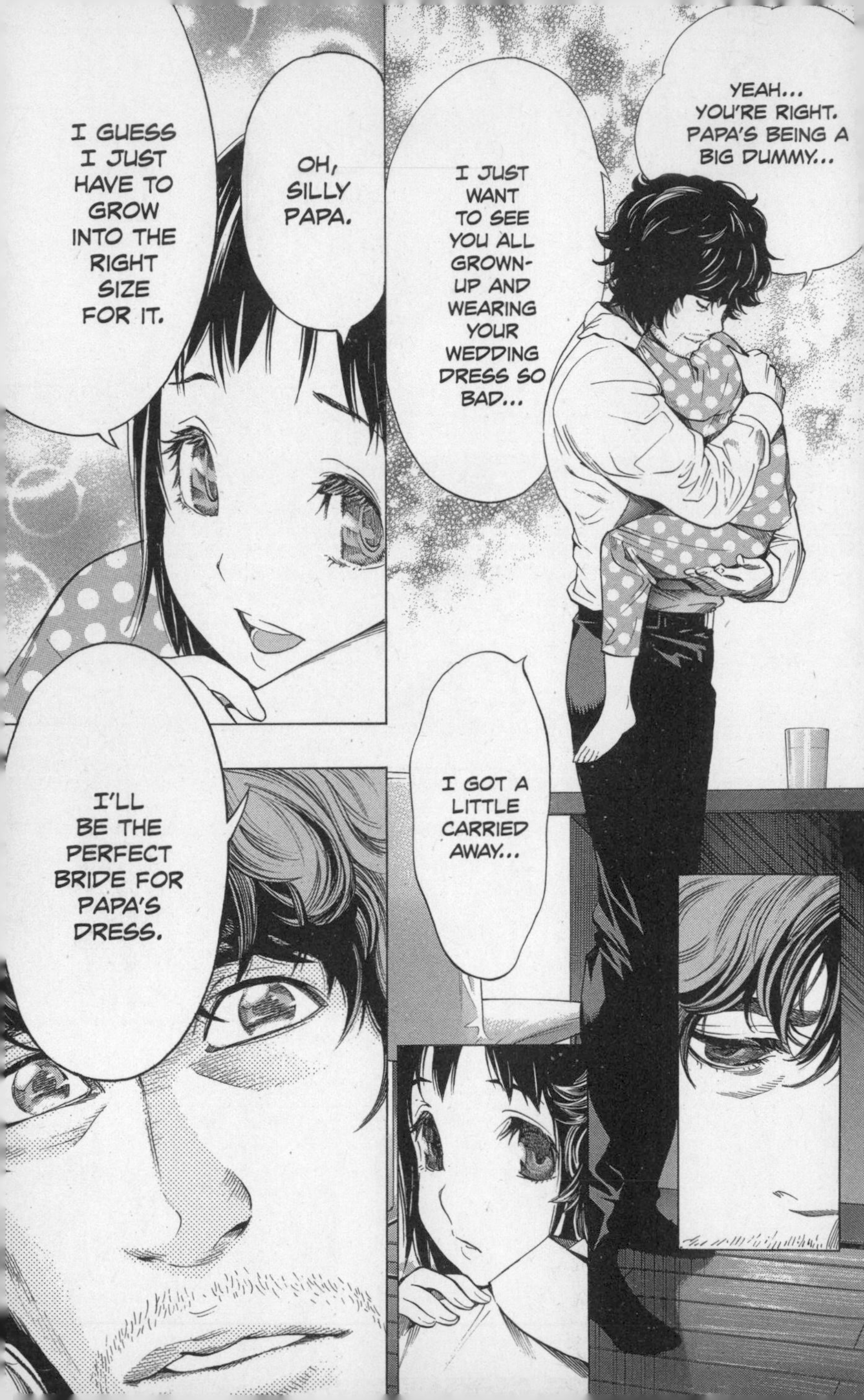
YEAH... YOU'RE RIGHT. PAPA'S BEING A BIG DUMMY...
I JUST WANT TO SEE YOU ALL GROWN-UP AND WEARING YOUR WEDDING DRESS SO BAD...
I GOT A LITTLE CARRIED AWAY...
OH, SILLY PAPA.
I GUESS I JUST HAVE TO GROW INTO THE RIGHT SIZE FOR IT.
I'LL BE THE PERFECT BRIDE FOR PAPA'S DRESS.

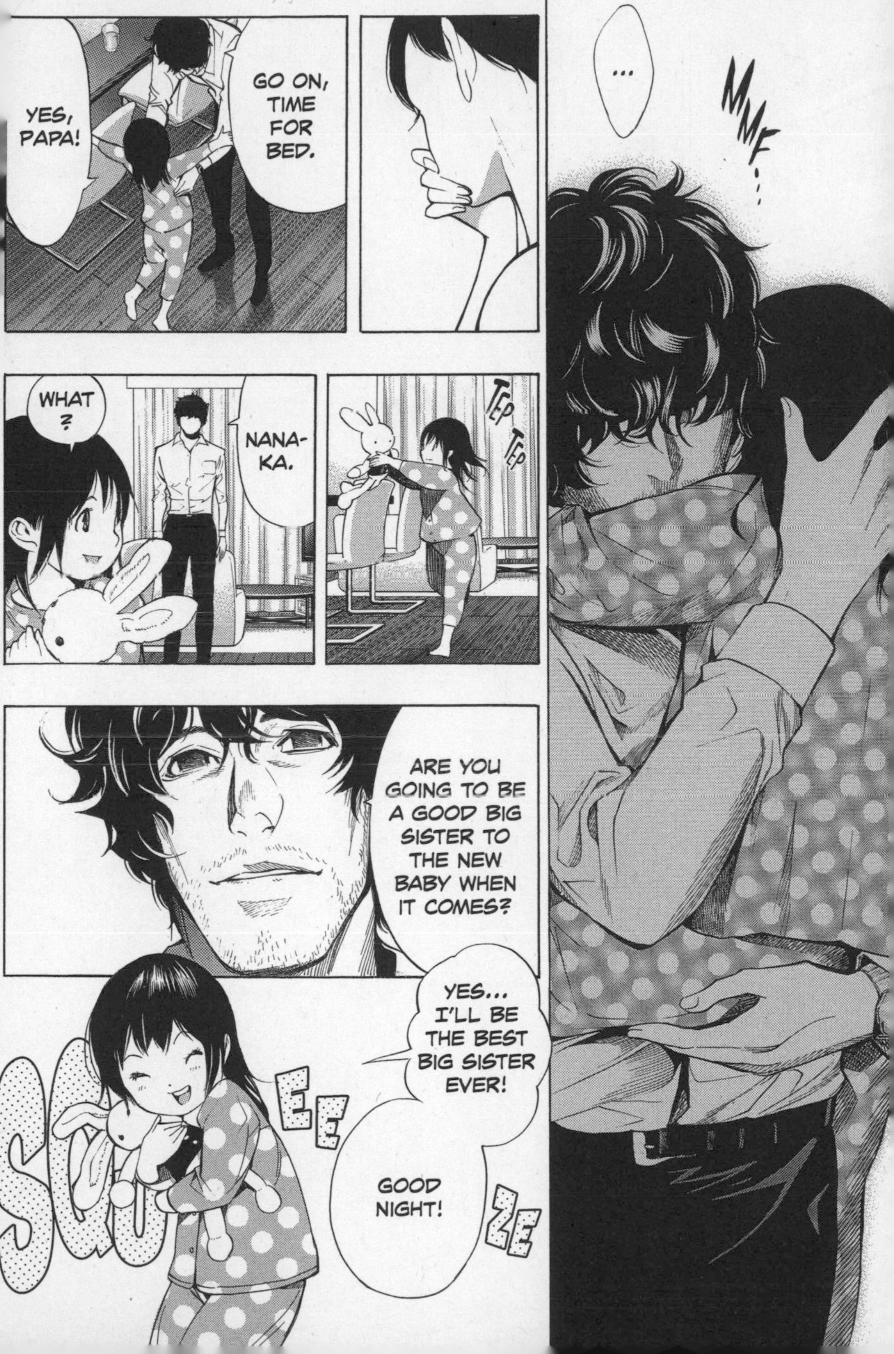
...
MMF...
TEP TEP
NANA-KA.
WHAT?
ARE YOU GOING TO BE A GOOD BIG SISTER TO THE NEW BABY WHEN IT COMES?
YES... I'LL BE THE BEST BIG SISTER EVER!
GOOD NIGHT!
SQUEEZE
GO ON, TIME FOR BED.
YES, PAPA!

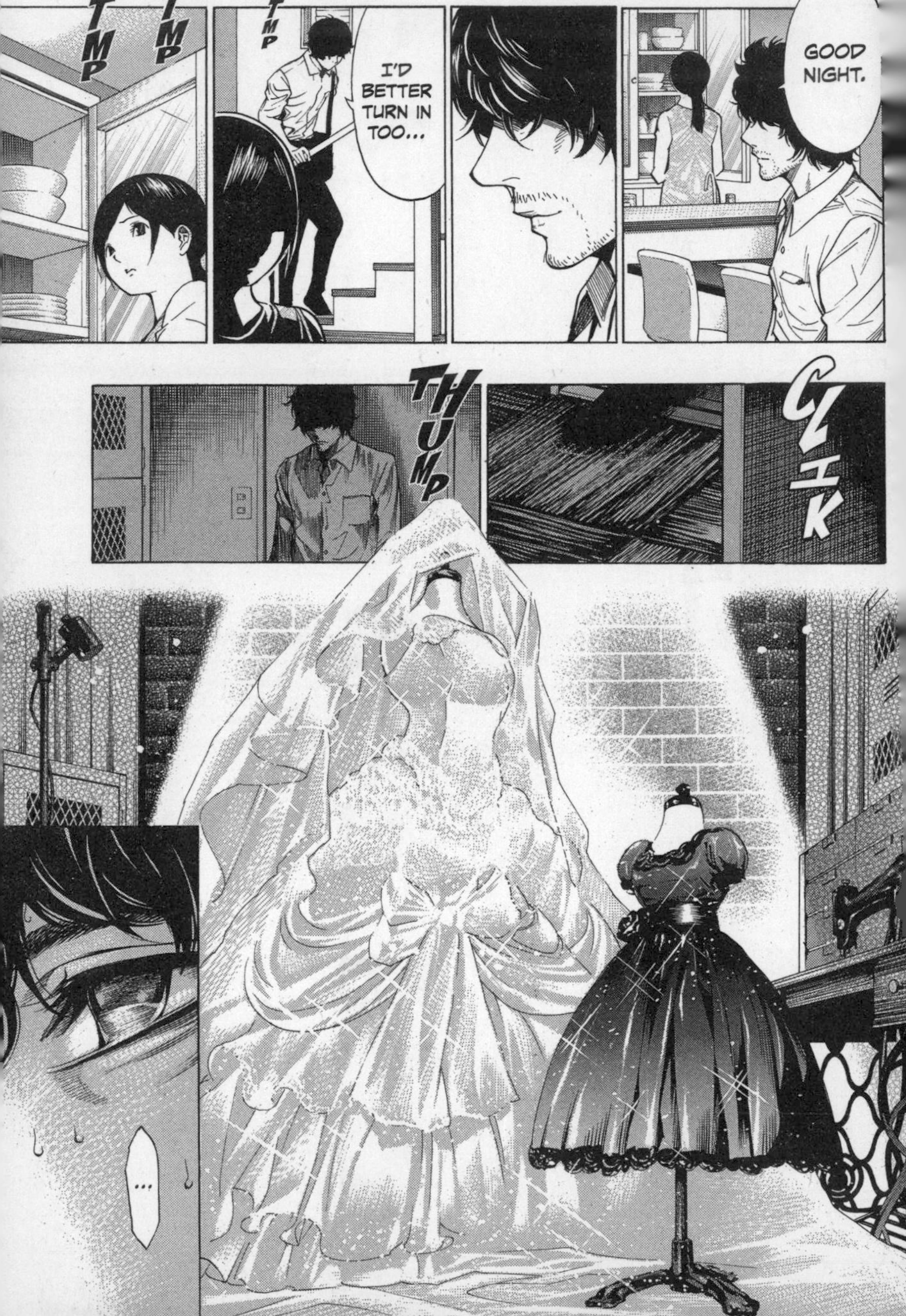
GOOD NIGHT.
TMP
I'D BETTER TURN IN TOO...
TMP
TMP
CLIK
THUMP
...

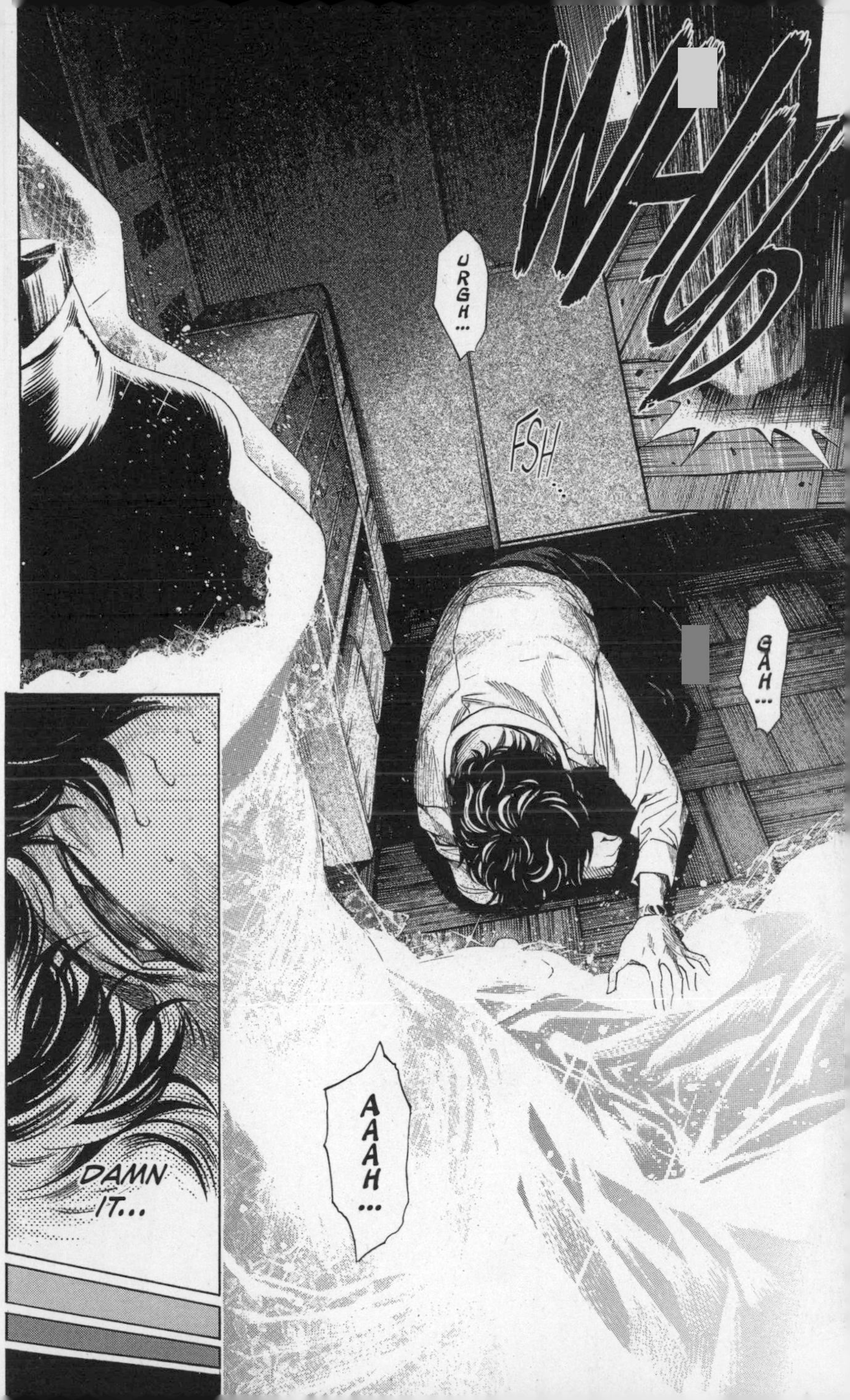
WHUD
URGH...
FSH...
GAH...
AAAH...
DAMN IT...

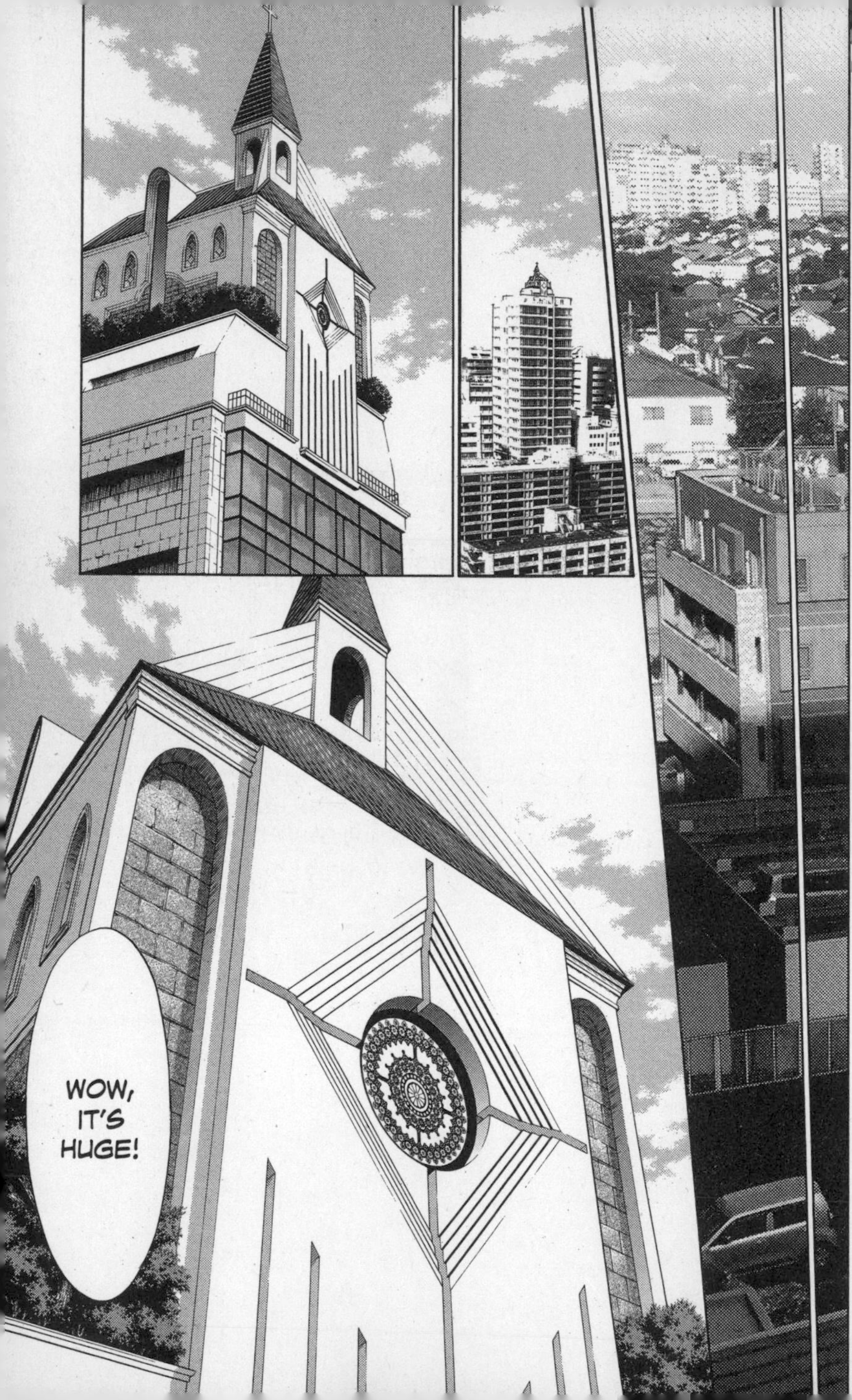
WOW, IT'S HUGE!

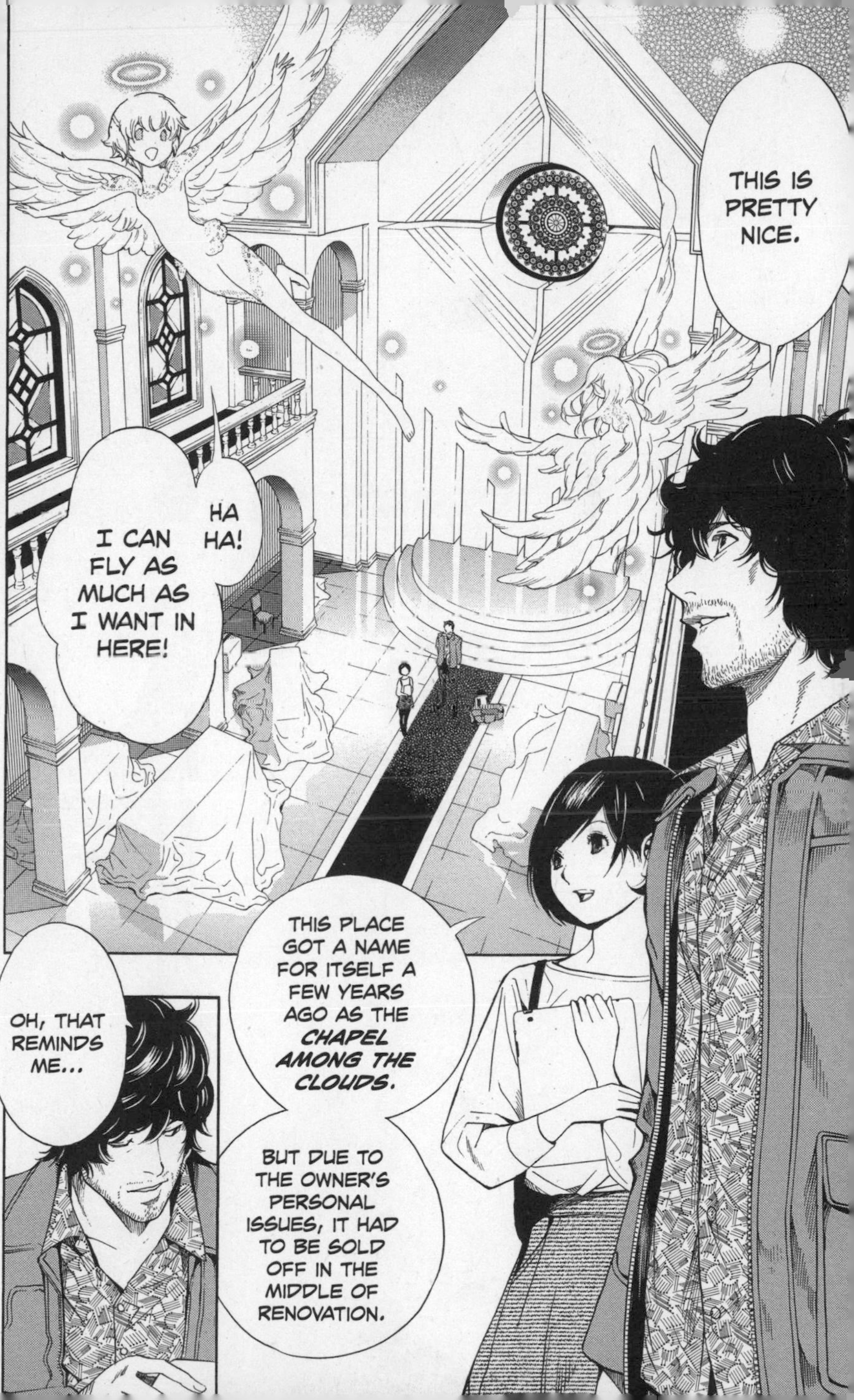
THIS IS PRETTY NICE.
I CAN FLY AS MUCH AS I WANT IN HERE!
HA HA!
THIS PLACE GOT A NAME FOR ITSELF A FEW YEARS AGO AS THE *CHAPEL AMONG THE CLOUDS*.
BUT DUE TO THE OWNER'S PERSONAL ISSUES, IT HAD TO BE SOLD OFF IN THE MIDDLE OF RENOVATION.
OH, THAT REMINDS ME...

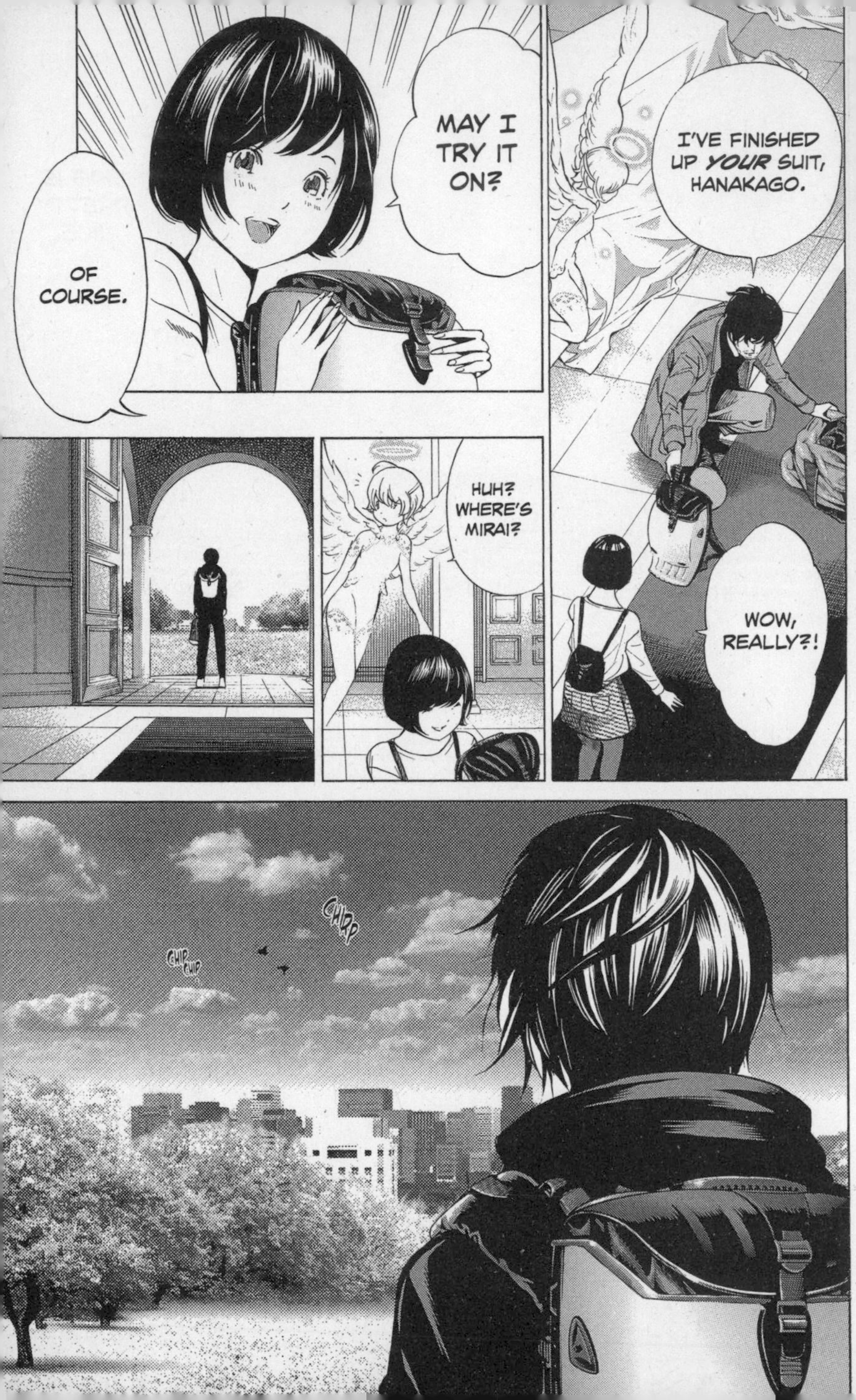
I'VE FINISHED UP *YOUR* SUIT, HANAKAGO.
WOW, REALLY?!
MAY I TRY IT ON?
OF COURSE.
HUH? WHERE'S MIRAI?
CHIRP
CHIP CHIP

CHIP CHIP
WHSH
WHSH
WHATCHA SPACIN' OUT FOR?
NOTH-ING...
JUST THINKING, THIS REMINDS ME OF THE PARK I USED TO VISIT WITH MY FAMILY...

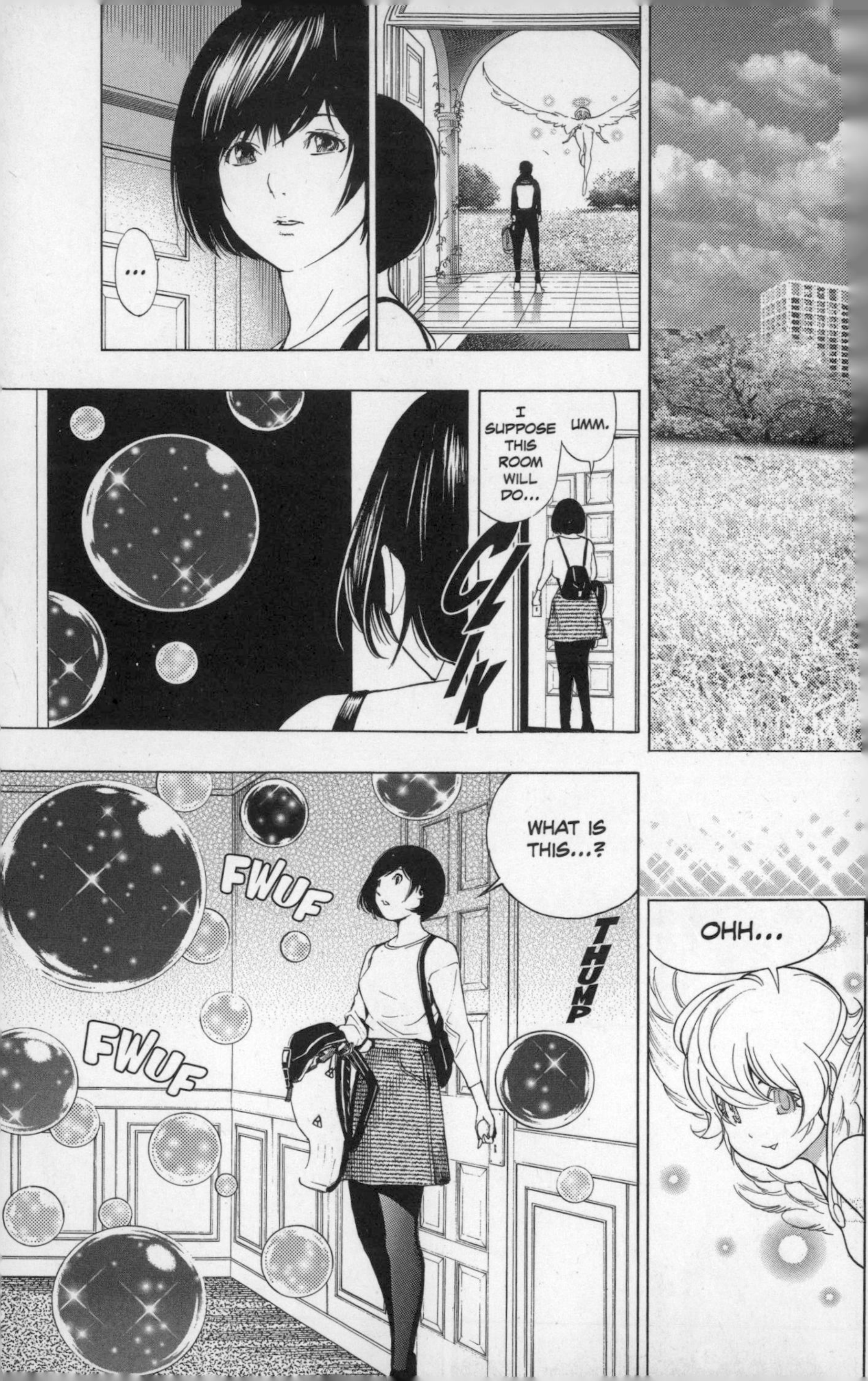
...
UMM.
I SUPPOSE THIS ROOM WILL DO...
CLICK
OHH...
WHAT IS THIS...?
THUMP
FWUF
FWUF

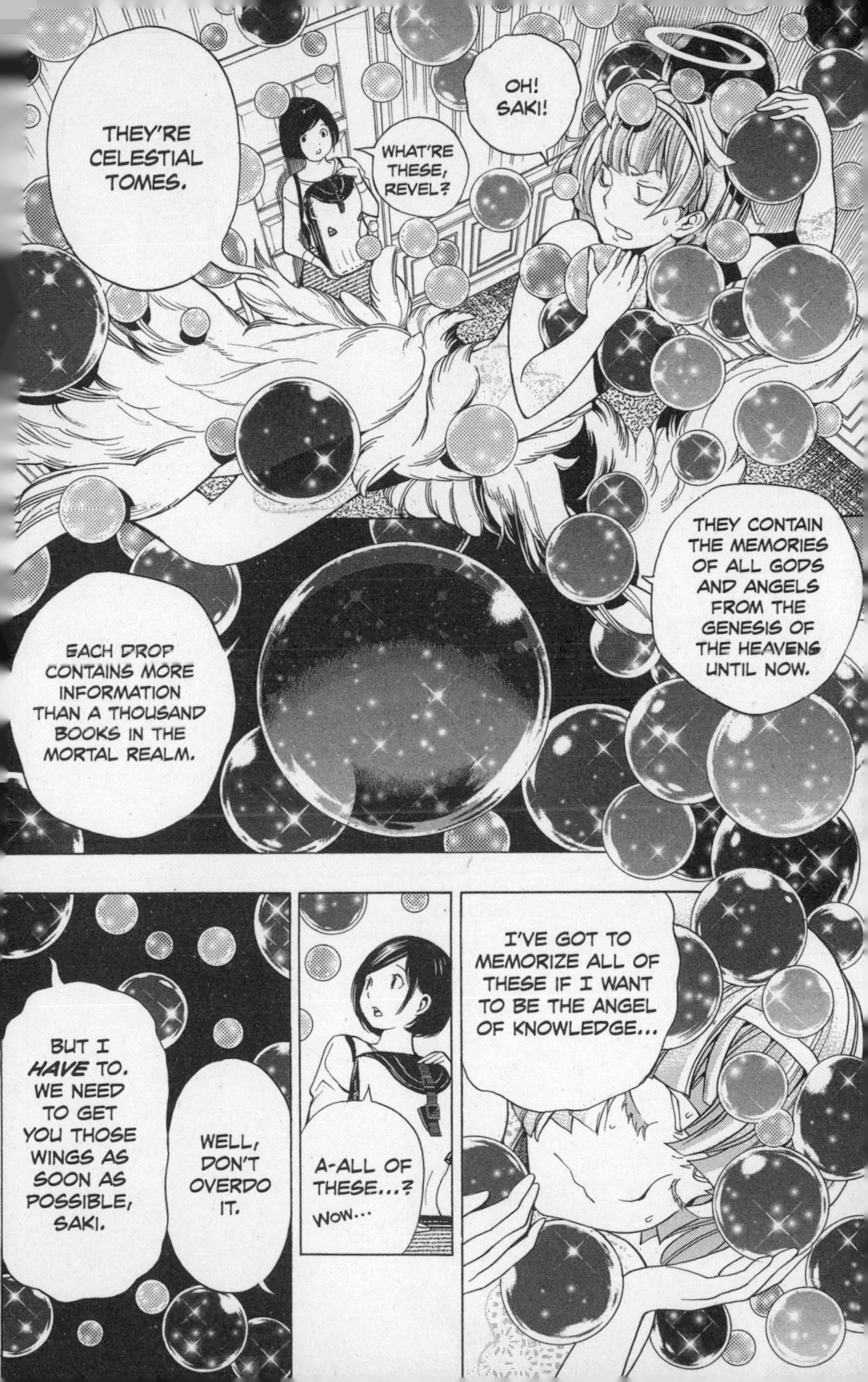
OH! SAKI!
WHAT'RE THESE, REVEL?
THEY'RE CELESTIAL TOMES.
THEY CONTAIN THE MEMORIES OF ALL GODS AND ANGELS FROM THE GENESIS OF THE HEAVENS UNTIL NOW.
EACH DROP CONTAINS MORE INFORMATION THAN A THOUSAND BOOKS IN THE MORTAL REALM.
I'VE GOT TO MEMORIZE ALL OF THESE IF I WANT TO BE THE ANGEL OF KNOWLEDGE...
A-ALL OF THESE...?
WOW...
WELL, DON'T OVERDO IT.
BUT I *HAVE* TO. WE NEED TO GET YOU THOSE WINGS AS SOON AS POSSIBLE, SAKI.

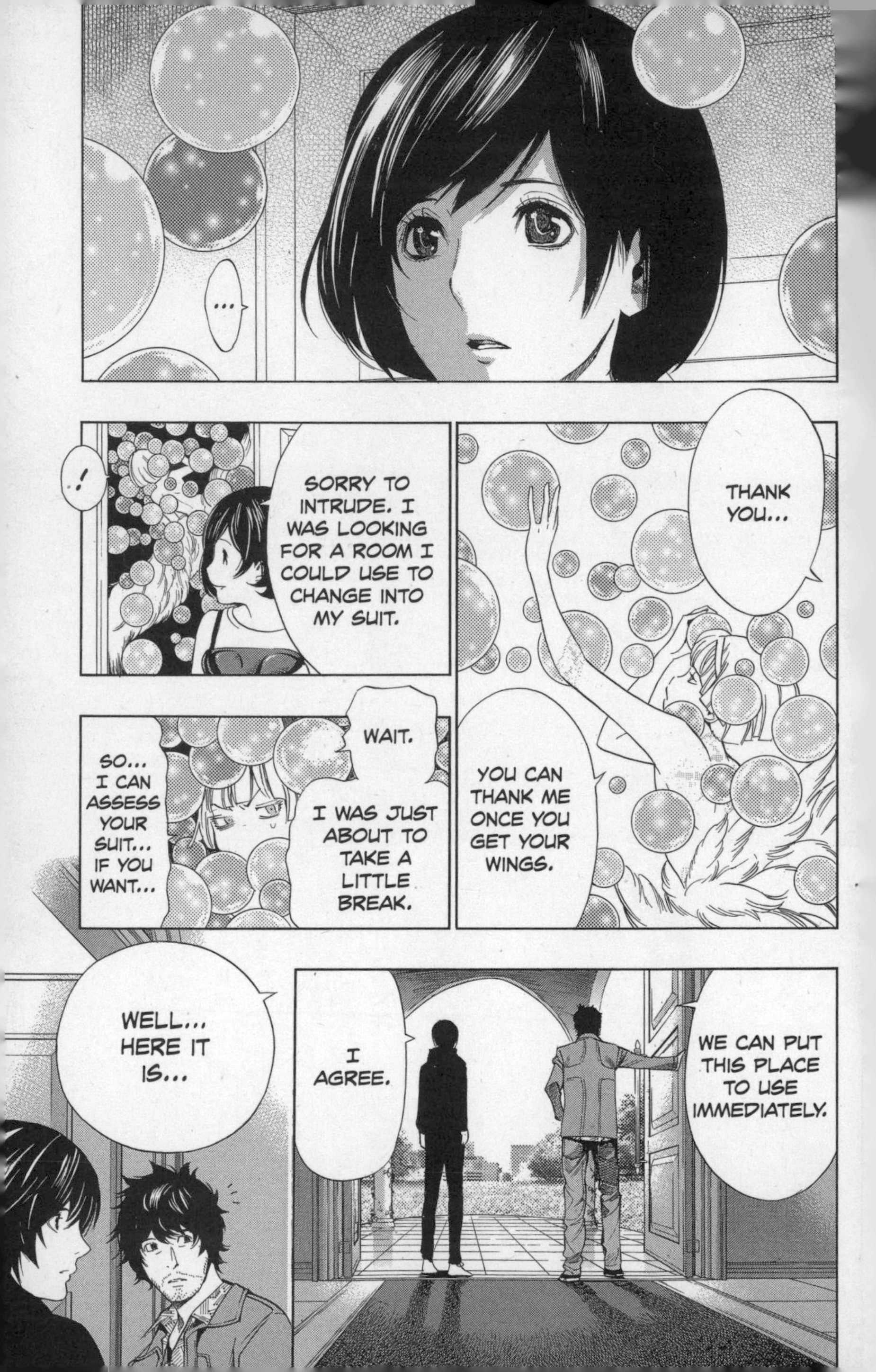
...
THANK YOU...
YOU CAN THANK ME ONCE YOU GET YOUR WINGS.
!
SORRY TO INTRUDE. I WAS LOOKING FOR A ROOM I COULD USE TO CHANGE INTO MY SUIT.
WAIT.
I WAS JUST ABOUT TO TAKE A LITTLE BREAK.
SO... I CAN ASSESS YOUR SUIT... IF YOU WANT...
WE CAN PUT THIS PLACE TO USE IMMEDIATELY.
I AGREE.
WELL... HERE IT IS...

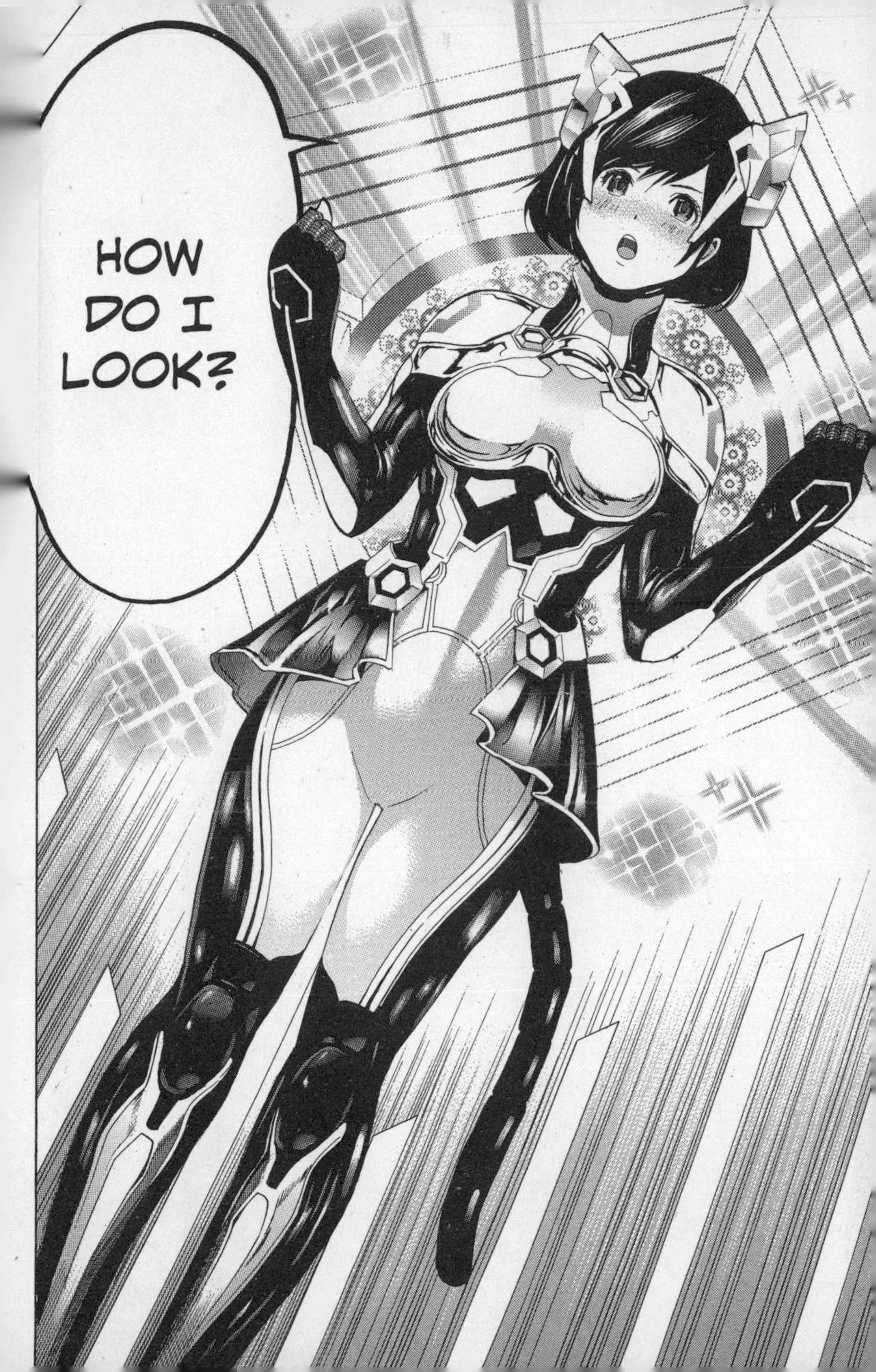
HOW DO I LOOK?

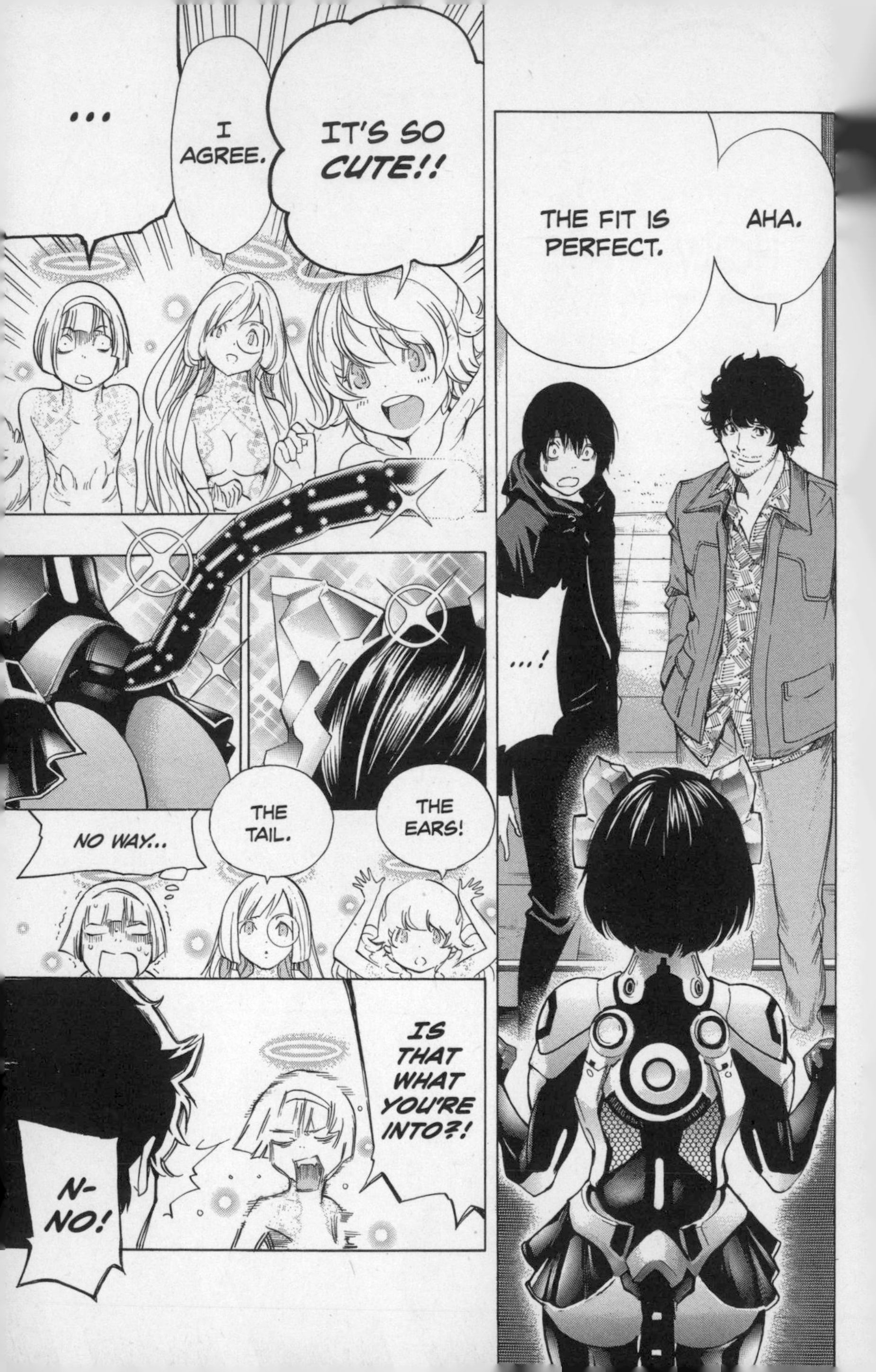
AHA.
THE FIT IS PERFECT.
...!
IT'S SO CUTE!!
I AGREE.
...
THE EARS!
THE TAIL.
NO WAY...
IS THAT WHAT YOU'RE INTO?!
N-NO!

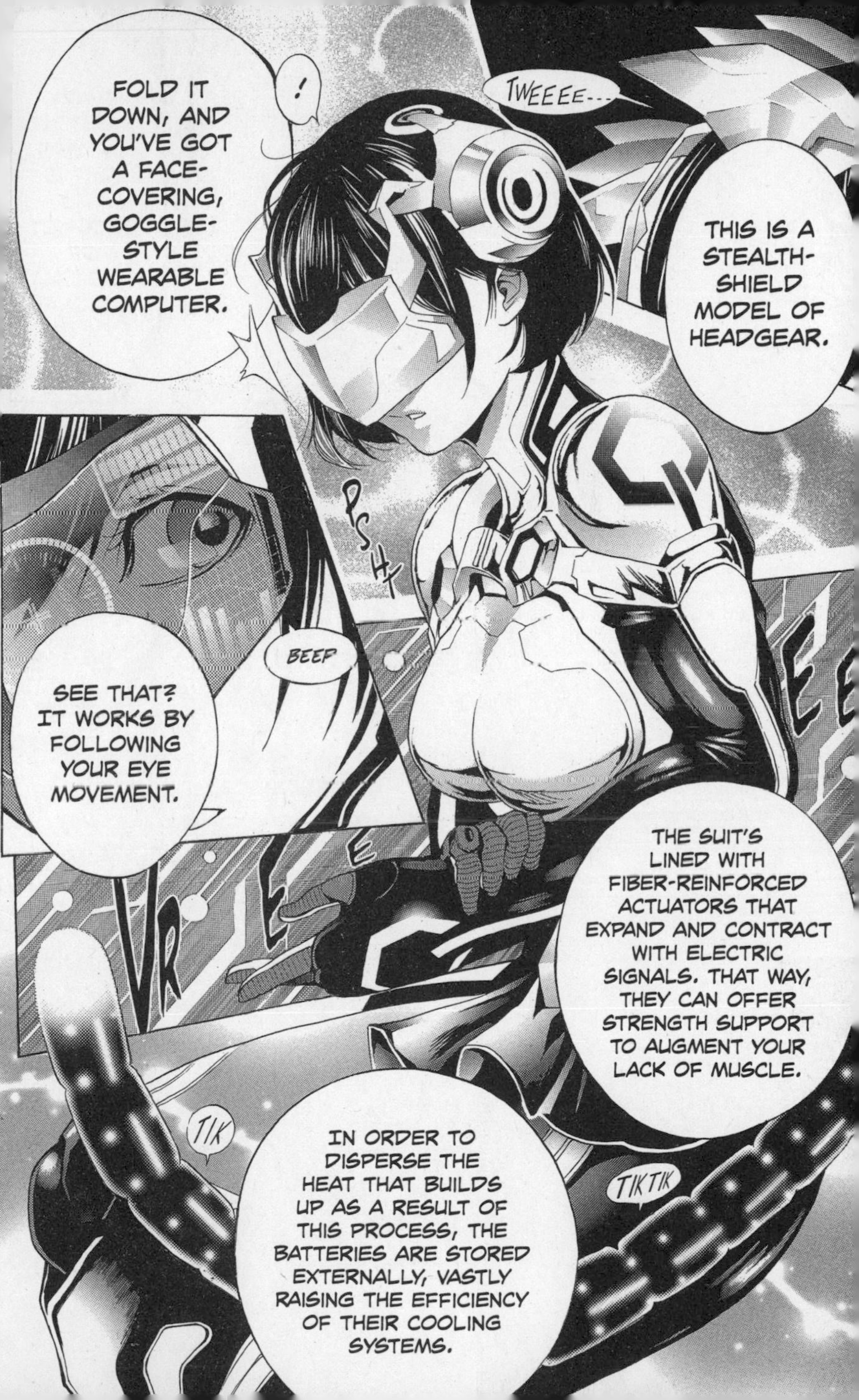
TWEEEE...
THIS IS A STEALTH-SHIELD MODEL OF HEADGEAR.
!
FOLD IT DOWN, AND YOU'VE GOT A FACE-COVERING, GOGGLE-STYLE WEARABLE COMPUTER.
PSHT
BEEP
SEE THAT? IT WORKS BY FOLLOWING YOUR EYE MOVEMENT.
THE SUIT'S LINED WITH FIBER-REINFORCED ACTUATORS THAT EXPAND AND CONTRACT WITH ELECTRIC SIGNALS. THAT WAY, THEY CAN OFFER STRENGTH SUPPORT TO AUGMENT YOUR LACK OF MUSCLE.
TIKTIK
TIK
IN ORDER TO DISPERSE THE HEAT THAT BUILDS UP AS A RESULT OF THIS PROCESS, THE BATTERIES ARE STORED EXTERNALLY, VASTLY RAISING THE EFFICIENCY OF THEIR COOLING SYSTEMS.

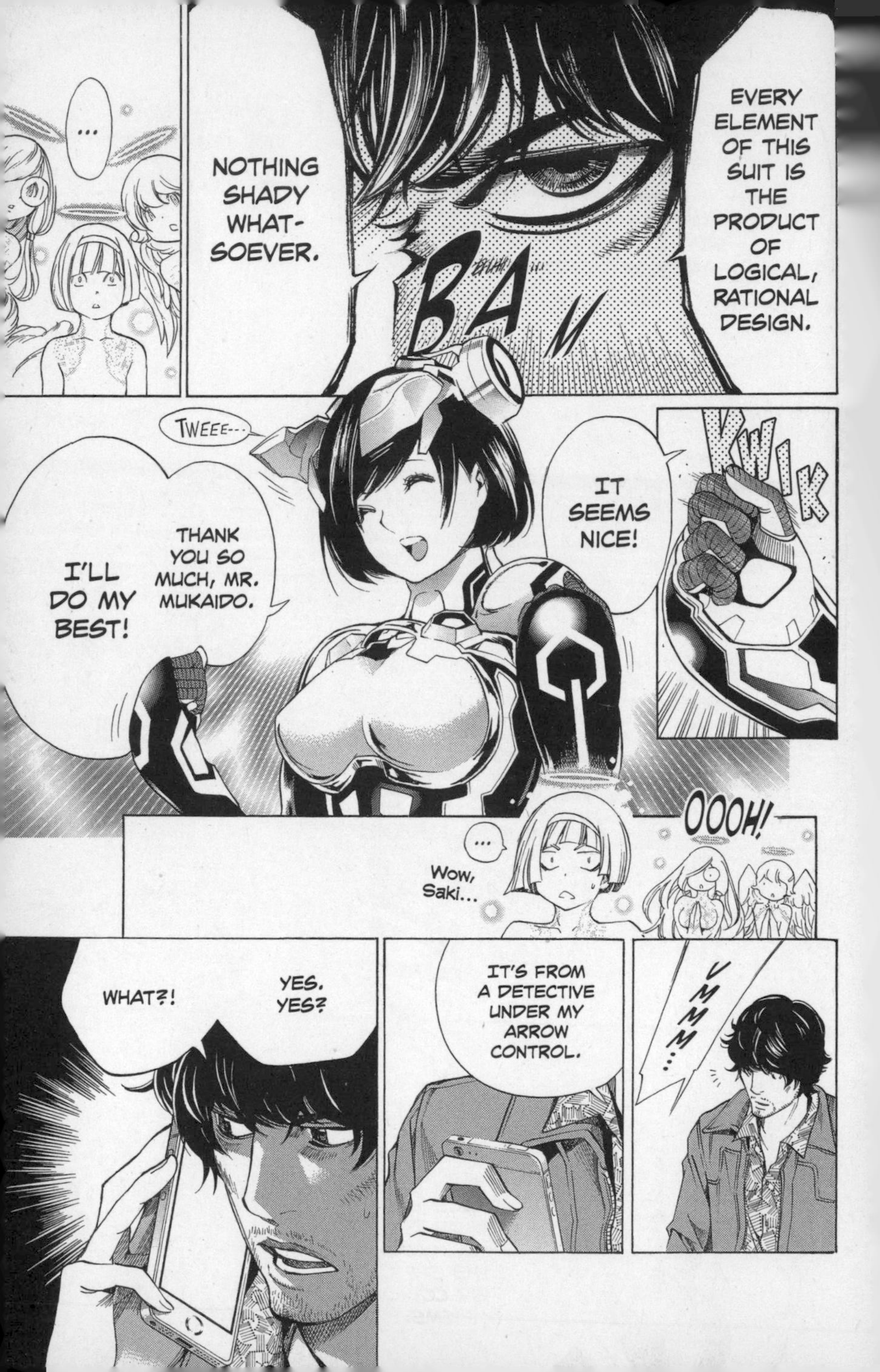
EVERY ELEMENT OF THIS SUIT IS THE PRODUCT OF LOGICAL, RATIONAL DESIGN.
BAM
NOTHING SHADY WHAT-SOEVER.
...
KWIK
IT SEEMS NICE!
TWEEE---
THANK YOU SO MUCH, MR. MUKAIDO.
I'LL DO MY BEST!
OOOH!
...
Wow, Saki...
VMMM...
IT'S FROM A DETECTIVE UNDER MY ARROW CONTROL.
YES. YES?
WHAT?!

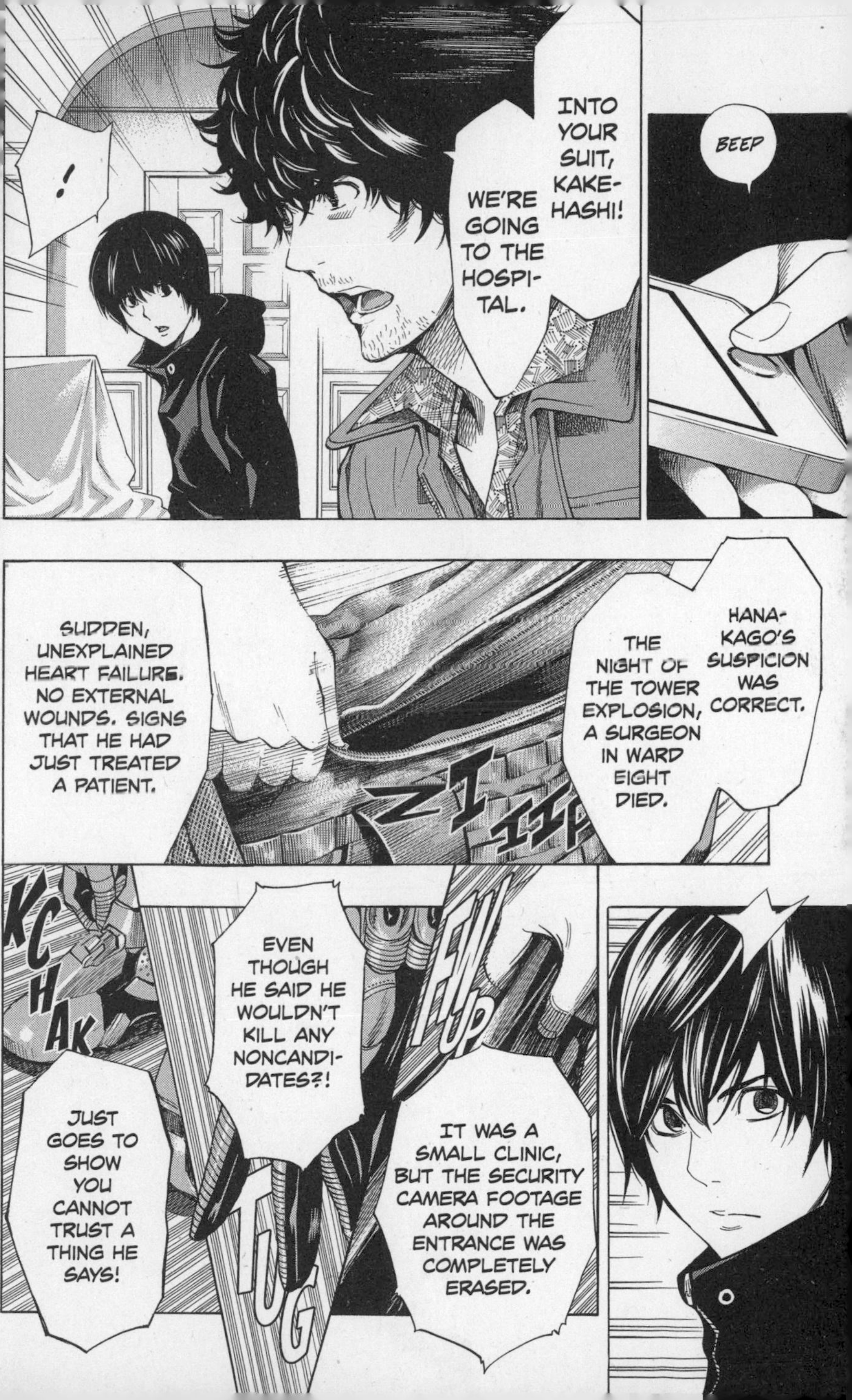
BEEP
INTO YOUR SUIT, KAKE-HASHI!
WE'RE GOING TO THE HOSPITAL.
!
HANA-KAGO'S SUSPICION WAS CORRECT.
THE NIGHT OF THE TOWER EXPLOSION, A SURGEON IN WARD EIGHT DIED.
SUDDEN, UNEXPLAINED HEART FAILURE. NO EXTERNAL WOUNDS. SIGNS THAT HE HAD JUST TREATED A PATIENT.
ZIIIP
IT WAS A SMALL CLINIC, BUT THE SECURITY CAMERA FOOTAGE AROUND THE ENTRANCE WAS COMPLETELY ERASED.
FWUP
EVEN THOUGH HE SAID HE WOULDN'T KILL ANY NONCANDI-DATES?!
TUG
KCHAK
JUST GOES TO SHOW YOU CANNOT TRUST A THING HE SAYS!

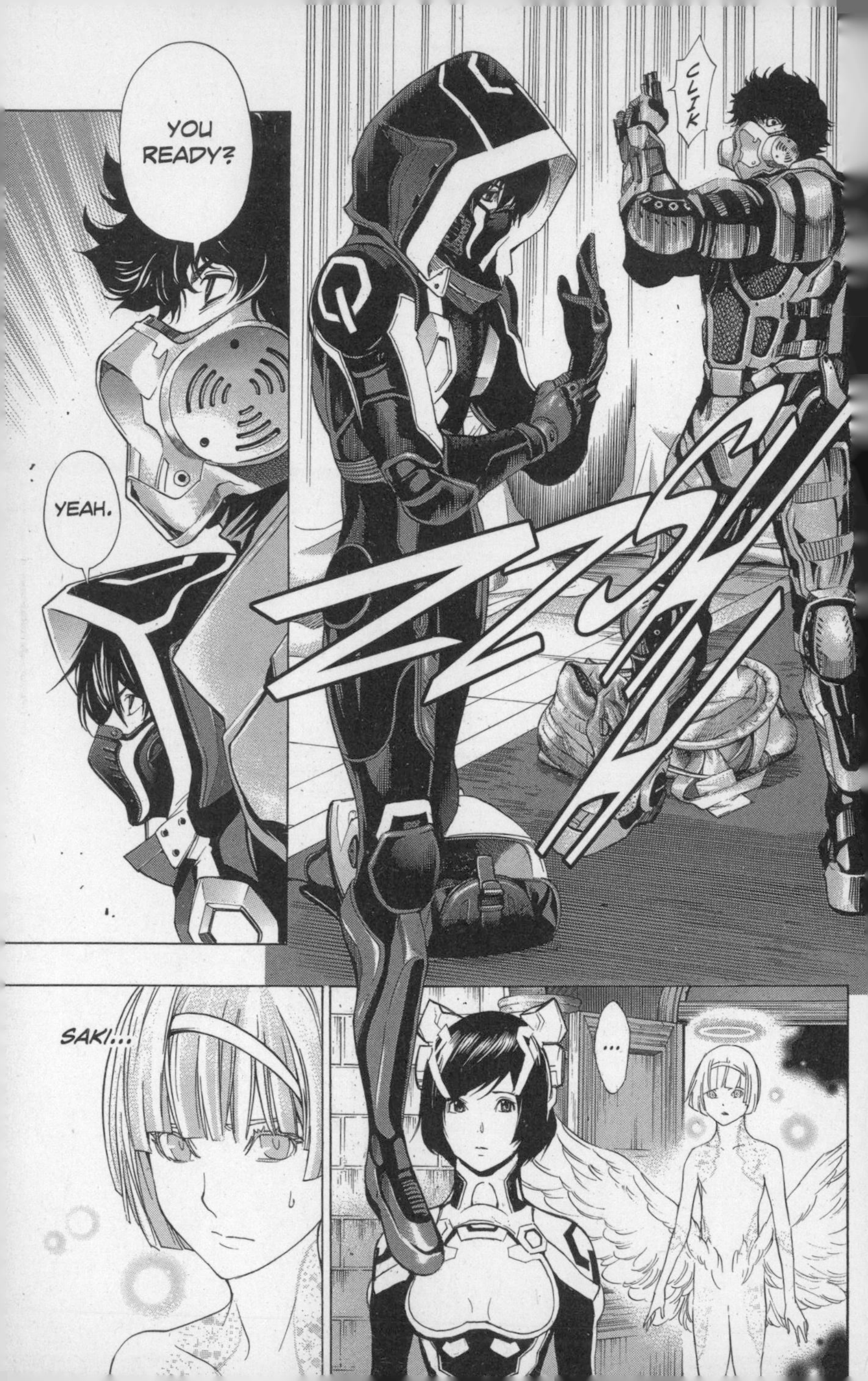
CLIK
YOU READY?
YEAH.
...
SAKI...

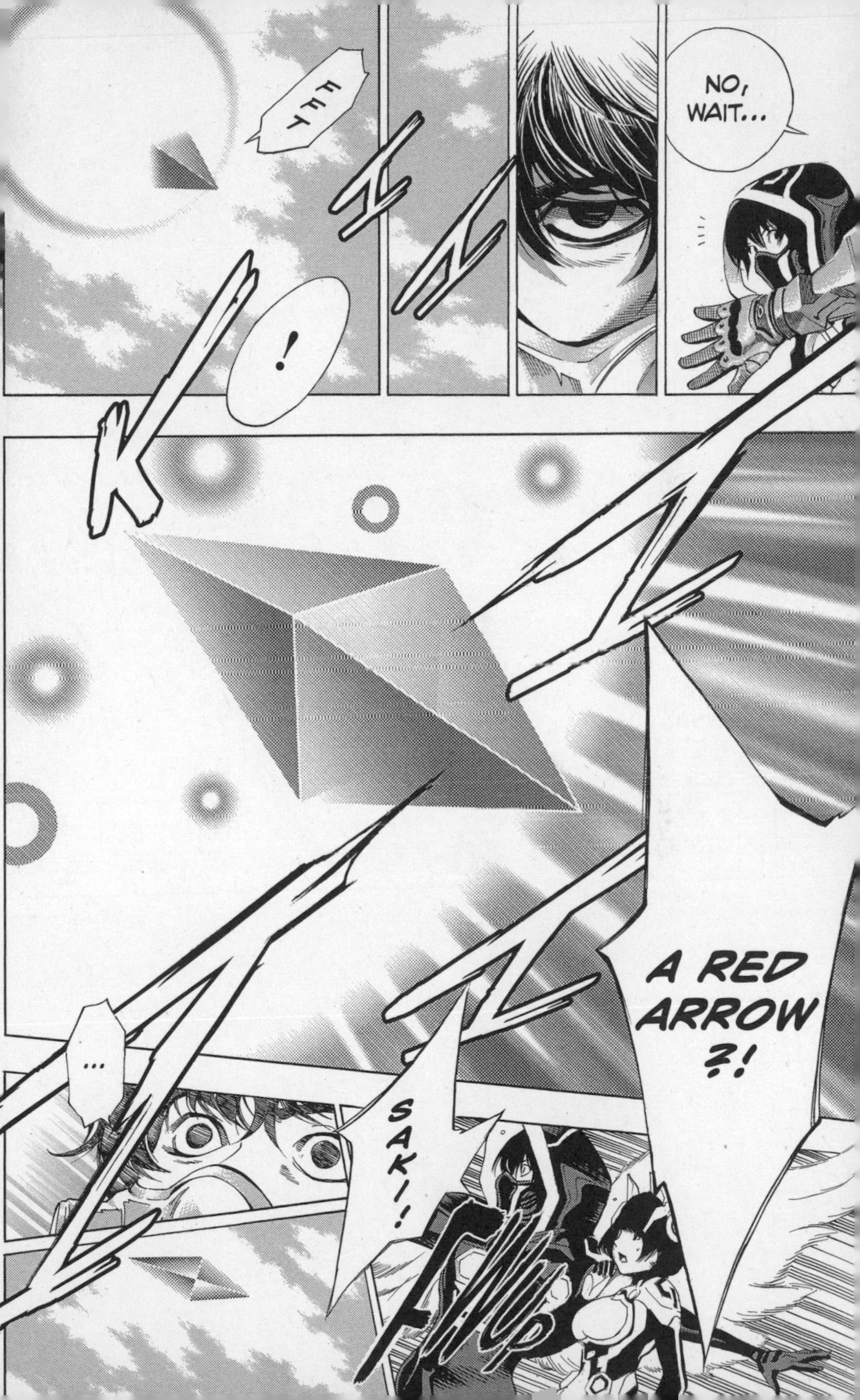
NO, WAIT...
FFT
!
A RED ARROW ?!
SAKI!!
...

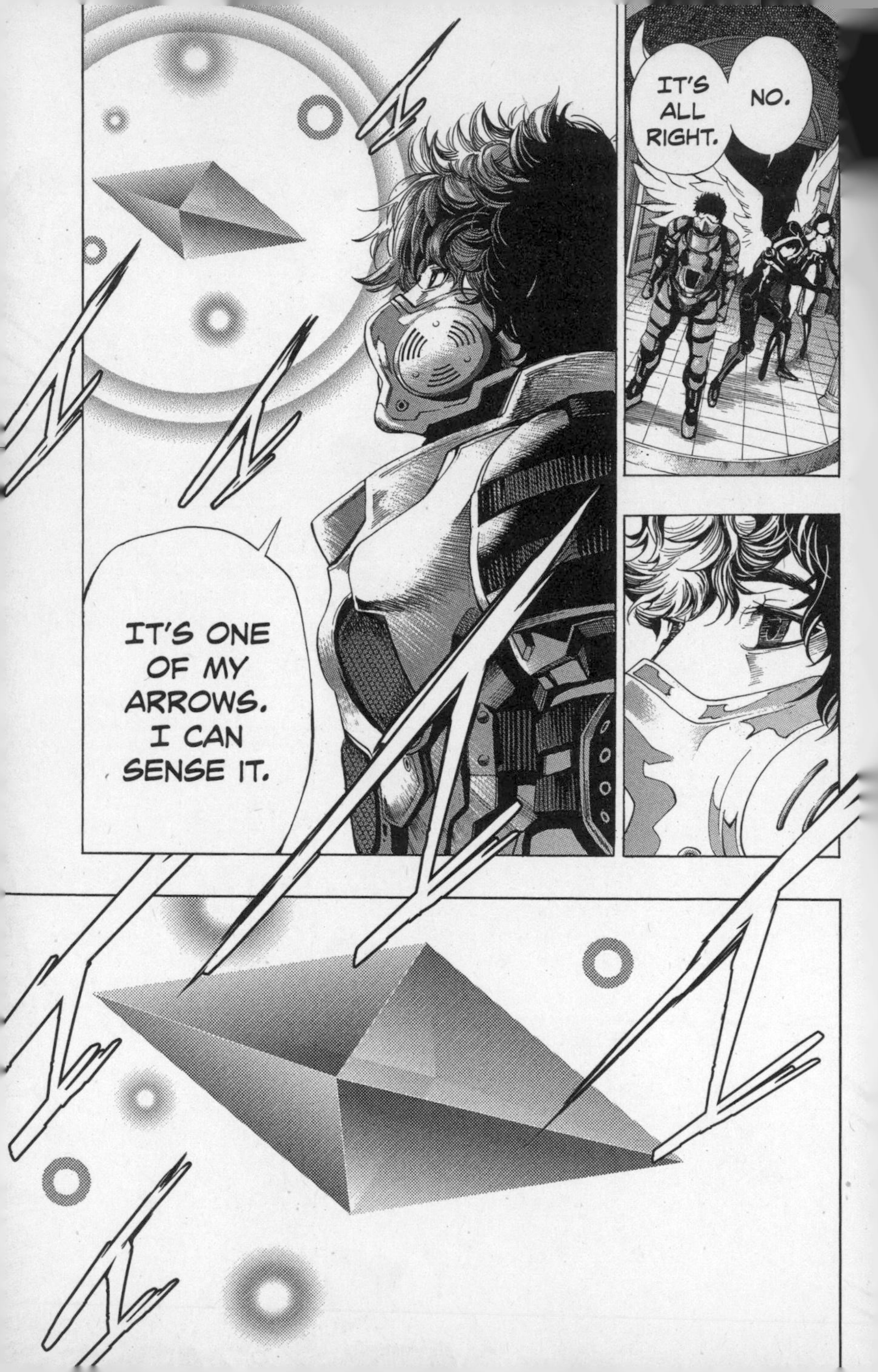
NO.
IT'S ALL RIGHT.
IT'S ONE OF MY ARROWS. I CAN SENSE IT.

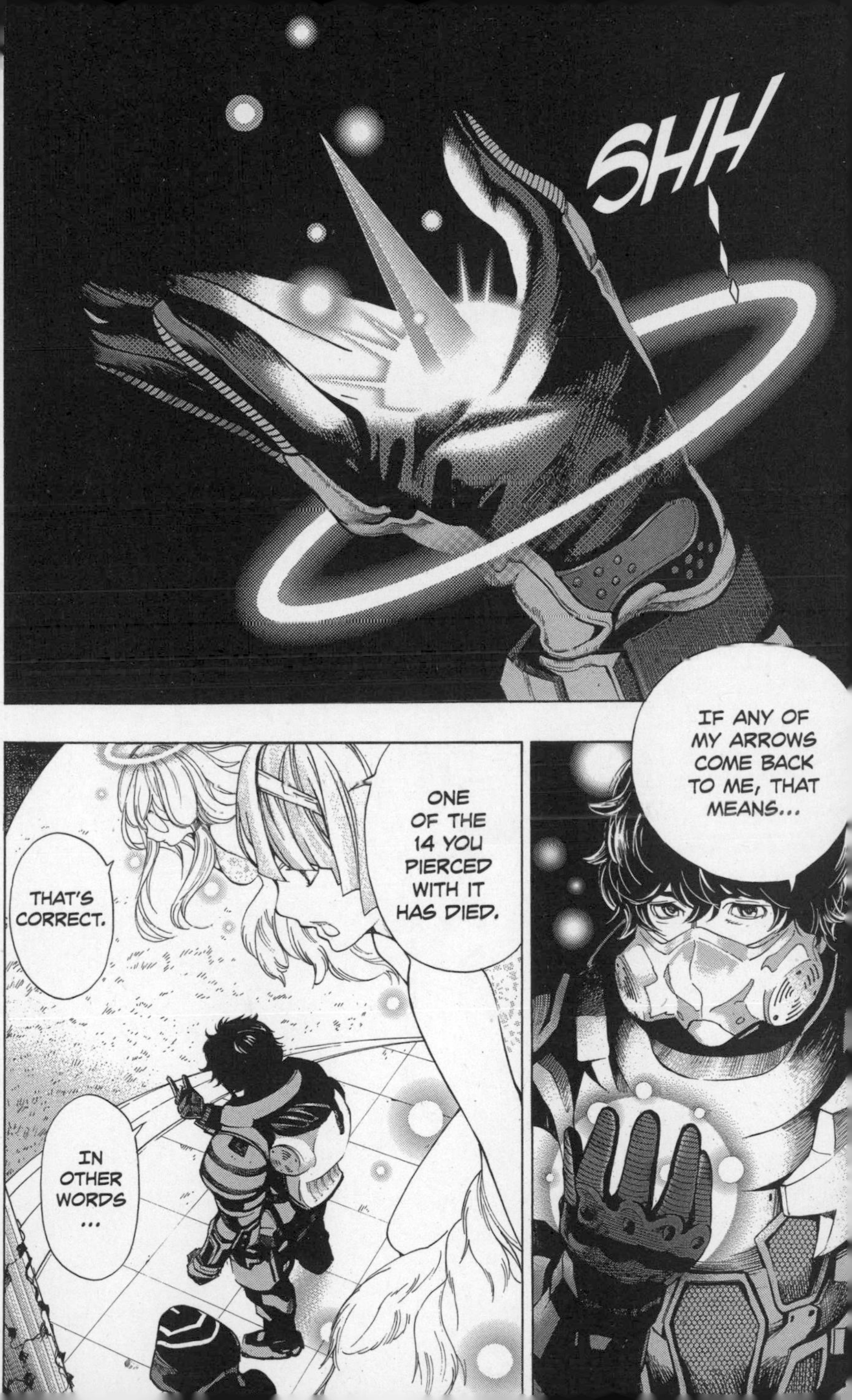
SHH
IF ANY OF MY ARROWS COME BACK TO ME, THAT MEANS...
ONE OF THE 14 YOU PIERCED WITH IT HAS DIED.
THAT'S CORRECT.
IN OTHER WORDS...

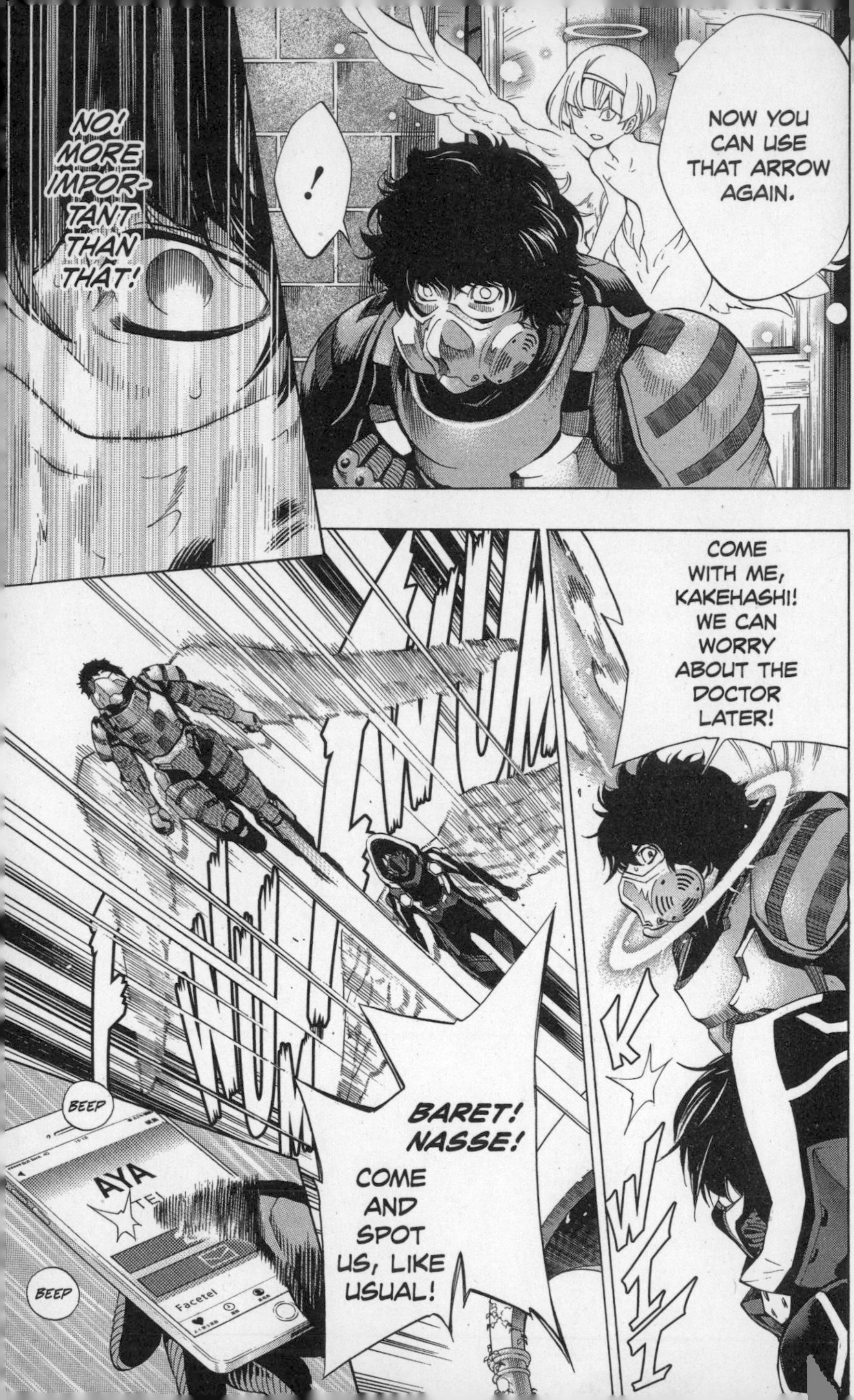
NOW YOU CAN USE THAT ARROW AGAIN.
!
NO! MORE IMPOR-TANT THAN THAT!
COME WITH ME, KAKEHASHI! WE CAN WORRY ABOUT THE DOCTOR LATER!
BARET! NASSE!
COME AND SPOT US, LIKE USUAL!
BEEP
AYA
Facetel
BEEP

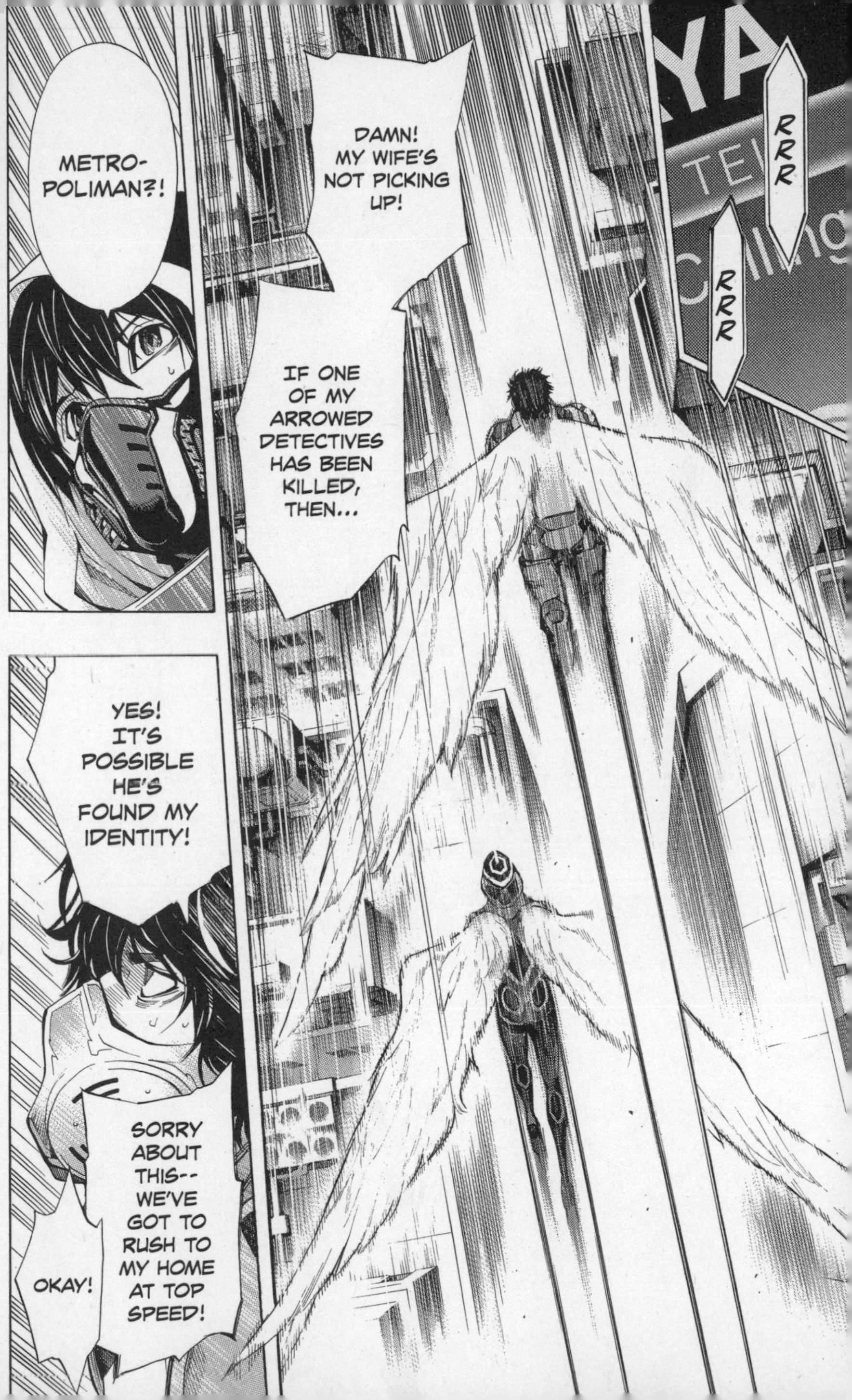
RRR
RRR
DAMN! MY WIFE'S NOT PICKING UP!
IF ONE OF MY ARROWED DETECTIVES HAS BEEN KILLED, THEN...
METRO-POLIMAN?!
YES! IT'S POSSIBLE HE'S FOUND MY IDENTITY!
SORRY ABOUT THIS-- WE'VE GOT TO RUSH TO MY HOME AT TOP SPEED!
OKAY!

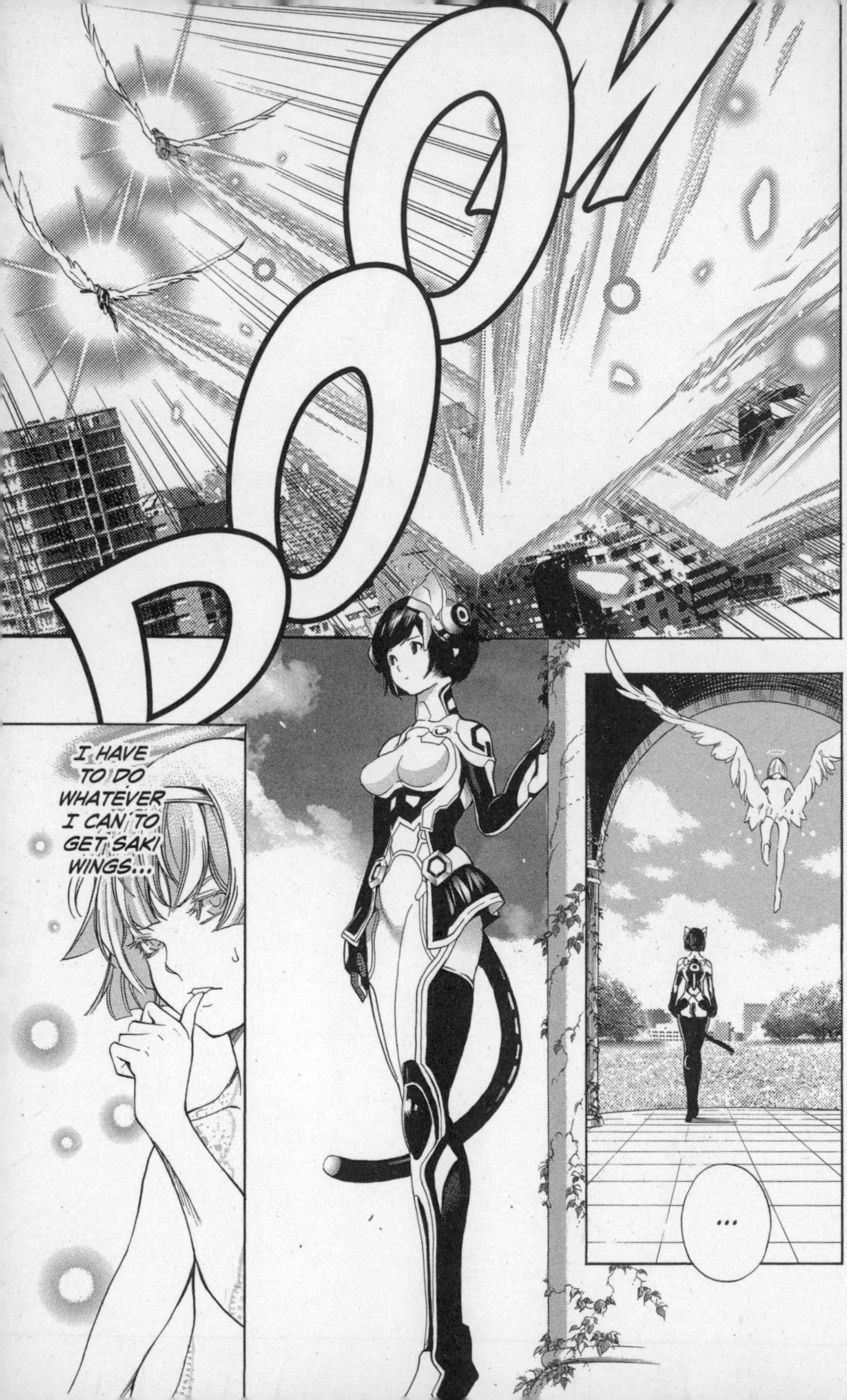
DOOOM
...
I HAVE TO DO WHATEVER I CAN TO GET SAKI WINGS...

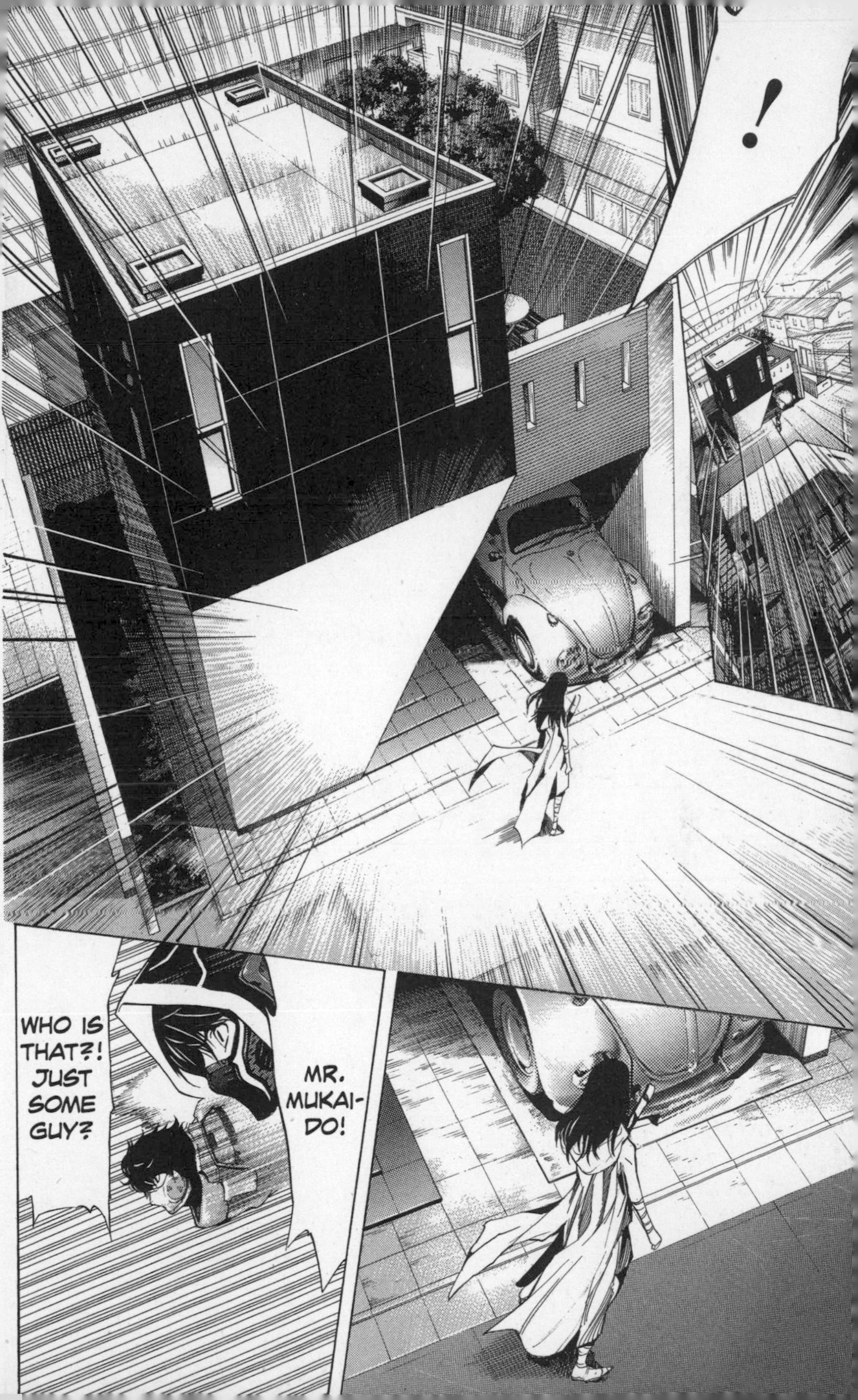
!
MR. MUKAI-DO!
WHO IS THAT?! JUST SOME GUY?

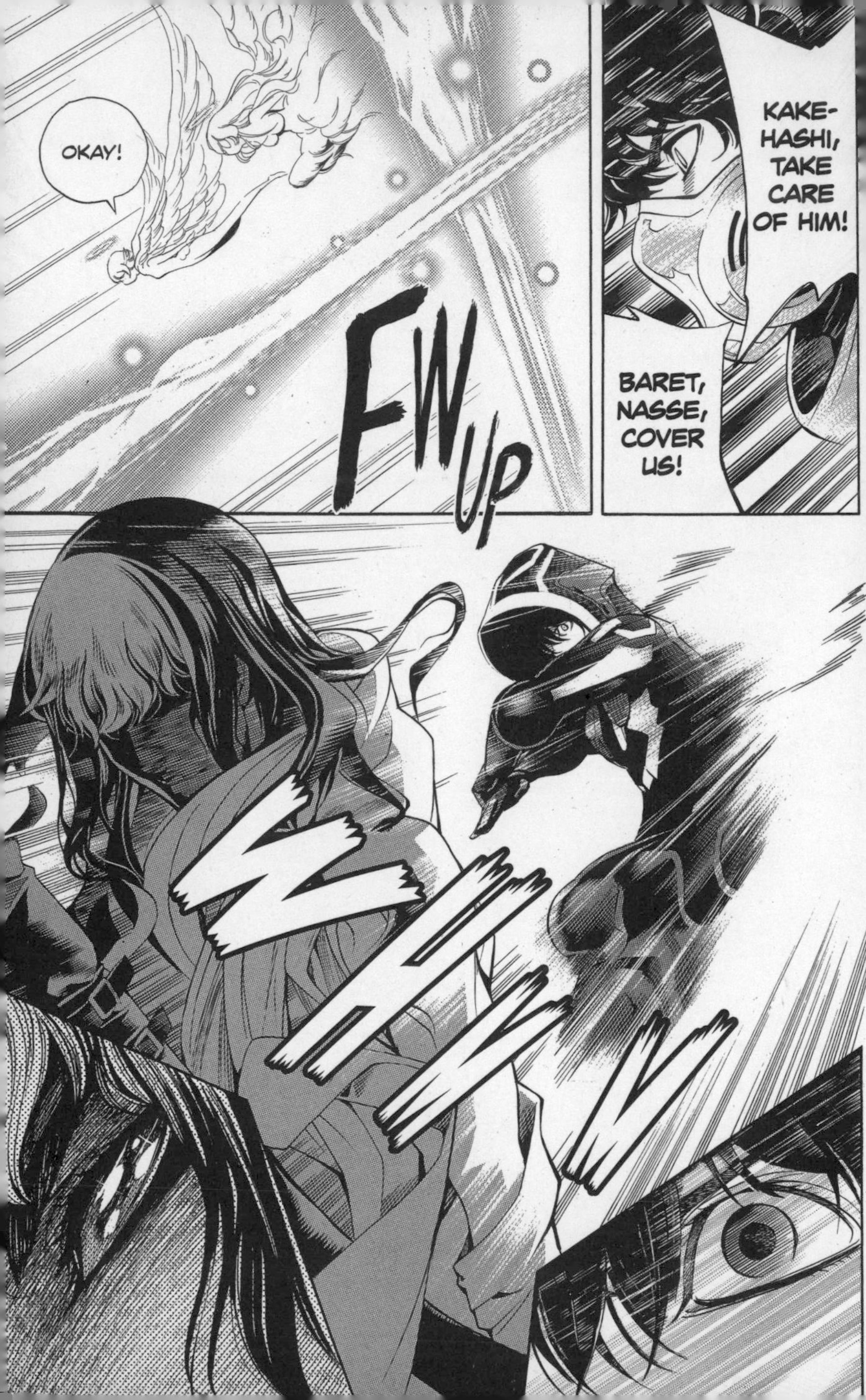
KAKE-HASHI, TAKE CARE OF HIM!
BARET, NASSE, COVER US!
OKAY!
FWUP

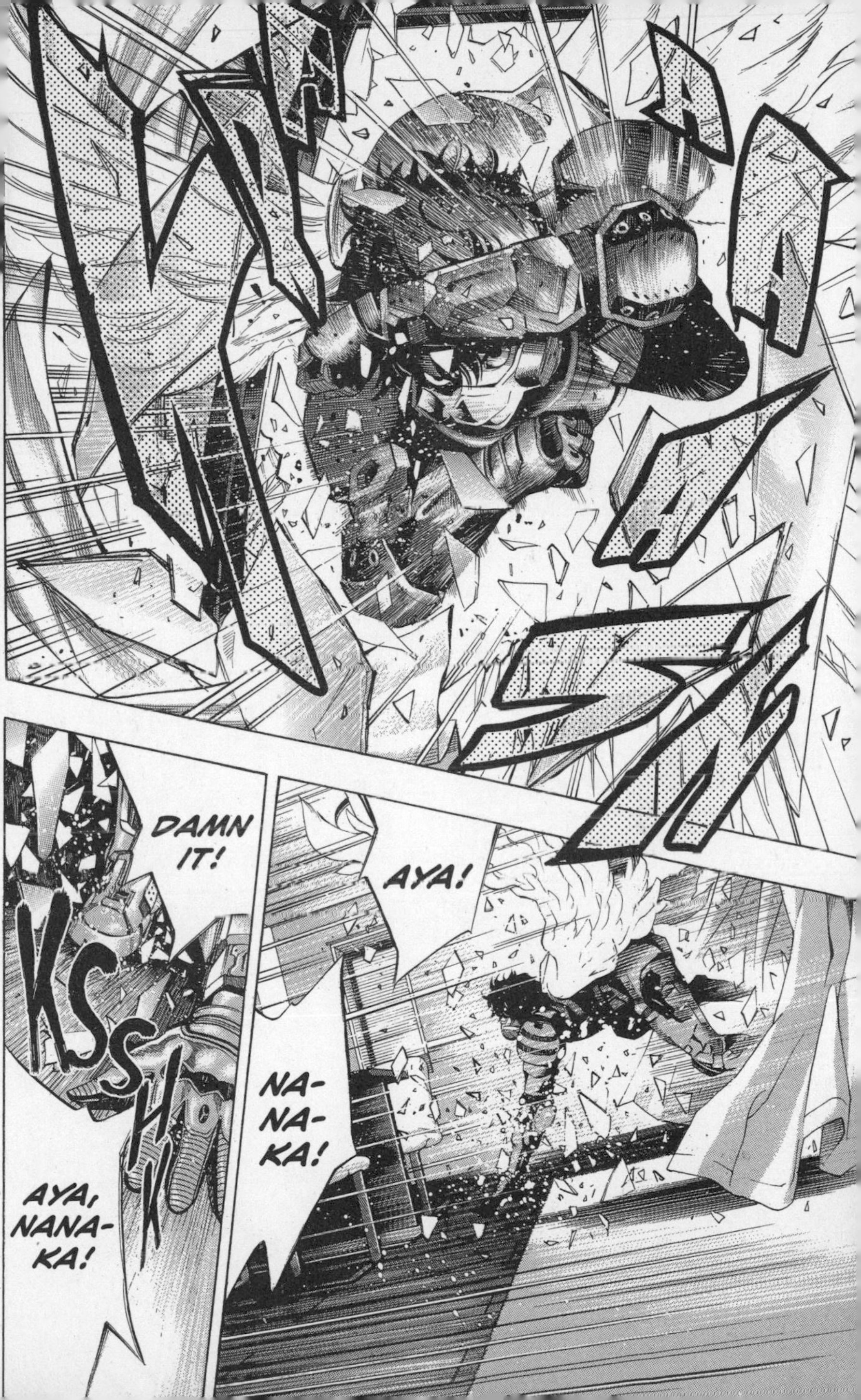
AYA!
NA-NA-KA!
DAMN IT!
KSSHK
AYA, NANA-KA!

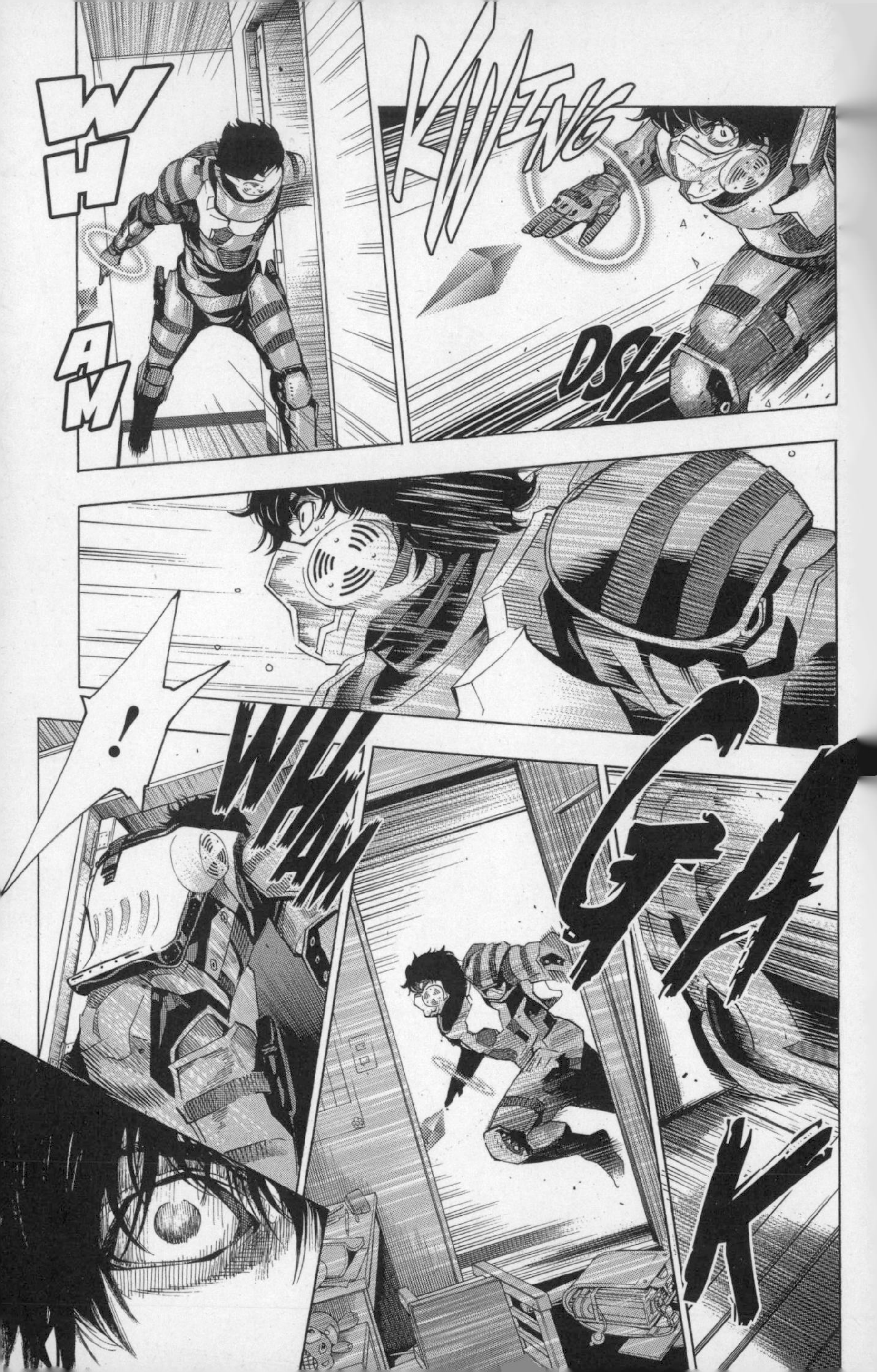
KWENG
DSH
WHAM
!
GAK
WHAM

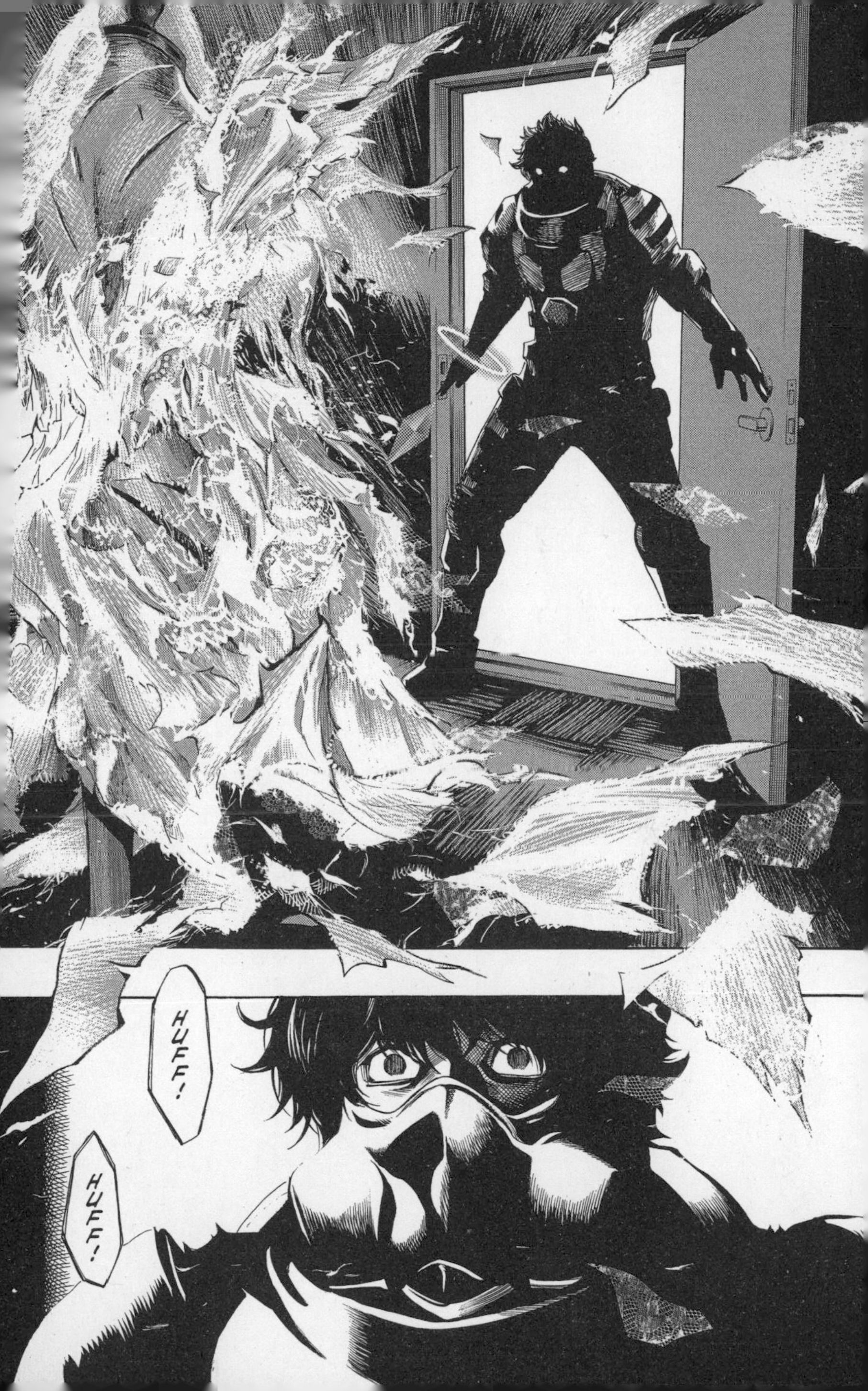
HUFF!
HUFF!

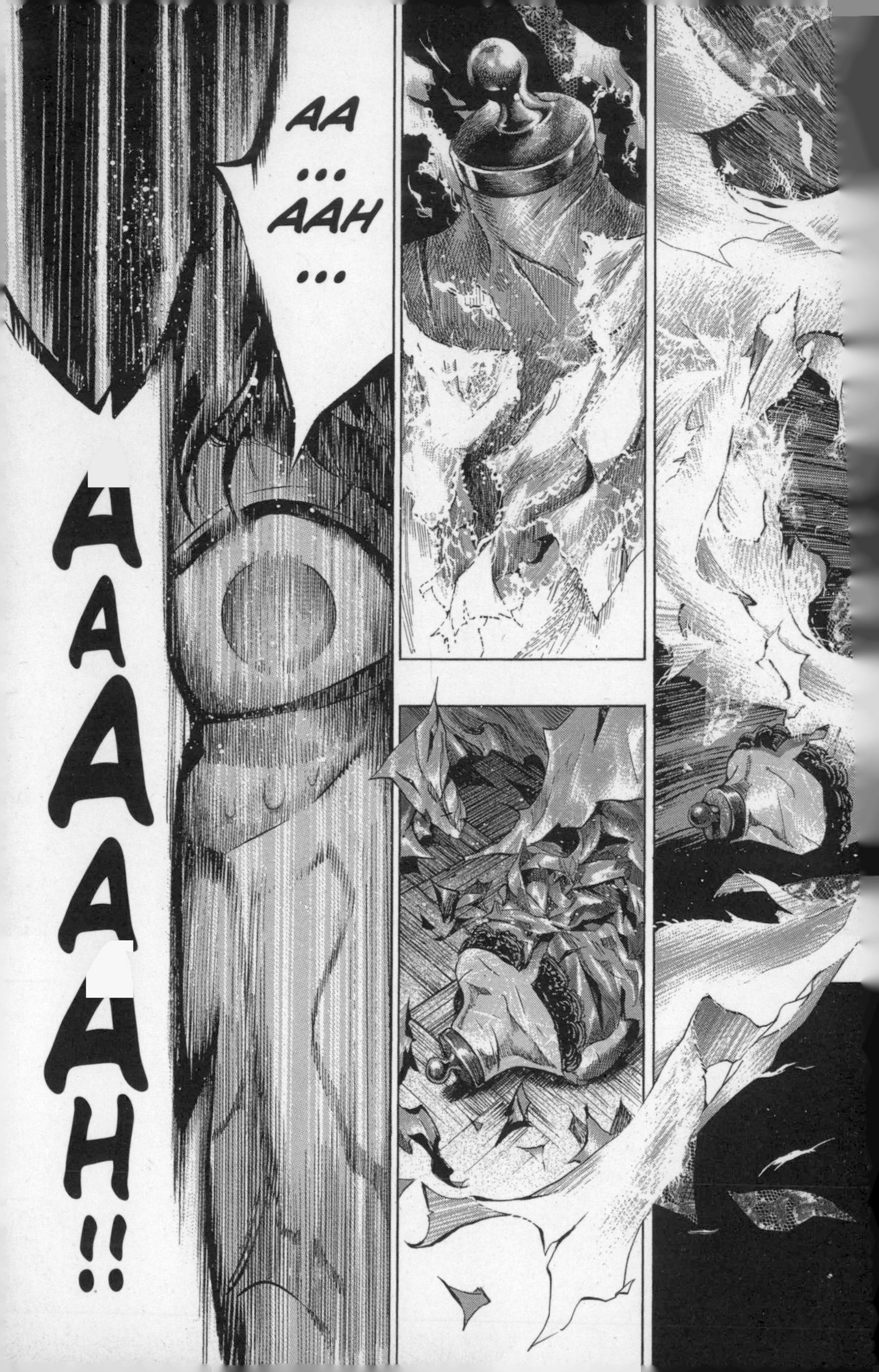
AA ... AAH ...
AAAAAAH!!

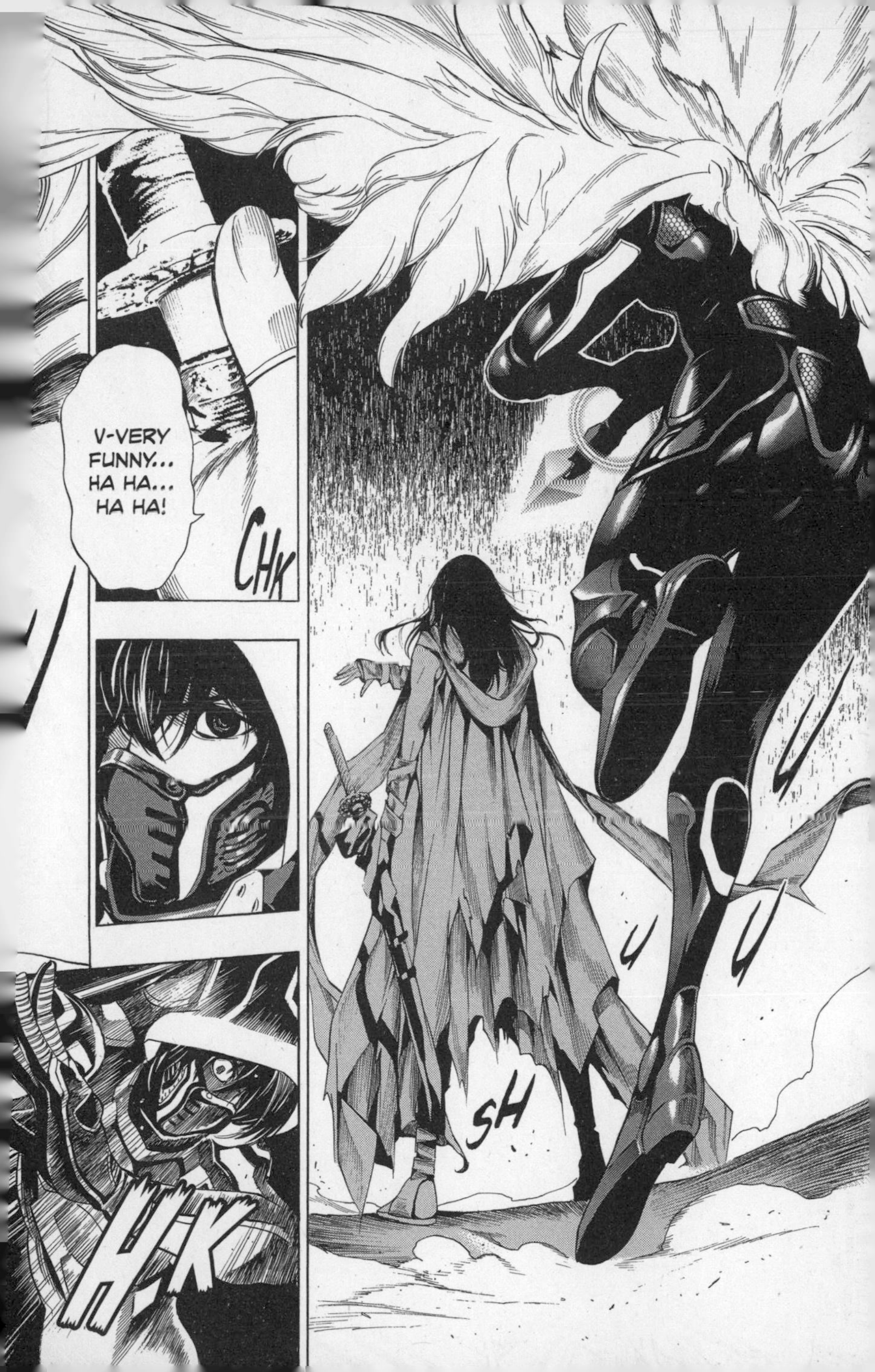
U
U
SH
V-VERY FUNNY... HA HA... HA HA!
CHK
HK

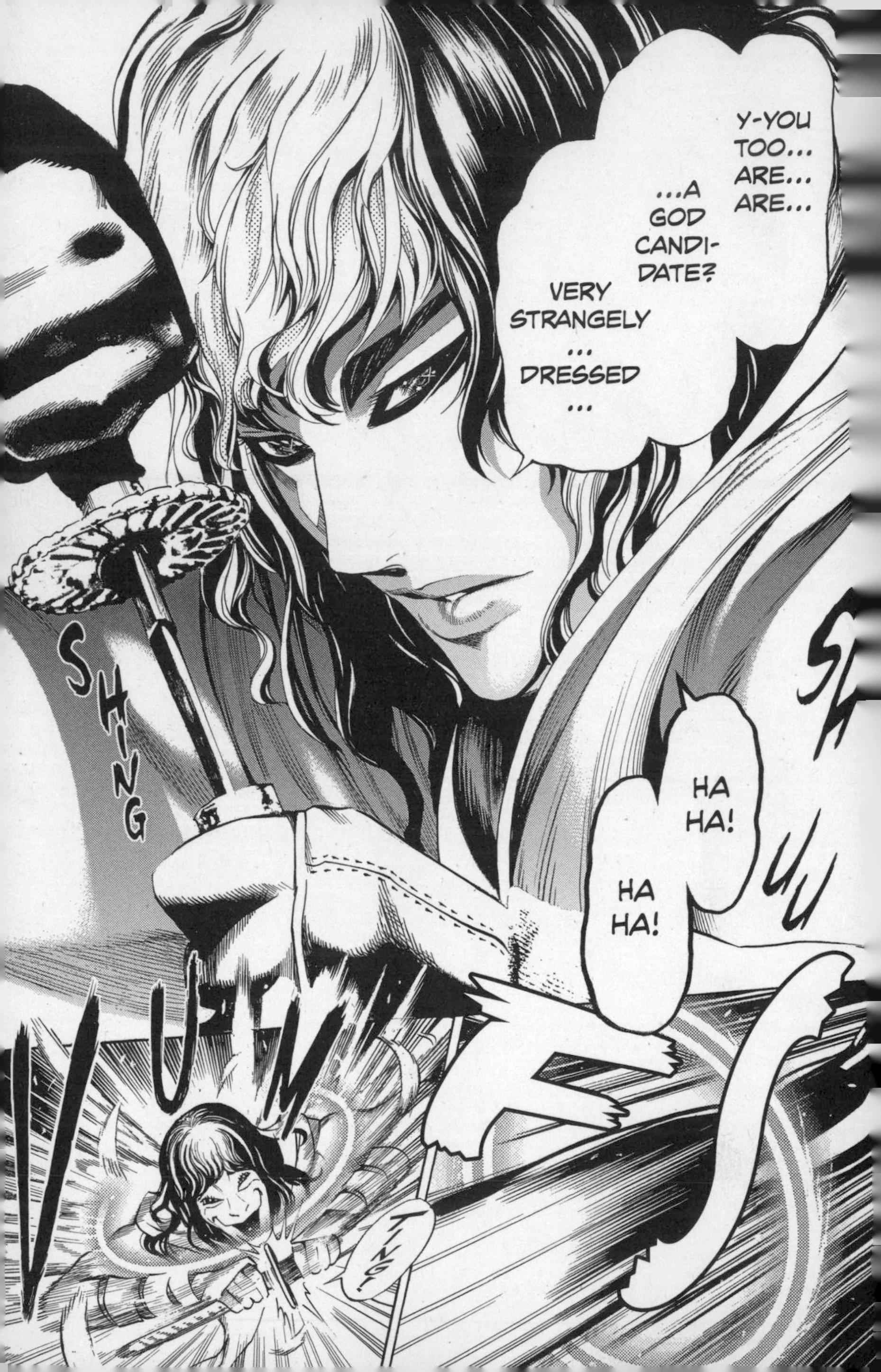

Y-YOU TOO... ARE... ARE...
...A GOD CANDI-DATE?
VERY STRANGELY ... DRESSED ...
SHUU
HA HA!
HA HA!
SHING
VUUM
TING!

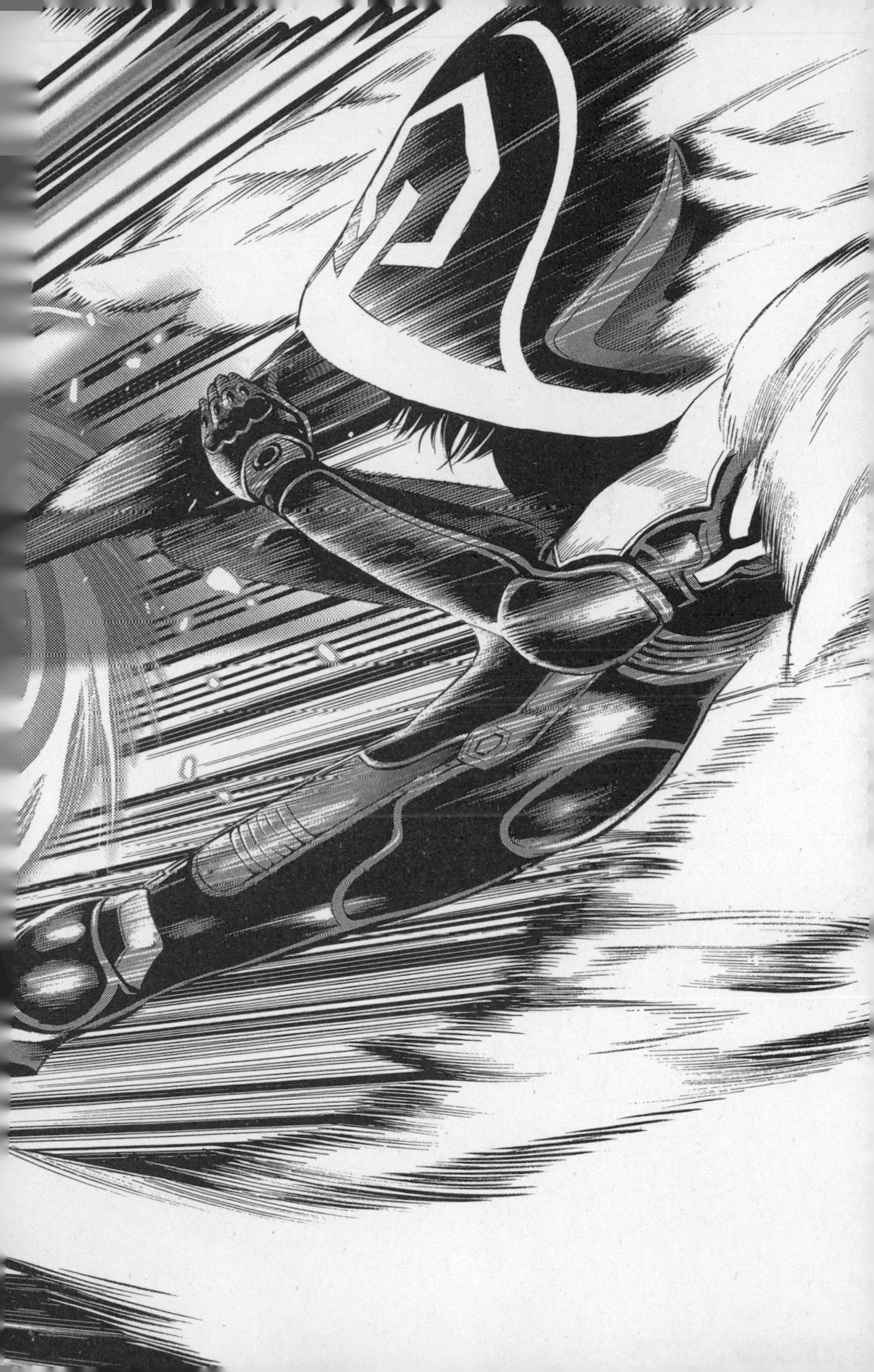

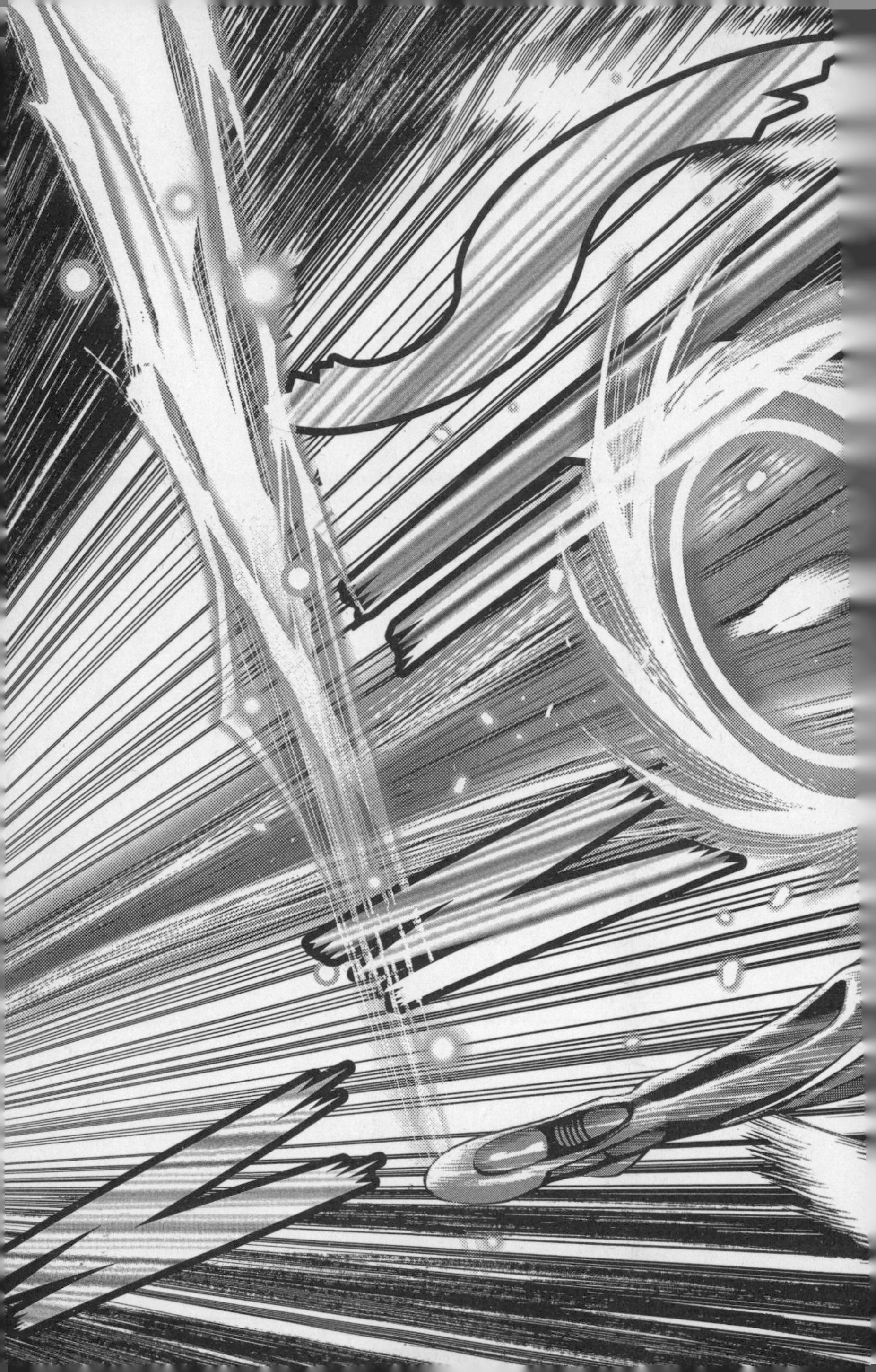

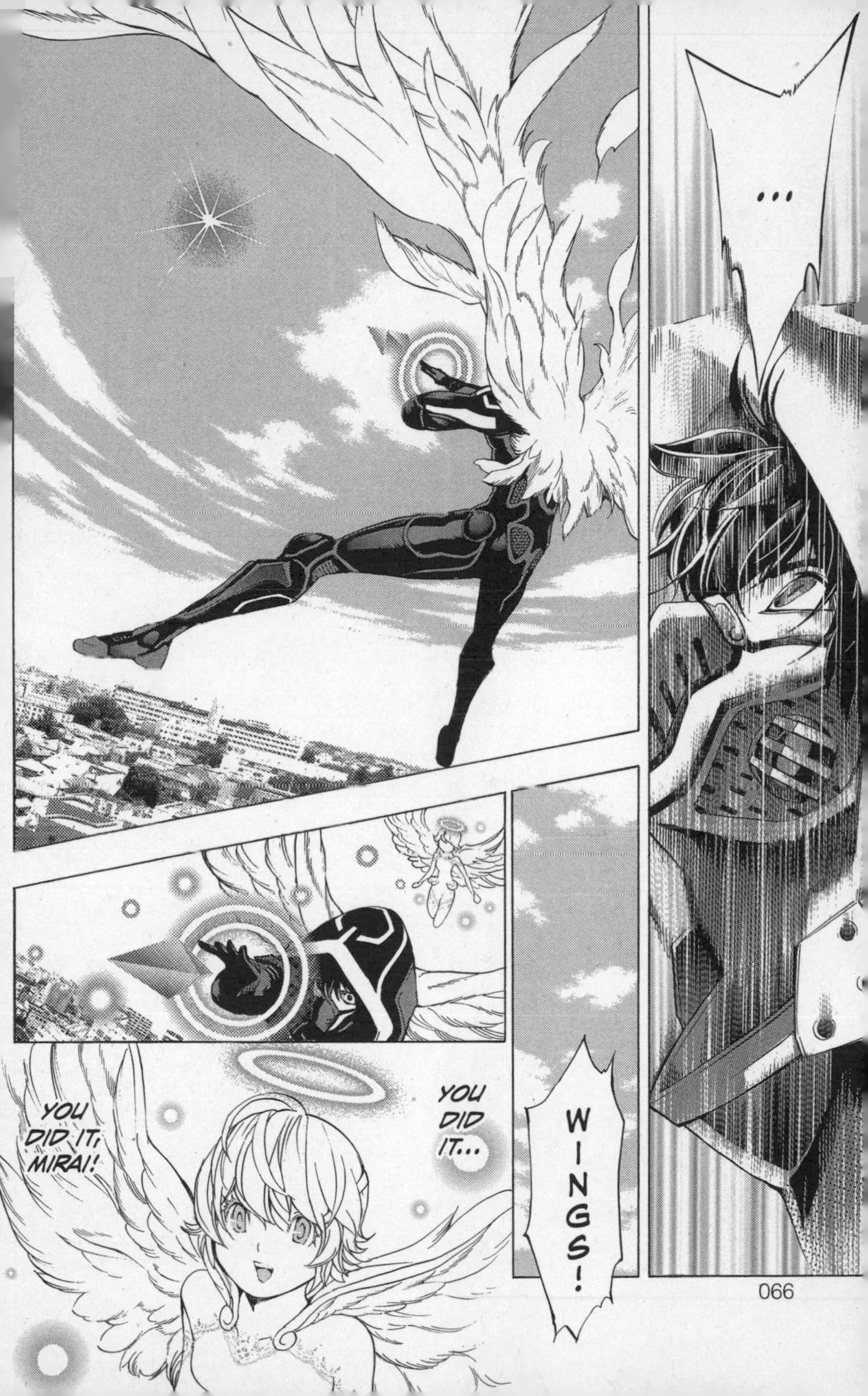
...
WINGS!
YOU DID IT...
YOU DID IT, MIRAI!

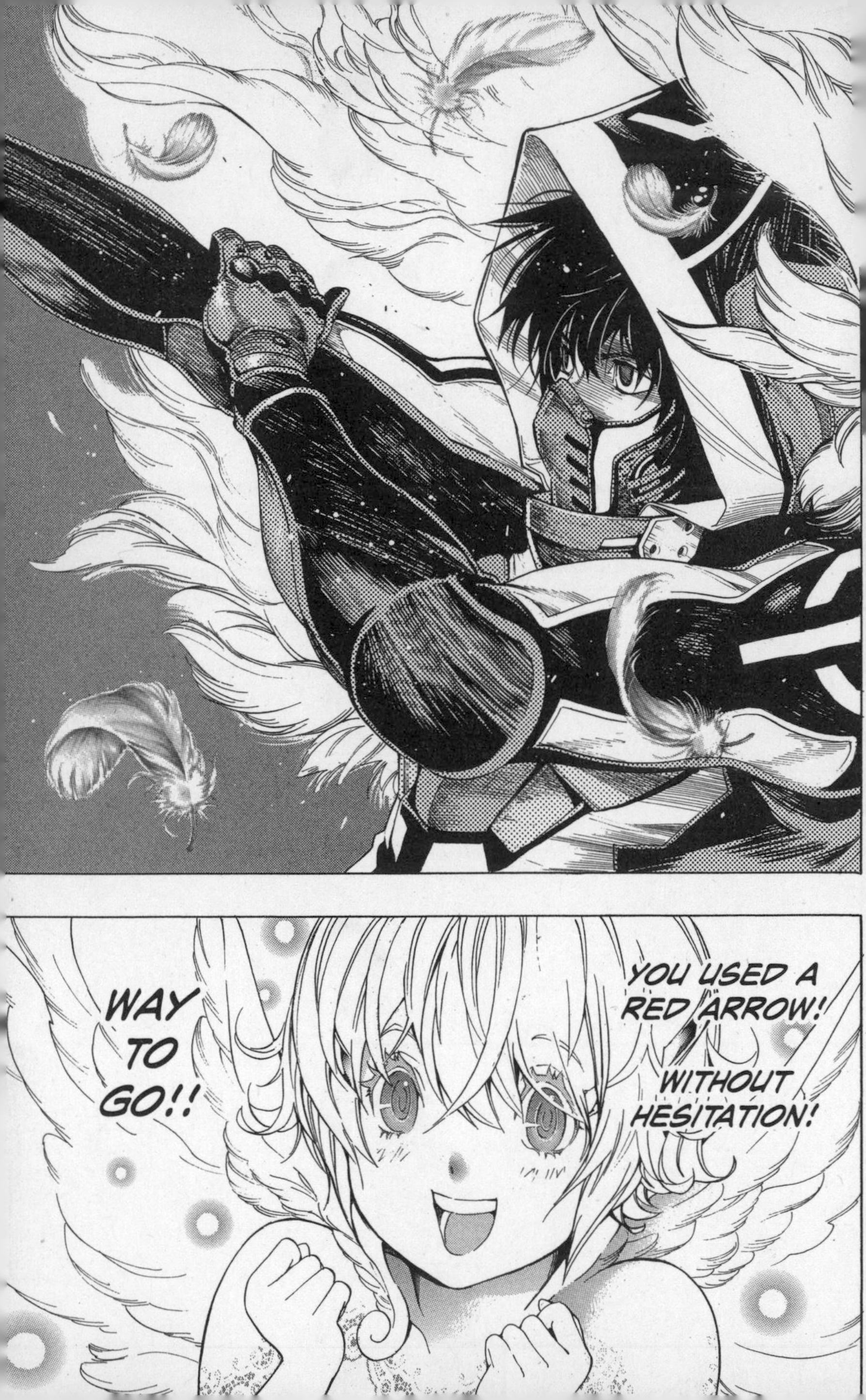
YOU USED A RED ARROW!
WITHOUT HESITATION!
WAY TO GO!!

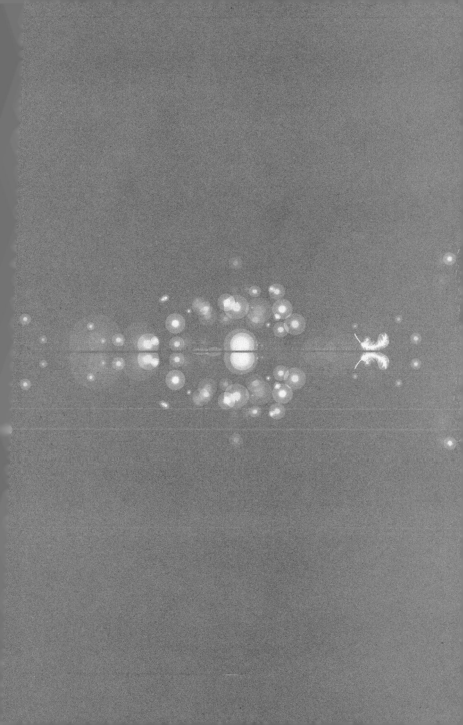

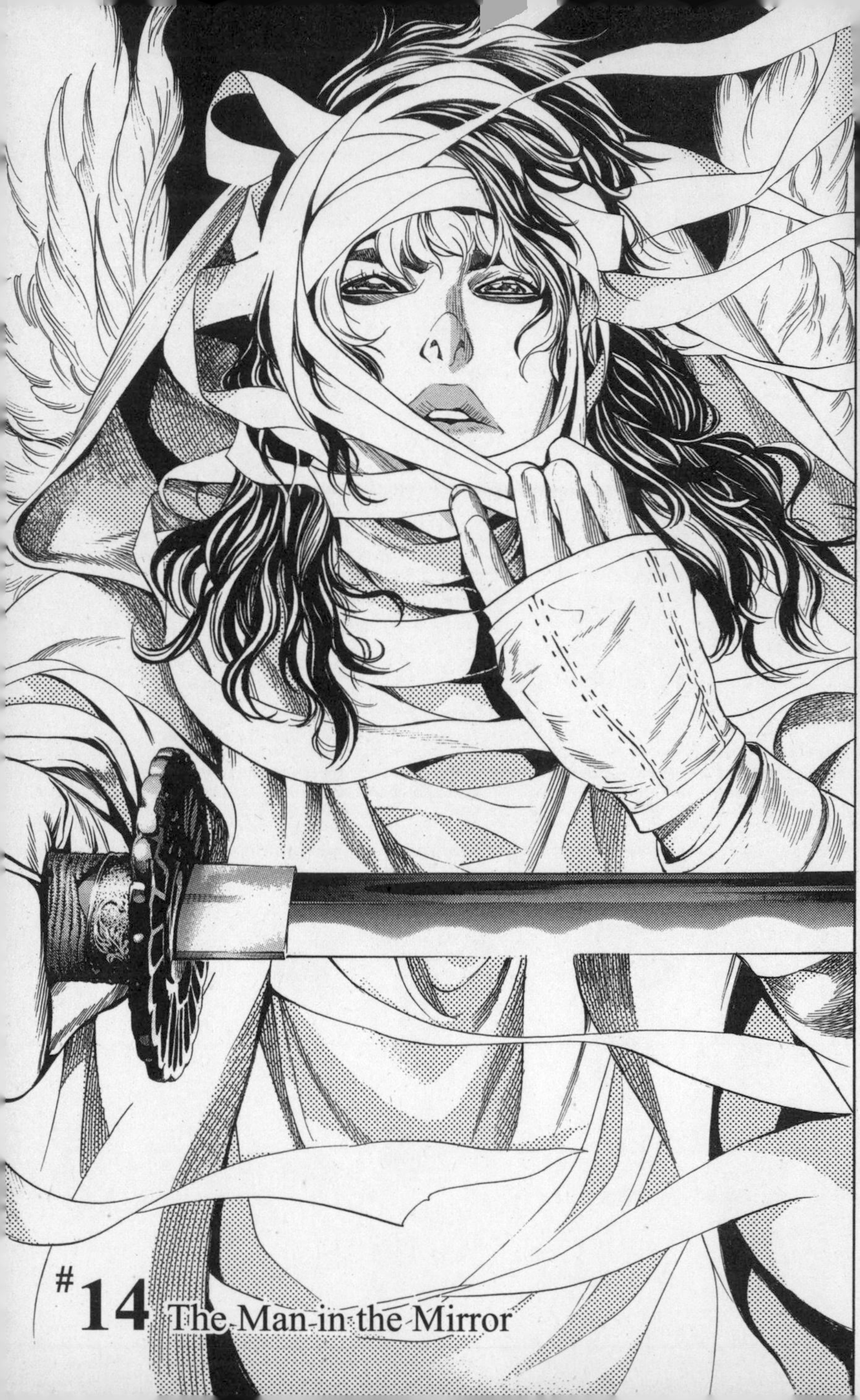
#14 The Man in the Mirror

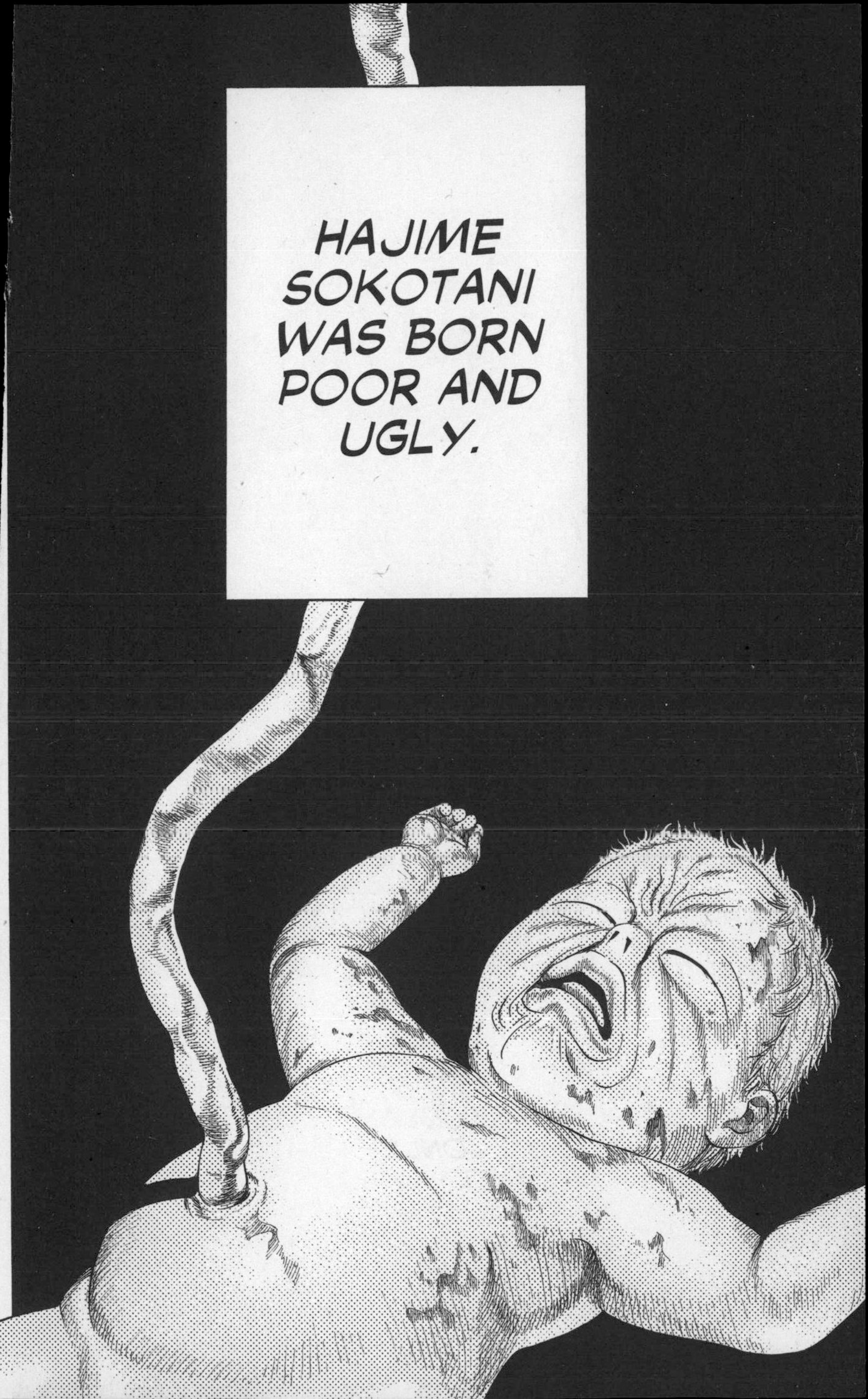
HAJIME SOKOTANI WAS BORN POOR AND UGLY.

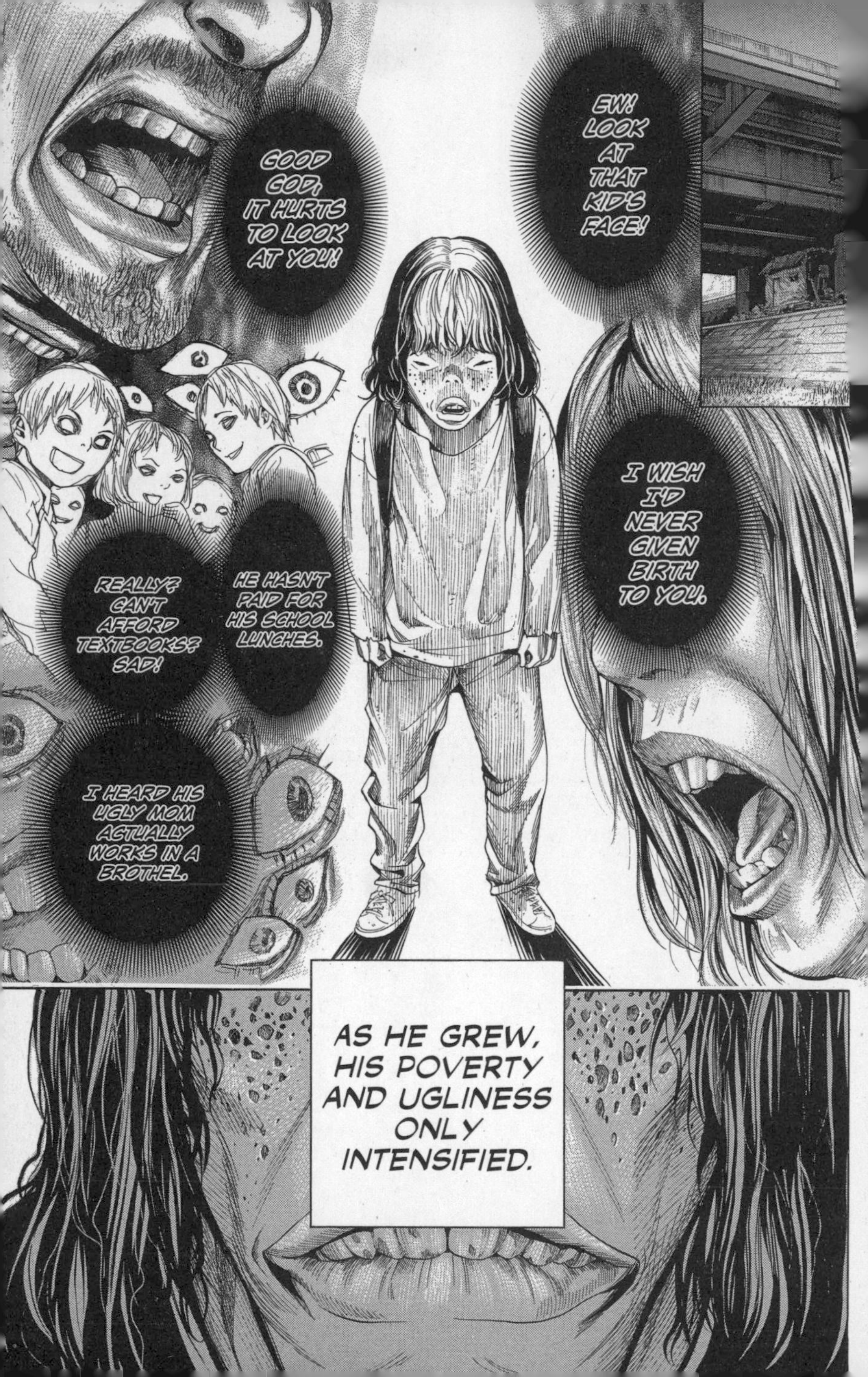
EW! LOOK AT THAT KID'S FACE!
GOOD GOD, IT HURTS TO LOOK AT YOU!
I WISH I'D NEVER GIVEN BIRTH TO YOU.
HE HASN'T PAID FOR HIS SCHOOL LUNCHES.
REALLY? CAN'T AFFORD TEXTBOOKS? SAD!
I HEARD HIS UGLY MOM ACTUALLY WORKS IN A BROTHEL.
AS HE GREW, HIS POVERTY AND UGLINESS ONLY INTENSIFIED.

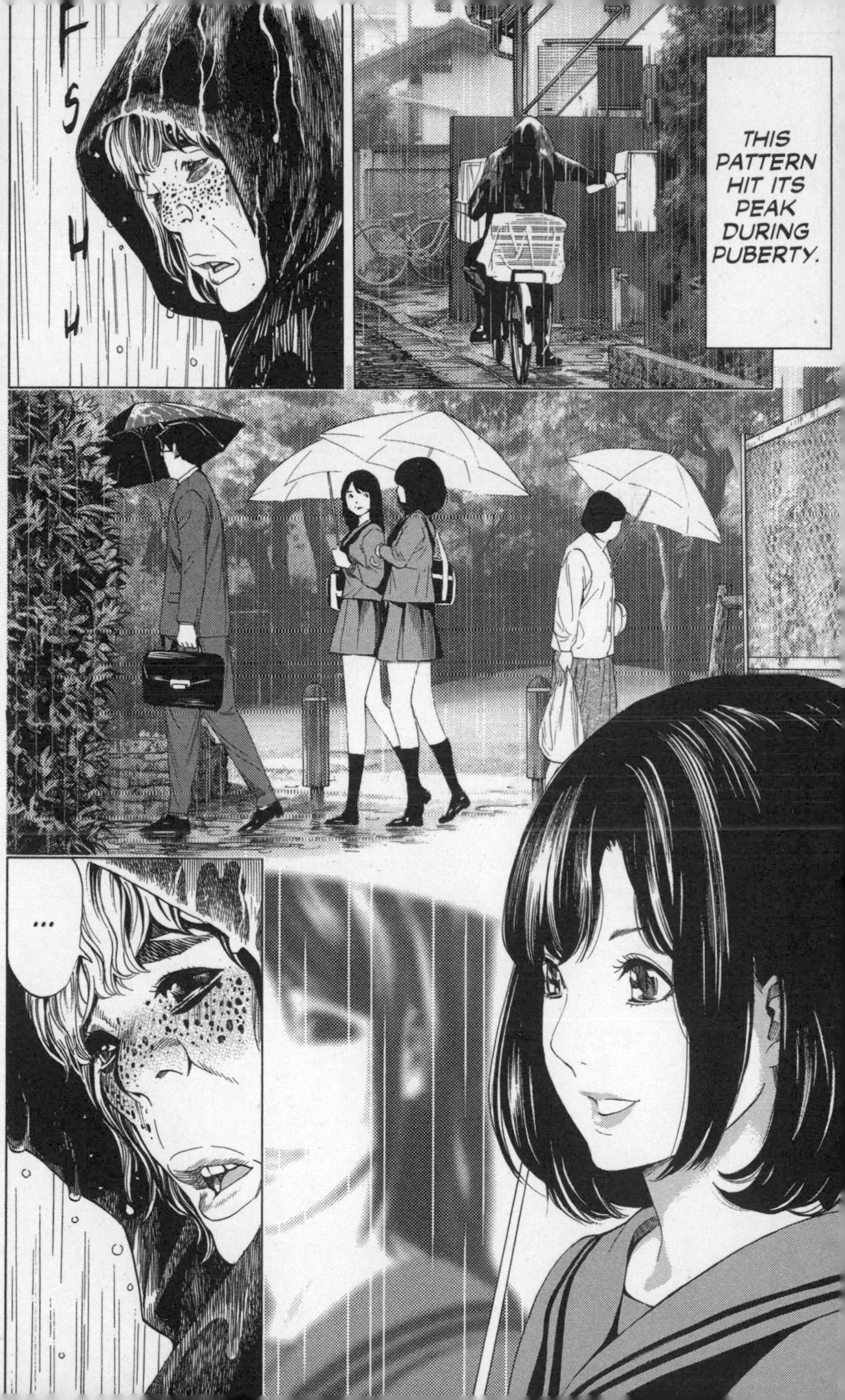
THIS PATTERN HIT ITS PEAK DURING PUBERTY.
FSHHH
...

...
SPLISH
SPLISH
KTUNK

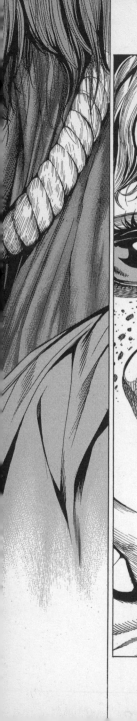

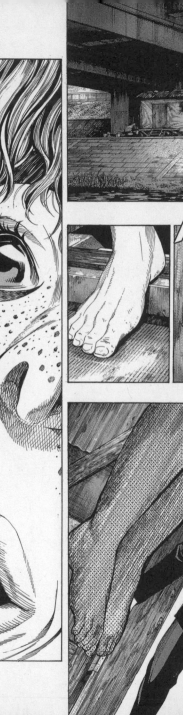

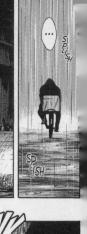

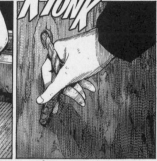

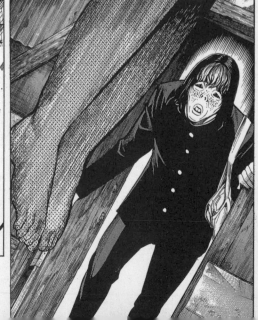

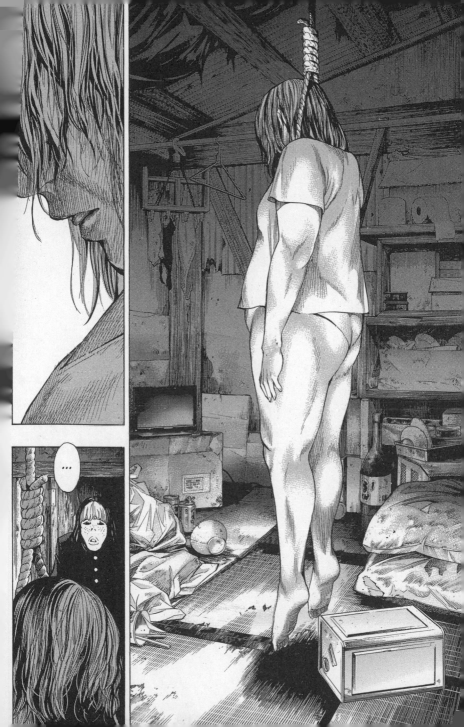

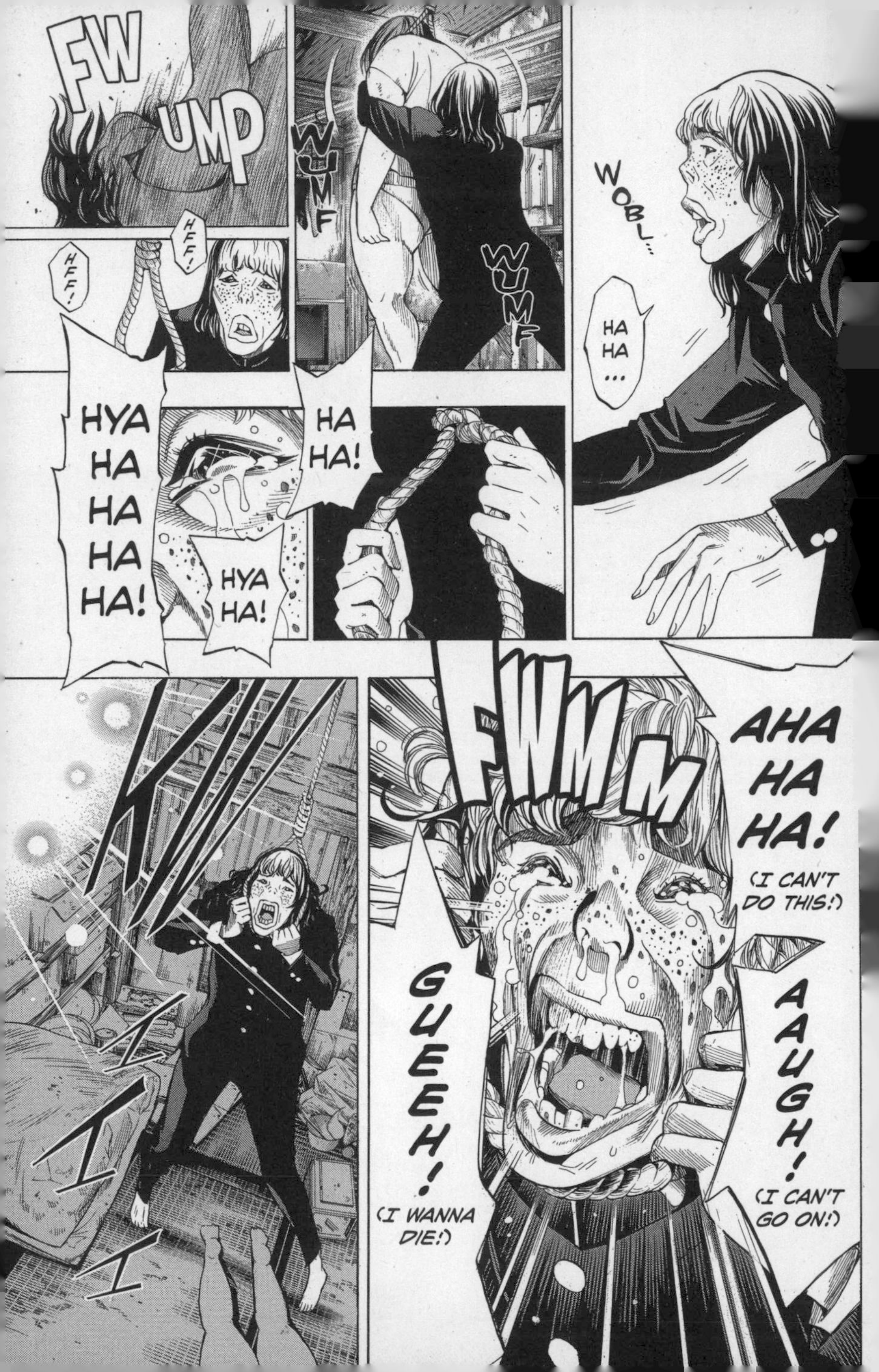
WOBL...
HA HA ...
WUMF
WUMF
FWUMP
HFF!
HFF!
HA HA!
HYA HA!
HYA HA HA HA HA HA!
FWMM
AHA HA HA HA!
(I CAN'T DO THIS!)
AAUGH!
(I CAN'T GO ON!)
GUEEH!
(I WANNA DIE!)
KIIII

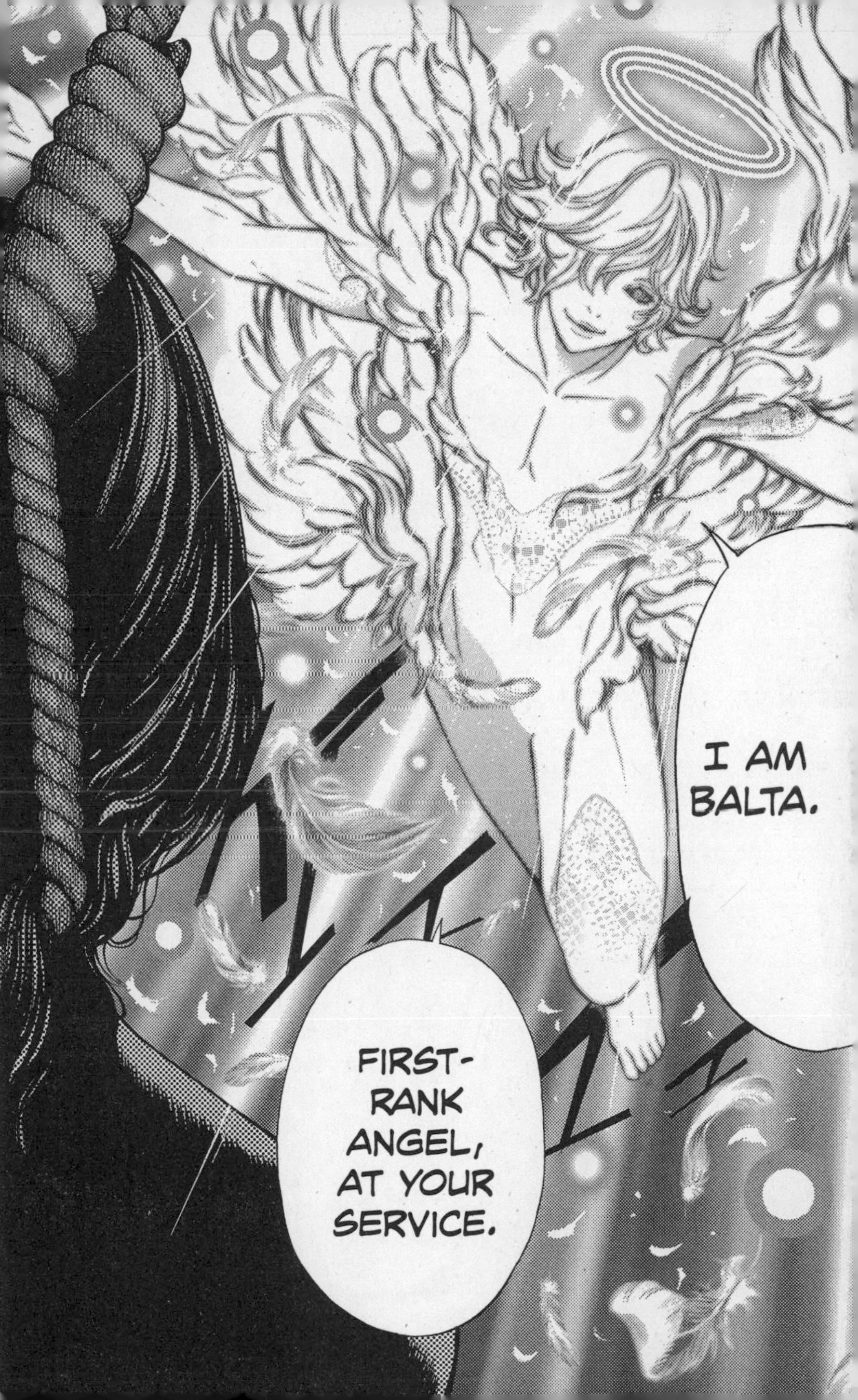
I AM BALTA.
FIRST-RANK ANGEL, AT YOUR SERVICE.

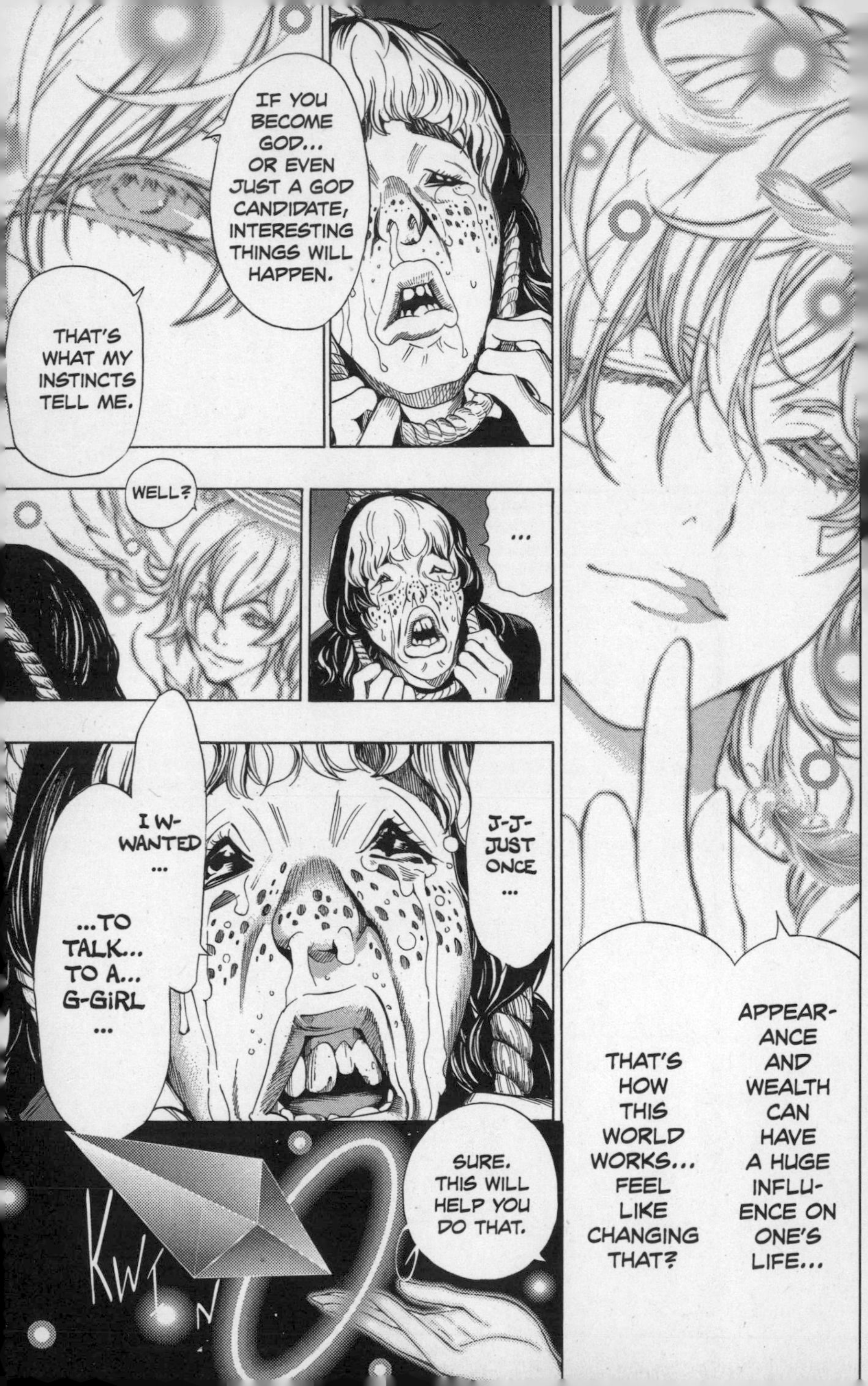
APPEARANCE AND WEALTH CAN HAVE A HUGE INFLUENCE ON ONE'S LIFE...
THAT'S HOW THIS WORLD WORKS... FEEL LIKE CHANGING THAT?
IF YOU BECOME GOD... OR EVEN JUST A GOD CANDIDATE, INTERESTING THINGS WILL HAPPEN.
THAT'S WHAT MY INSTINCTS TELL ME.
...
WELL?
J-J-JUST ONCE...
I W-WANTED...
...TO TALK... TO A... G-GIRL...
SURE. THIS WILL HELP YOU DO THAT.
KWIN

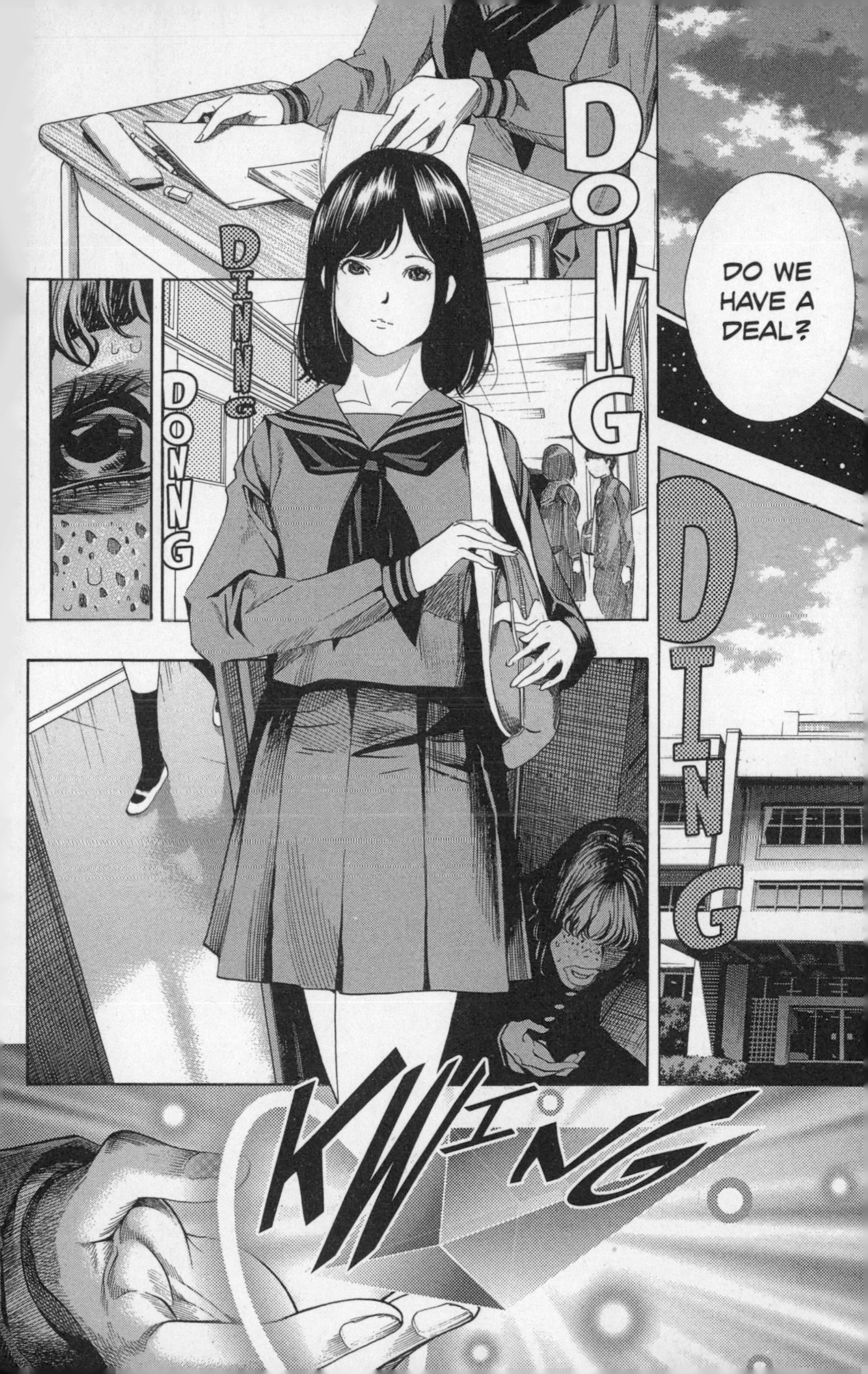
DO WE HAVE A DEAL?
DONG
DING
DONG
DING
DONG
KWING

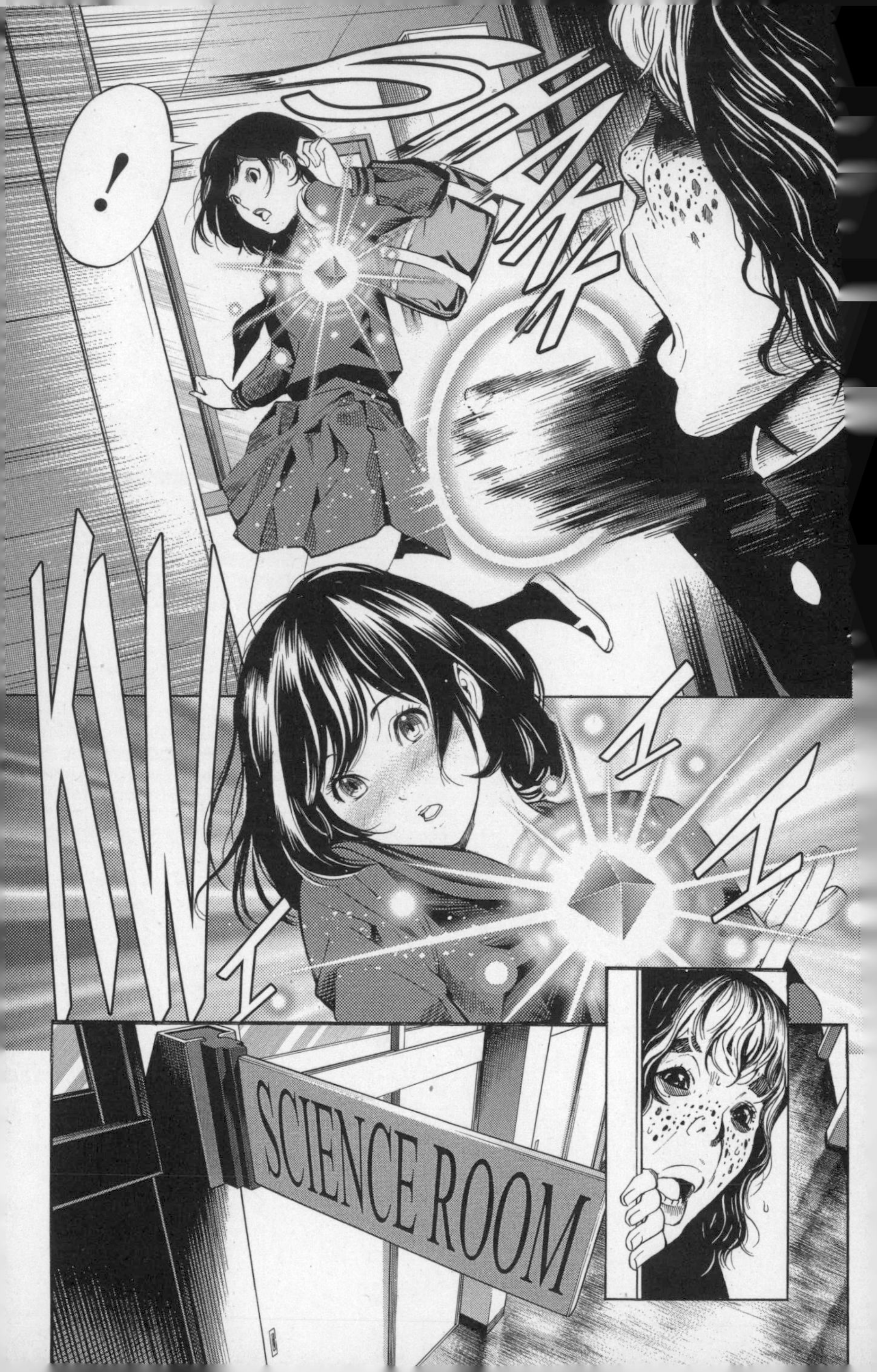
SHAKK
!
KWINN
SCIENCE ROOM

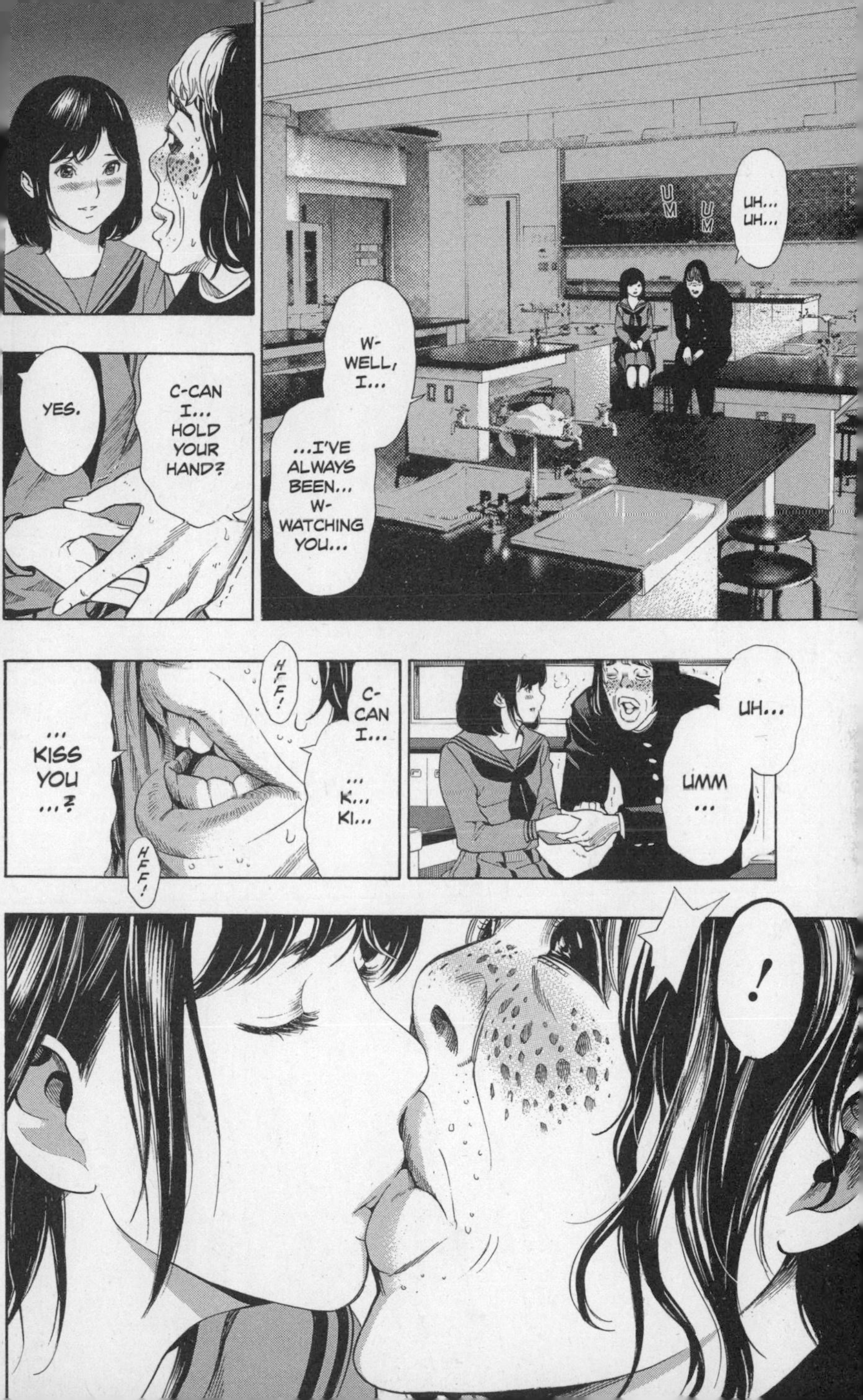
UM
UM
UH... UH...
W-WELL, I...
...I'VE ALWAYS BEEN... W-WATCHING YOU...
C-CAN I... HOLD YOUR HAND?
YES.
UH...
UMM...
C-CAN I...
HFF!
...K... KI...
...KISS YOU...?
HFF!
!

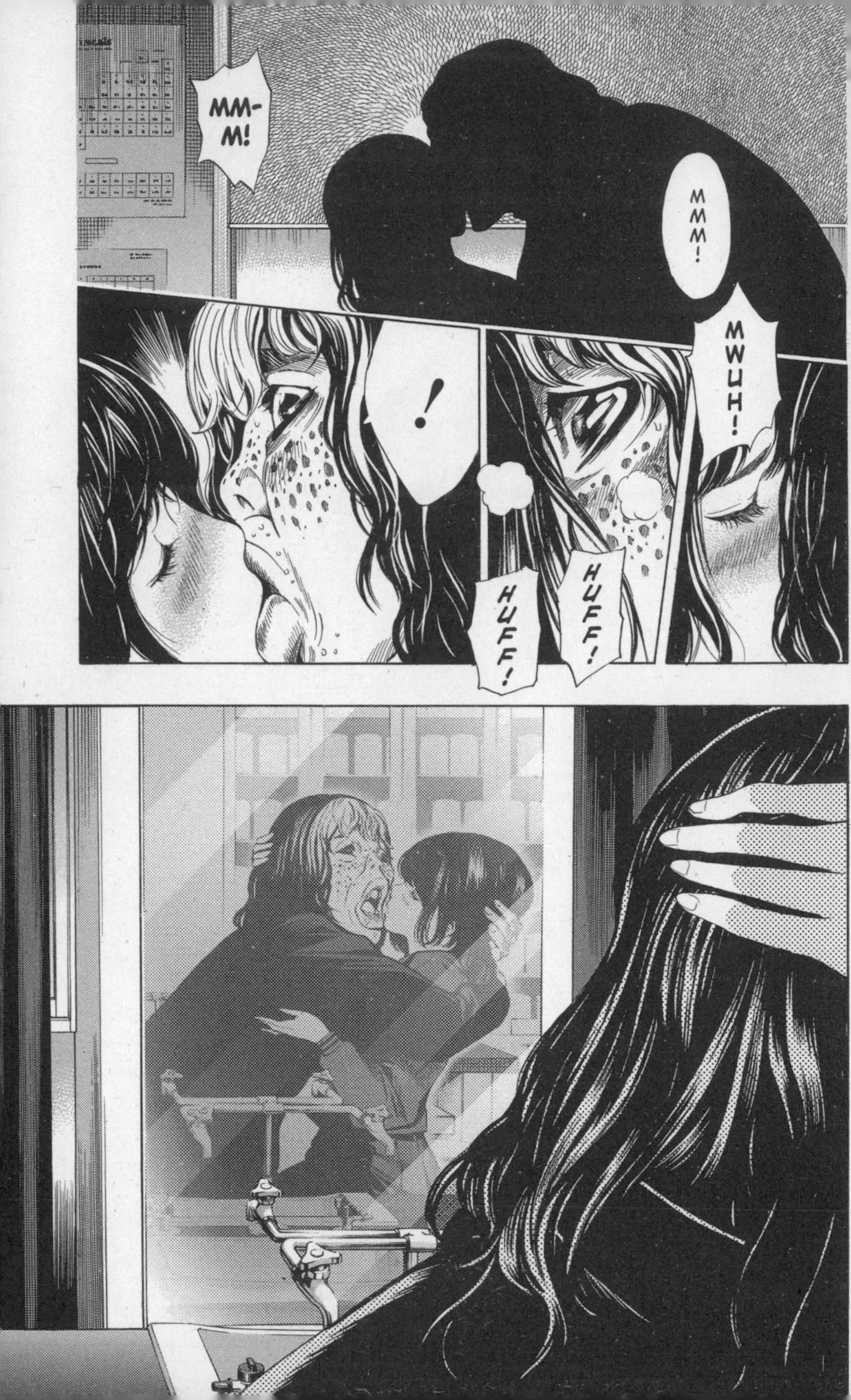
MMM!
MM-M!
MWUH!
HUFF!
!
HUFF!

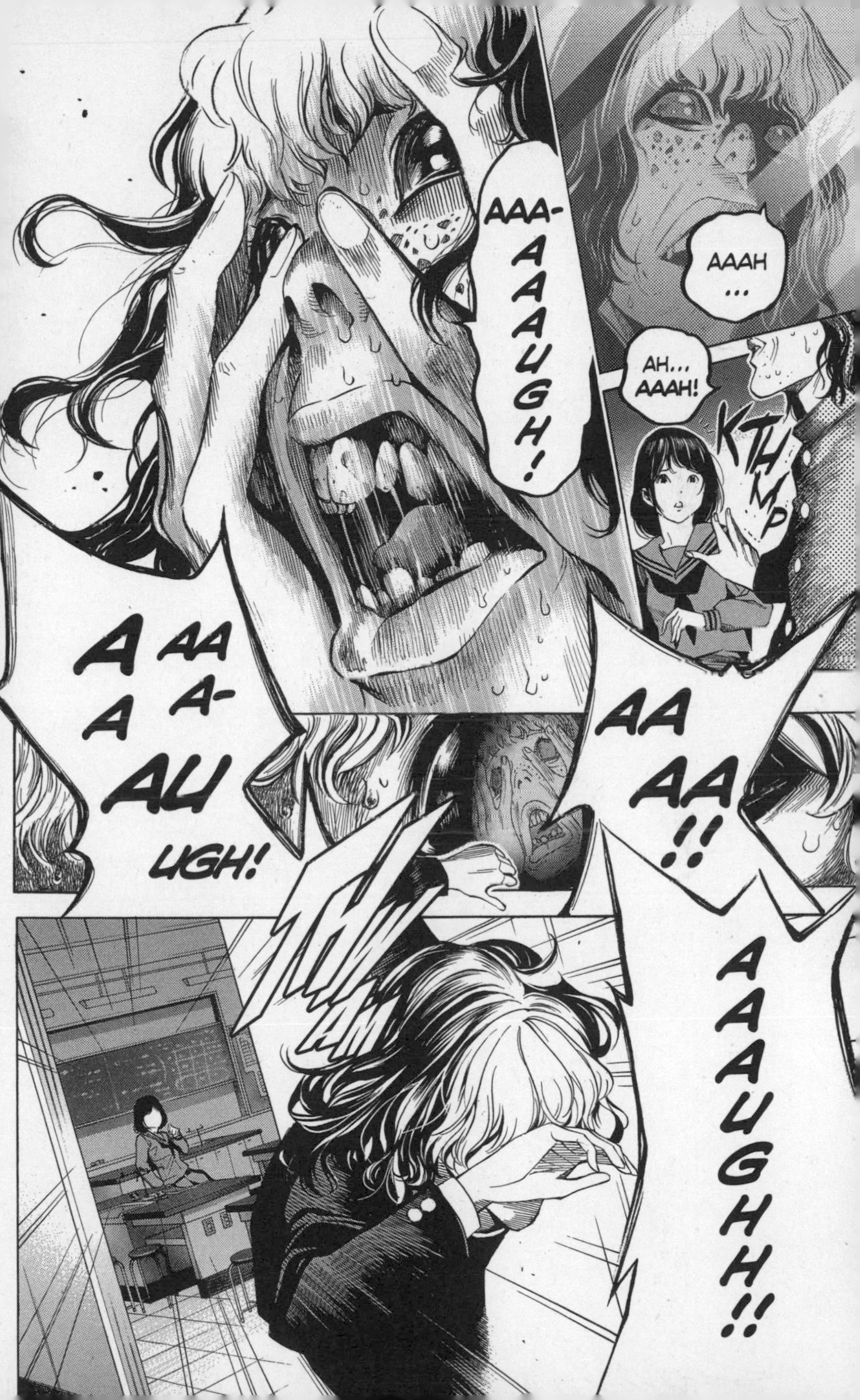
AAAH ...
AH... AAAH!
KTHMP
AAA-AAAAUGH!
AAAA!!
AAAA-AUUGH!
AAAAUGHH!!

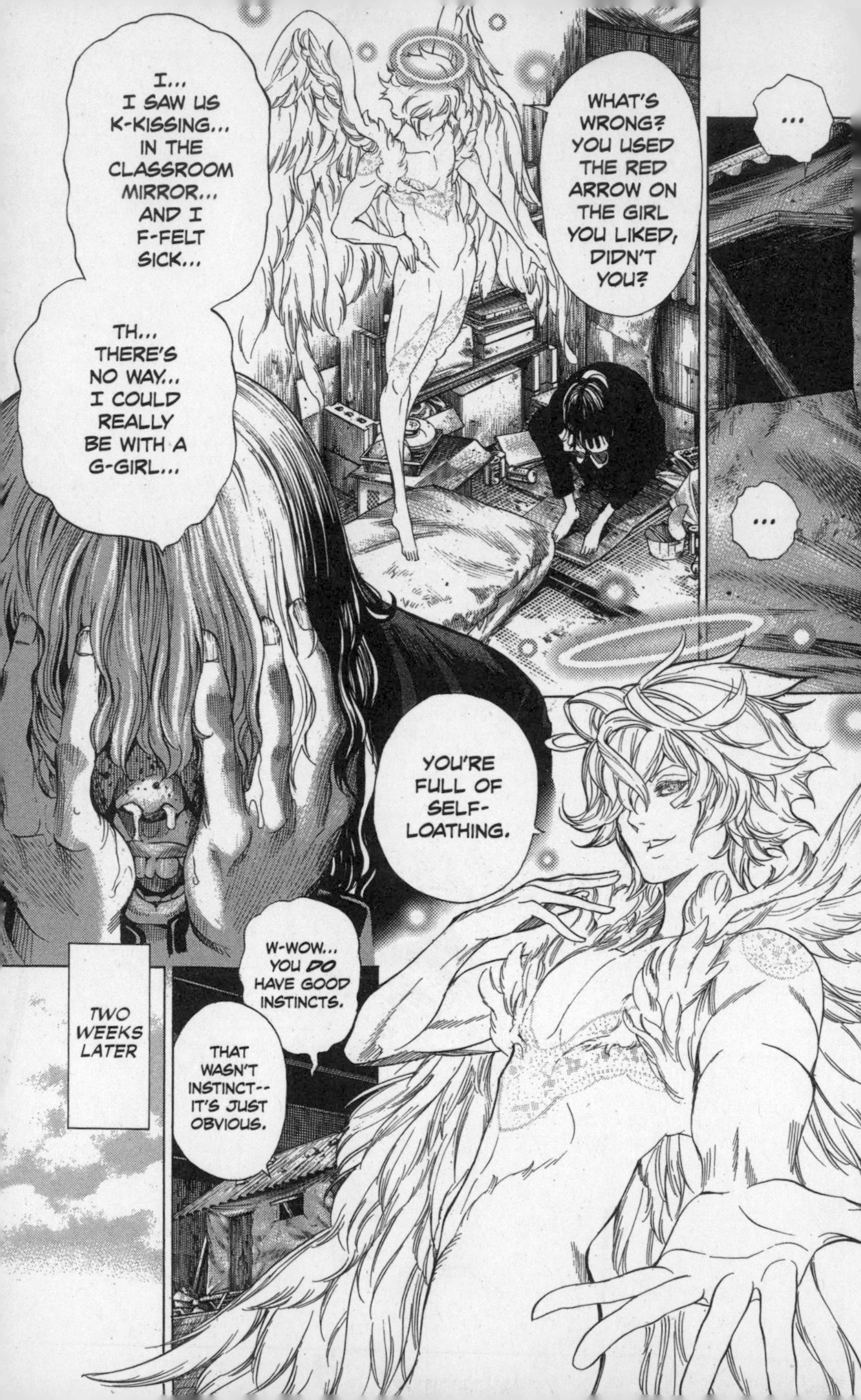
...
...
WHAT'S WRONG? YOU USED THE RED ARROW ON THE GIRL YOU LIKED, DIDN'T YOU?
I... I SAW US K-KISSING... IN THE CLASSROOM MIRROR... AND I F-FELT SICK...
TH... THERE'S NO WAY... I COULD REALLY BE WITH A G-GIRL...
YOU'RE FULL OF SELF-LOATHING.
W-WOW... YOU *DO* HAVE GOOD INSTINCTS.
THAT WASN'T INSTINCT-- IT'S JUST OBVIOUS.
TWO WEEKS LATER

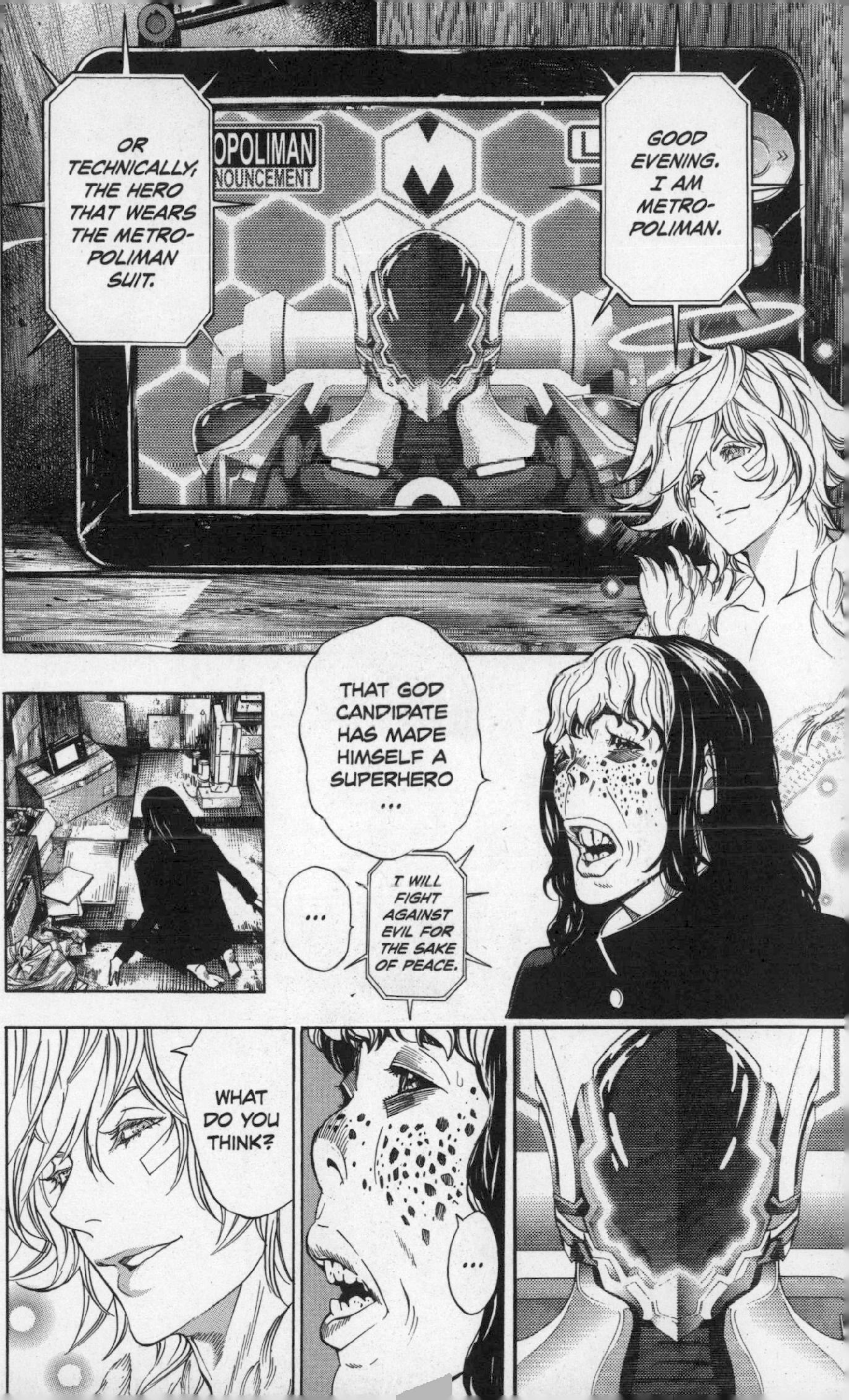
GOOD EVENING. I AM METRO-POLIMAN.
OPOLIMAN
NOUNCEMENT
OR TECHNICALLY, THE HERO THAT WEARS THE METRO-POLIMAN SUIT.
THAT GOD CANDIDATE HAS MADE HIMSELF A SUPERHERO ...
I WILL FIGHT AGAINST EVIL FOR THE SAKE OF PEACE.
...
...
WHAT DO YOU THINK?

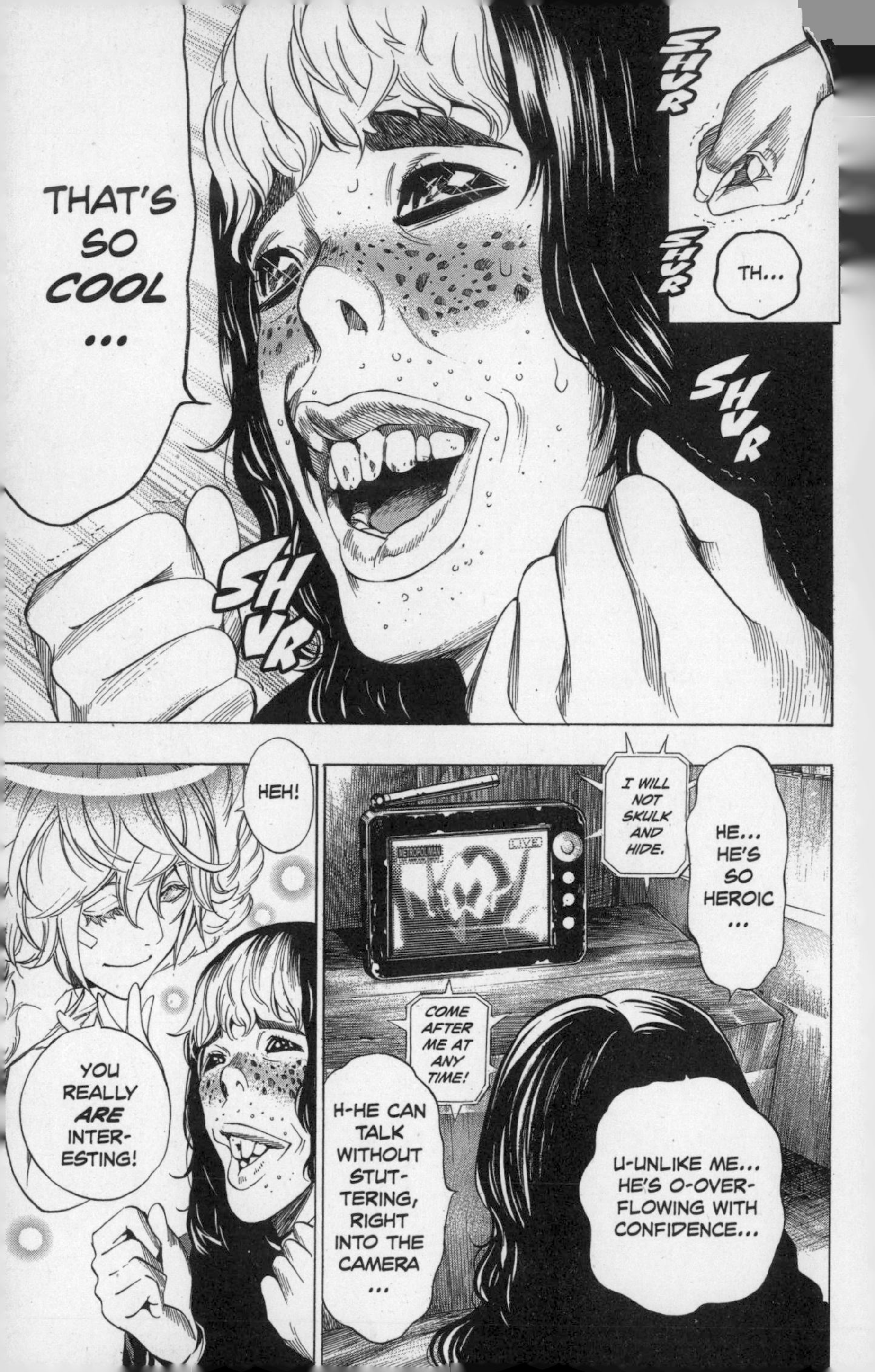
SHUR
SHUR
TH...
SHUR
THAT'S SO COOL ...
SHUR
HE... HE'S SO HEROIC ...
I WILL NOT SKULK AND HIDE.
METROPOLIMAN
LIVE
COME AFTER ME AT ANY TIME!
U-UNLIKE ME... HE'S O-OVER-FLOWING WITH CONFIDENCE...
H-HE CAN TALK WITHOUT STUT-TERING, RIGHT INTO THE CAMERA ...
HEH!
YOU REALLY *ARE* INTER-ESTING!

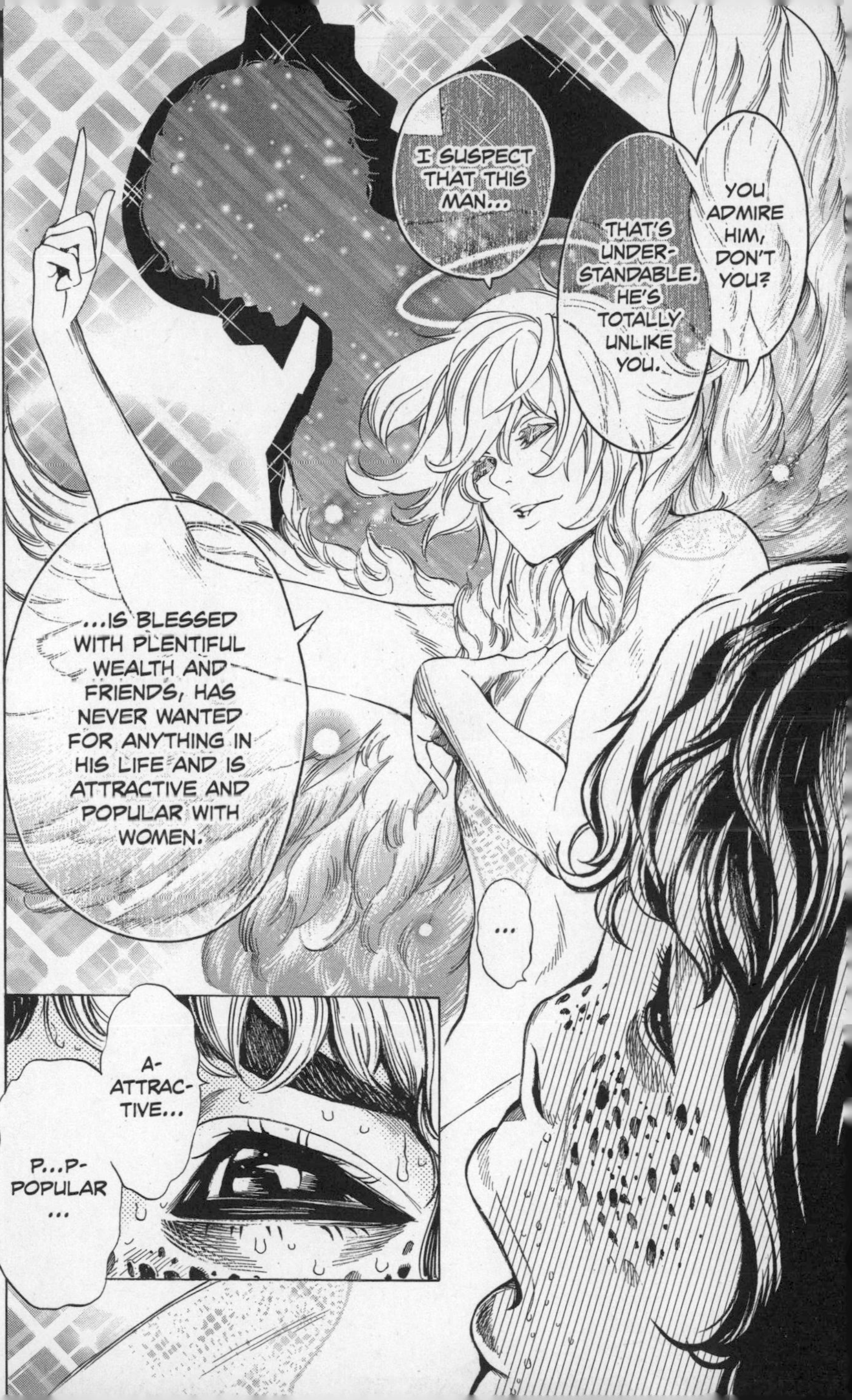
YOU ADMIRE HIM, DON'T YOU?
THAT'S UNDER-STANDABLE. HE'S TOTALLY UNLIKE YOU.
I SUSPECT THAT THIS MAN...
...IS BLESSED WITH PLENTIFUL WEALTH AND FRIENDS, HAS NEVER WANTED FOR ANYTHING IN HIS LIFE AND IS ATTRACTIVE AND POPULAR WITH WOMEN.
...
A-ATTRAC-TIVE...
P...P-POPULAR...

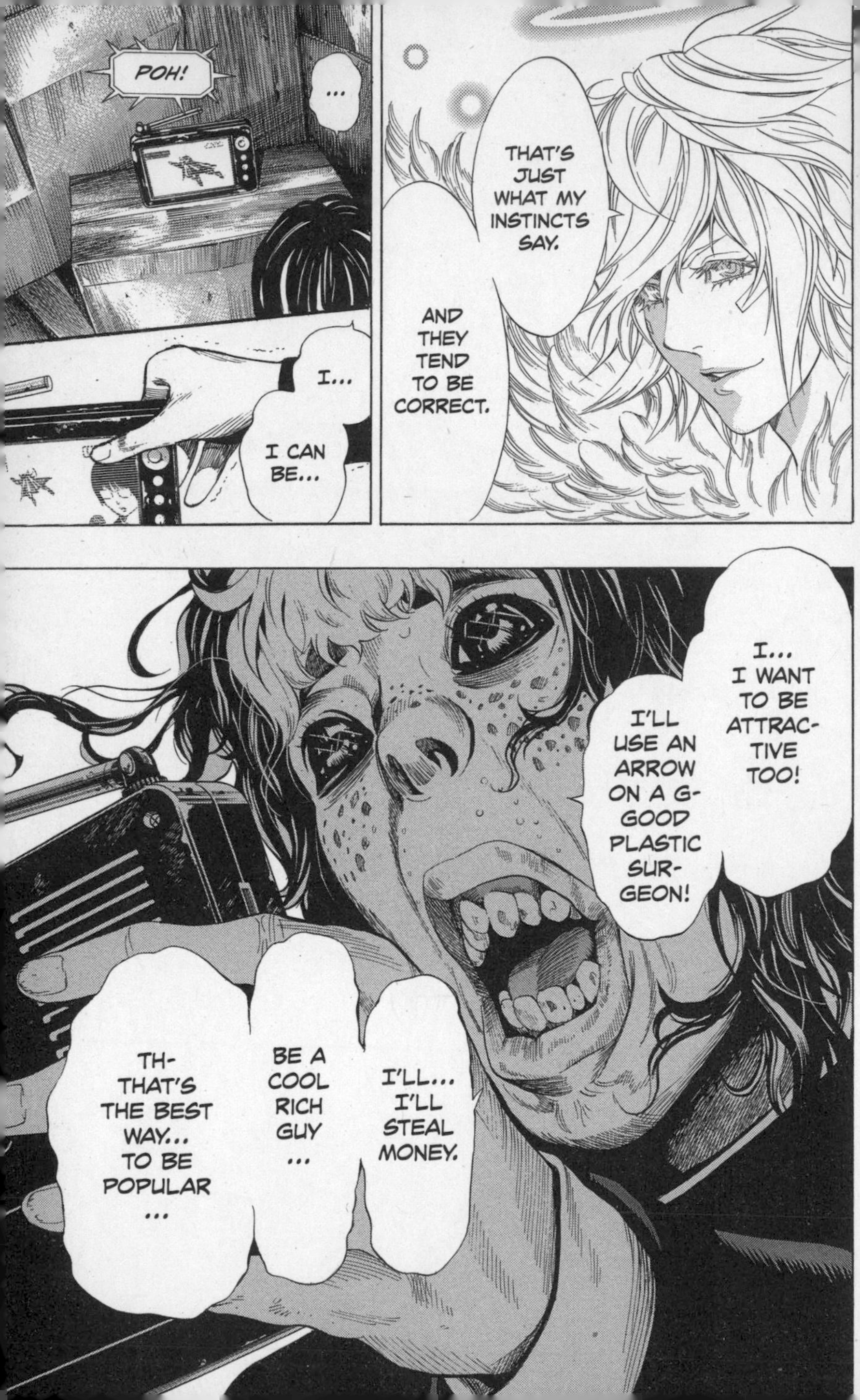
THAT'S JUST WHAT MY INSTINCTS SAY.
AND THEY TEND TO BE CORRECT.
...
POH!
I...
I CAN BE...
I... I WANT TO BE ATTRAC-TIVE TOO!
I'LL USE AN ARROW ON A G-GOOD PLASTIC SUR-GEON!
I'LL... I'LL STEAL MONEY.
BE A COOL RICH GUY ...
TH-THAT'S THE BEST WAY... TO BE POPULAR ...

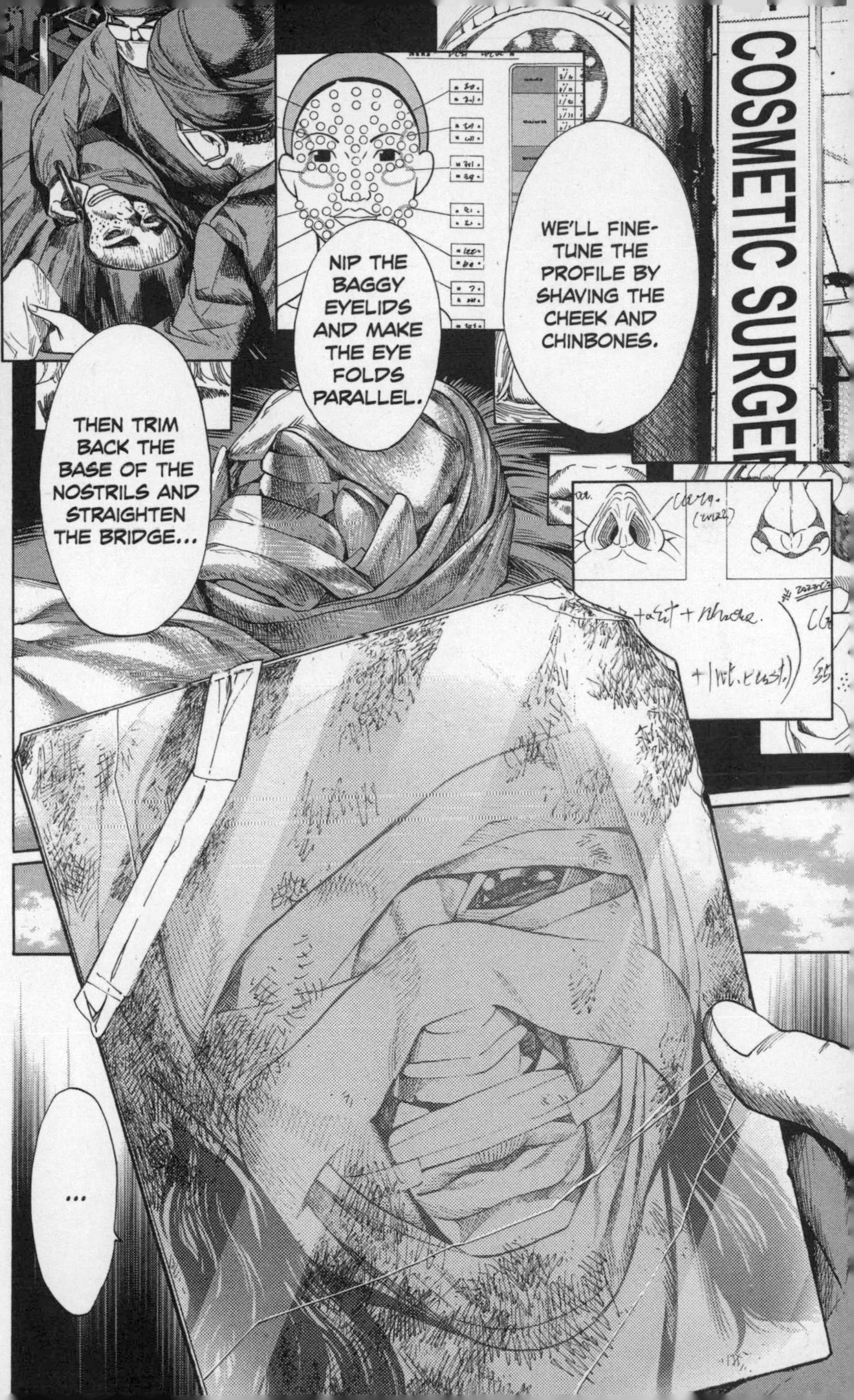
COSMETIC SURGER
WE'LL FINE-TUNE THE PROFILE BY SHAVING THE CHEEK AND CHINBONES.
NIP THE BAGGY EYELIDS AND MAKE THE EYE FOLDS PARALLEL.
THEN TRIM BACK THE BASE OF THE NOSTRILS AND STRAIGHTEN THE BRIDGE...
...

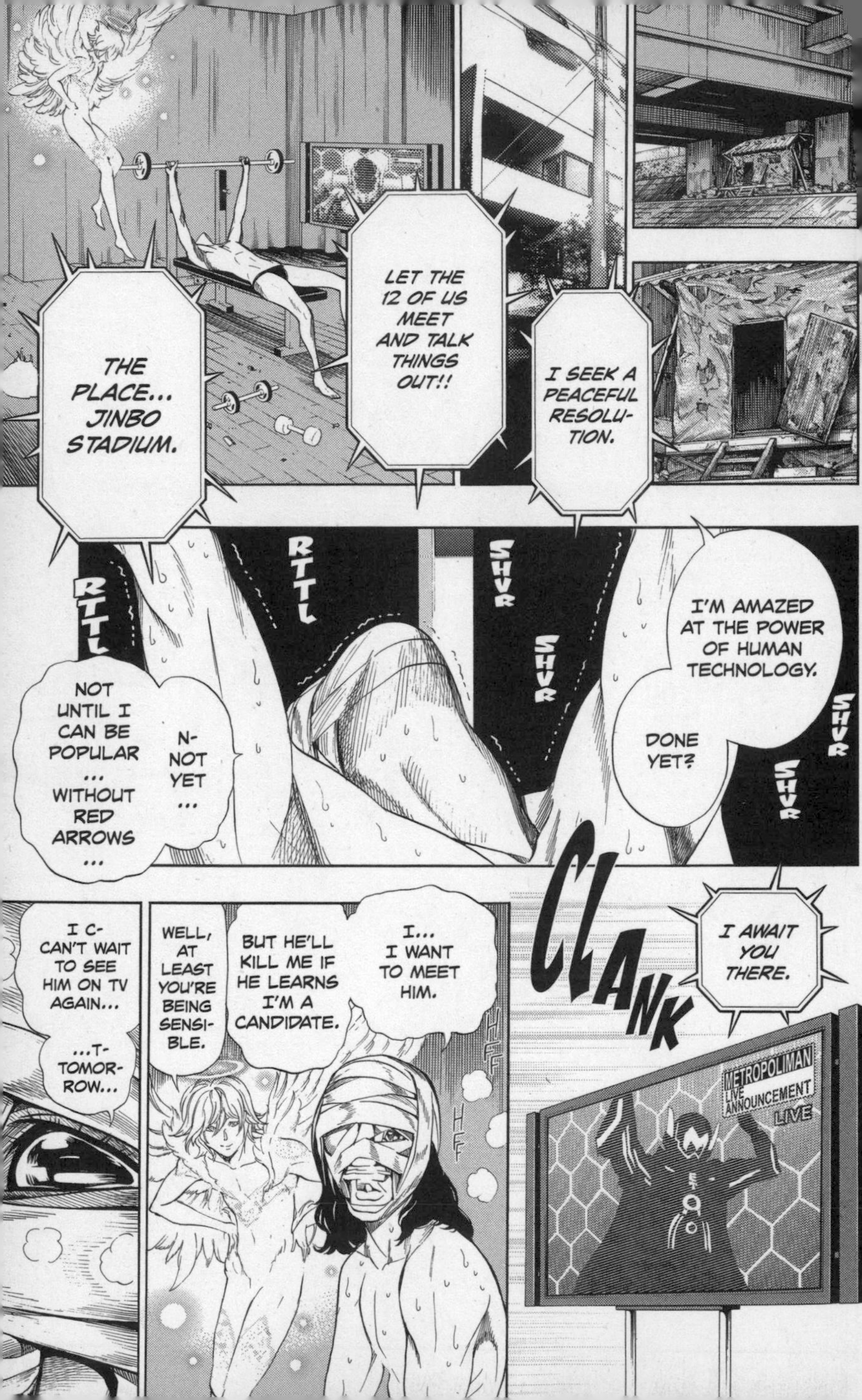
I SEEK A PEACEFUL RESOLUTION.
LET THE 12 OF US MEET AND TALK THINGS OUT!!
THE PLACE... JINBO STADIUM.
I'M AMAZED AT THE POWER OF HUMAN TECHNOLOGY.
DONE YET?
SHVR
SHVR
SHVR
SHVR
RTTL
N-NOT YET...
NOT UNTIL I CAN BE POPULAR... WITHOUT RED ARROWS...
RTTL
CLANK
I AWAIT YOU THERE.
METROPOLIMAN
LIVE ANNOUNCEMENT
LIVE
I... I WANT TO MEET HIM.
BUT HE'LL KILL ME IF HE LEARNS I'M A CANDIDATE.
WELL, AT LEAST YOU'RE BEING SENSIBLE.
HFF
HFF
I C-CAN'T WAIT TO SEE HIM ON TV AGAIN...
...T-TOMORROW...

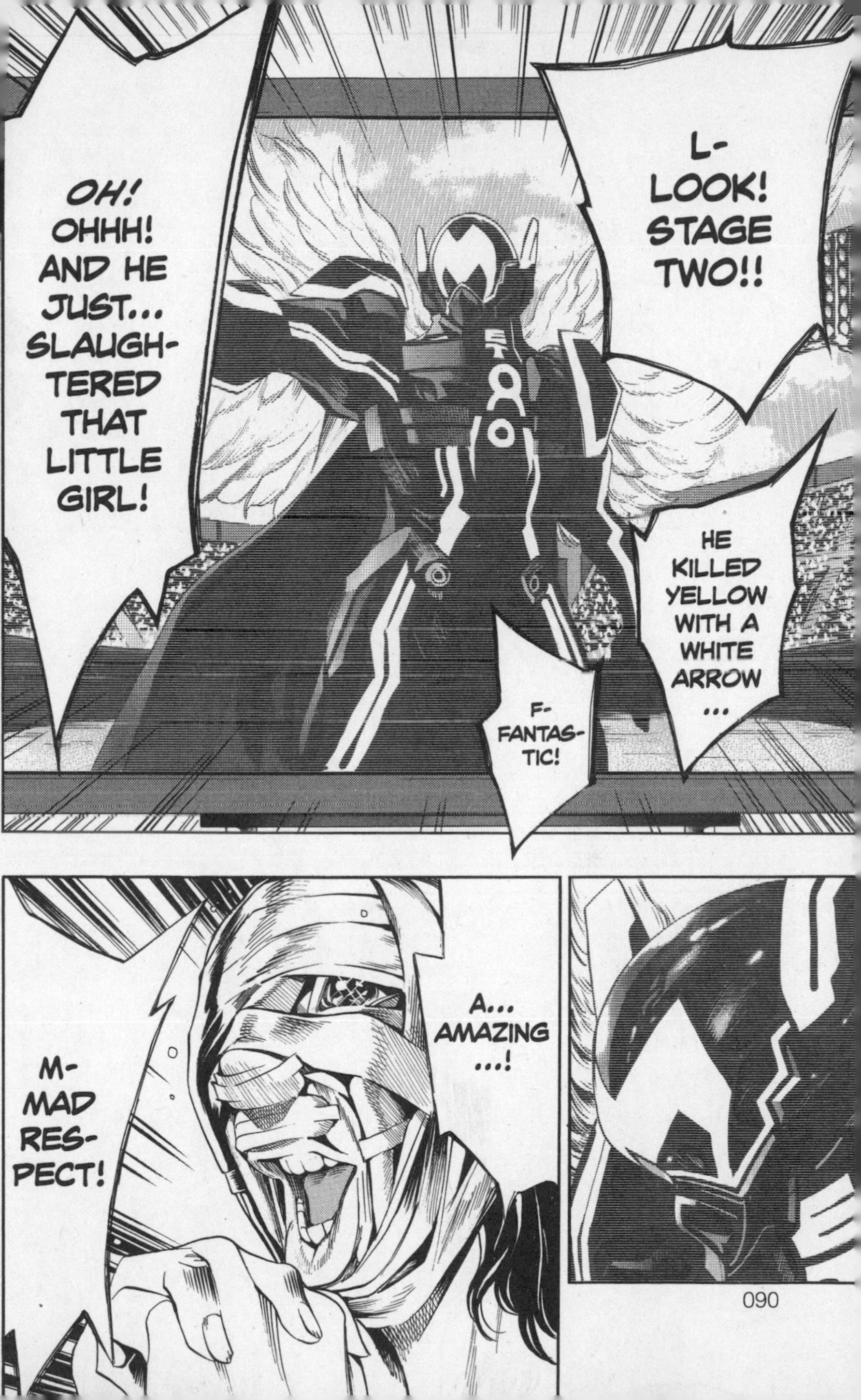
L- LOOK! STAGE TWO!!
OH! OHHH! AND HE JUST... SLAUGH-TERED THAT LITTLE GIRL!
HE KILLED YELLOW WITH A WHITE ARROW...
F- FANTAS-TIC!
A... AMAZING...!
M- MAD RES-PECT!

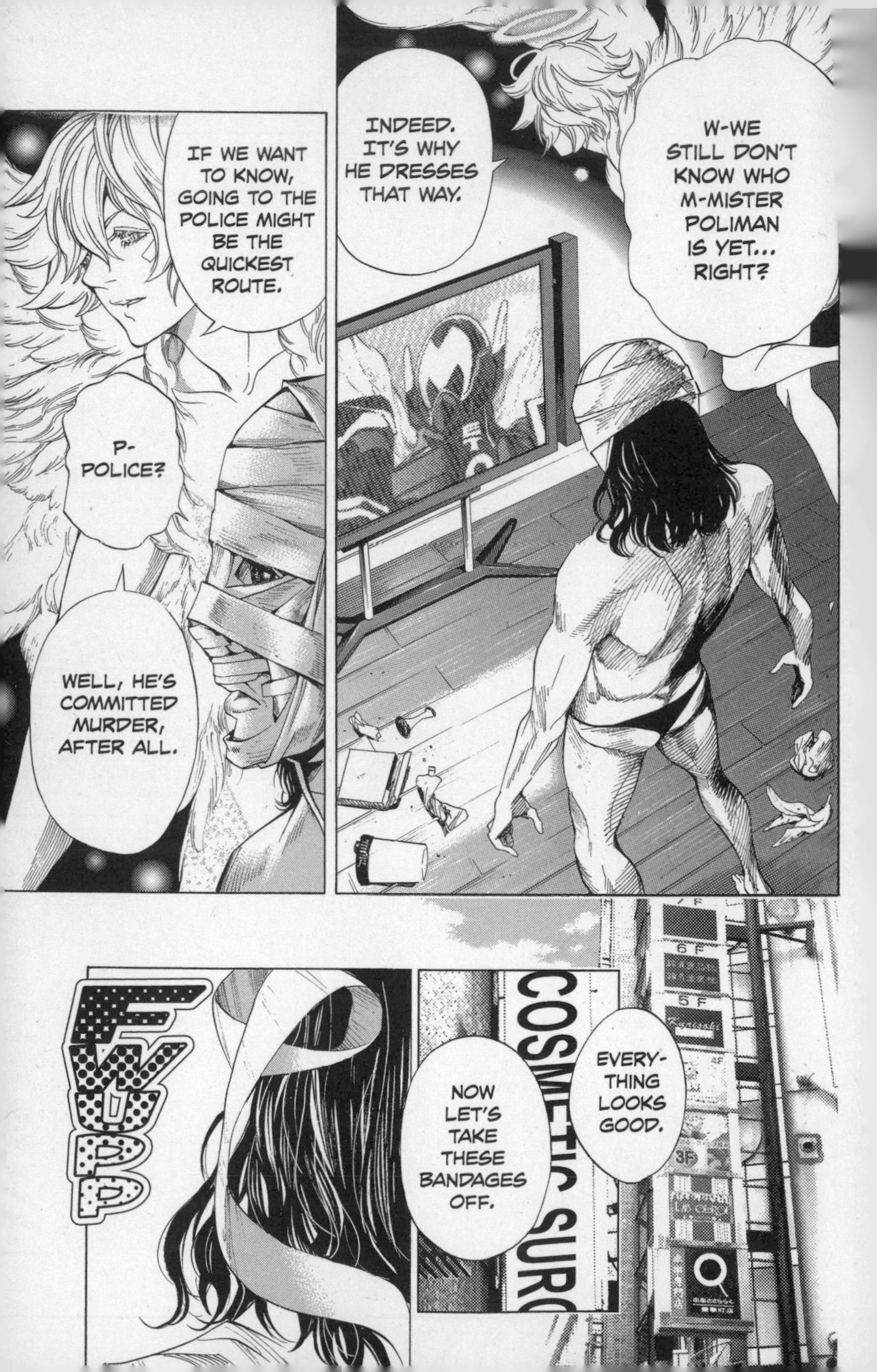
W-WE STILL DON'T KNOW WHO M-MISTER POLIMAN IS YET... RIGHT?
INDEED. IT'S WHY HE DRESSES THAT WAY.
IF WE WANT TO KNOW, GOING TO THE POLICE MIGHT BE THE QUICKEST ROUTE.
P-POLICE?
WELL, HE'S COMMITTED MURDER, AFTER ALL.
COSMETIC SURG
EVERY-THING LOOKS GOOD.
NOW LET'S TAKE THESE BANDAGES OFF.
FWUPP

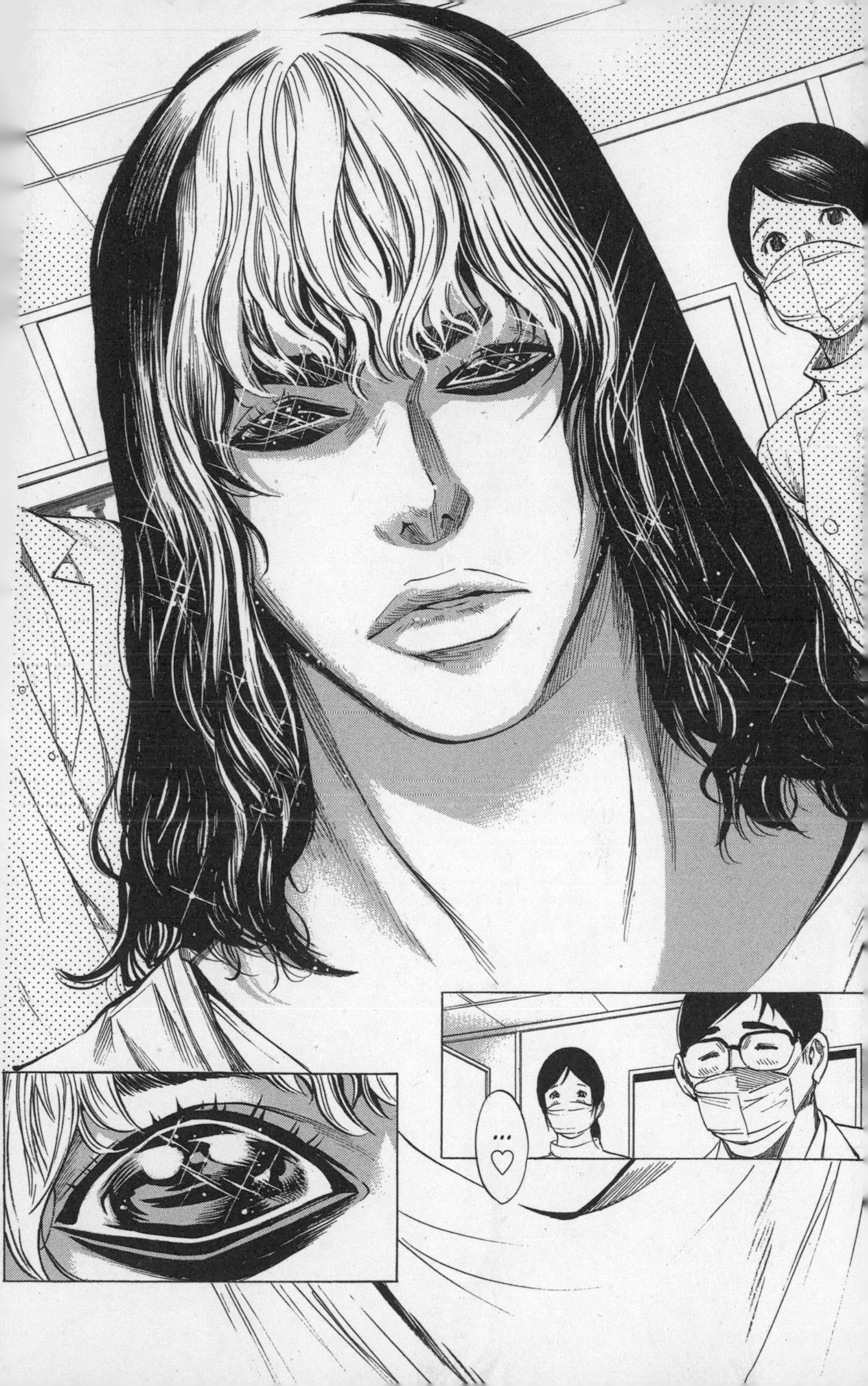
...
♡

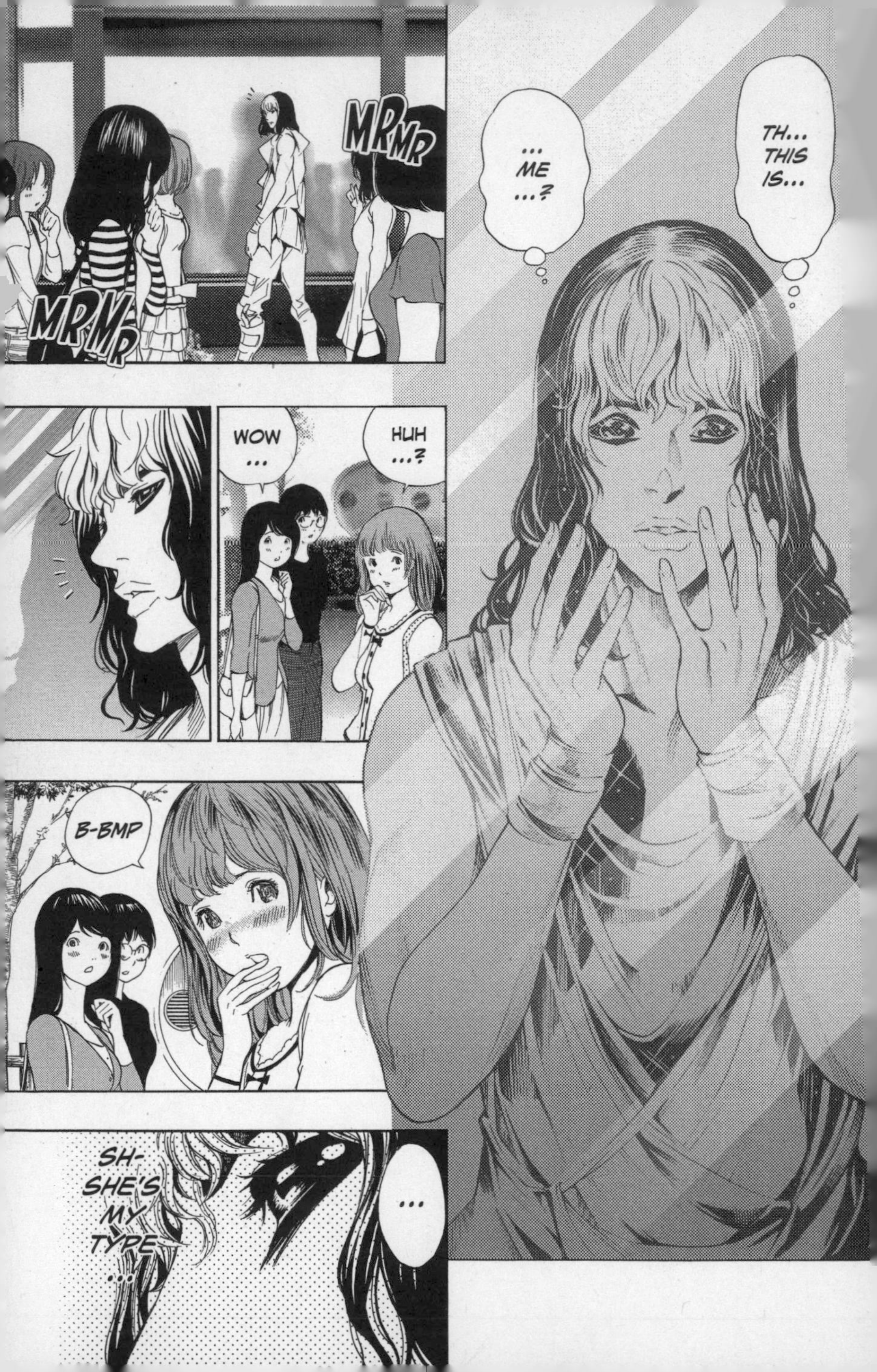
TH... THIS IS...
... ME ...?
MRMR
MRMR
HUH ...?
WOW ...
B-BMP
...
SH- SHE'S MY TYPE ...

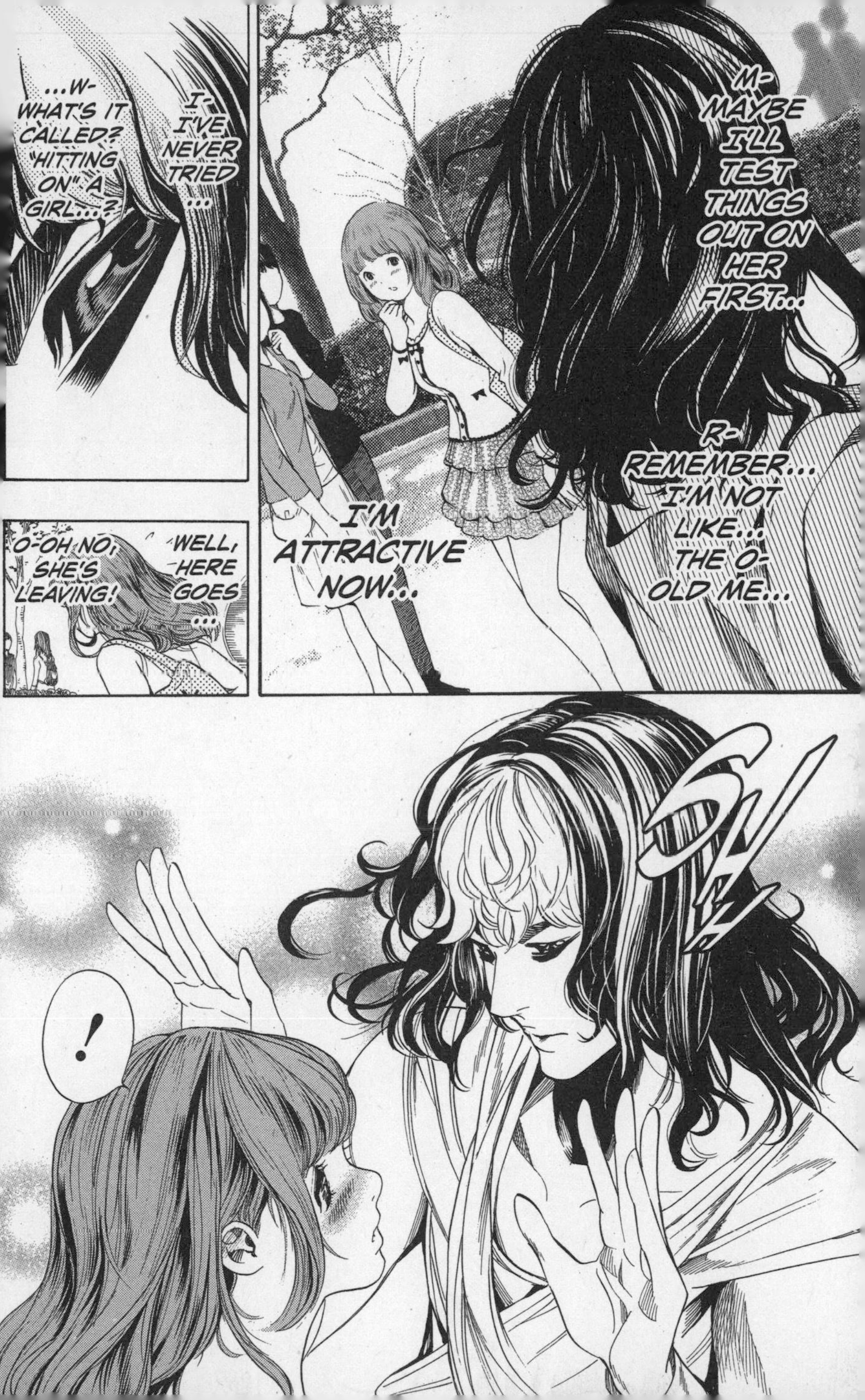
M-MAYBE I'LL TEST THINGS OUT ON HER FIRST...
R-REMEMBER... I'M NOT LIKE... THE O-OLD ME...
I'M ATTRACTIVE NOW...
I-I'VE NEVER TRIED...
...W-WHAT'S IT CALLED? "HITTING ON" A GIRL...?
WELL, HERE GOES...
O-OH NO, SHE'S LEAVING!
SHH
!

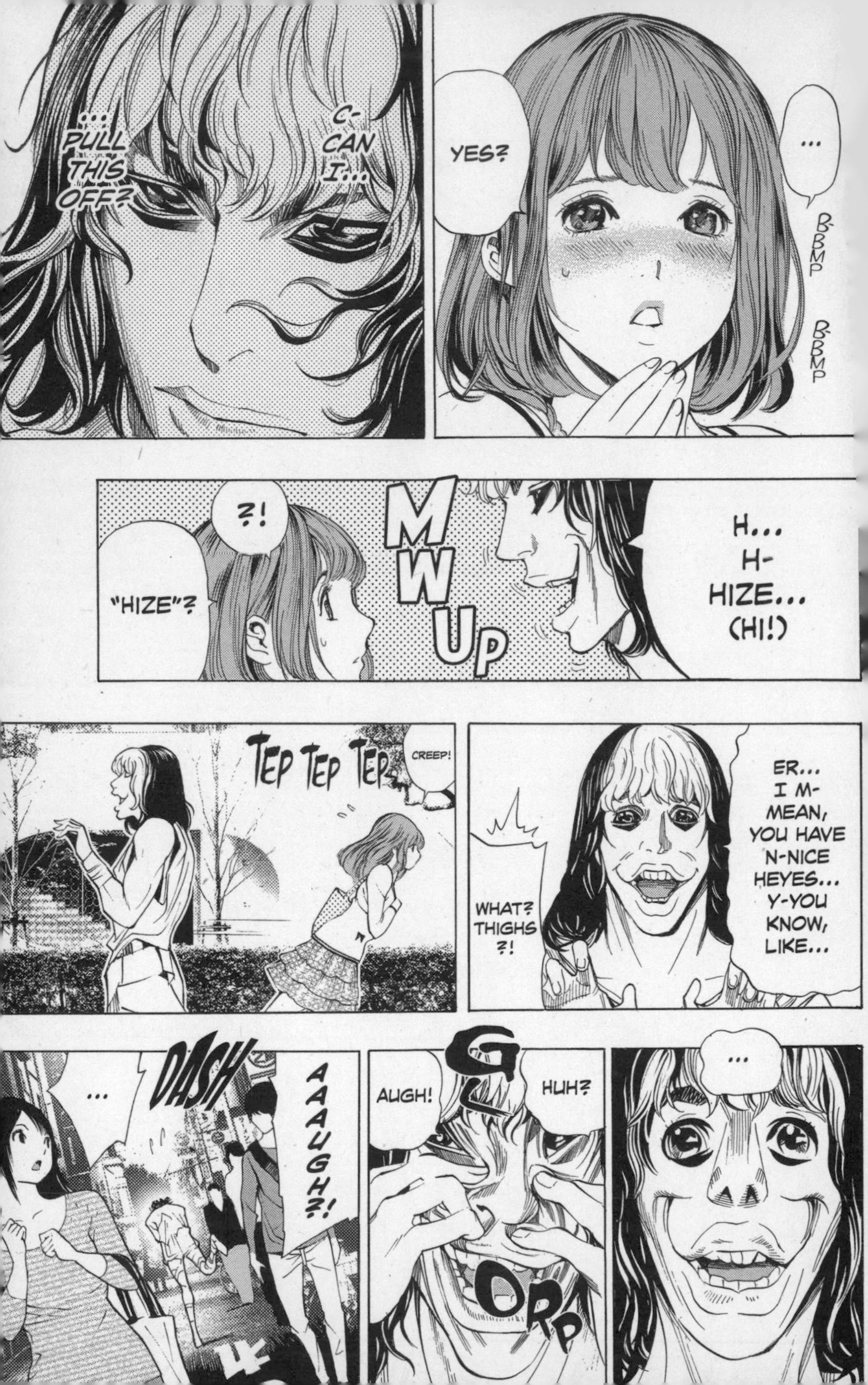
...
B-BBMP
B-BBMP
YES?
C-CAN I...
...PULL THIS OFF?
H... H-HIZE... (HI!)
MWUP
?!
"HIZE"?
ER... I M-MEAN, YOU HAVE N-NICE HEYES... Y-YOU KNOW, LIKE...
WHAT? THIGHS ?!
CREEP!
TEP TEP TEP
...
HUH?
GLORP
AUGH!
AAAAUGH?!
DASH
...

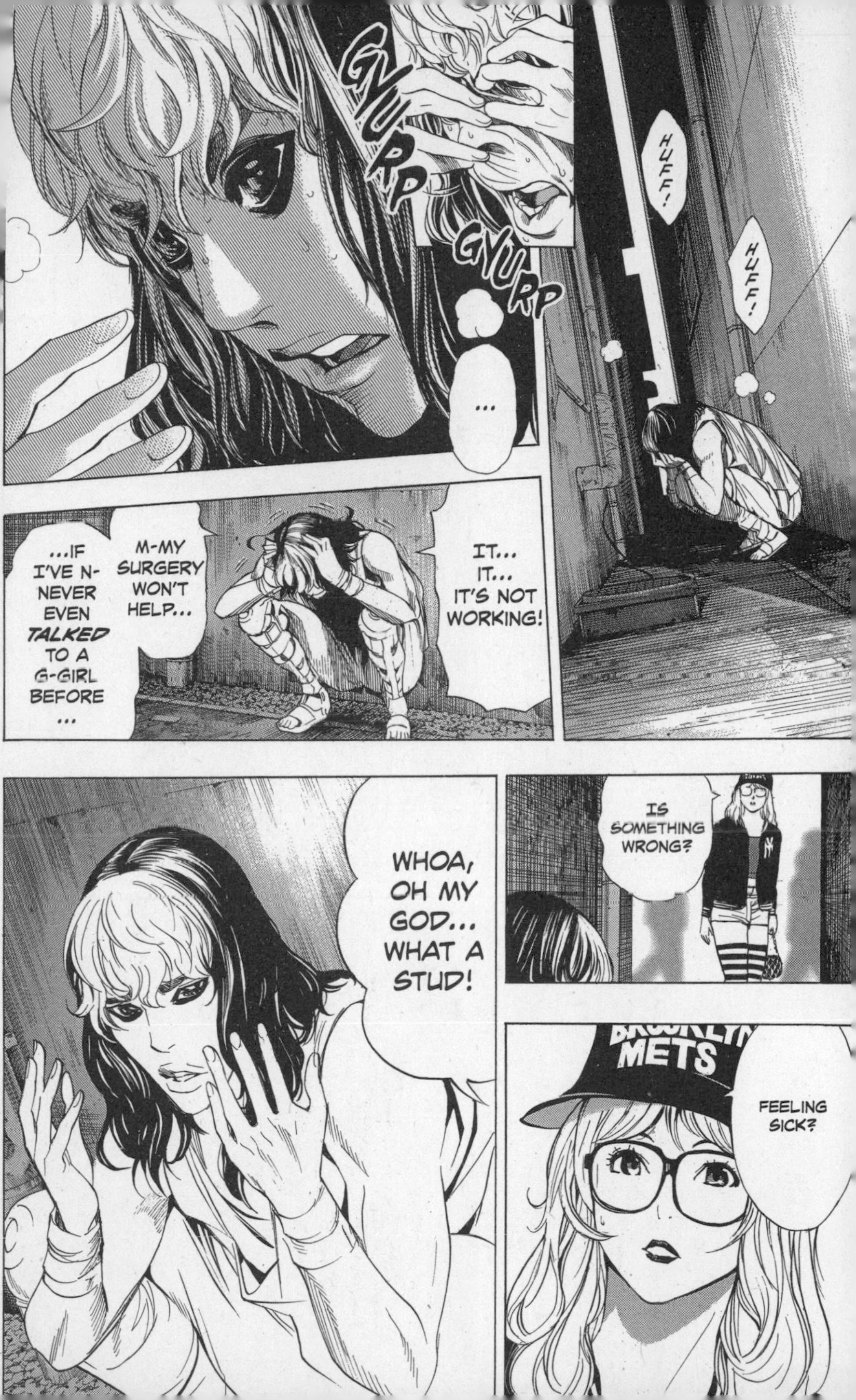
HUFF!
HUFF!
GYURP
GYURP
...
IT... IT... IT'S NOT WORKING!
M-MY SURGERY WON'T HELP...
...IF I'VE N-NEVER EVEN TALKED TO A G-GIRL BEFORE...
IS SOMETHING WRONG?
METS
FEELING SICK?
WHOA, OH MY GOD... WHAT A STUD!

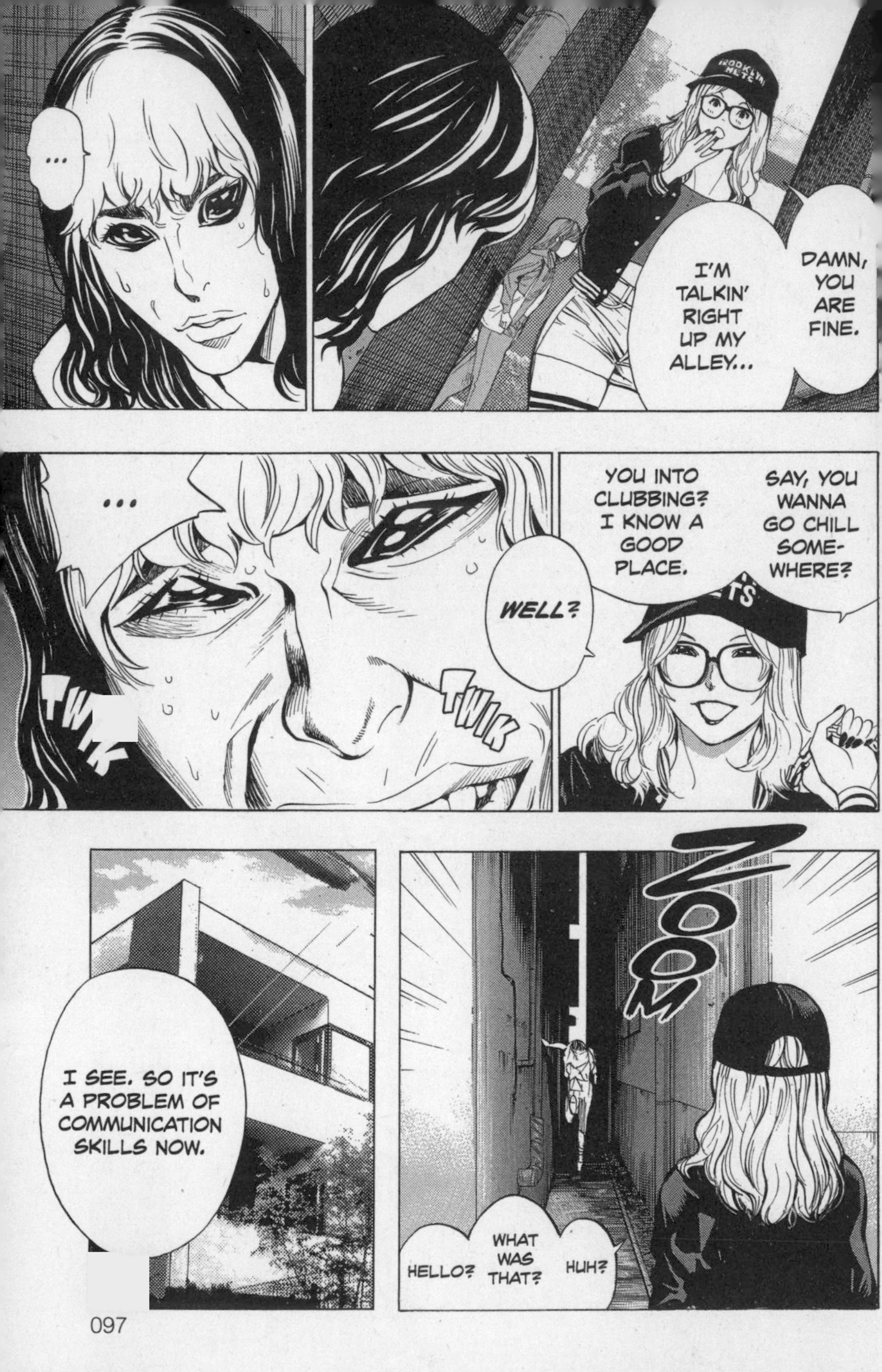
DAMN, YOU ARE FINE.
I'M TALKIN' RIGHT UP MY ALLEY...
...
SAY, YOU WANNA GO CHILL SOME-WHERE?
YOU INTO CLUBBING? I KNOW A GOOD PLACE.
WELL?
...
TWIK
TWIK
ZOOM
HUH?
WHAT WAS THAT?
HELLO?
I SEE. SO IT'S A PROBLEM OF COMMUNICATION SKILLS NOW.

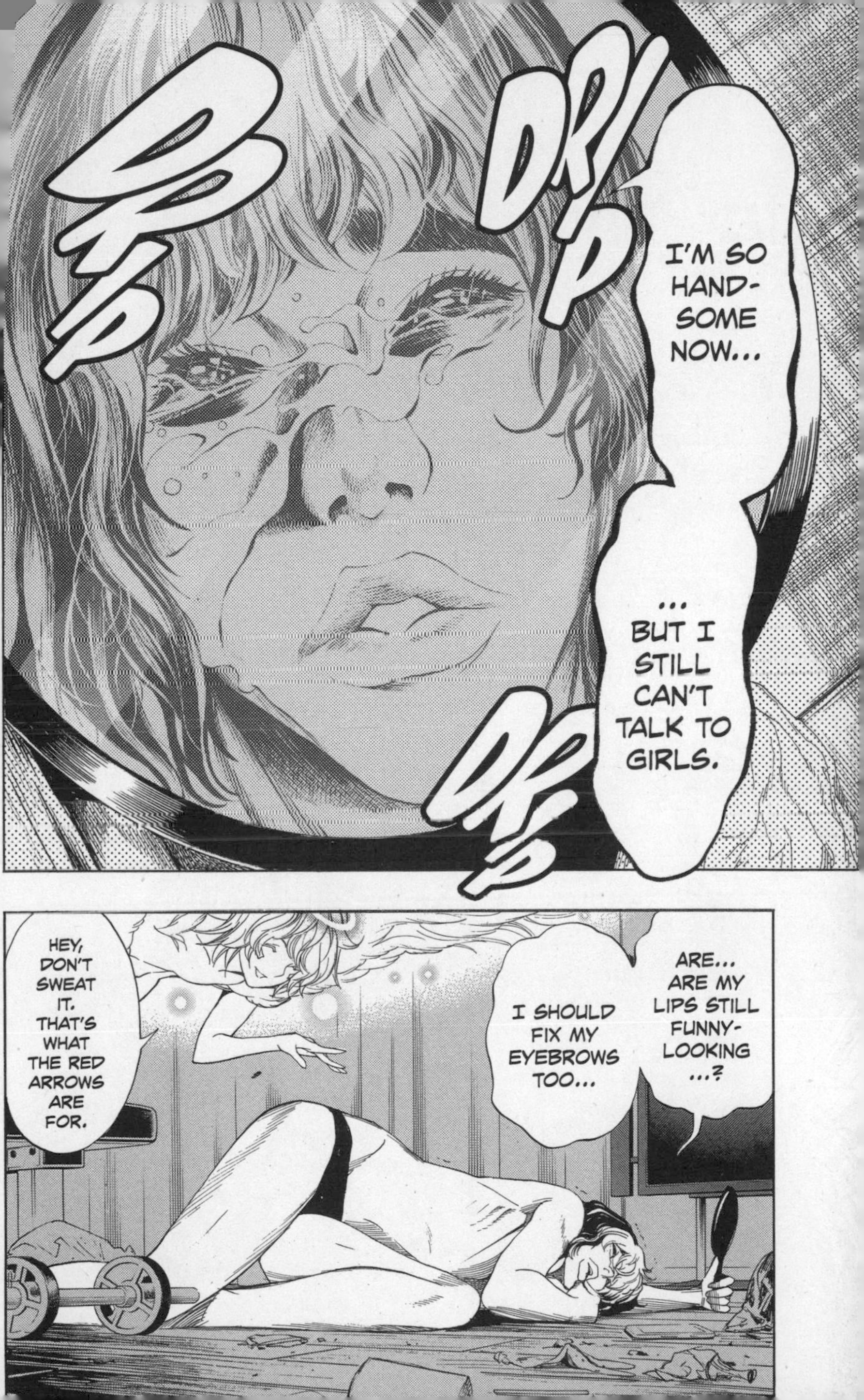
DRIP
DRIP
I'M SO HANDSOME NOW...
... BUT I STILL CAN'T TALK TO GIRLS.
DRIP
ARE... ARE MY LIPS STILL FUNNY-LOOKING ...?
I SHOULD FIX MY EYEBROWS TOO...
HEY, DON'T SWEAT IT. THAT'S WHAT THE RED ARROWS ARE FOR.

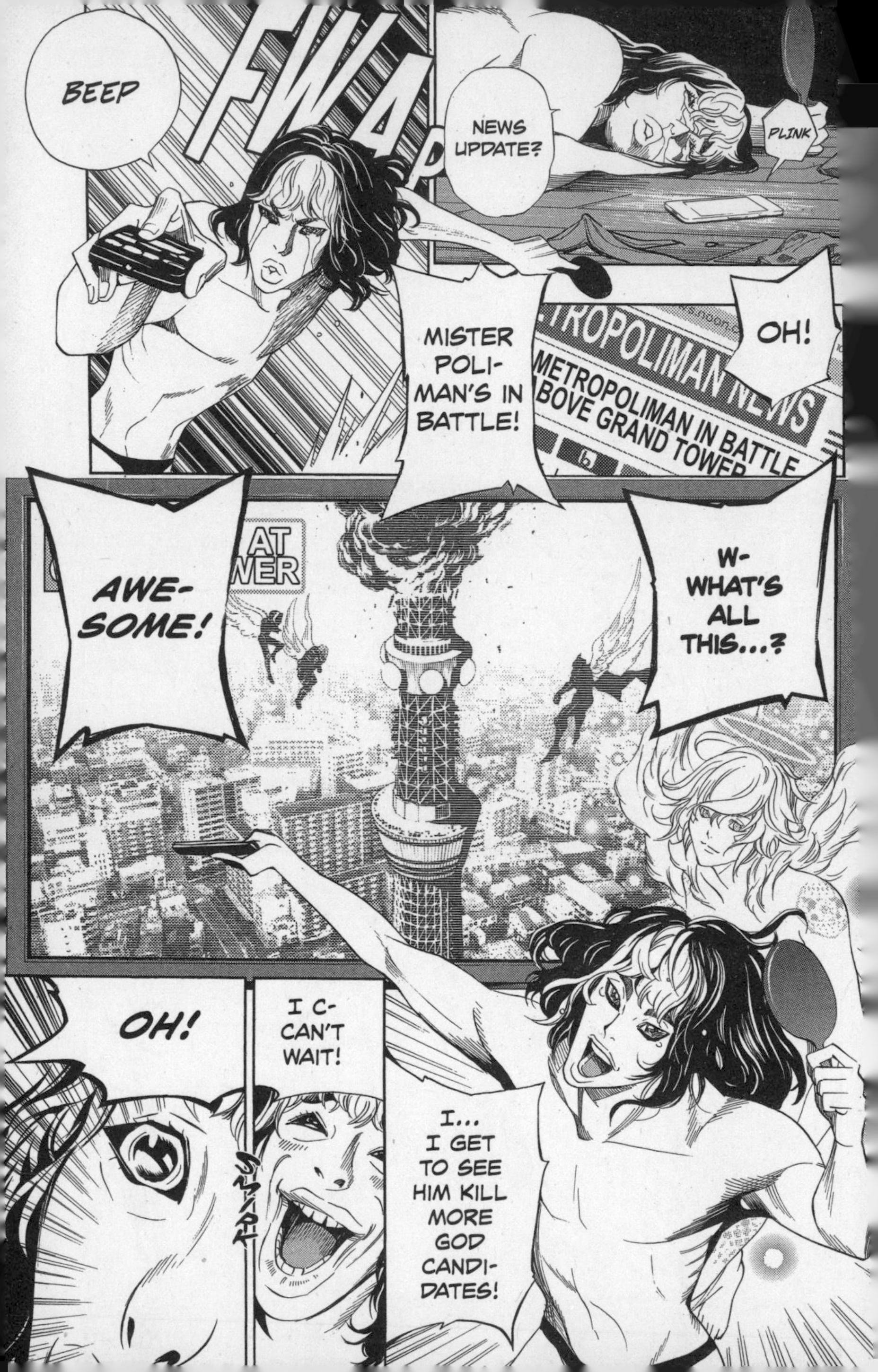
PLINK
NEWS UPDATE?
BEEP
FWAP
OH!
TROPOLIMAN NEWS
METROPOLIMAN IN BATTLE
BOVE GRAND TOWER
MISTER POLI-MAN'S IN BATTLE!
W-WHAT'S ALL THIS...?
AWE-SOME!
I... I GET TO SEE HIM KILL MORE GOD CANDI-DATES!
I C-CAN'T WAIT!
SMIRK
OH!

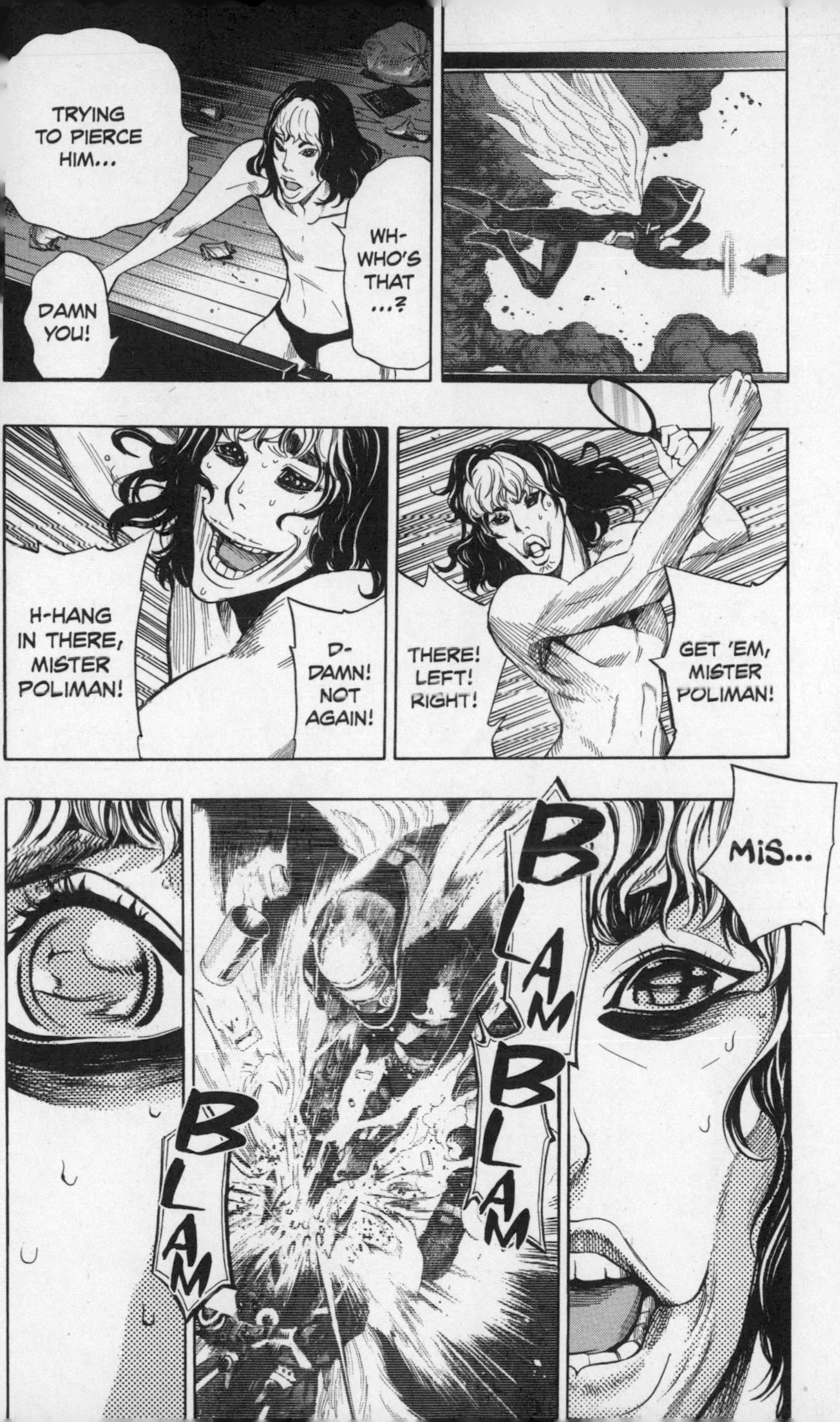
TRYING TO PIERCE HIM...
WH- WHO'S THAT ...?
DAMN YOU!
GET 'EM, MISTER POLIMAN!
THERE! LEFT! RIGHT!
D- DAMN! NOT AGAIN!
H-HANG IN THERE, MISTER POLIMAN!
MIS...
BLAM
BLAM
BLAM

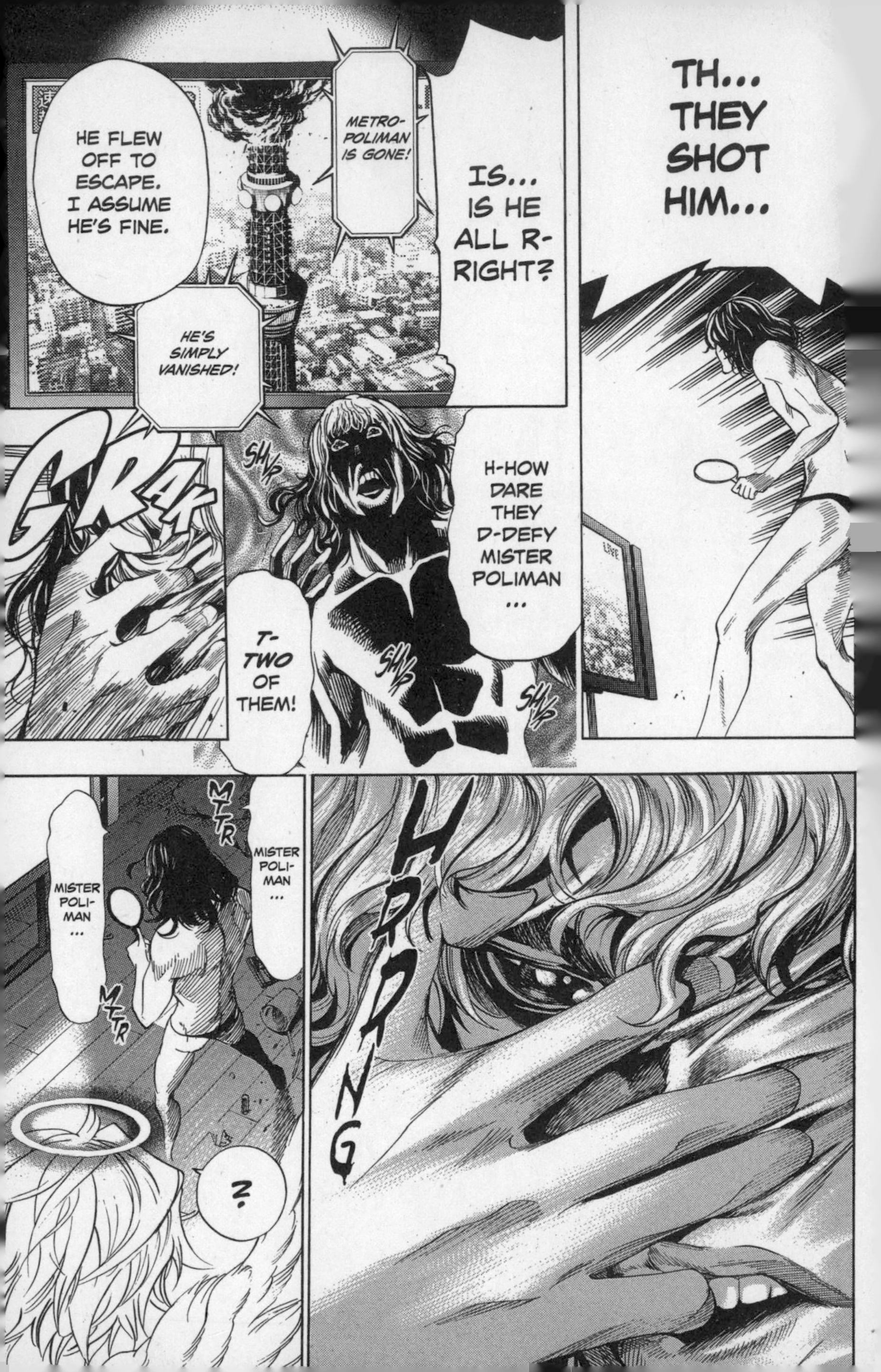

TH... THEY SHOT HIM...
IS... IS HE ALL R-RIGHT?
METRO-POLIMAN IS GONE!
HE FLEW OFF TO ESCAPE. I ASSUME HE'S FINE.
HE'S SIMPLY VANISHED!
H-HOW DARE THEY D-DEFY MISTER POLIMAN ...
SHVP
SHVP
T-TWO OF THEM!
SHVP
GRAK
HDRANG
MTTR
MISTER POLI-MAN ...
MISTER POLI-MAN ...
MTTR
?

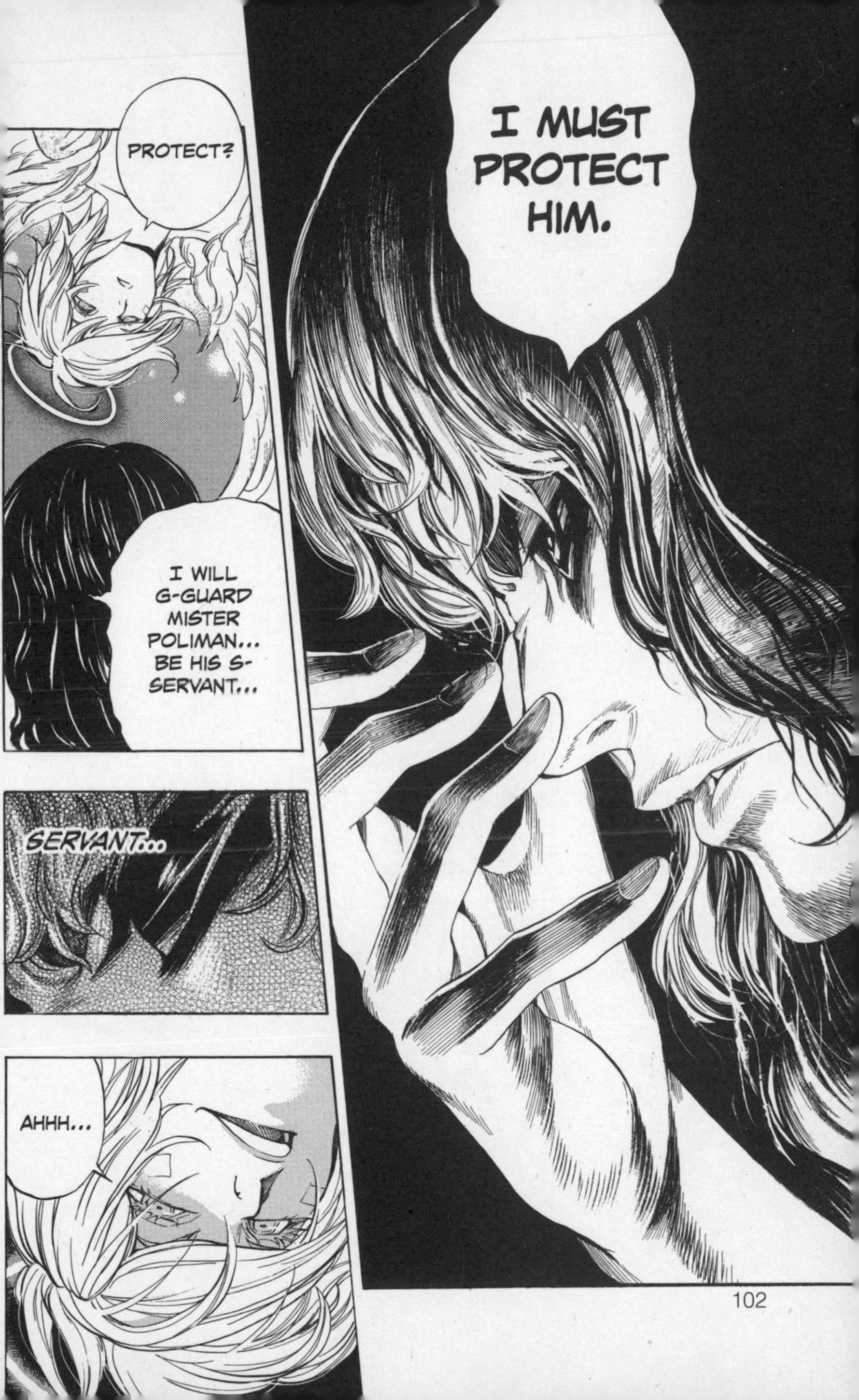
I MUST PROTECT HIM.
PROTECT?
I WILL G-GUARD MISTER POLIMAN... BE HIS S-SERVANT...
SERVANT...
AHHH...

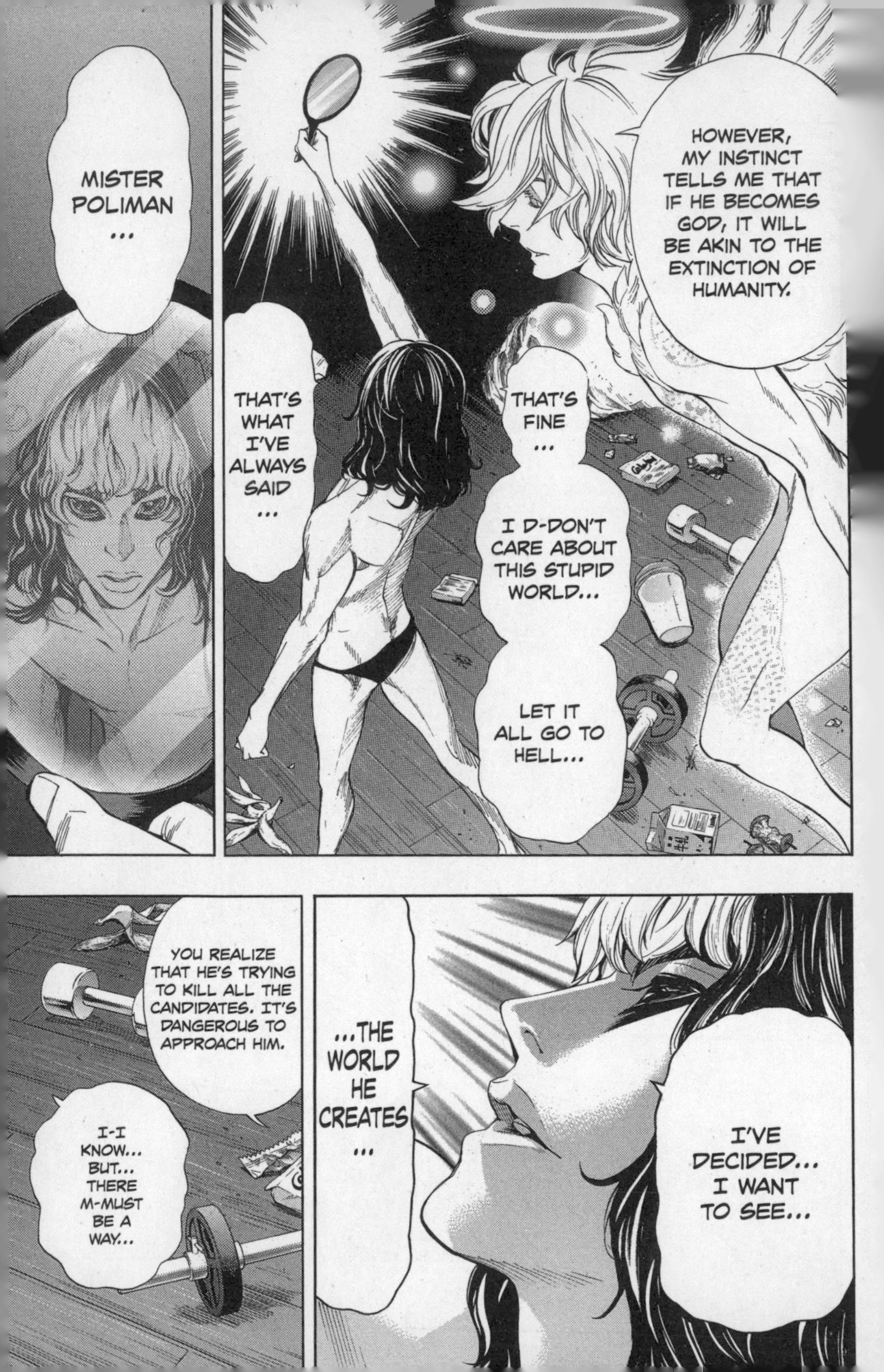
HOWEVER, MY INSTINCT TELLS ME THAT IF HE BECOMES GOD, IT WILL BE AKIN TO THE EXTINCTION OF HUMANITY.
THAT'S FINE ...
I D-DON'T CARE ABOUT THIS STUPID WORLD...
LET IT ALL GO TO HELL...
THAT'S WHAT I'VE ALWAYS SAID ...
MISTER POLIMAN ...
I'VE DECIDED... I WANT TO SEE...
...THE WORLD HE CREATES ...
YOU REALIZE THAT HE'S TRYING TO KILL ALL THE CANDIDATES. IT'S DANGEROUS TO APPROACH HIM.
I-I KNOW... BUT... THERE M-MUST BE A WAY...

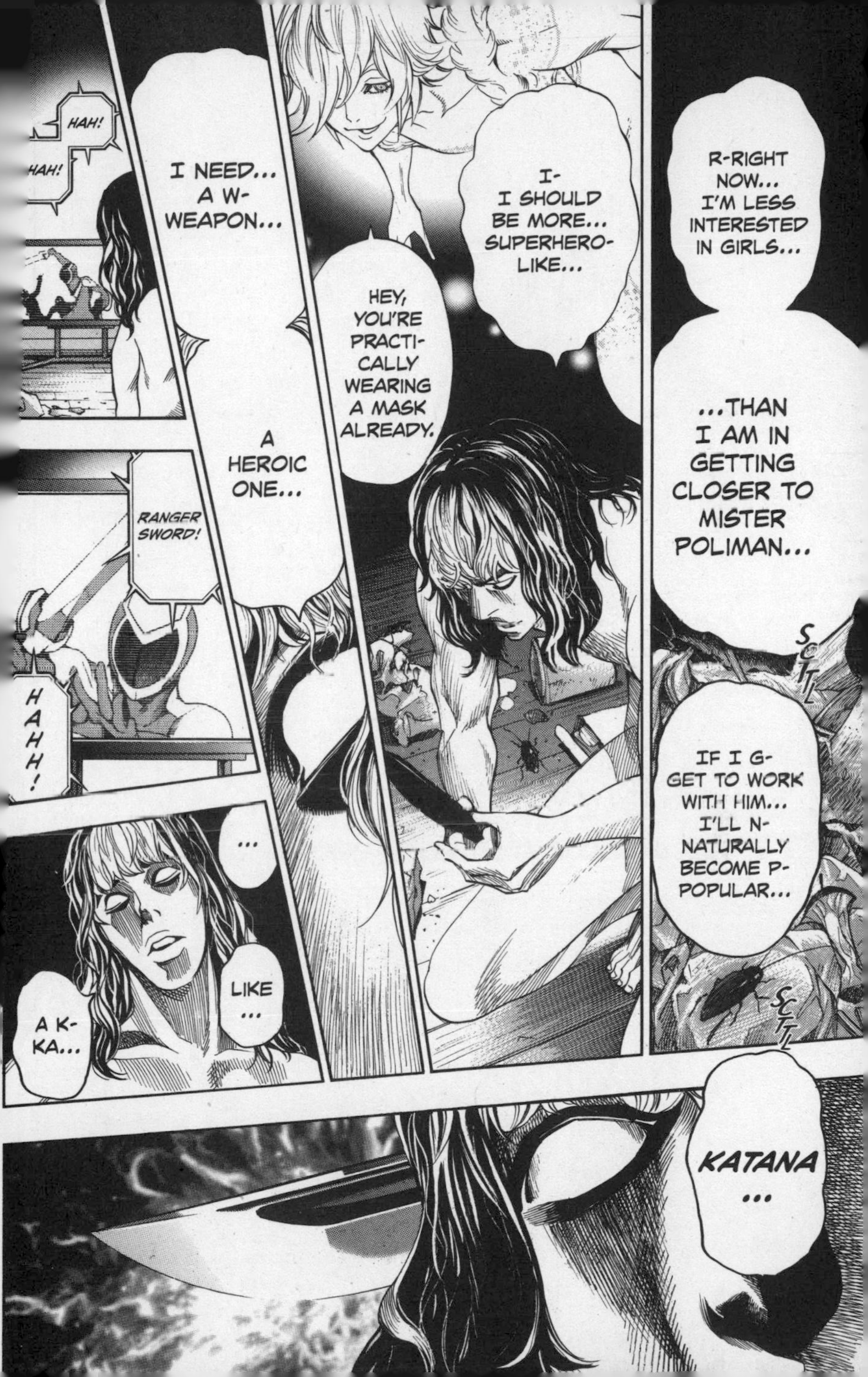
R-RIGHT NOW... I'M LESS INTERESTED IN GIRLS...
...THAN I AM IN GETTING CLOSER TO MISTER POLIMAN...
SCTTL
IF I G-GET TO WORK WITH HIM... I'LL N-NATURALLY BECOME P-POPULAR...
SCTTL
I- I SHOULD BE MORE... SUPERHERO-LIKE...
HEY, YOU'RE PRACTI-CALLY WEARING A MASK ALREADY.
I NEED... A W-WEAPON...
A HEROIC ONE...
HAH!
HAH!
RANGER SWORD!
HAHH!
...
LIKE ...
A K-KA...
KATANA ...

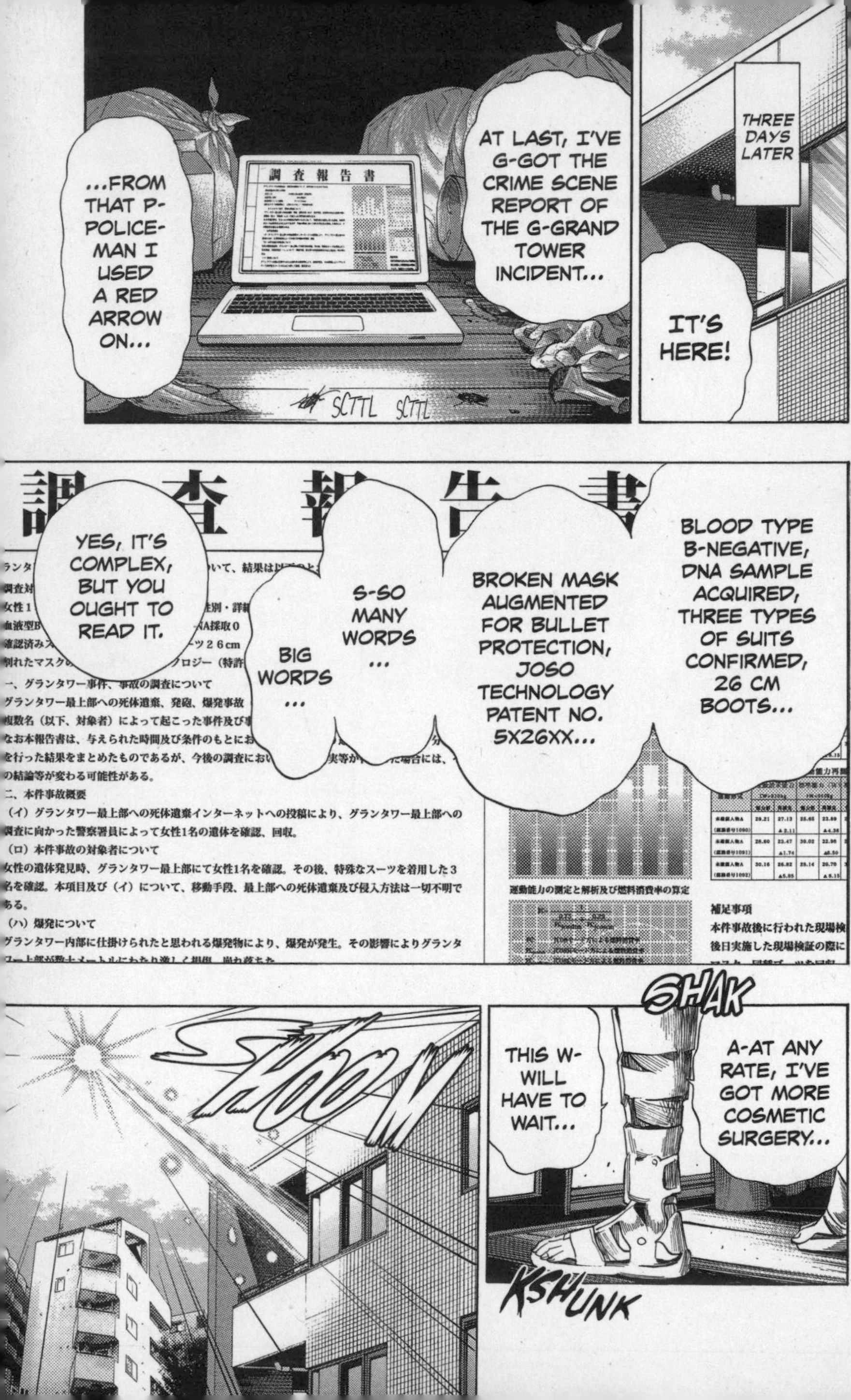
THREE DAYS LATER
IT'S HERE!
AT LAST, I'VE G-GOT THE CRIME SCENE REPORT OF THE G-GRAND TOWER INCIDENT...
...FROM THAT P-POLICEMAN I USED A RED ARROW ON...
SCTTL SCTTL
調査報告書
BLOOD TYPE B-NEGATIVE, DNA SAMPLE ACQUIRED, THREE TYPES OF SUITS CONFIRMED, 26 CM BOOTS...
BROKEN MASK AUGMENTED FOR BULLET PROTECTION, JOSO TECHNOLOGY PATENT NO. 5X26XX...
S-SO MANY WORDS...
BIG WORDS...
YES, IT'S COMPLEX, BUT YOU OUGHT TO READ IT.
一、グランタワー事件、事故の調査について
二、本件事故概要
（イ）グランタワー最上部への死体遺棄インターネットへの投稿により、グランタワー最上部への
調査に向かった警察署員によって女性1名の遺体を確認、回収。
（ロ）本件事故の対象者について
女性の遺体発見時、グランタワー最上部にて女性1名を確認。その後、特殊なスーツを着用した3
名を確認。本項目及び（イ）について、移動手段、最上部への死体遺棄及び侵入方法は一切不明で
ある。
（ハ）爆発について
運動能力の測定と解析及び燃料消費率の算定
補足事項
SHAK
A-AT ANY RATE, I'VE GOT MORE COSMETIC SURGERY...
THIS W-WILL HAVE TO WAIT...
KSHUNK
SHOOM

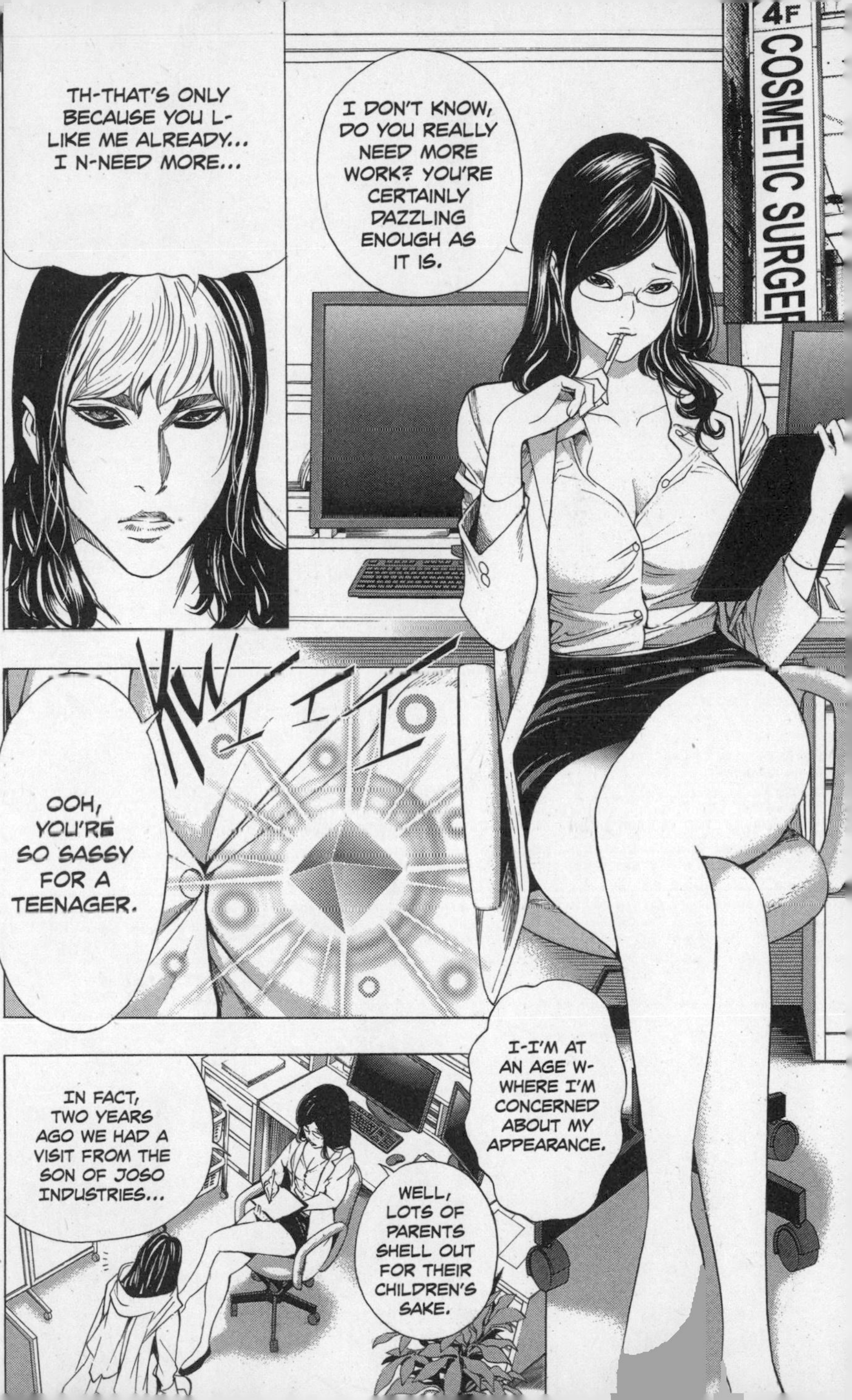
4F COSMETIC SURGER
I DON'T KNOW, DO YOU REALLY NEED MORE WORK? YOU'RE CERTAINLY DAZZLING ENOUGH AS IT IS.
TH-THAT'S ONLY BECAUSE YOU L-LIKE ME ALREADY... I N-NEED MORE...
KWIIII
OOH, YOU'RE SO SASSY FOR A TEENAGER.
I-I'M AT AN AGE W-WHERE I'M CONCERNED ABOUT MY APPEARANCE.
WELL, LOTS OF PARENTS SHELL OUT FOR THEIR CHILDREN'S SAKE.
IN FACT, TWO YEARS AGO WE HAD A VISIT FROM THE SON OF JOSO INDUSTRIES...

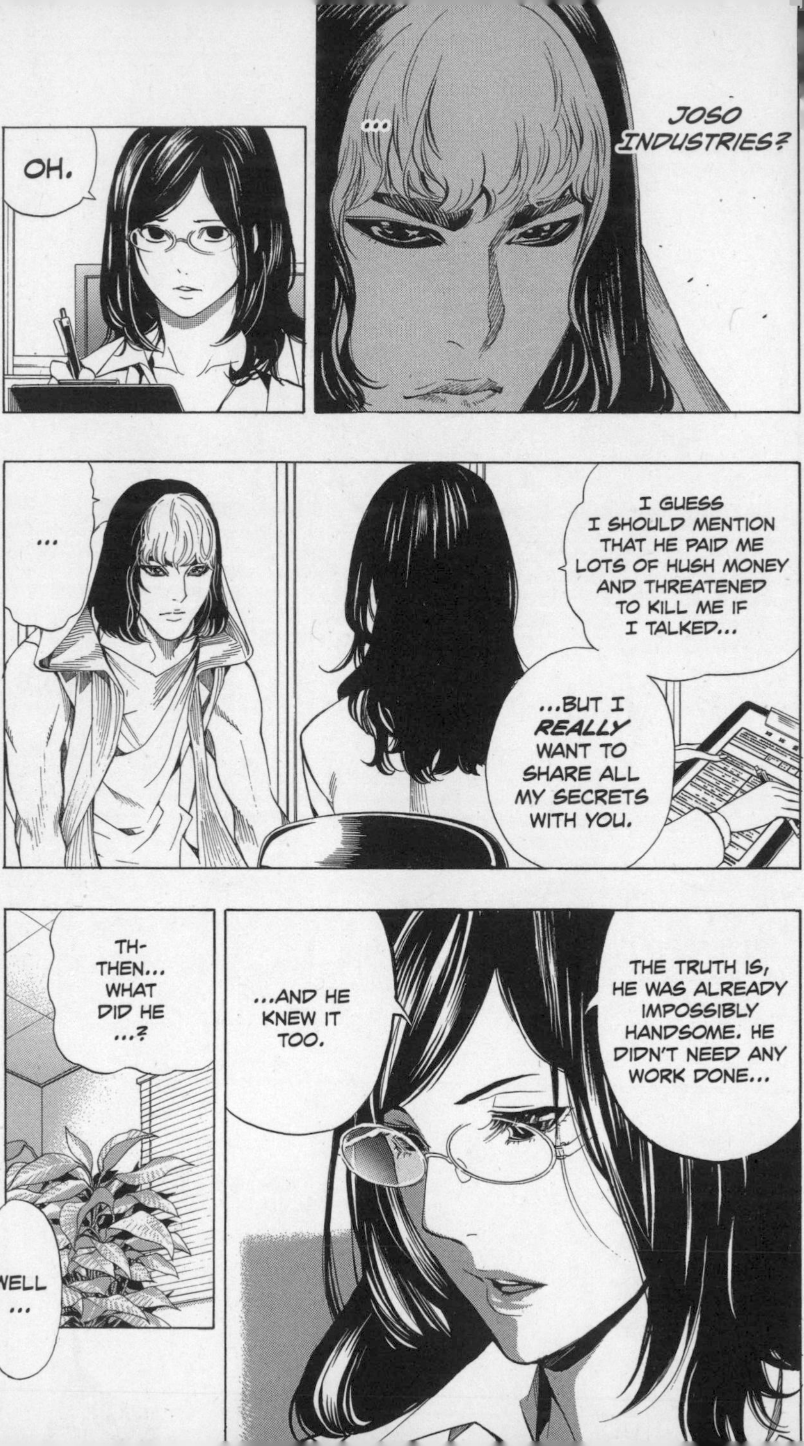
JOSO INDUSTRIES?
...
OH.
I GUESS I SHOULD MENTION THAT HE PAID ME LOTS OF HUSH MONEY AND THREATENED TO KILL ME IF I TALKED...
...BUT I *REALLY* WANT TO SHARE ALL MY SECRETS WITH YOU.
...
THE TRUTH IS, HE WAS ALREADY IMPOSSIBLY HANDSOME. HE DIDN'T NEED ANY WORK DONE...
...AND HE KNEW IT TOO.
TH- THEN... WHAT DID HE ...?
WELL ...

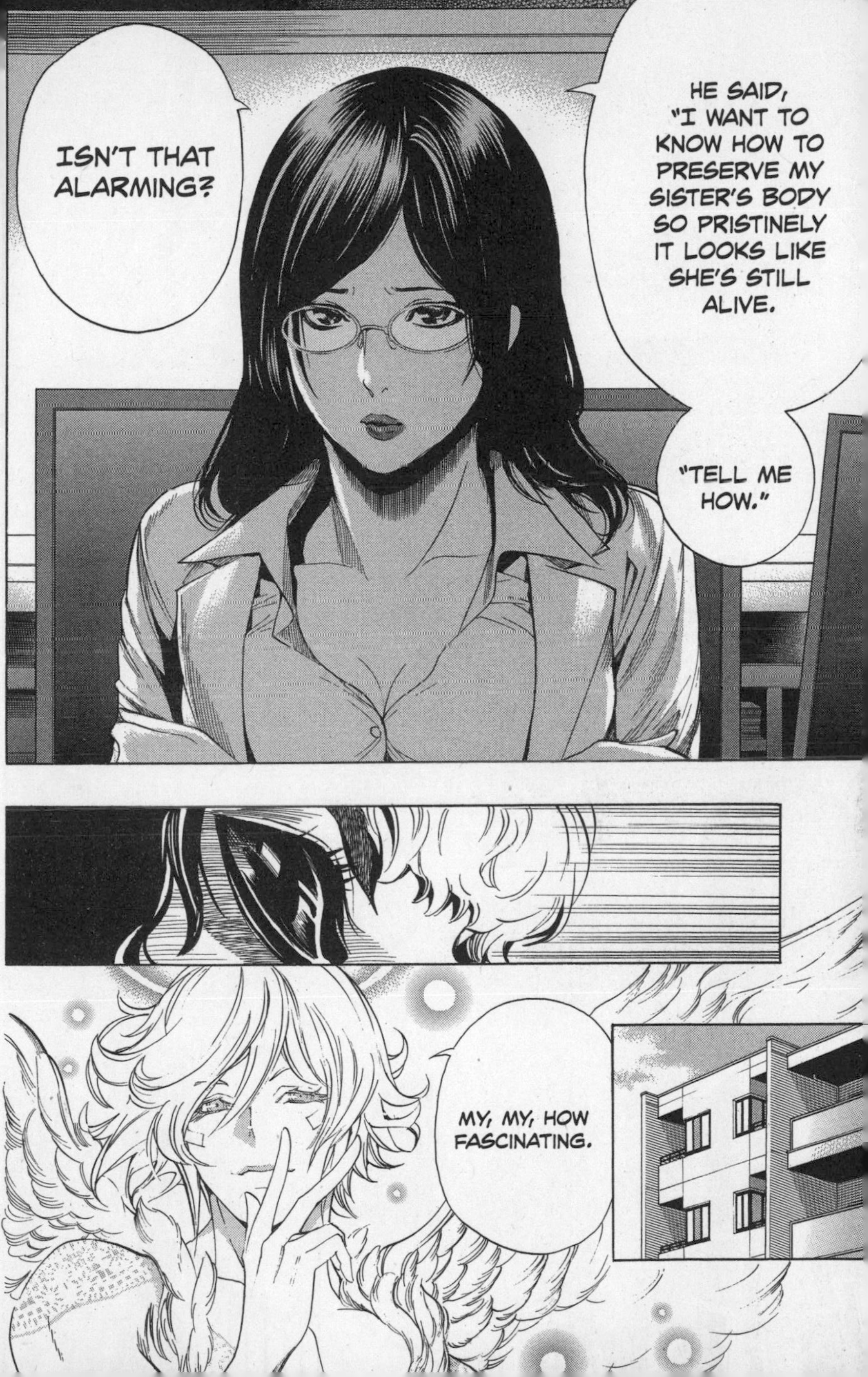
HE SAID, "I WANT TO KNOW HOW TO PRESERVE MY SISTER'S BODY SO PRISTINELY IT LOOKS LIKE SHE'S STILL ALIVE.
"TELL ME HOW."
ISN'T THAT ALARMING?
MY, MY, HOW FASCINATING.

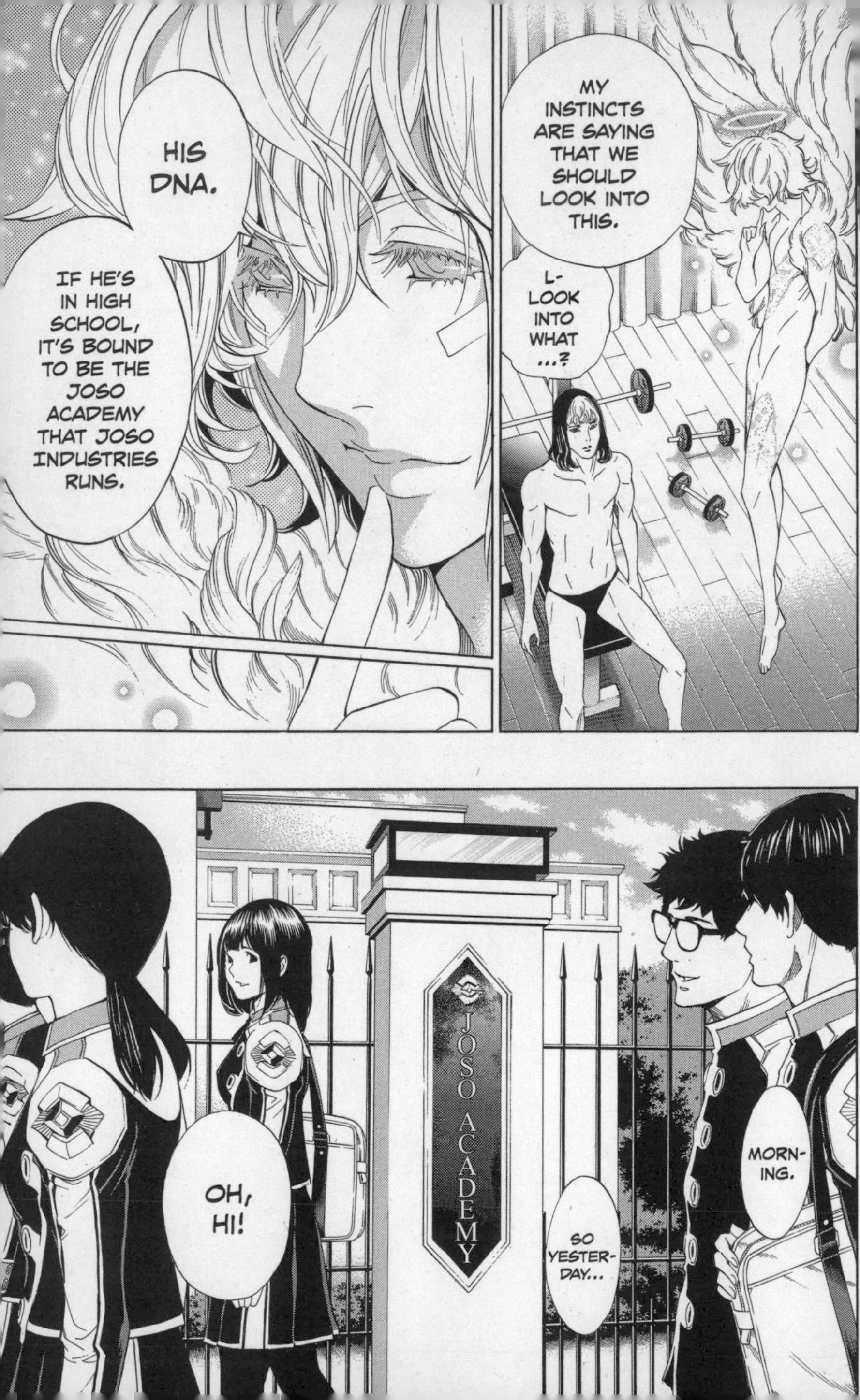
MY INSTINCTS ARE SAYING THAT WE SHOULD LOOK INTO THIS.
L-LOOK INTO WHAT...?
HIS DNA.
IF HE'S IN HIGH SCHOOL, IT'S BOUND TO BE THE JOSO ACADEMY THAT JOSO INDUSTRIES RUNS.
MORN-ING.
SO YESTER-DAY...
JOSO ACADEMY
OH, HI!

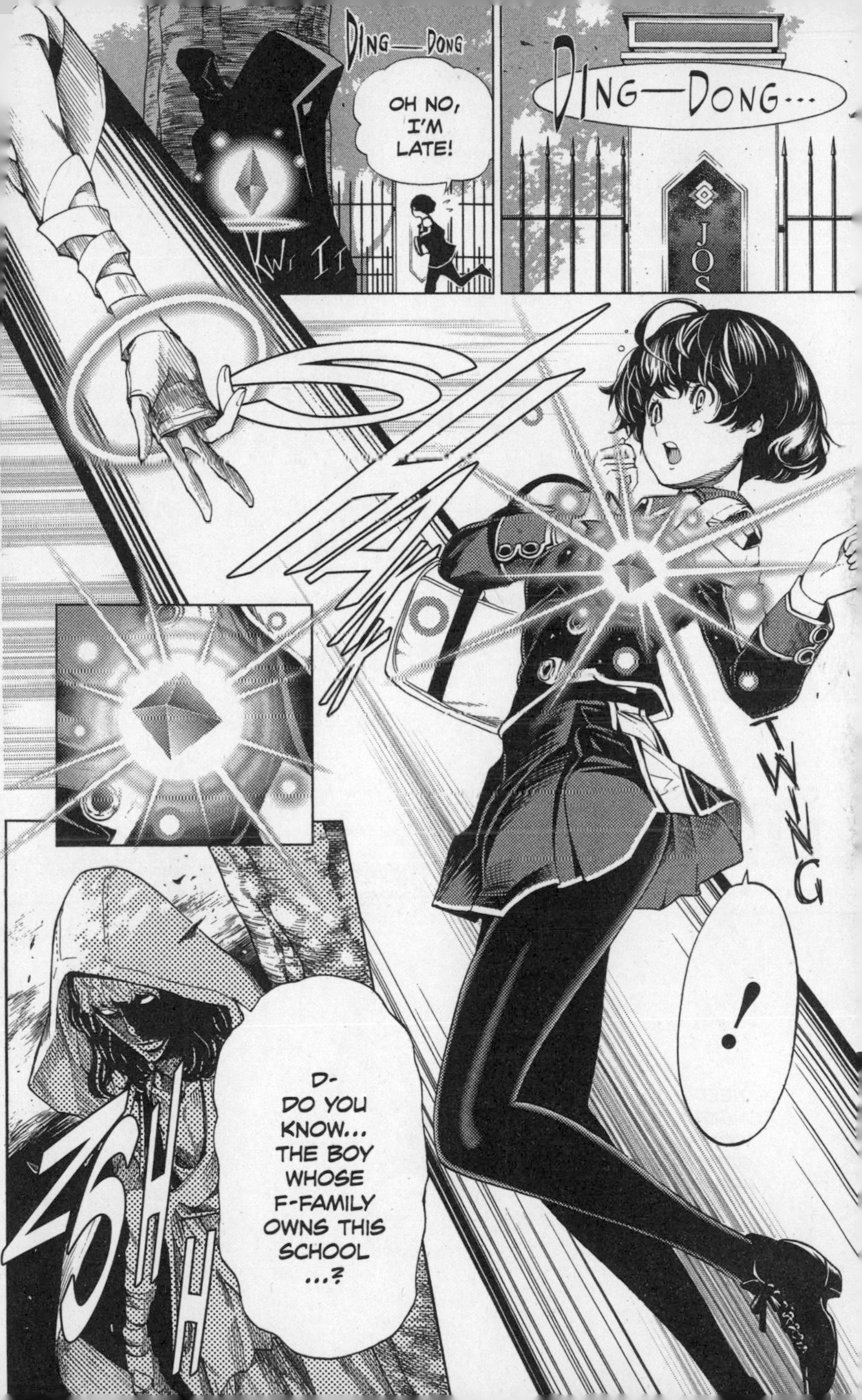
DING—DONG...
JOS
DING—DONG
OH NO, I'M LATE!
KWI II
TWING
!
D- DO YOU KNOW... THE BOY WHOSE F-FAMILY OWNS THIS SCHOOL ...?

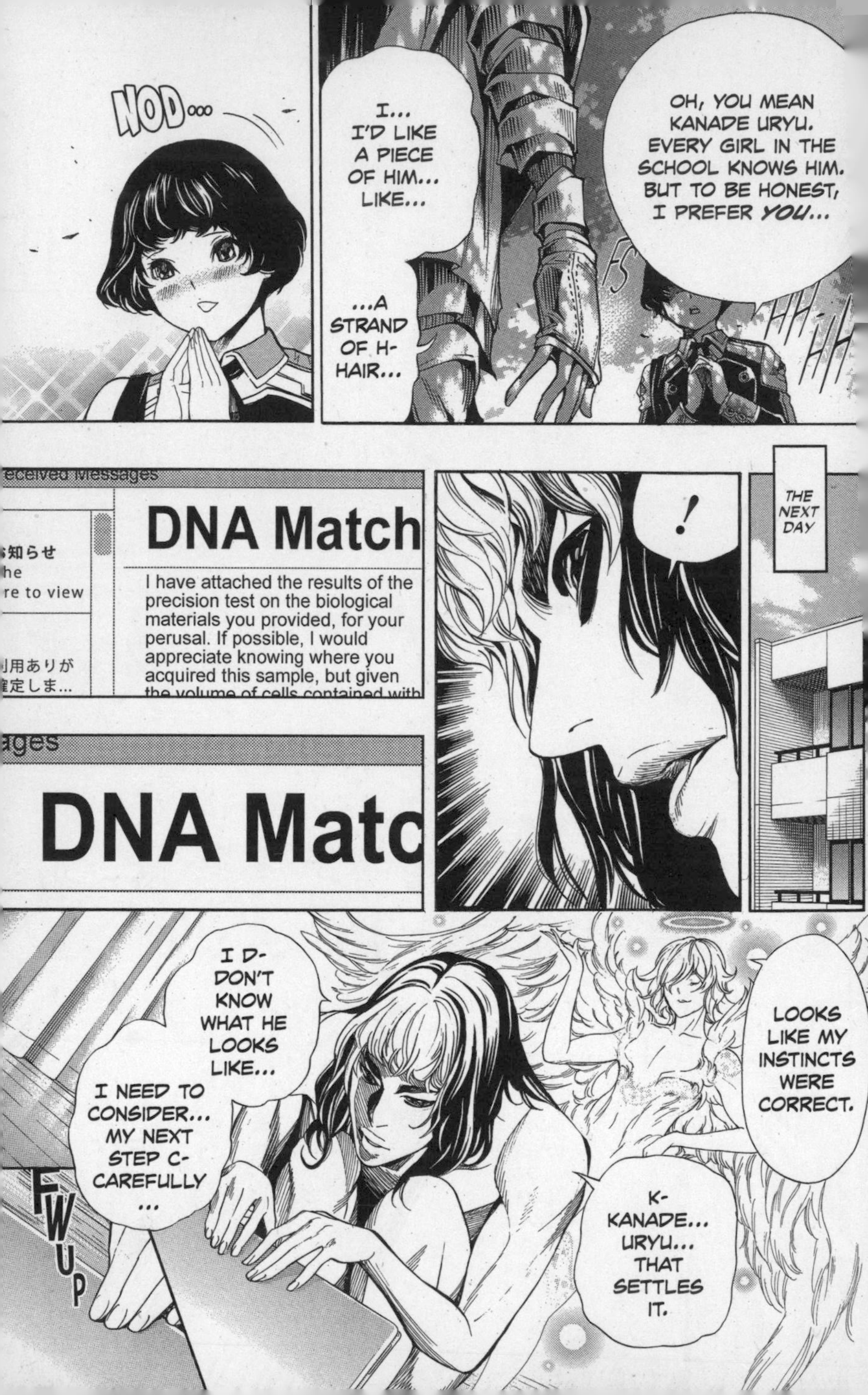
OH, YOU MEAN KANADE URYU. EVERY GIRL IN THE SCHOOL KNOWS HIM. BUT TO BE HONEST, I PREFER *YOU*...
I... I'D LIKE A PIECE OF HIM... LIKE...
...A STRAND OF H- HAIR...
NOD...
THE NEXT DAY
!
eceived Messages
DNA Match
知らせ
he
re to view
利用ありが
確定しま...
I have attached the results of the precision test on the biological materials you provided, for your perusal. If possible, I would appreciate knowing where you acquired this sample, but given
ages
DNA Matc
LOOKS LIKE MY INSTINCTS WERE CORRECT.
K- KANADE... URYU... THAT SETTLES IT.
I D- DON'T KNOW WHAT HE LOOKS LIKE...
I NEED TO CONSIDER... MY NEXT STEP C- CAREFULLY...
FWUP

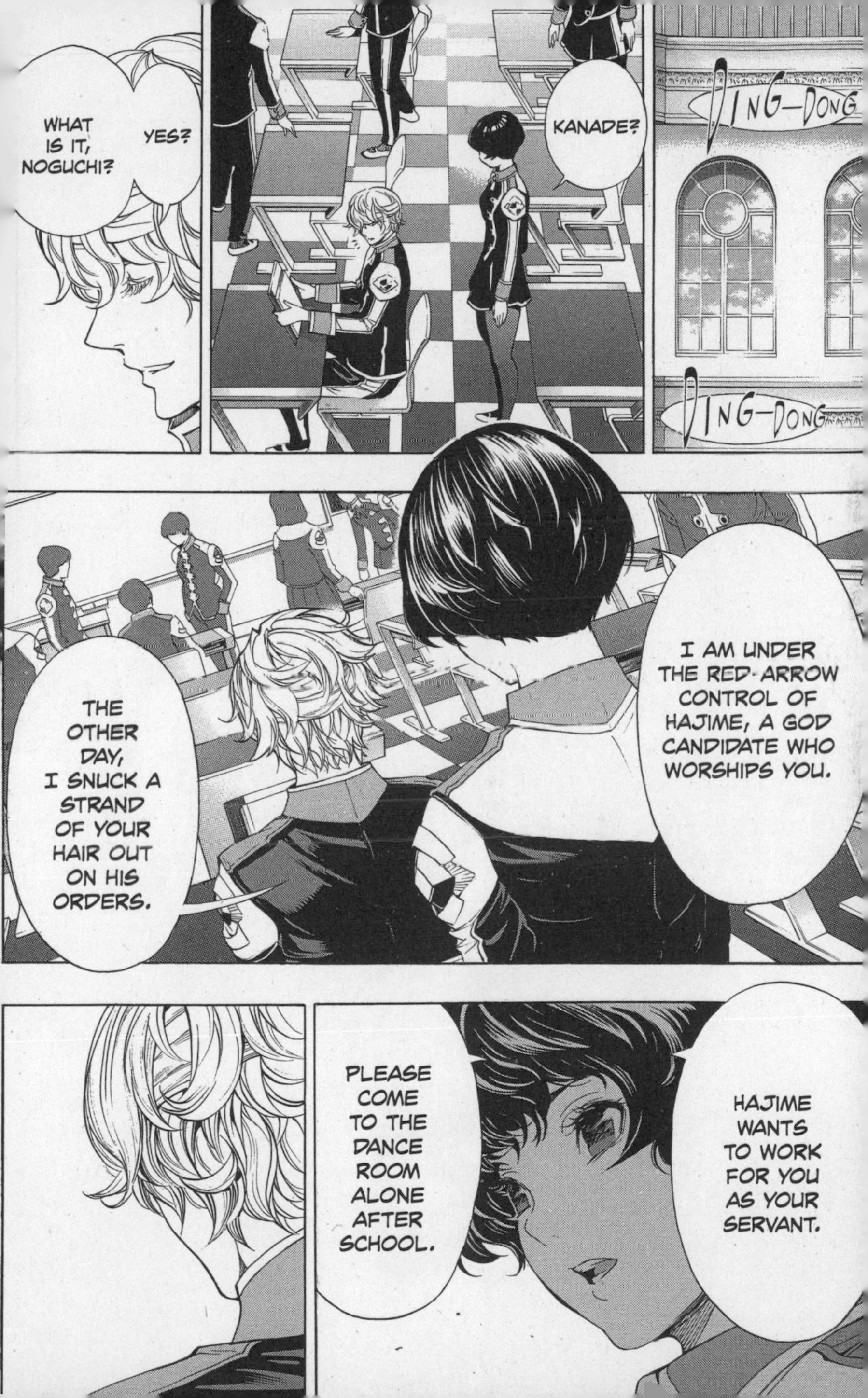
DING-DONG
DING-DONG
KANADE?
YES?
WHAT IS IT, NOGUCHI?
I AM UNDER THE RED-ARROW CONTROL OF HAJIME, A GOD CANDIDATE WHO WORSHIPS YOU.
THE OTHER DAY, I SNUCK A STRAND OF YOUR HAIR OUT ON HIS ORDERS.
HAJIME WANTS TO WORK FOR YOU AS YOUR SERVANT.
PLEASE COME TO THE DANCE ROOM ALONE AFTER SCHOOL.

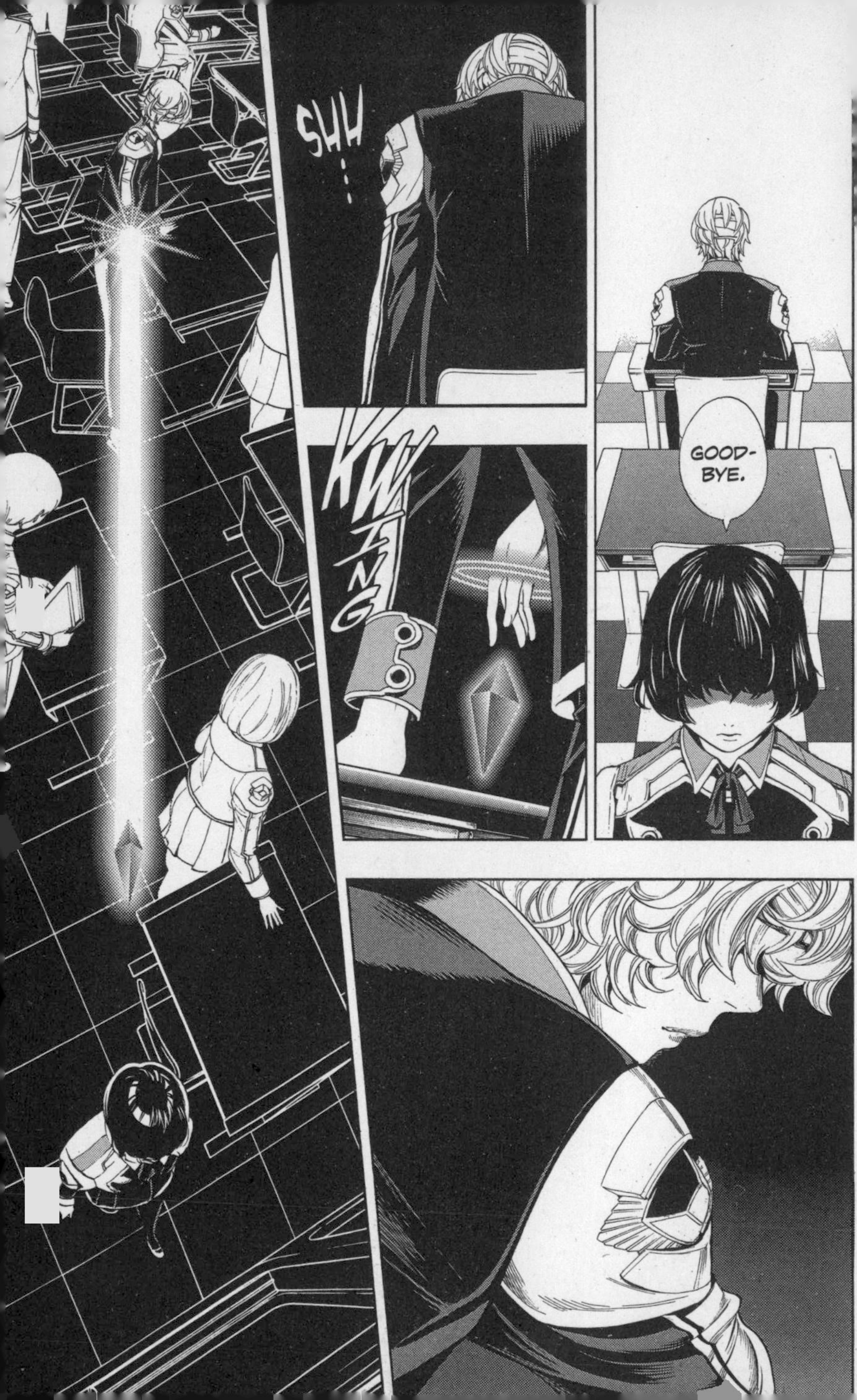
GOOD-BYE.
SHH...
KWIING

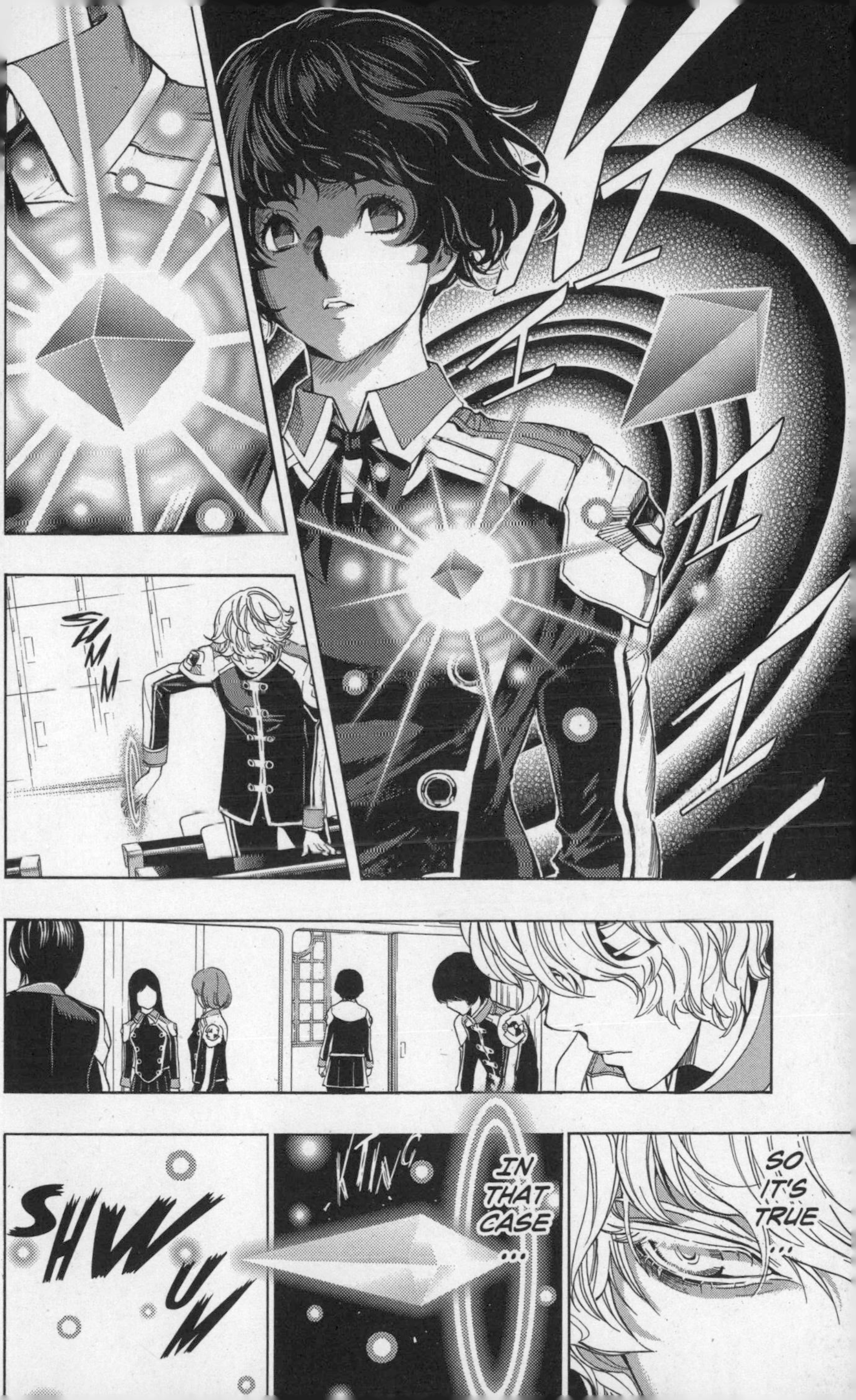
SO IT'S TRUE...
IN THAT CASE...
KTING
SHWUM

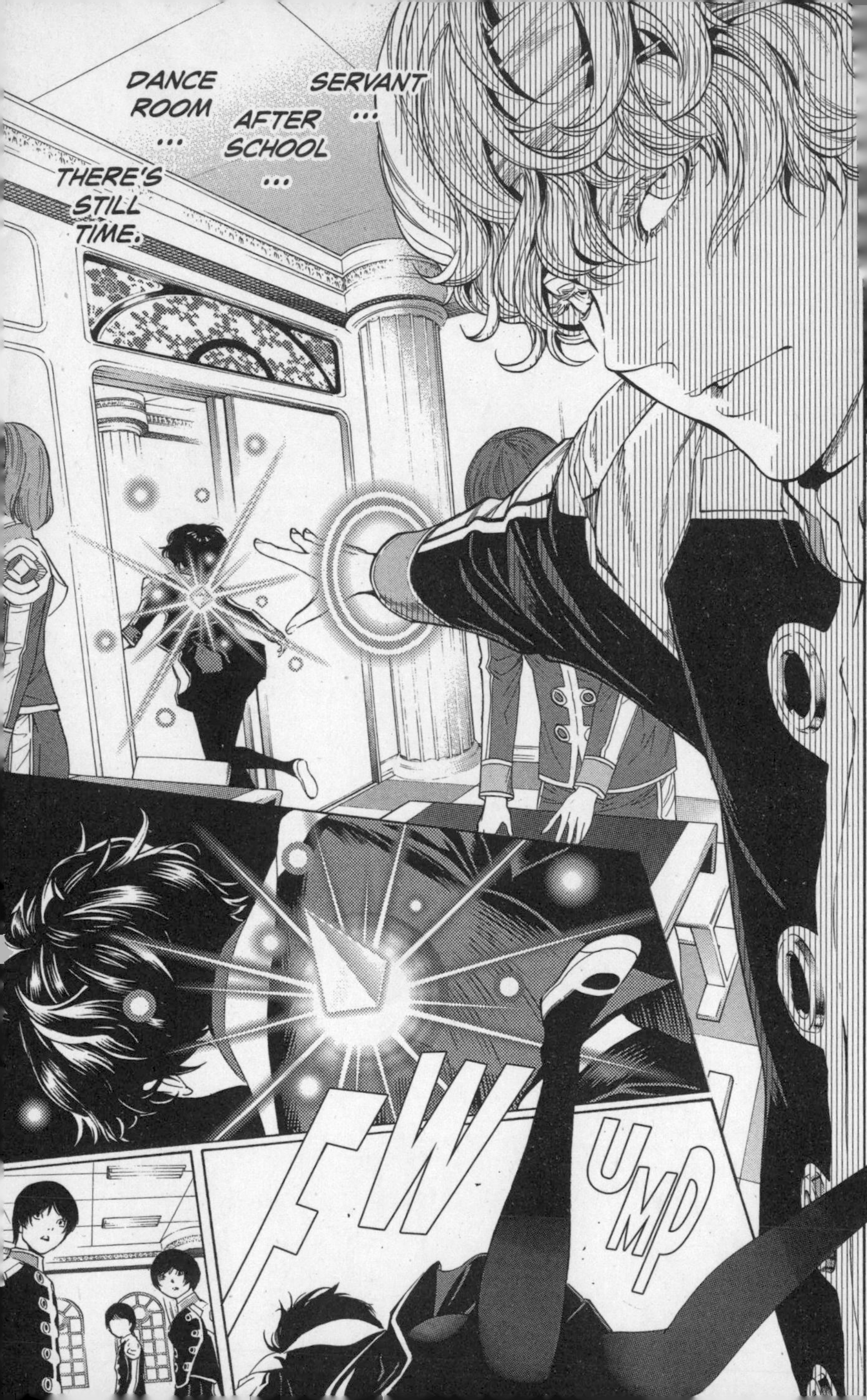
SERVANT ...
AFTER SCHOOL ...
DANCE ROOM ...
THERE'S STILL TIME.
FWUMP

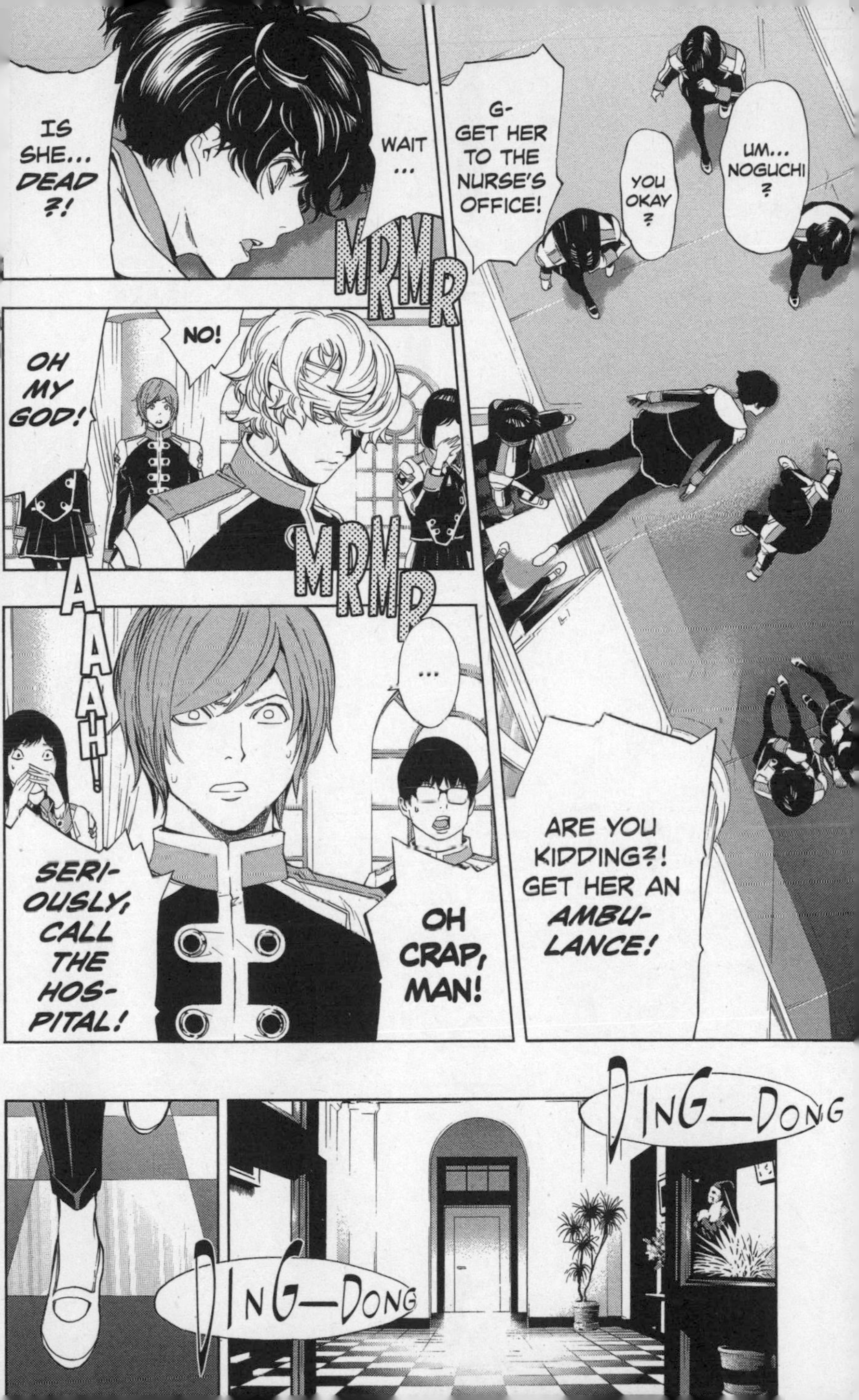
UM... NOGUCHI?
YOU OKAY?
G- GET HER TO THE NURSE'S OFFICE!
ARE YOU KIDDING?! GET HER AN AMBULANCE!
WAIT...
MRMR
IS SHE... DEAD?!
NO!
MRMR
OH MY GOD!
...
OH CRAP, MAN!
AAAAH!
SERIOUSLY, CALL THE HOSPITAL!
DING—DONG
DING—DONG

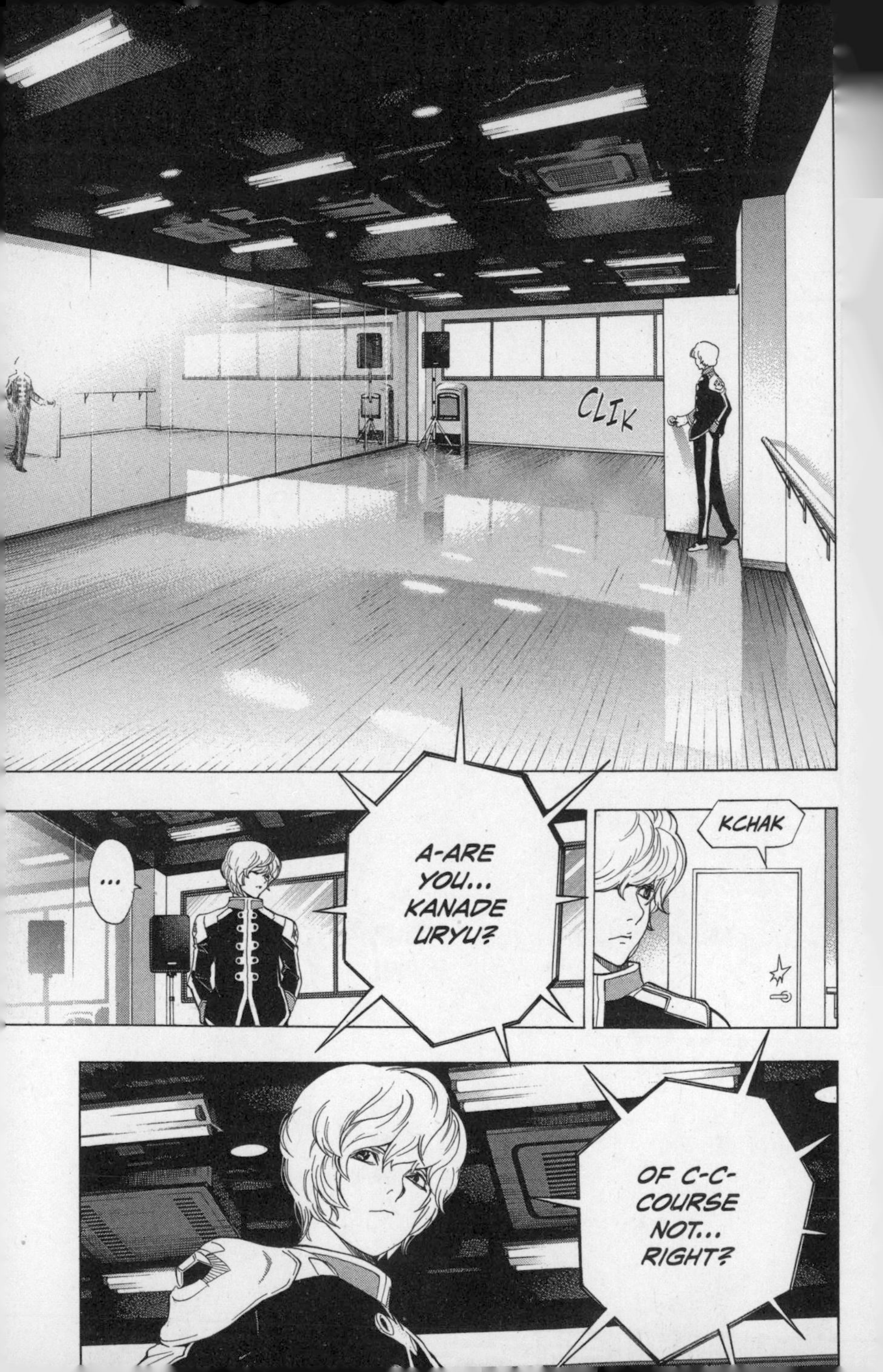
CLIK
KCHAK
A-ARE YOU... KANADE URYU?
...
OF C-C-COURSE NOT... RIGHT?

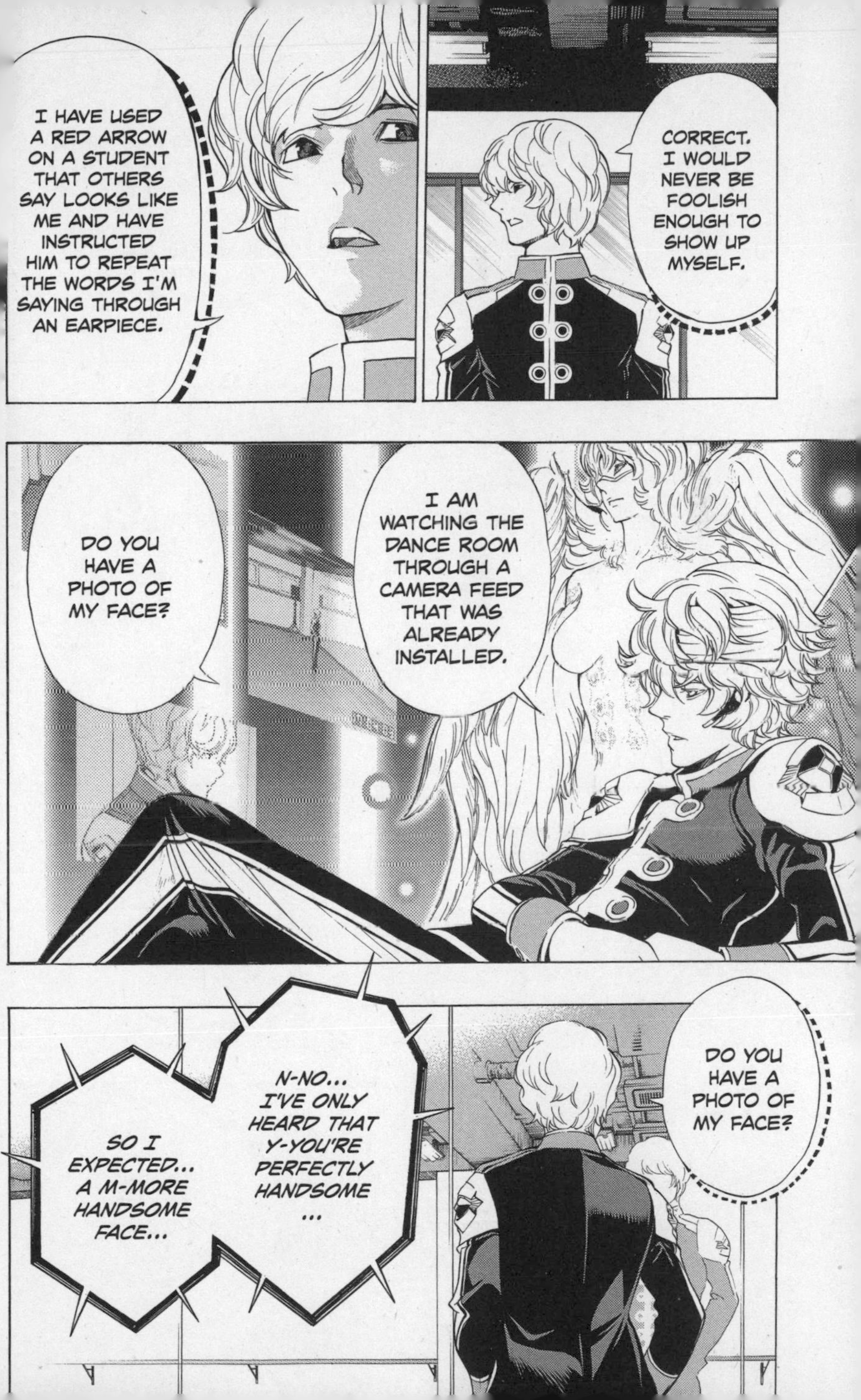
CORRECT. I WOULD NEVER BE FOOLISH ENOUGH TO SHOW UP MYSELF.
I HAVE USED A RED ARROW ON A STUDENT THAT OTHERS SAY LOOKS LIKE ME AND HAVE INSTRUCTED HIM TO REPEAT THE WORDS I'M SAYING THROUGH AN EARPIECE.
I AM WATCHING THE DANCE ROOM THROUGH A CAMERA FEED THAT WAS ALREADY INSTALLED.
DO YOU HAVE A PHOTO OF MY FACE?
DO YOU HAVE A PHOTO OF MY FACE?
N-NO... I'VE ONLY HEARD THAT Y-YOU'RE PERFECTLY HANDSOME ...
SO I EXPECTED... A M-MORE HANDSOME FACE...

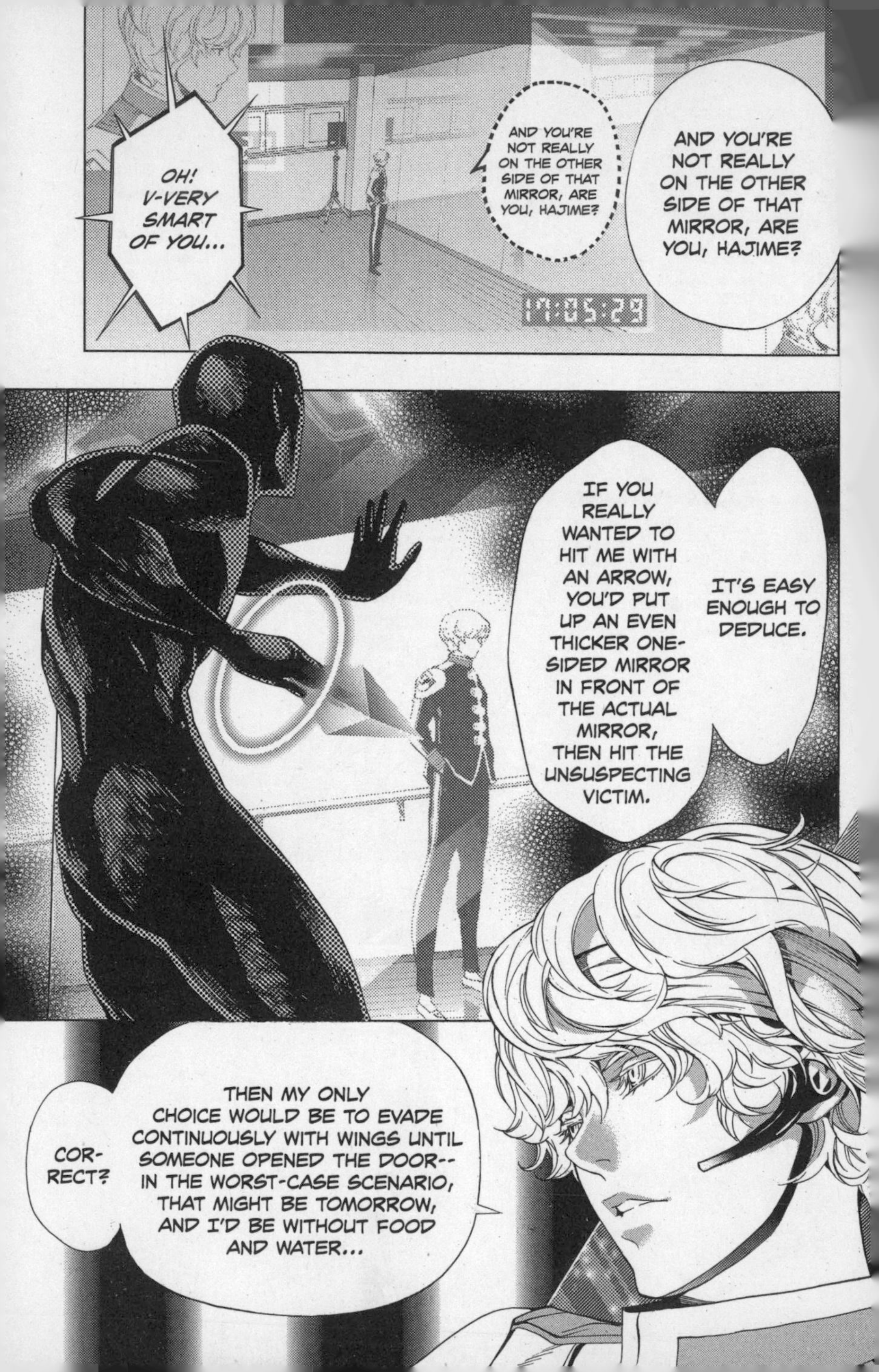
AND YOU'RE NOT REALLY ON THE OTHER SIDE OF THAT MIRROR, ARE YOU, HAJIME?
AND YOU'RE NOT REALLY ON THE OTHER SIDE OF THAT MIRROR, ARE YOU, HAJIME?
17:05:29
OH! V-VERY SMART OF YOU...
IT'S EASY ENOUGH TO DEDUCE.
IF YOU REALLY WANTED TO HIT ME WITH AN ARROW, YOU'D PUT UP AN EVEN THICKER ONE-SIDED MIRROR IN FRONT OF THE ACTUAL MIRROR, THEN HIT THE UNSUSPECTING VICTIM.
THEN MY ONLY CHOICE WOULD BE TO EVADE CONTINUOUSLY WITH WINGS UNTIL SOMEONE OPENED THE DOOR--IN THE WORST-CASE SCENARIO, THAT MIGHT BE TOMORROW, AND I'D BE WITHOUT FOOD AND WATER...
COR-RECT?

SO IF THE REAL ME SHOWED UP, YOU COULD JUST HOLD YOUR ARROW AT THE READY ON THE OTHER SIDE OF THE MIRROR AND THREATEN ME.
R-RIGHT...
SO WHAT WERE YOU GOING TO THREATEN ME INTO DOING?
N-NO, NO THREATS. I J-JUST WANT TO BE YOUR SERVANT...
THAT'S R-REALLY ALL THERE IS TO IT...
TO KILL SOMEONE WITH WINGS, TRAP THEM IN A BOX.
A ONE-SIDED MIRROR BOX IS THE IDEAL SCENARIO.
ANYONE COULD COME UP WITH YOUR IDEA. IT'S NOT THE MOST CONVINCING PITCH FOR YOUR INTELLECT.
...

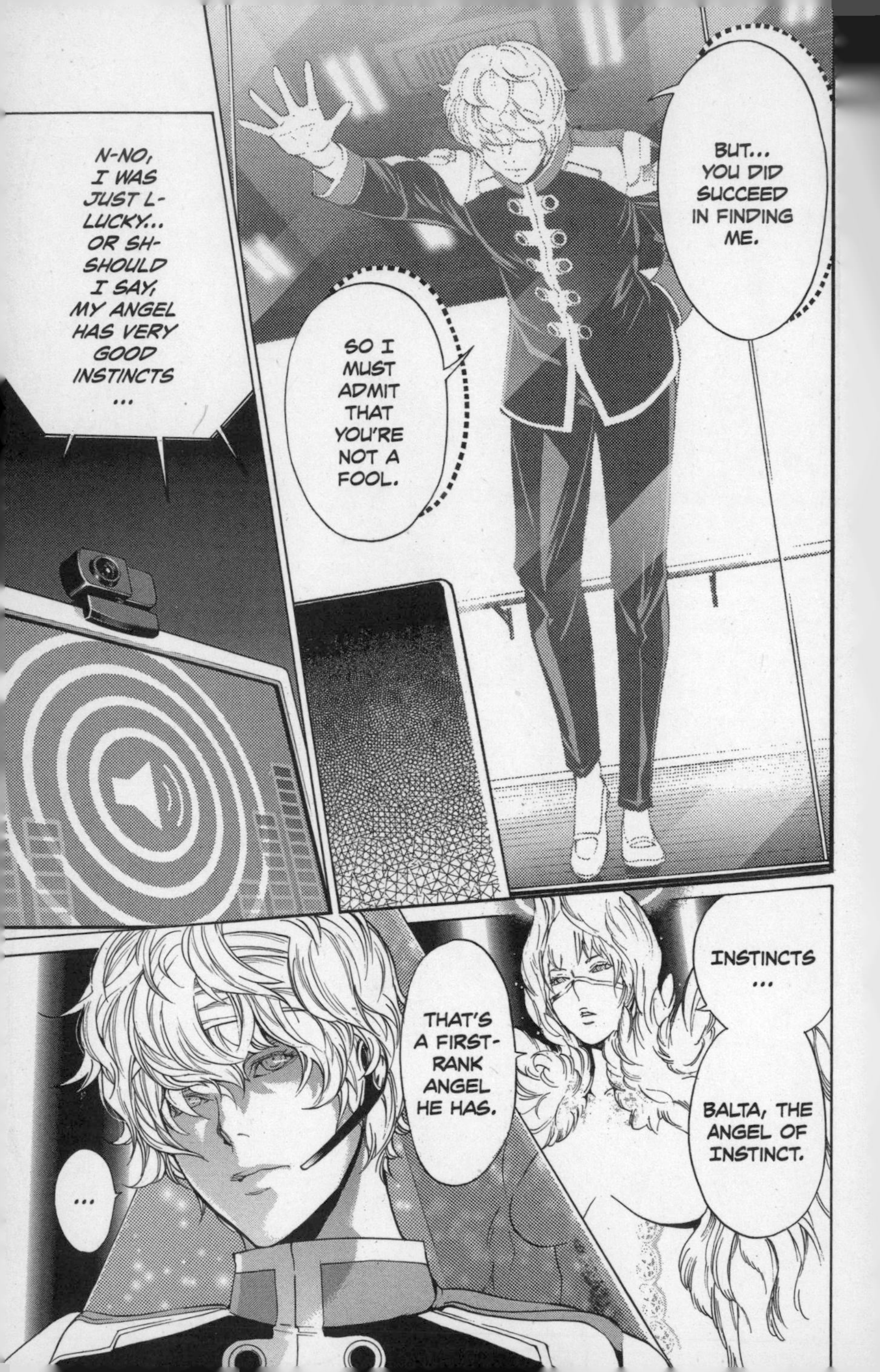
BUT... YOU DID SUCCEED IN FINDING ME.
SO I MUST ADMIT THAT YOU'RE NOT A FOOL.
N-NO, I WAS JUST L-LUCKY... OR SH-SHOULD I SAY, MY ANGEL HAS VERY GOOD INSTINCTS...
INSTINCTS...
BALTA, THE ANGEL OF INSTINCT.
THAT'S A FIRST-RANK ANGEL HE HAS.
...

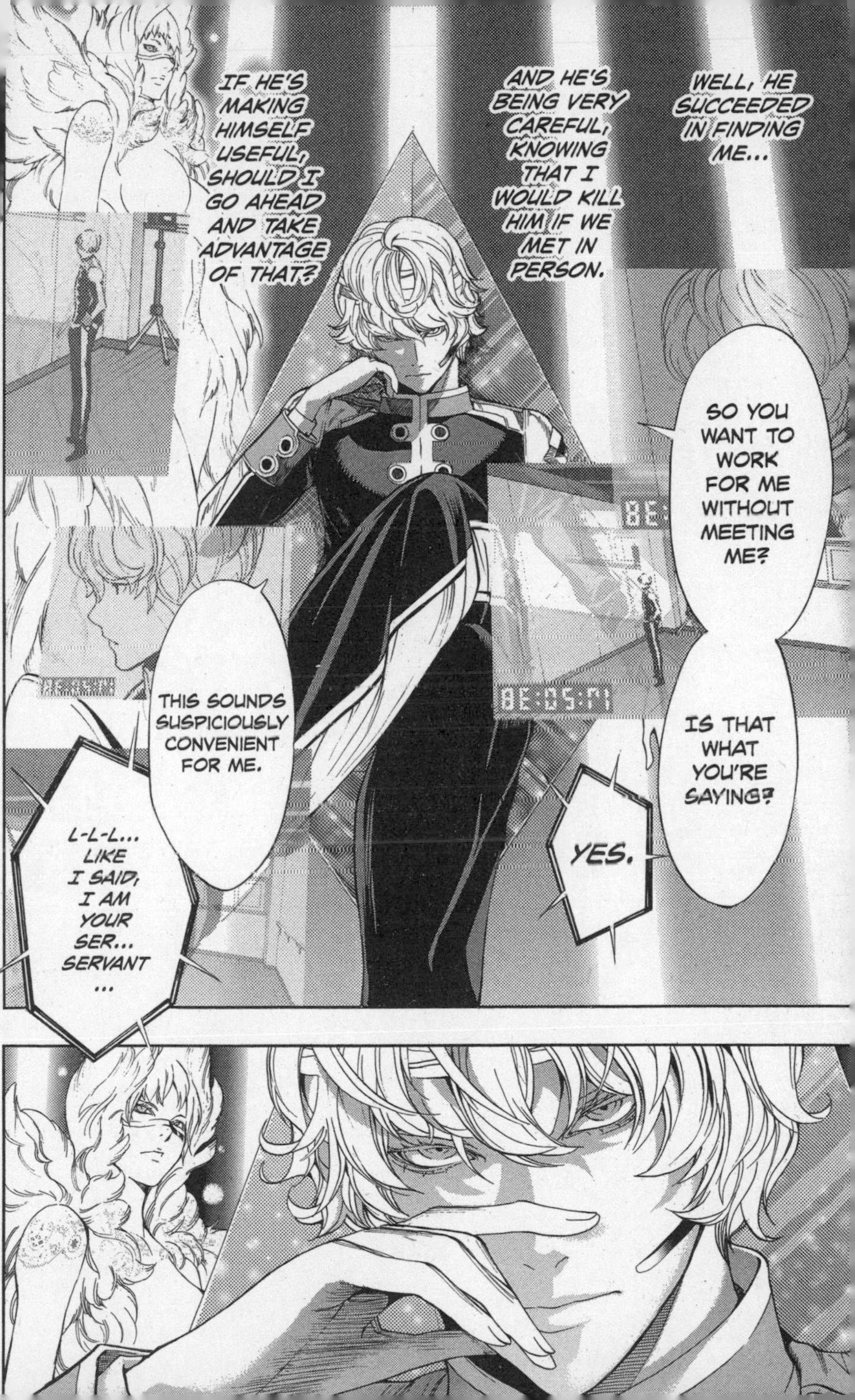
WELL, HE SUCCEEDED IN FINDING ME...
AND HE'S BEING VERY CAREFUL, KNOWING THAT I WOULD KILL HIM IF WE MET IN PERSON.
IF HE'S MAKING HIMSELF USEFUL, SHOULD I GO AHEAD AND TAKE ADVANTAGE OF THAT?
SO YOU WANT TO WORK FOR ME WITHOUT MEETING ME?
IS THAT WHAT YOU'RE SAYING?
YES.
THIS SOUNDS SUSPICIOUSLY CONVENIENT FOR ME.
L-L-L... LIKE I SAID, I AM YOUR SER... SERVANT ...

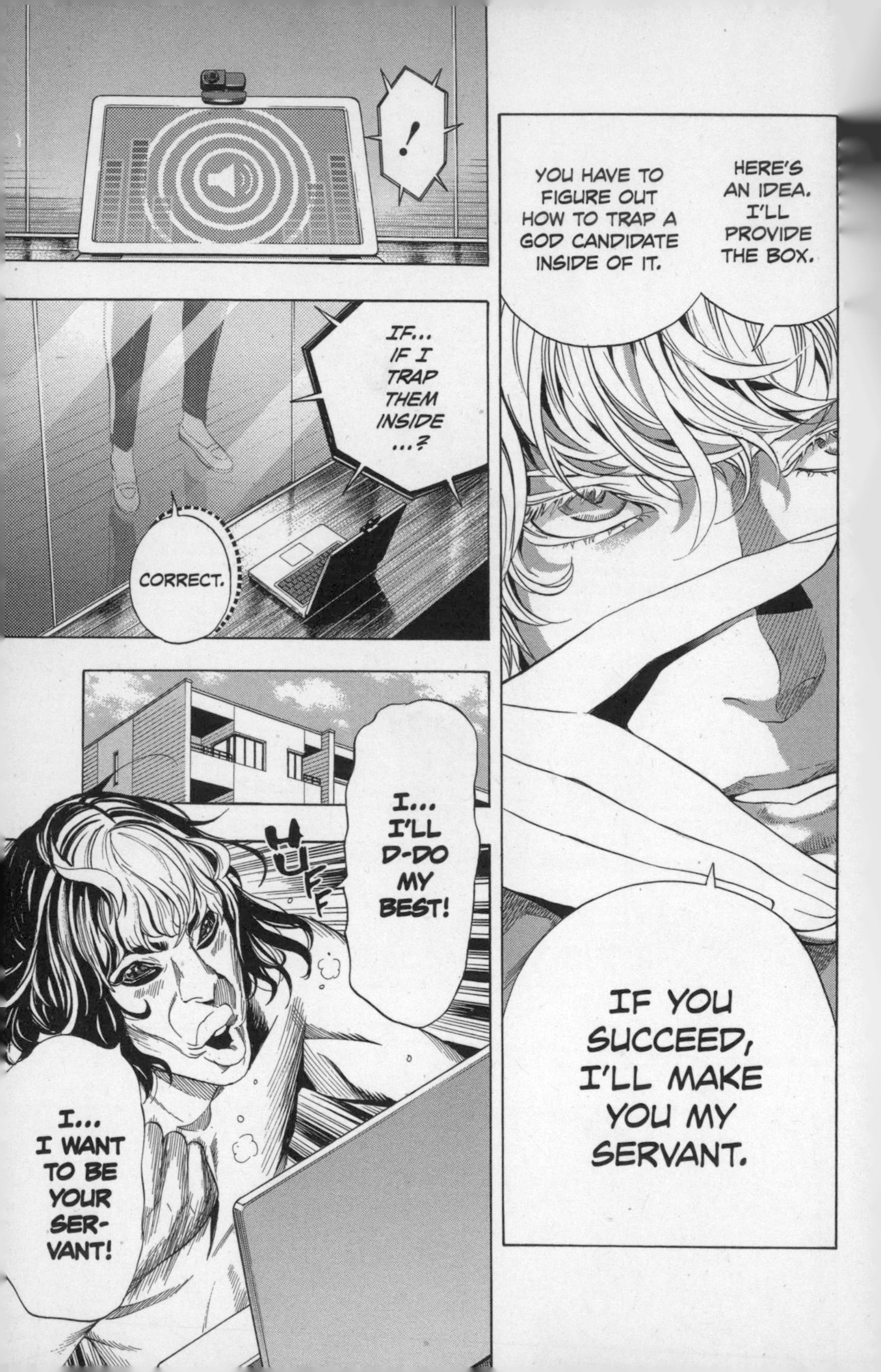
HERE'S AN IDEA. I'LL PROVIDE THE BOX.
YOU HAVE TO FIGURE OUT HOW TO TRAP A GOD CANDIDATE INSIDE OF IT.
IF YOU SUCCEED, I'LL MAKE YOU MY SERVANT.
!
IF... IF I TRAP THEM INSIDE ...?
CORRECT.
I... I'LL D-DO MY BEST!
HUFF
I... I WANT TO BE YOUR SER-VANT!

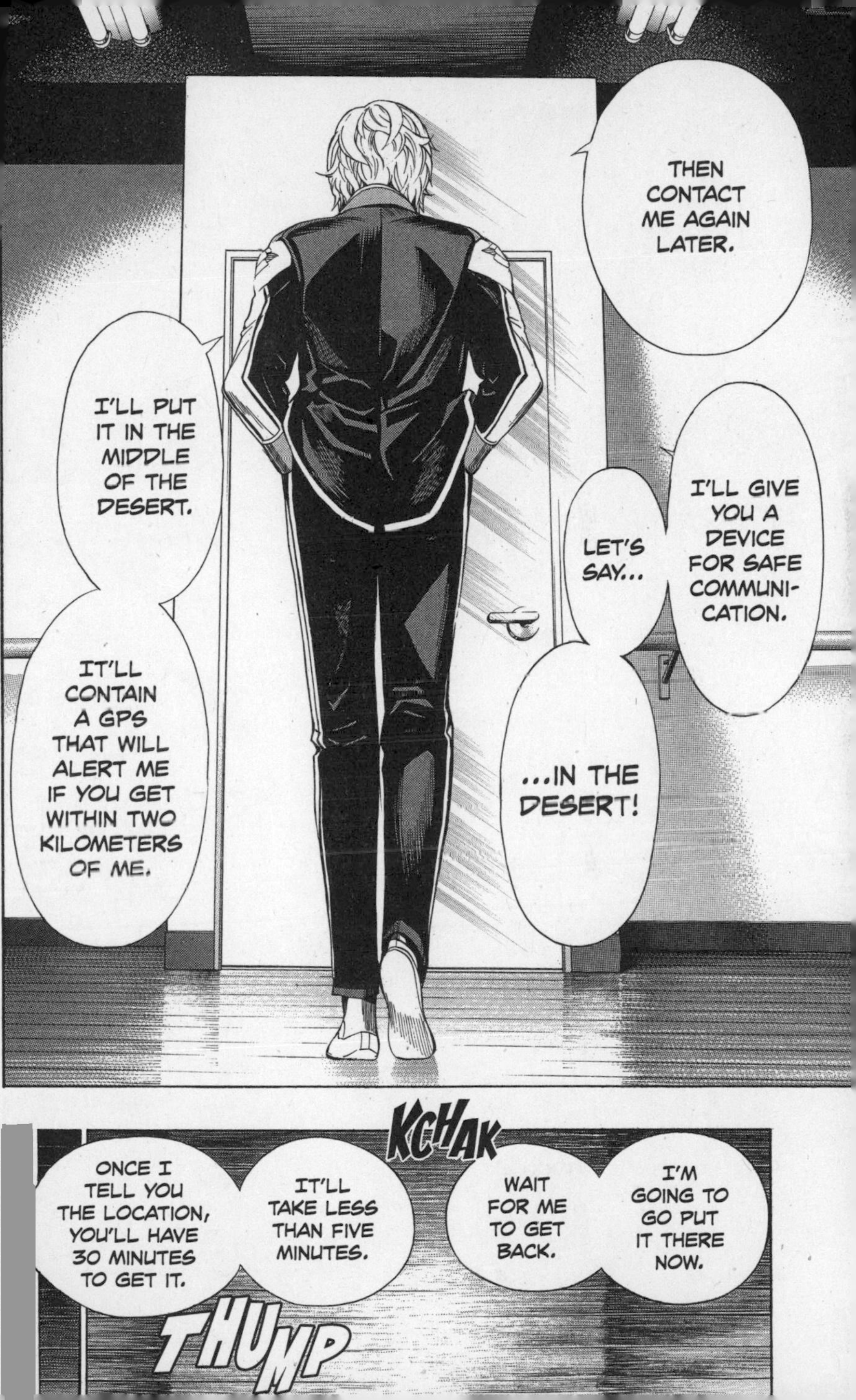
THEN CONTACT ME AGAIN LATER.
I'LL GIVE YOU A DEVICE FOR SAFE COMMUNICATION.
LET'S SAY...
...IN THE DESERT!
I'LL PUT IT IN THE MIDDLE OF THE DESERT.
IT'LL CONTAIN A GPS THAT WILL ALERT ME IF YOU GET WITHIN TWO KILOMETERS OF ME.
I'M GOING TO GO PUT IT THERE NOW.
KCHAK
WAIT FOR ME TO GET BACK.
IT'LL TAKE LESS THAN FIVE MINUTES.
ONCE I TELL YOU THE LOCATION, YOU'LL HAVE 30 MINUTES TO GET IT.
THUMP

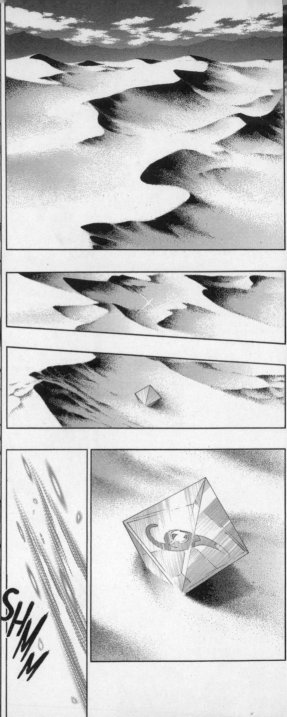

SHMM

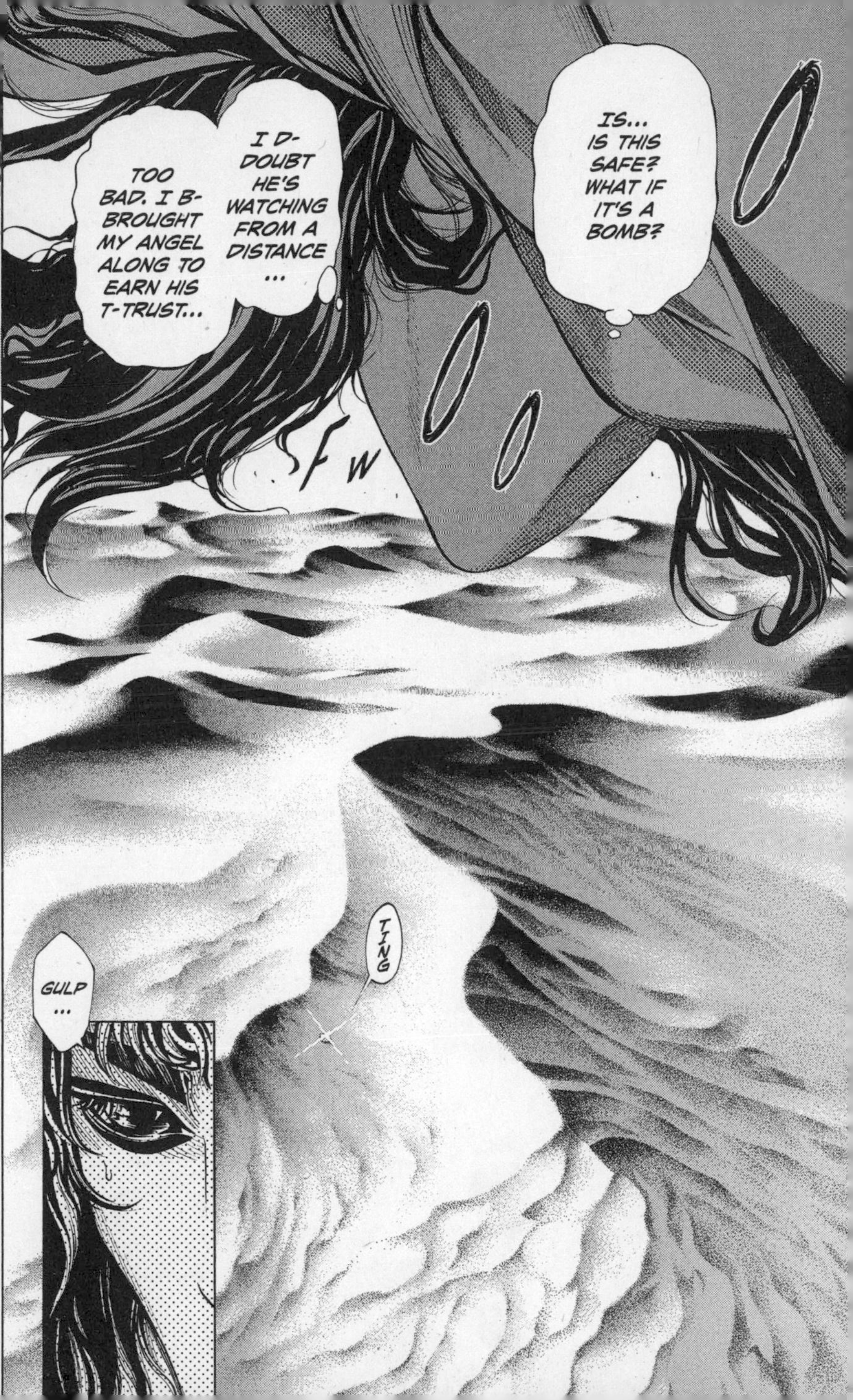
IS... IS THIS SAFE? WHAT IF IT'S A BOMB?
I D-DOUBT HE'S WATCHING FROM A DISTANCE...
TOO BAD. I B-BROUGHT MY ANGEL ALONG TO EARN HIS T-TRUST...
FW
TING
GULP...

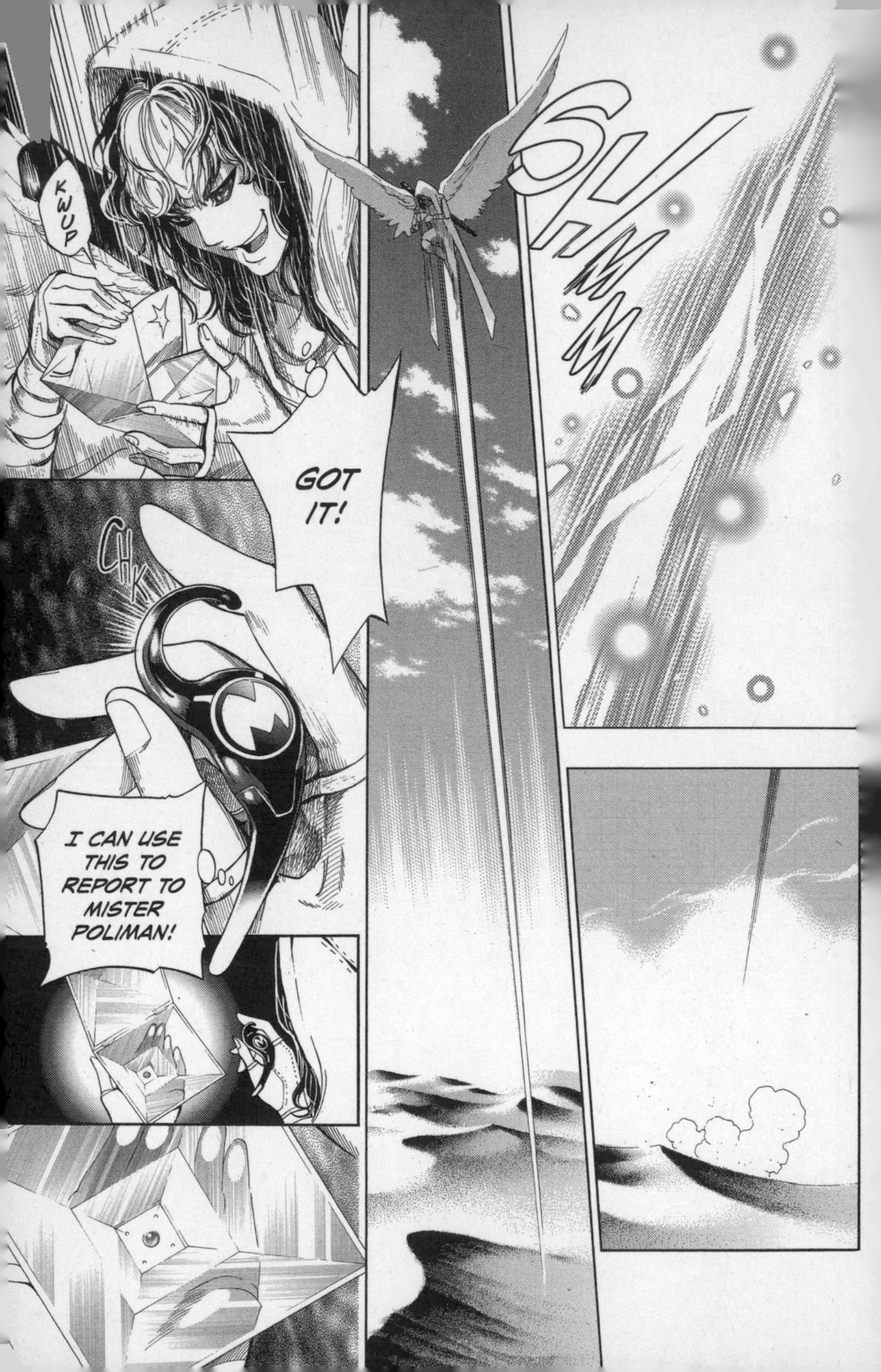
SHMMM
KWUP
GOT IT!
CHK
I CAN USE THIS TO REPORT TO MISTER POLIMAN!

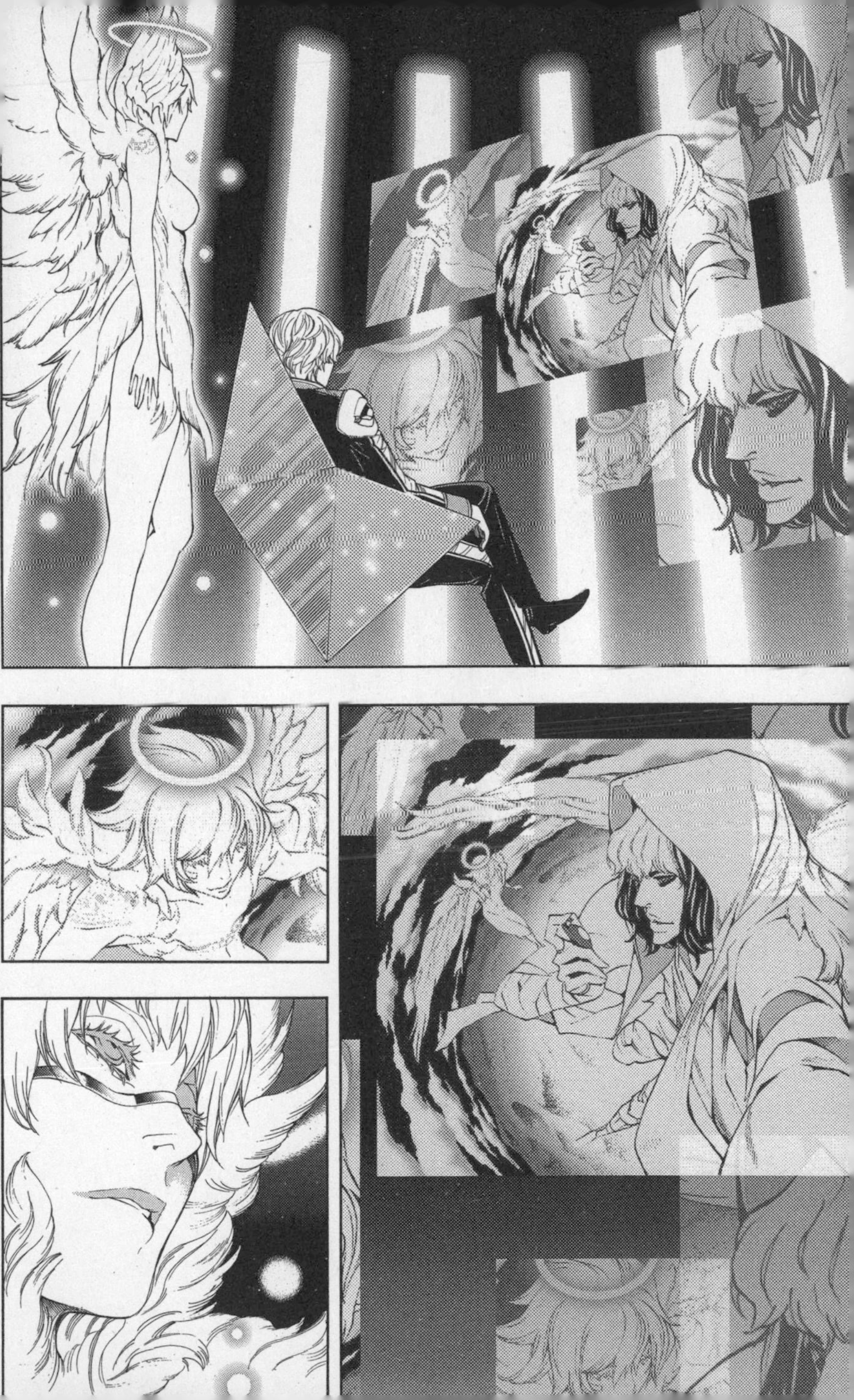

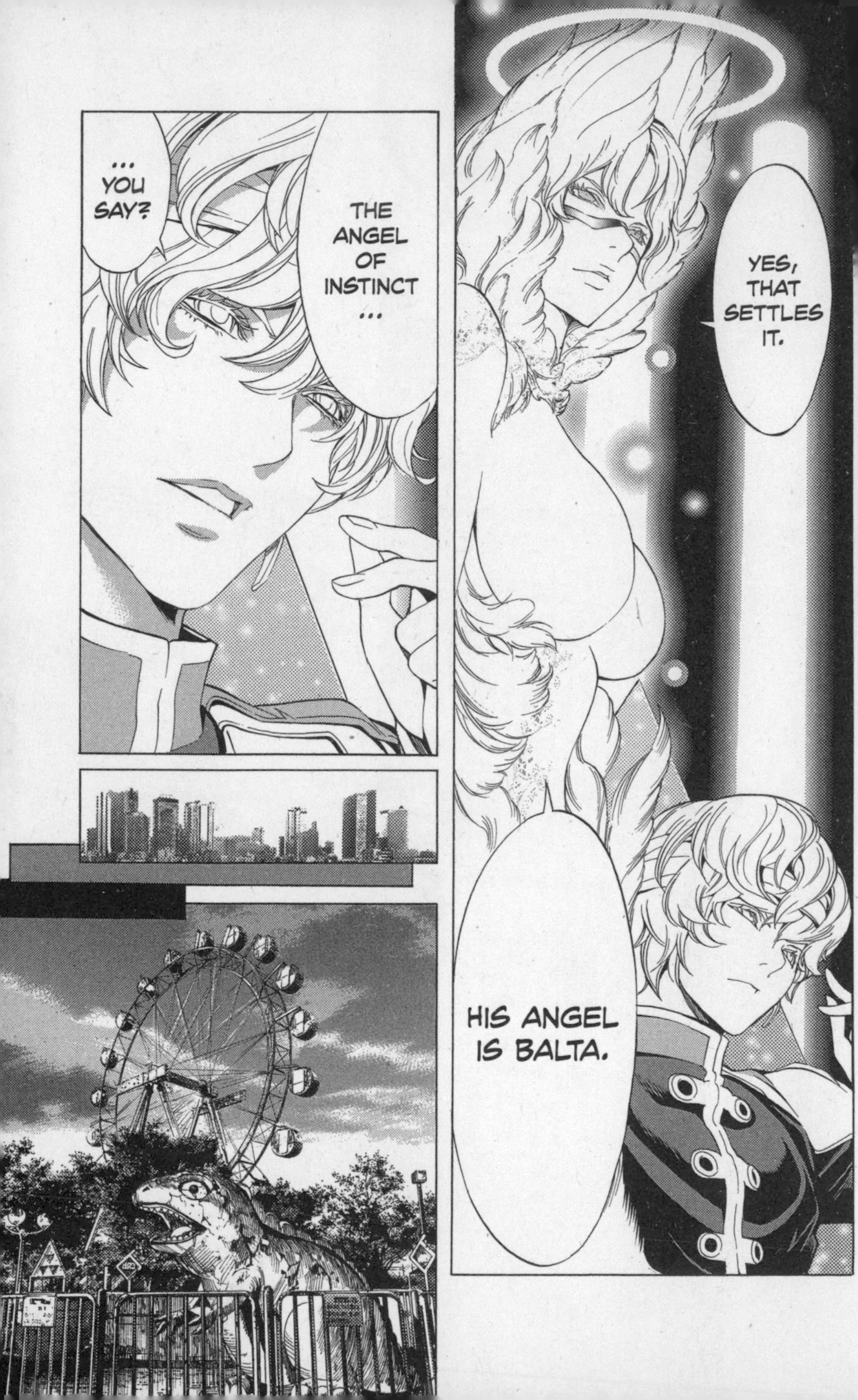
YES, THAT SETTLES IT.
HIS ANGEL IS BALTA.
THE ANGEL OF INSTINCT ...
... YOU SAY?

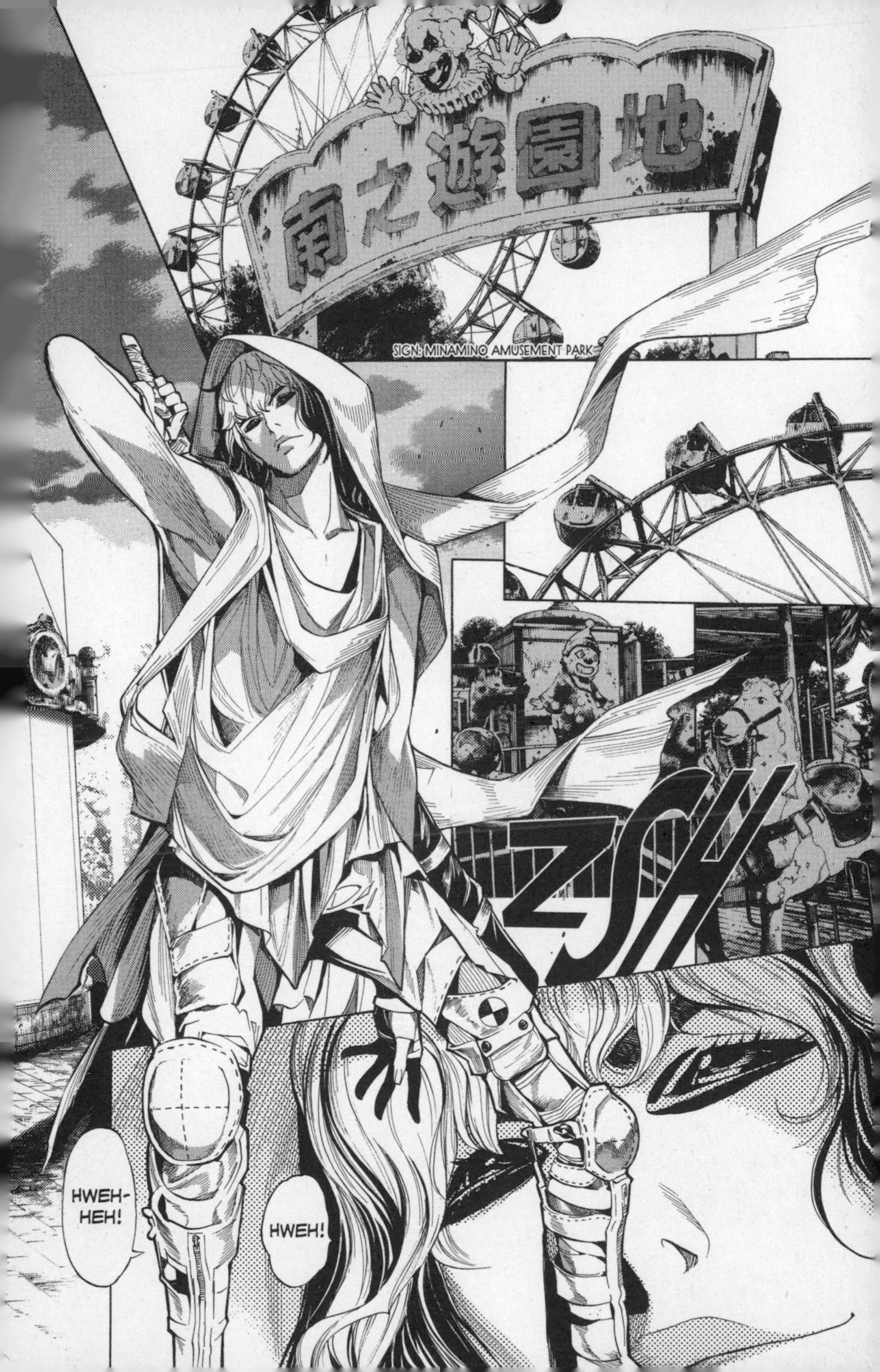
南之遊園地
SIGN: MINAMINO AMUSEMENT PARK
ZSH
HWEH!
HWEH-HEH!

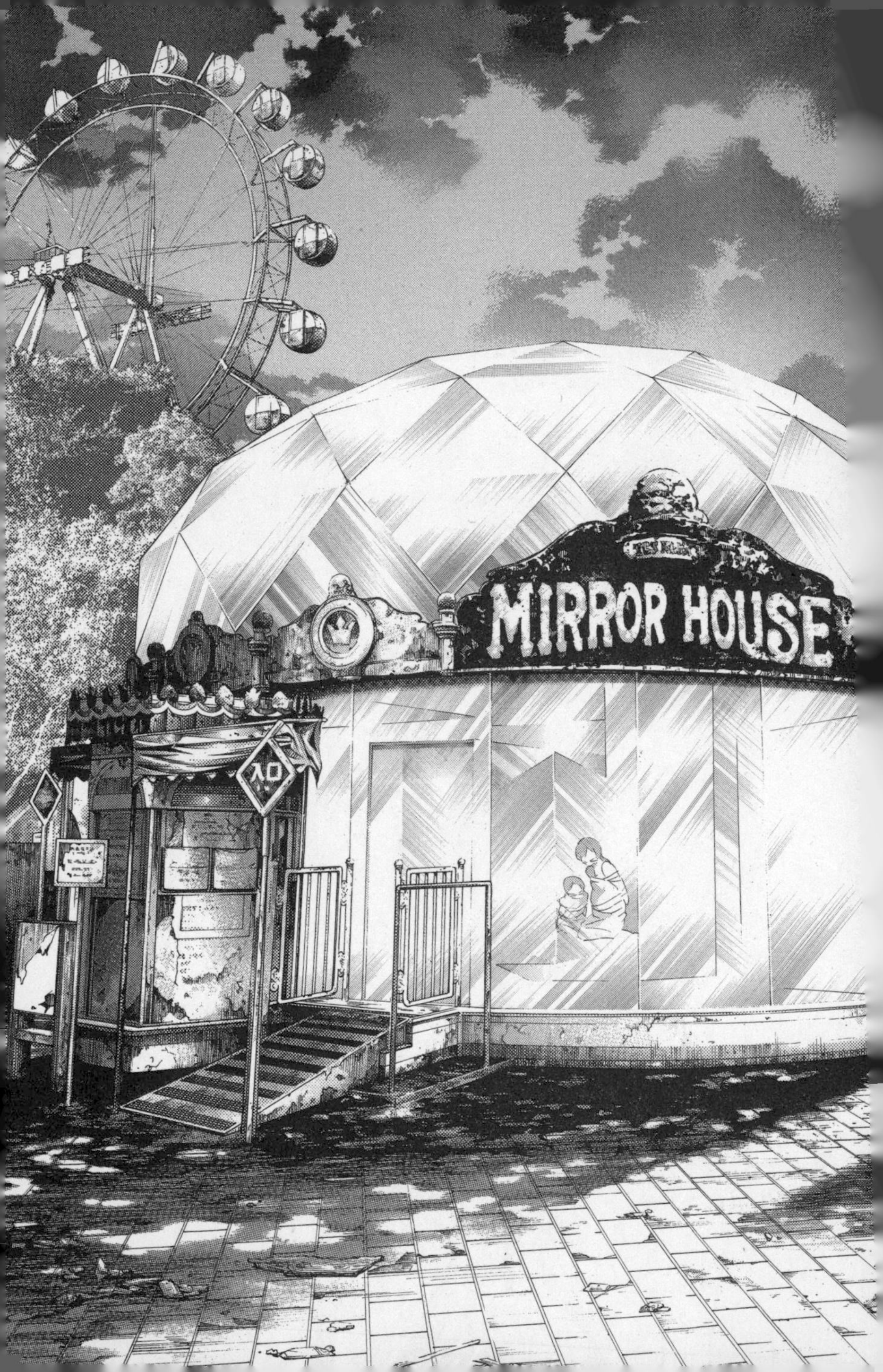
MIRROR HOUSE
入口

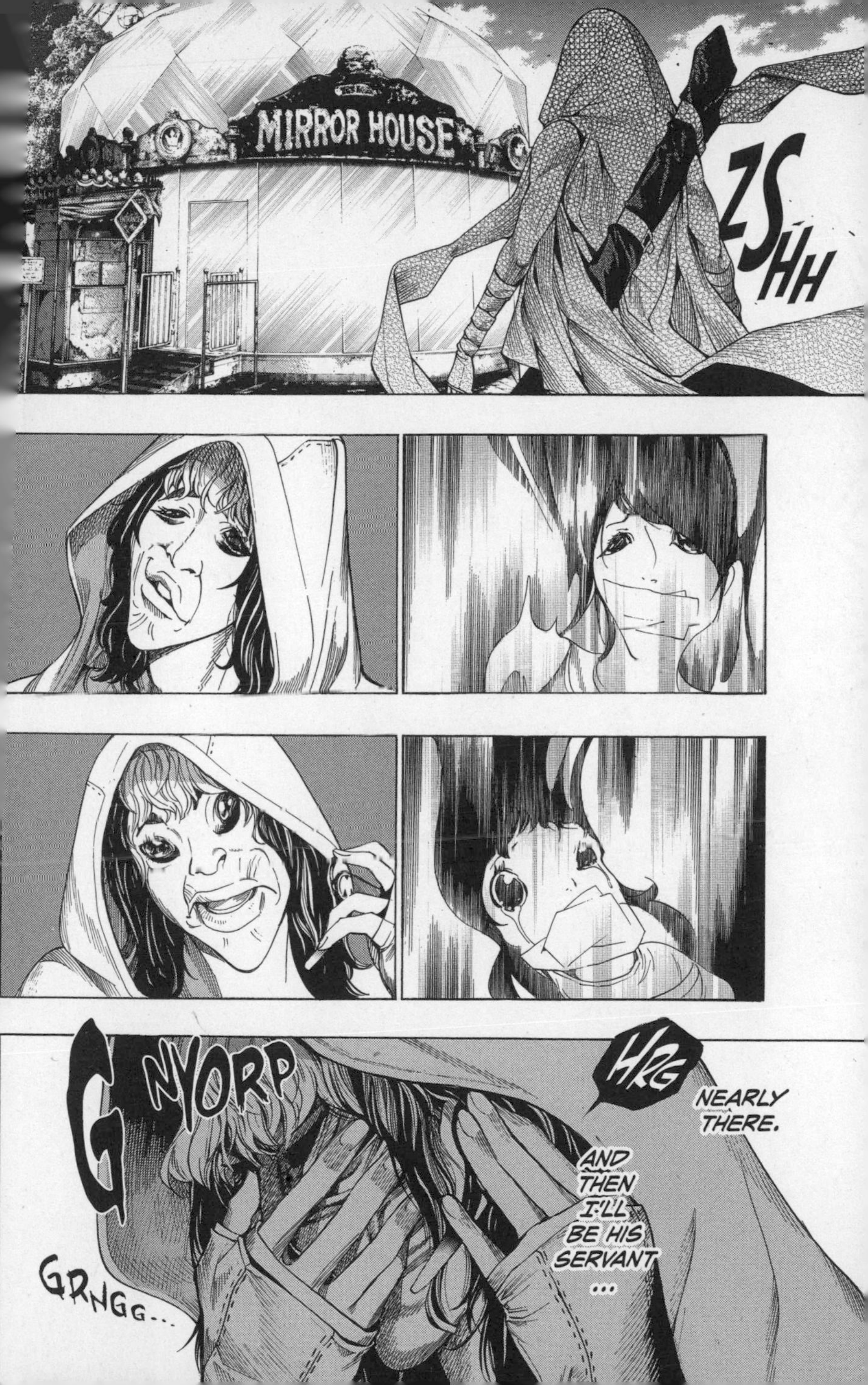
MIRROR HOUSE
ZSHH
HRG
NEARLY THERE.
AND THEN I'LL BE HIS SERVANT...
GNYORP
GRNGG...

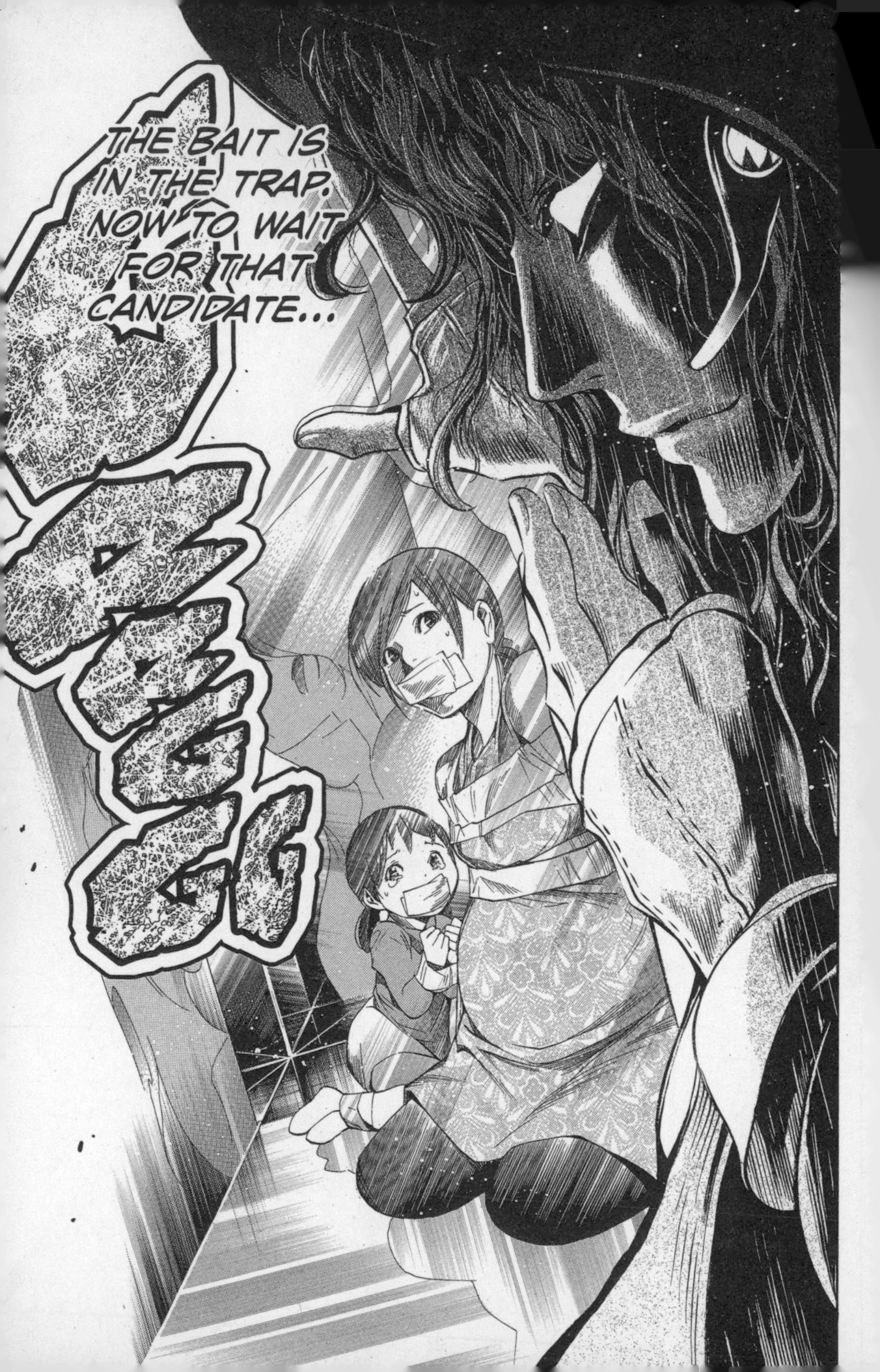
THE BAIT IS IN THE TRAP. NOW TO WAIT FOR THAT CANDIDATE...

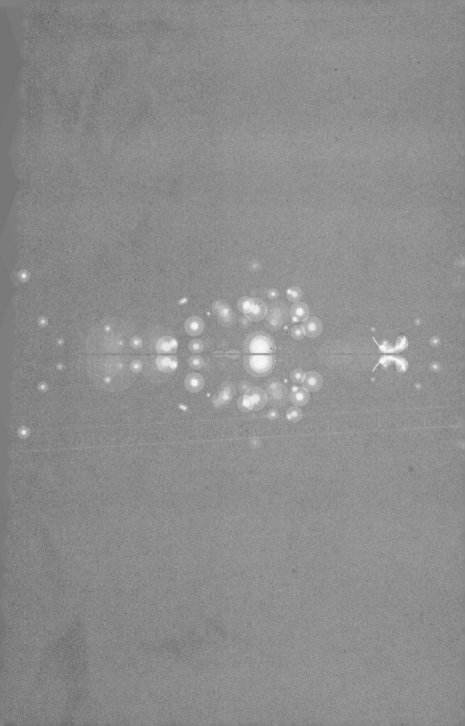

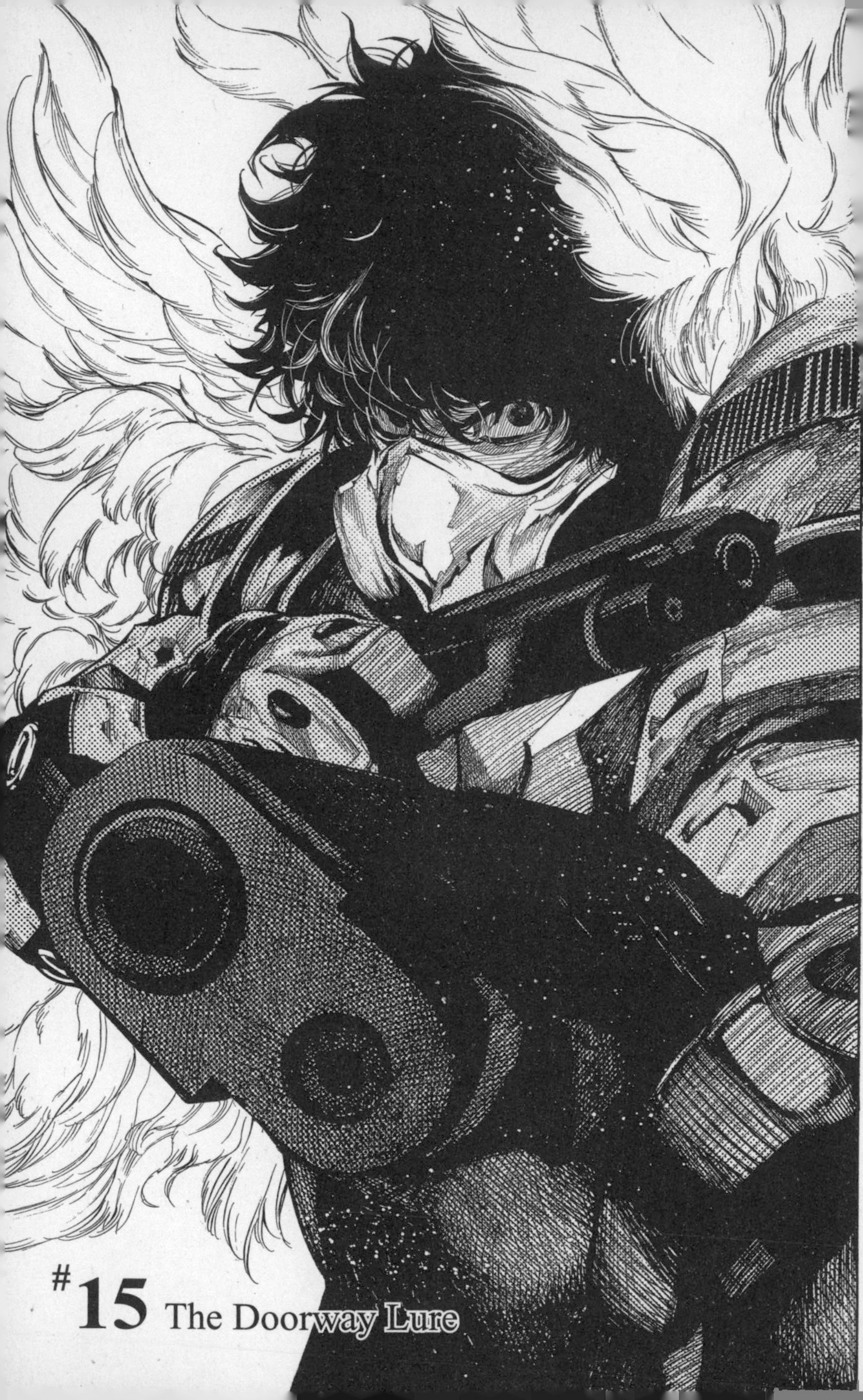

#15 The Doorway Lure

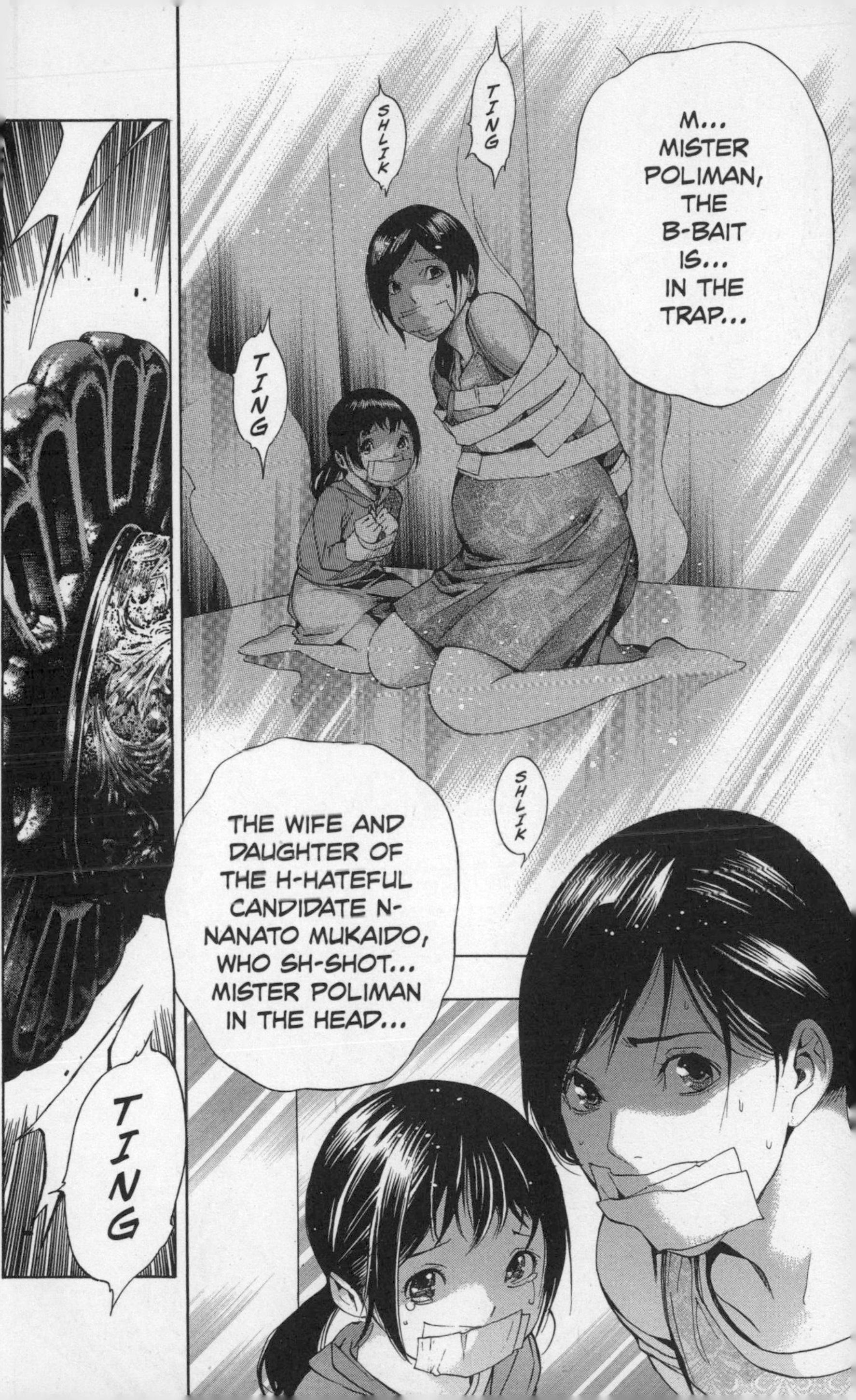
M... MISTER POLIMAN, THE B-BAIT IS... IN THE TRAP...
TING
SHLIK
TING
SHLIK
THE WIFE AND DAUGHTER OF THE H-HATEFUL CANDIDATE N-NANATO MUKAIDO, WHO SH-SHOT... MISTER POLIMAN IN THE HEAD...
TING

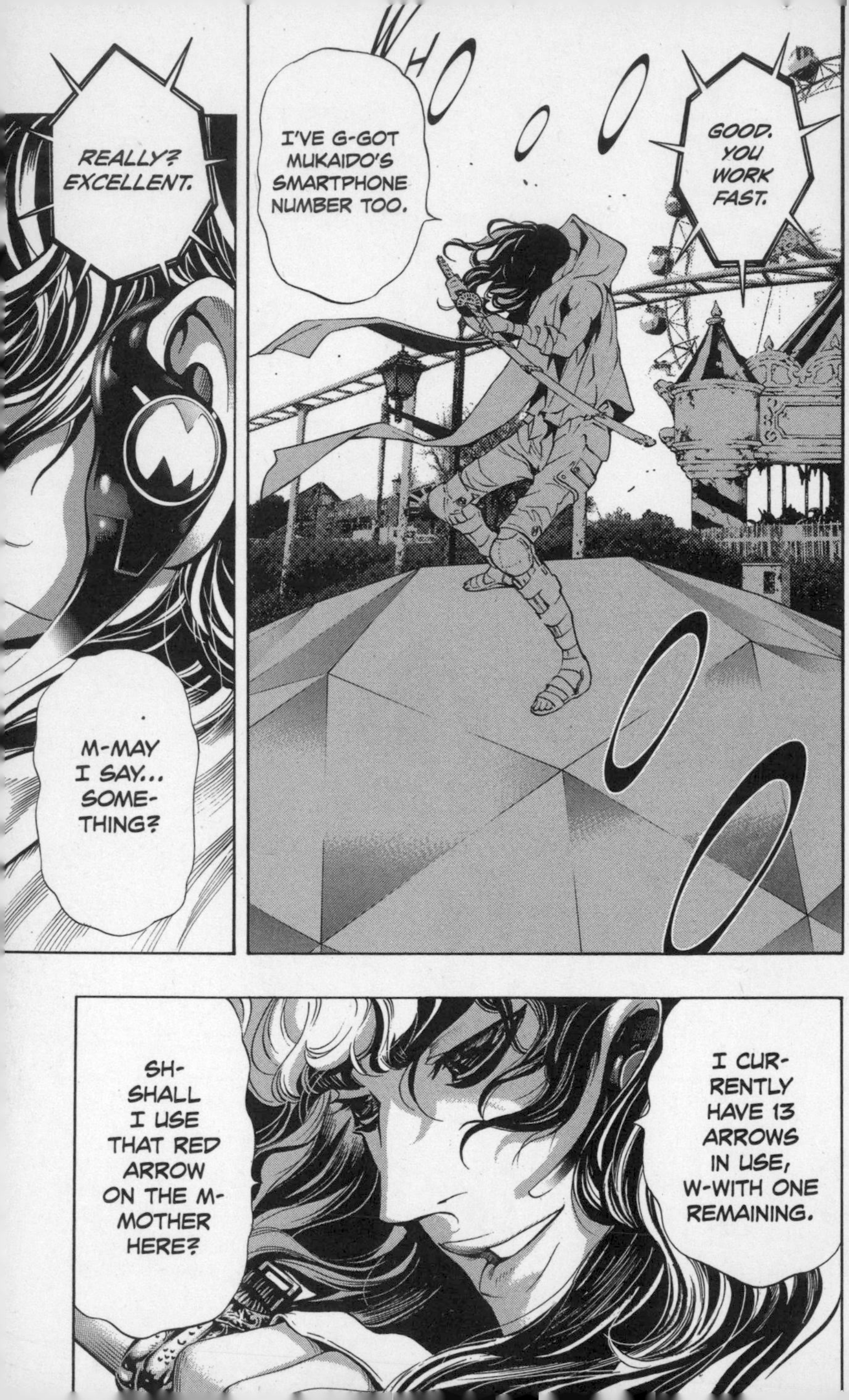
WHOOOO
I'VE G-GOT MUKAIDO'S SMARTPHONE NUMBER TOO.
GOOD. YOU WORK FAST.
REALLY? EXCELLENT.
M-MAY I SAY... SOME-THING?
I CUR-RENTLY HAVE 13 ARROWS IN USE, W-WITH ONE REMAINING.
SH-SHALL I USE THAT RED ARROW ON THE M-MOTHER HERE?

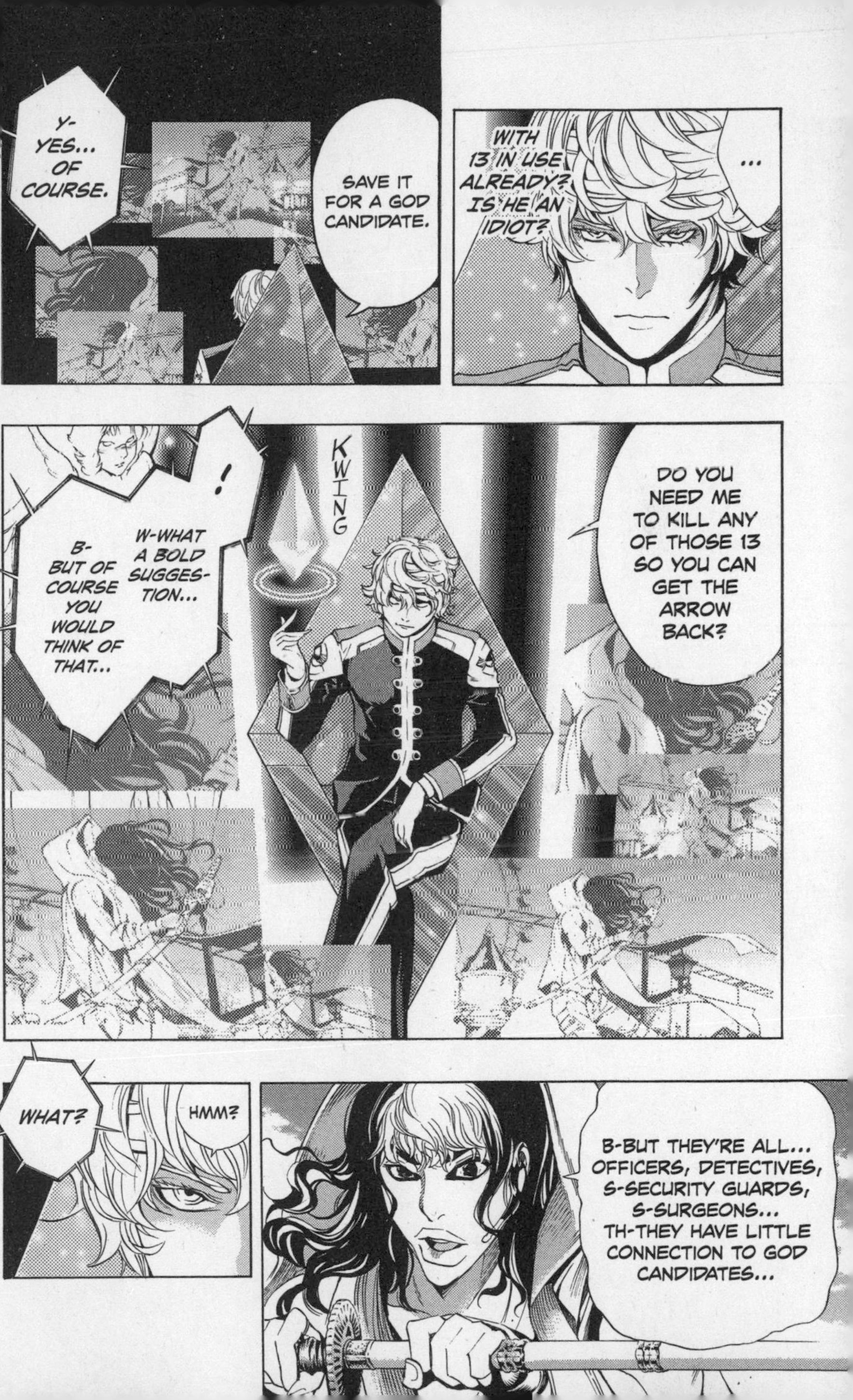
...
WITH 13 IN USE ALREADY? IS HE AN IDIOT?
SAVE IT FOR A GOD CANDIDATE.
Y-YES... OF COURSE.
DO YOU NEED ME TO KILL ANY OF THOSE 13 SO YOU CAN GET THE ARROW BACK?
KWING
!
W-WHAT A BOLD SUGGESTION...
B-BUT OF COURSE YOU WOULD THINK OF THAT...
B-BUT THEY'RE ALL... OFFICERS, DETECTIVES, S-SECURITY GUARDS, S-SURGEONS... TH-THEY HAVE LITTLE CONNECTION TO GOD CANDIDATES...
HMM?
WHAT?

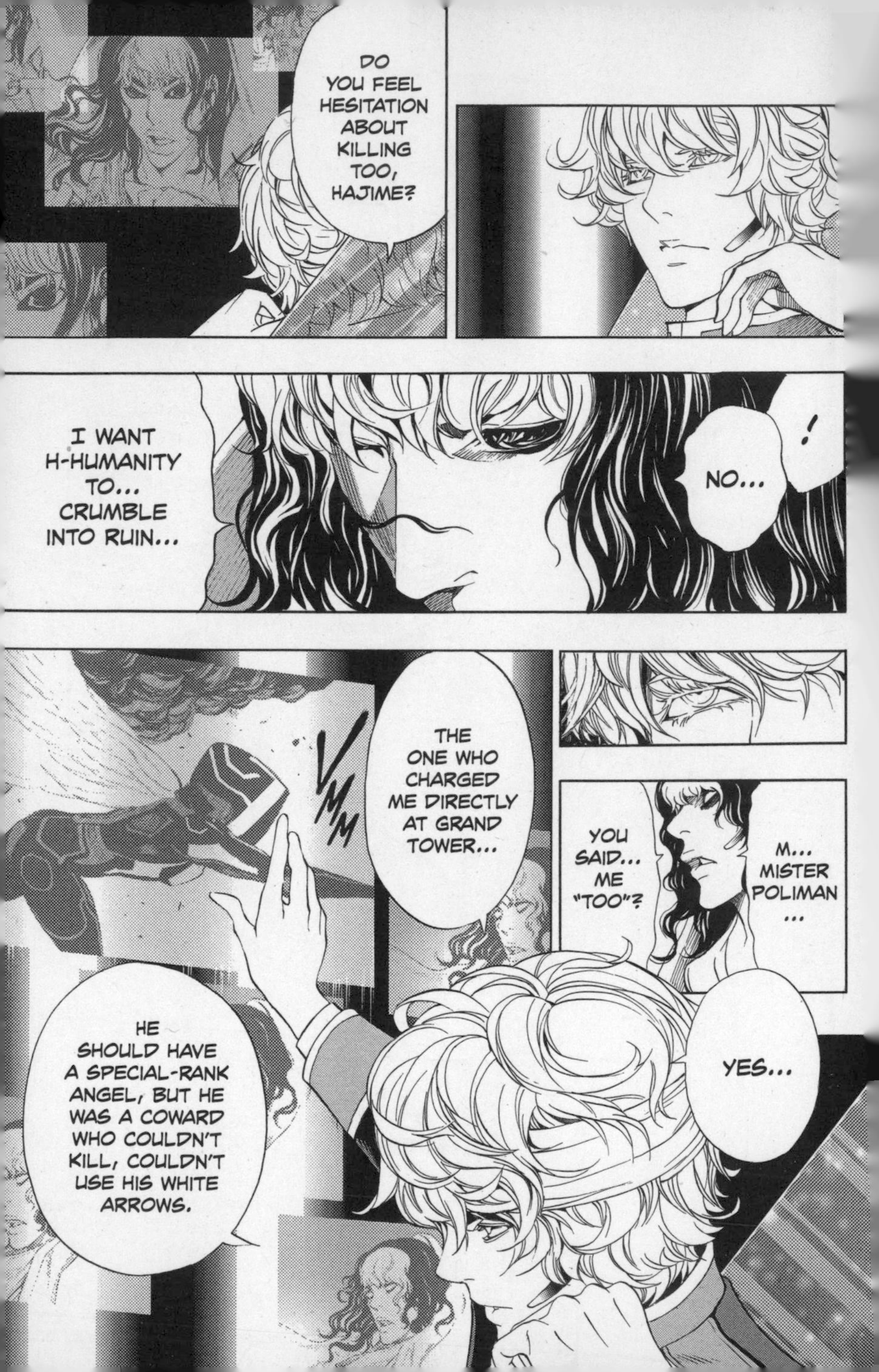
DO YOU FEEL HESITATION ABOUT KILLING TOO, HAJIME?
!
NO...
I WANT H-HUMANITY TO... CRUMBLE INTO RUIN...
M... MISTER POLIMAN ...
YOU SAID... ME "TOO"?
VMM
THE ONE WHO CHARGED ME DIRECTLY AT GRAND TOWER...
YES...
HE SHOULD HAVE A SPECIAL-RANK ANGEL, BUT HE WAS A COWARD WHO COULDN'T KILL, COULDN'T USE HIS WHITE ARROWS.

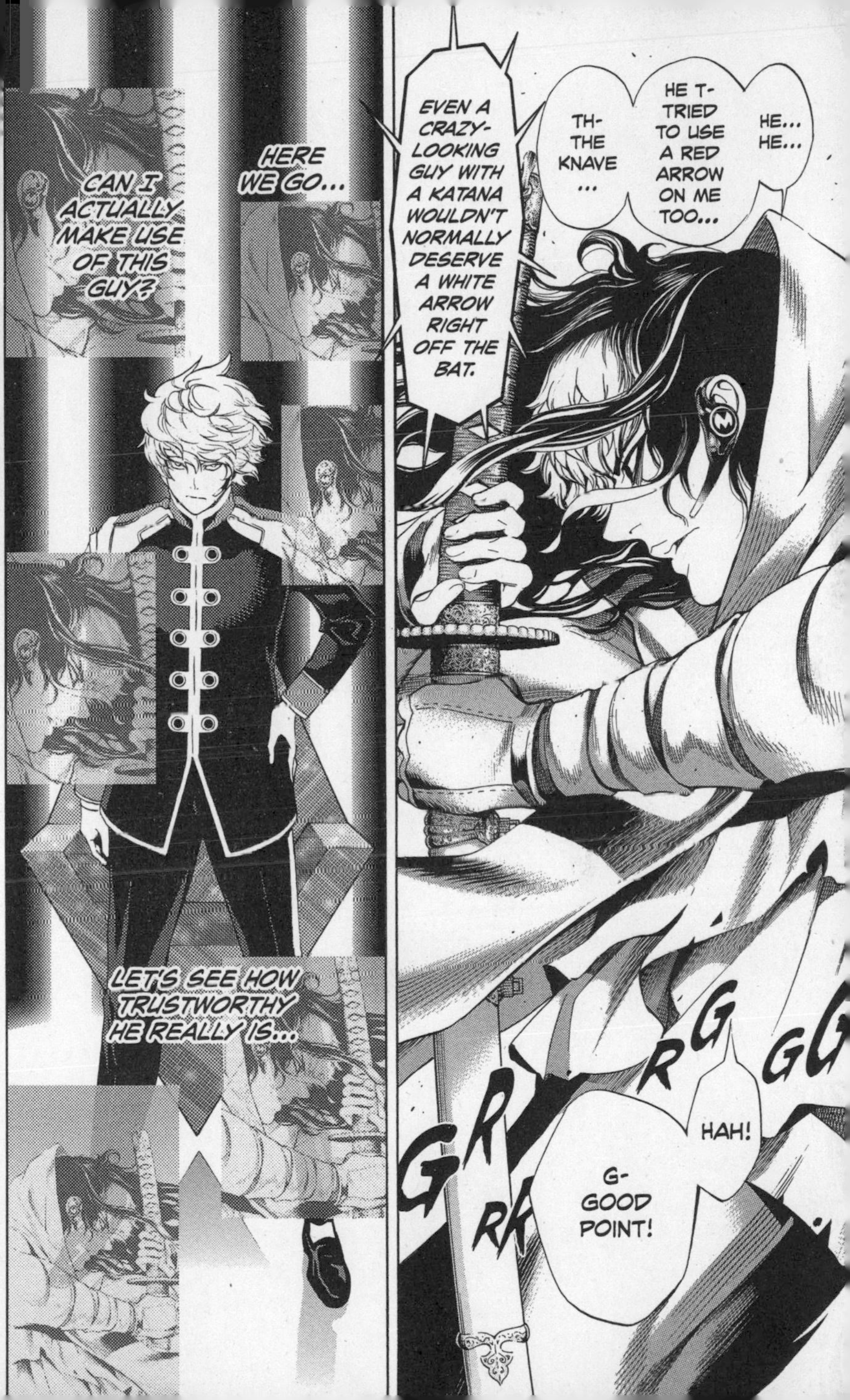
HE... HE...
HE T-TRIED TO USE A RED ARROW ON ME TOO...
TH-THE KNAVE...
EVEN A CRAZY-LOOKING GUY WITH A KATANA WOULDN'T NORMALLY DESERVE A WHITE ARROW RIGHT OFF THE BAT.
HAH!
G-GOOD POINT!
HERE WE GO...
CAN I ACTUALLY MAKE USE OF THIS GUY?
LET'S SEE HOW TRUSTWORTHY HE REALLY IS...

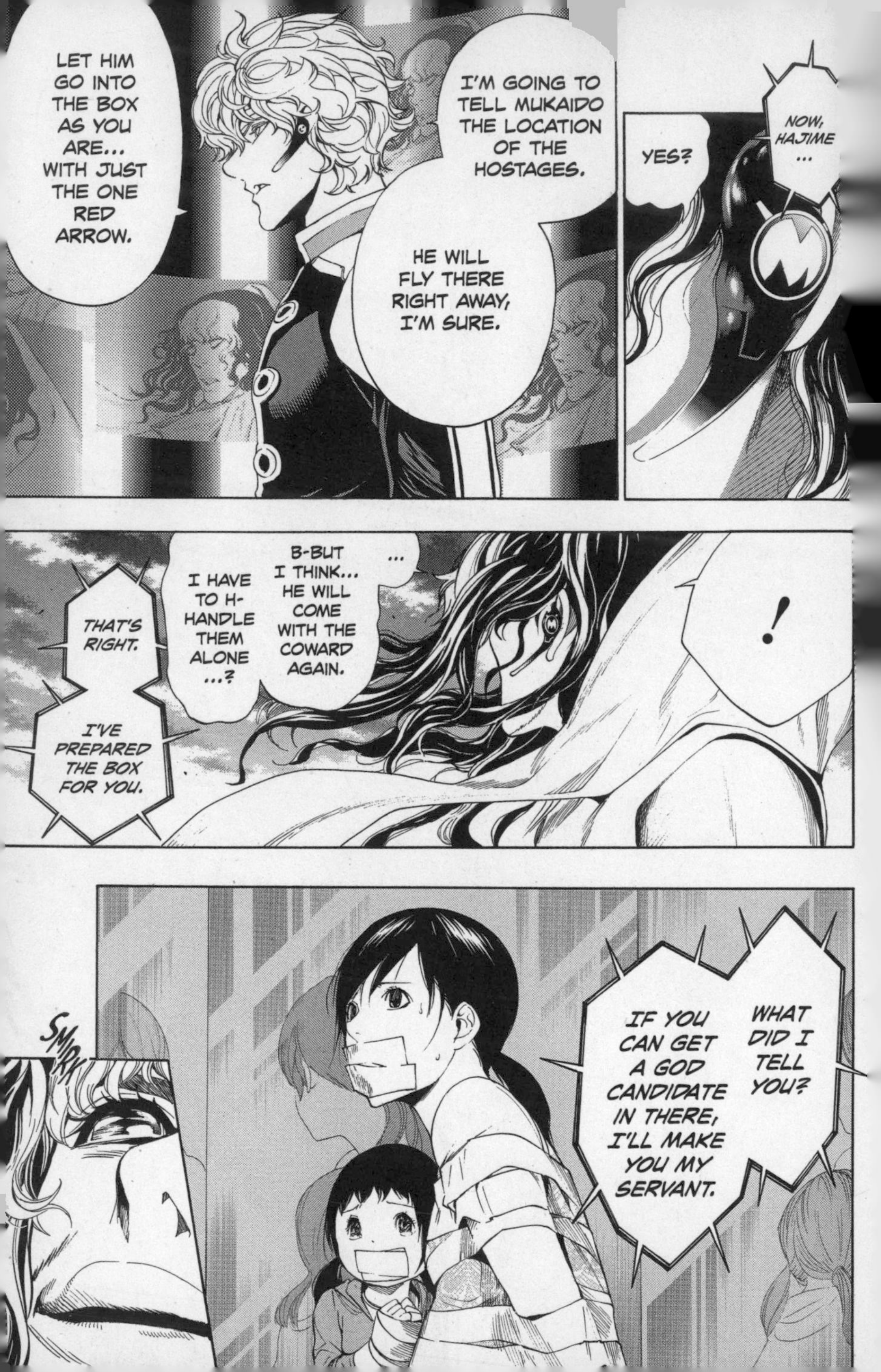
NOW, HAJIME ...
YES?
I'M GOING TO TELL MUKAIDO THE LOCATION OF THE HOSTAGES.
HE WILL FLY THERE RIGHT AWAY, I'M SURE.
LET HIM GO INTO THE BOX AS YOU ARE... WITH JUST THE ONE RED ARROW.
!
...
B-BUT I THINK... HE WILL COME WITH THE COWARD AGAIN.
I HAVE TO H-HANDLE THEM ALONE ...?
THAT'S RIGHT.
I'VE PREPARED THE BOX FOR YOU.
WHAT DID I TELL YOU?
IF YOU CAN GET A GOD CANDIDATE IN THERE, I'LL MAKE YOU MY SERVANT.
SMIRK

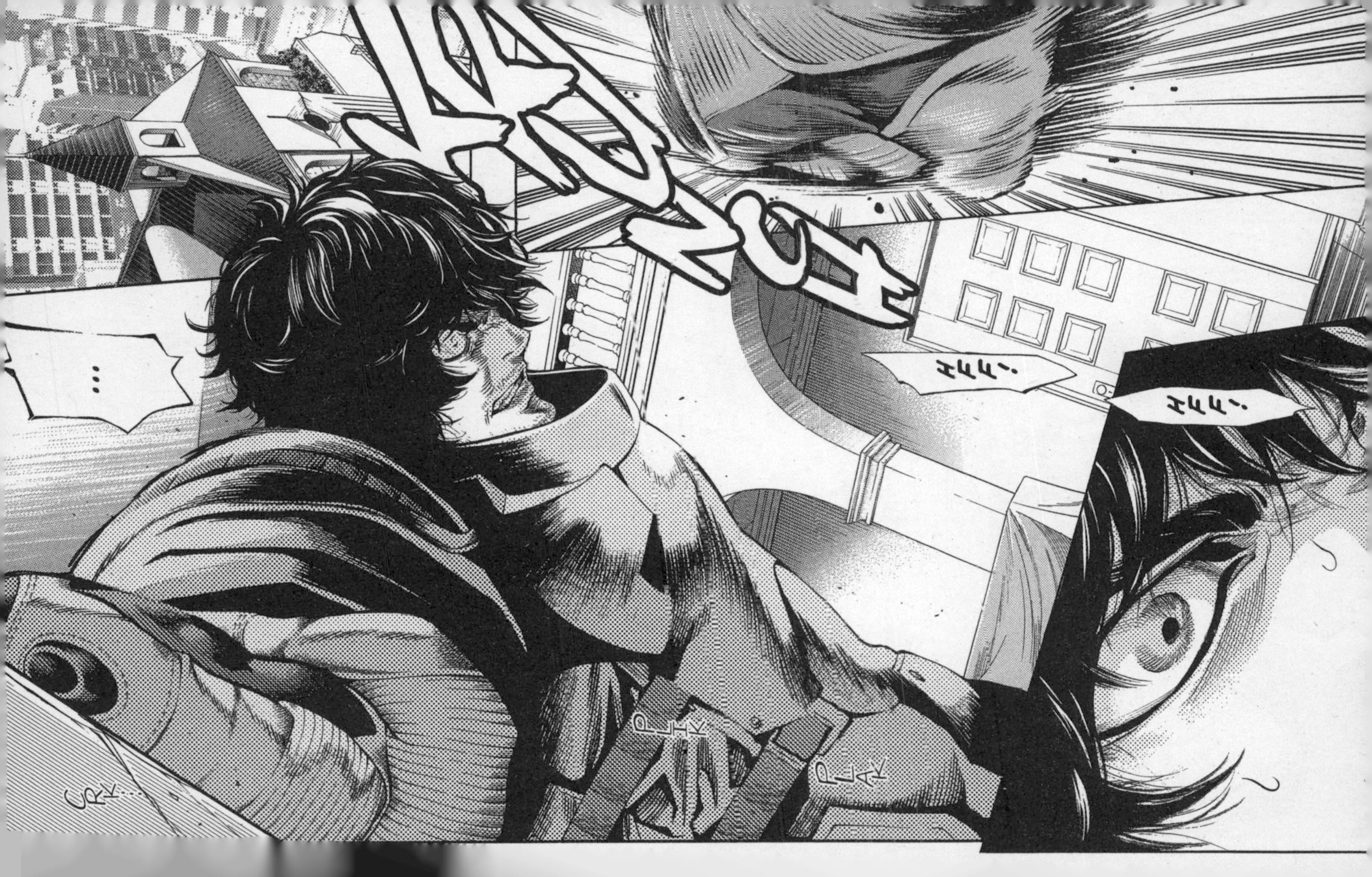
HFF!
HFF!
...
PLIK
PLAK
CRK...

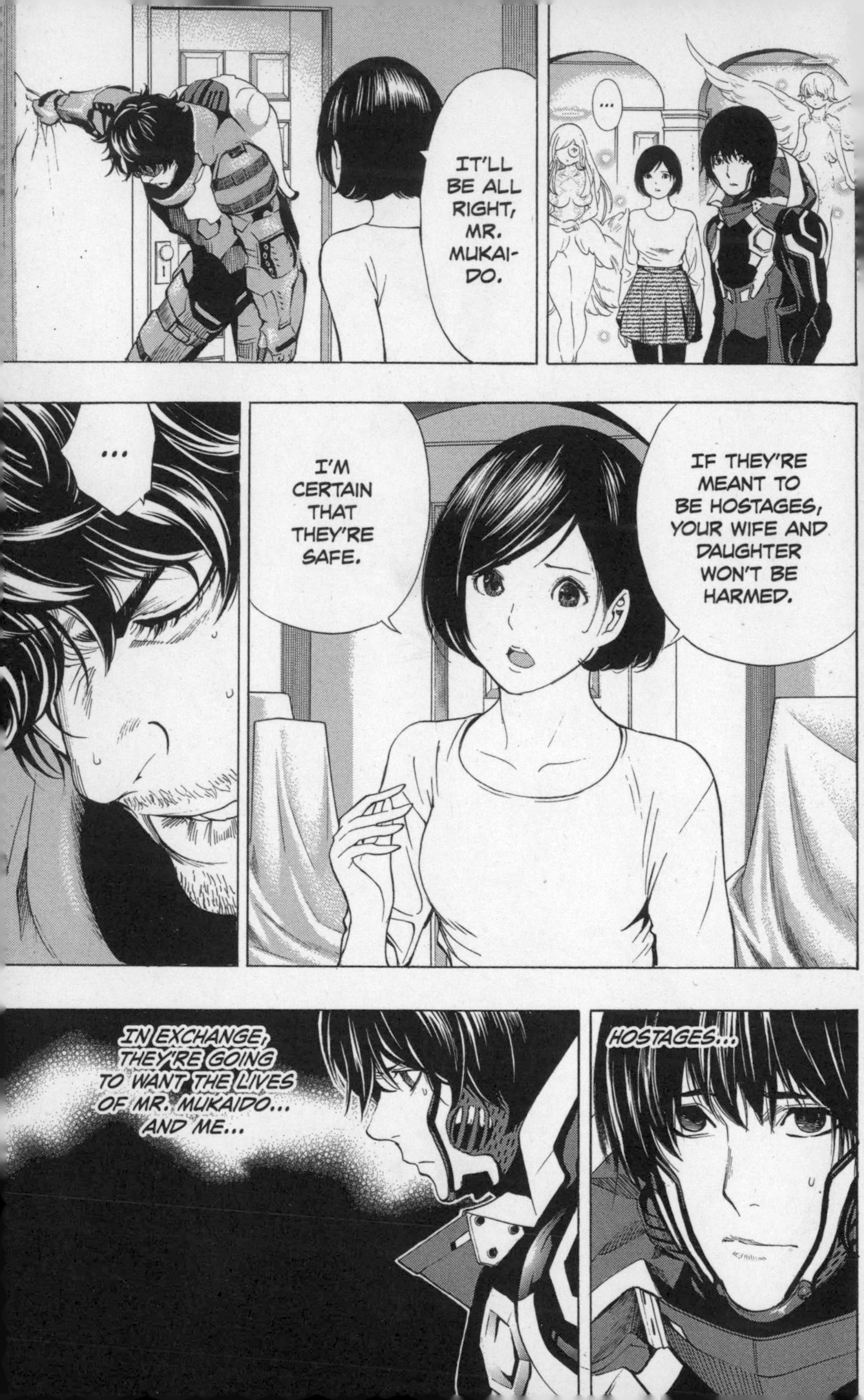
...
IT'LL BE ALL RIGHT, MR. MUKAIDO.
IF THEY'RE MEANT TO BE HOSTAGES, YOUR WIFE AND DAUGHTER WON'T BE HARMED.
I'M CERTAIN THAT THEY'RE SAFE.
...
HOSTAGES...
IN EXCHANGE, THEY'RE GOING TO WANT THE LIVES OF MR. MUKAIDO... AND ME...

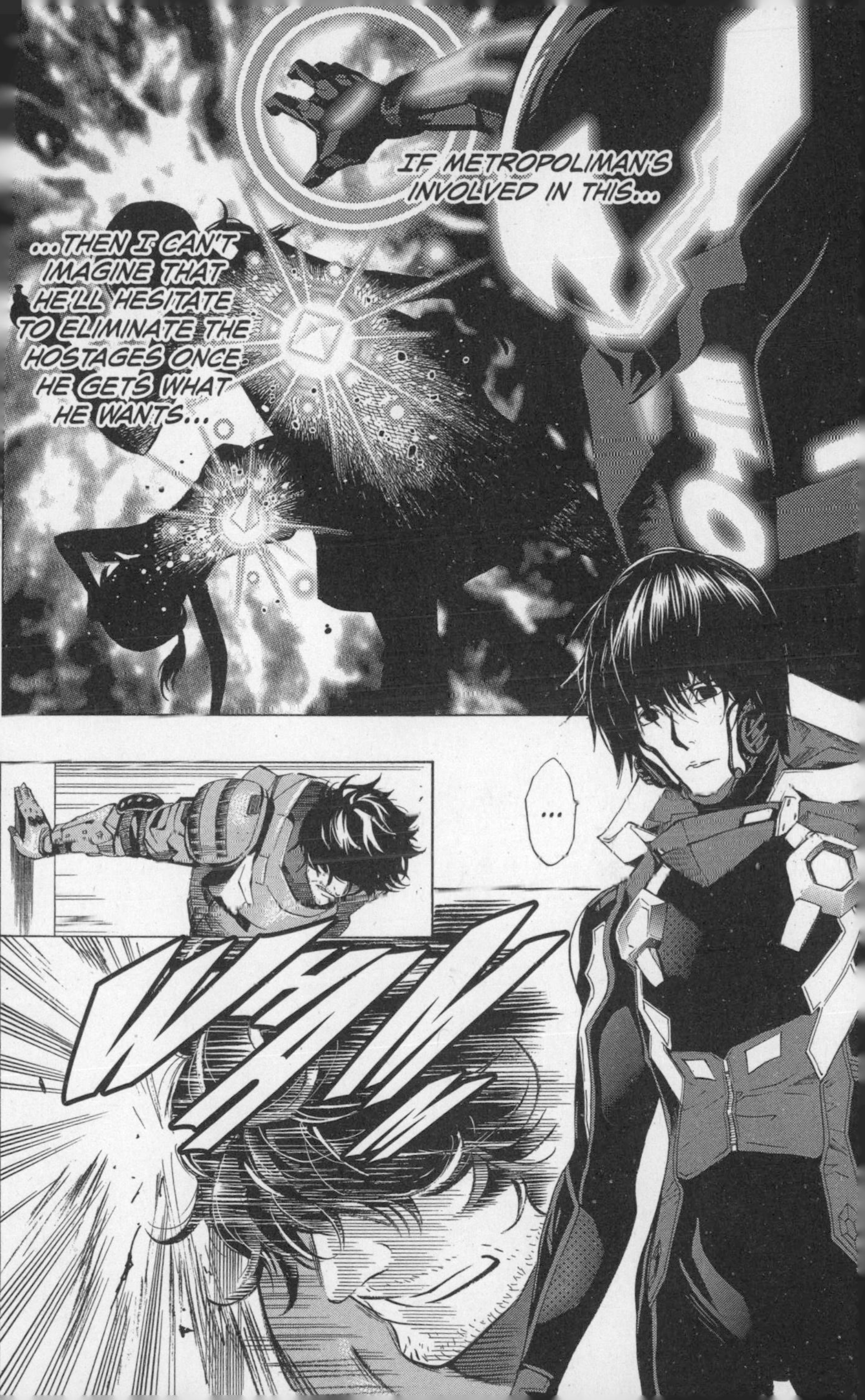
IF METROPOLIMAN'S INVOLVED IN THIS...
...THEN I CAN'T IMAGINE THAT HE'LL HESITATE TO ELIMINATE THE HOSTAGES ONCE HE GETS WHAT HE WANTS...
...

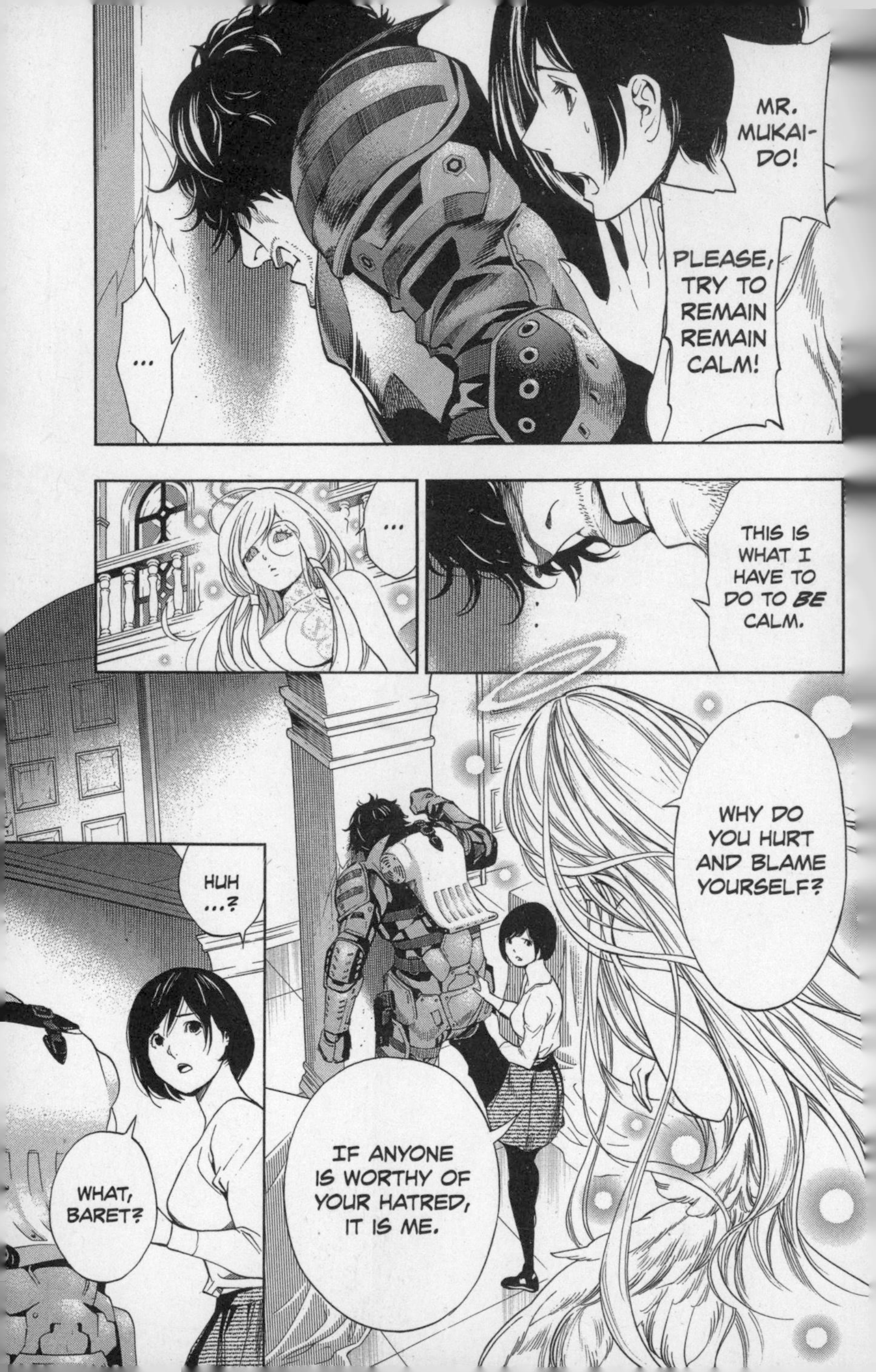
MR. MUKAI-DO!
PLEASE, TRY TO REMAIN REMAIN CALM!
...
THIS IS WHAT I HAVE TO DO TO *BE* CALM.
...
WHY DO YOU HURT AND BLAME YOURSELF?
IF ANYONE IS WORTHY OF YOUR HATRED, IT IS ME.
HUH ...?
WHAT, BARET?

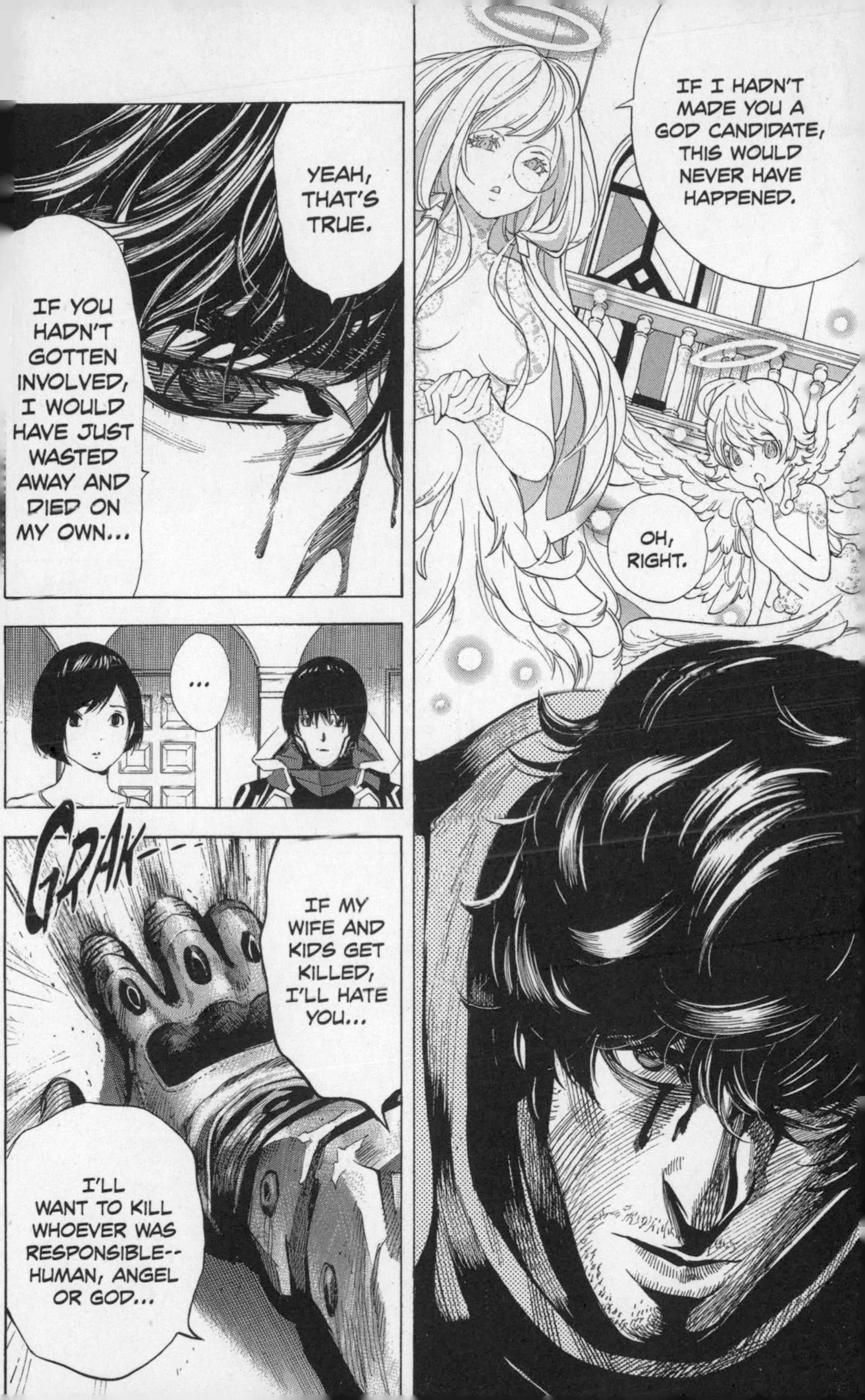
IF I HADN'T MADE YOU A GOD CANDIDATE, THIS WOULD NEVER HAVE HAPPENED.
OH, RIGHT.
YEAH, THAT'S TRUE.
IF YOU HADN'T GOTTEN INVOLVED, I WOULD HAVE JUST WASTED AWAY AND DIED ON MY OWN...
...
GRAK---
IF MY WIFE AND KIDS GET KILLED, I'LL HATE YOU...
I'LL WANT TO KILL WHOEVER WAS RESPONSIBLE-- HUMAN, ANGEL OR GOD...

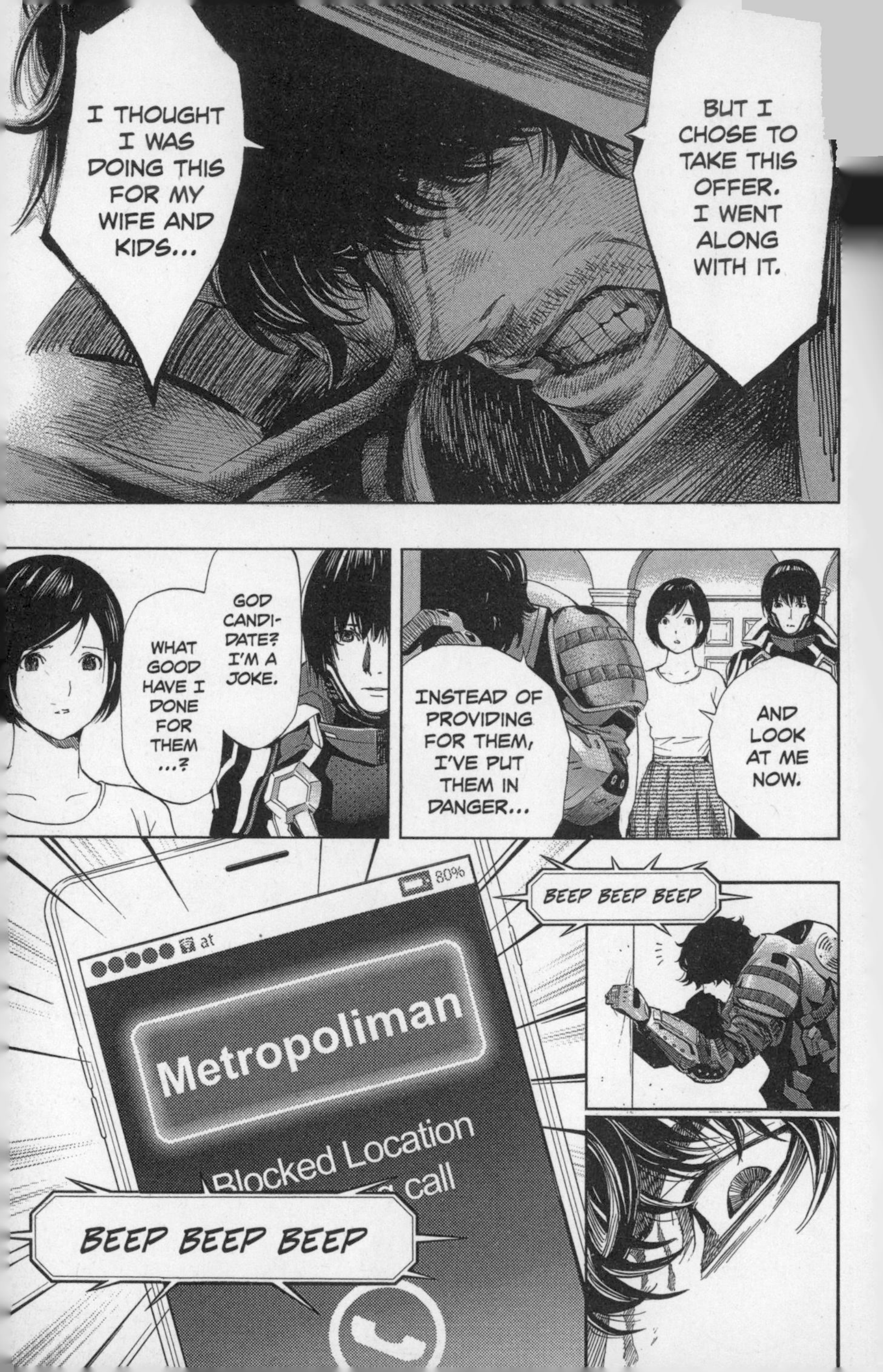
BUT I CHOSE TO TAKE THIS OFFER. I WENT ALONG WITH IT.
I THOUGHT I WAS DOING THIS FOR MY WIFE AND KIDS...
AND LOOK AT ME NOW.
INSTEAD OF PROVIDING FOR THEM, I'VE PUT THEM IN DANGER...
GOD CANDIDATE? I'M A JOKE.
WHAT GOOD HAVE I DONE FOR THEM ...?
BEEP BEEP BEEP
80%
Metropoliman
Blocked Location
BEEP BEEP BEEP

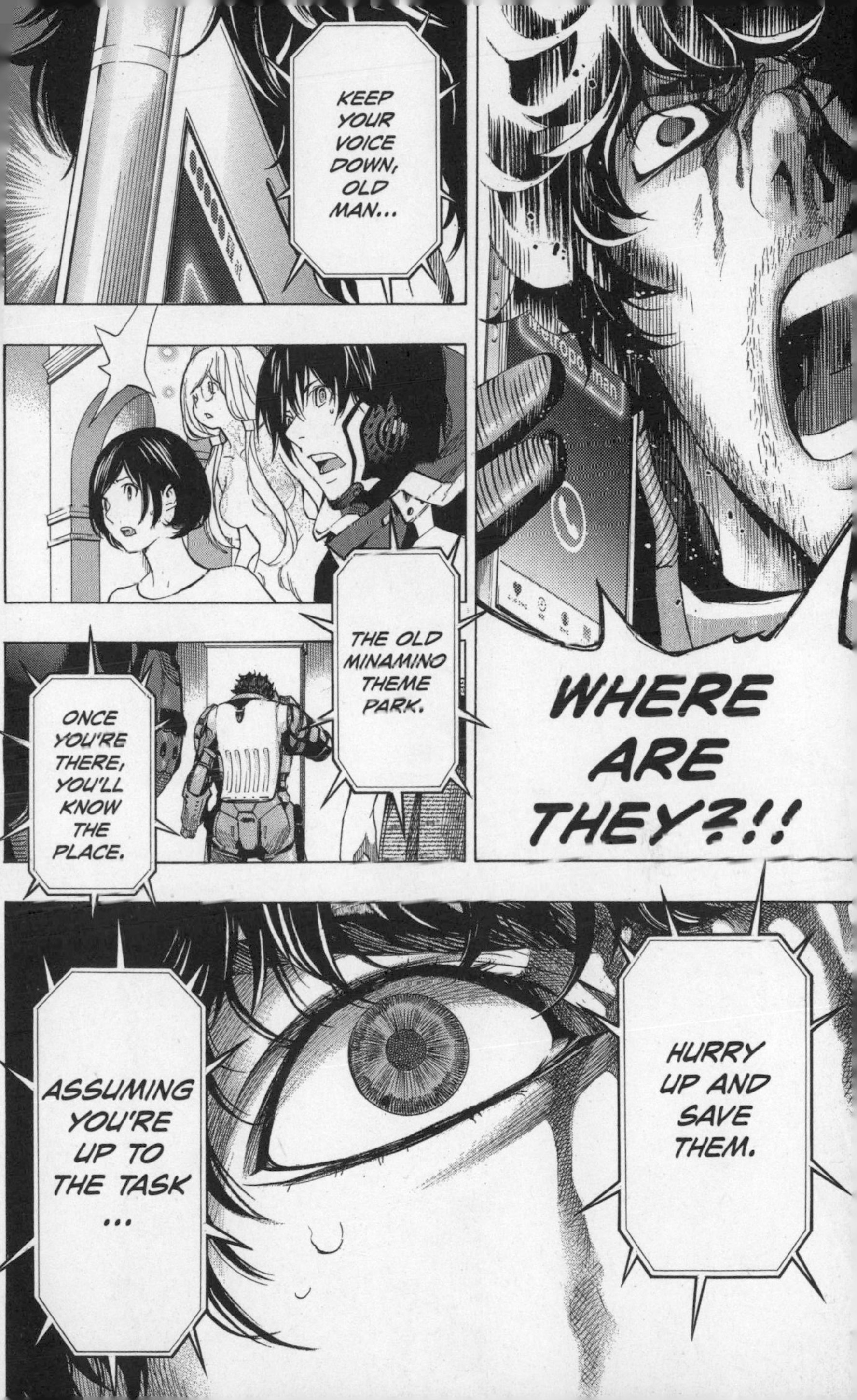
WHERE ARE THEY?!!
KEEP YOUR VOICE DOWN, OLD MAN...
THE OLD MINAMINO THEME PARK.
ONCE YOU'RE THERE, YOU'LL KNOW THE PLACE.
HURRY UP AND SAVE THEM.
ASSUMING YOU'RE UP TO THE TASK ...

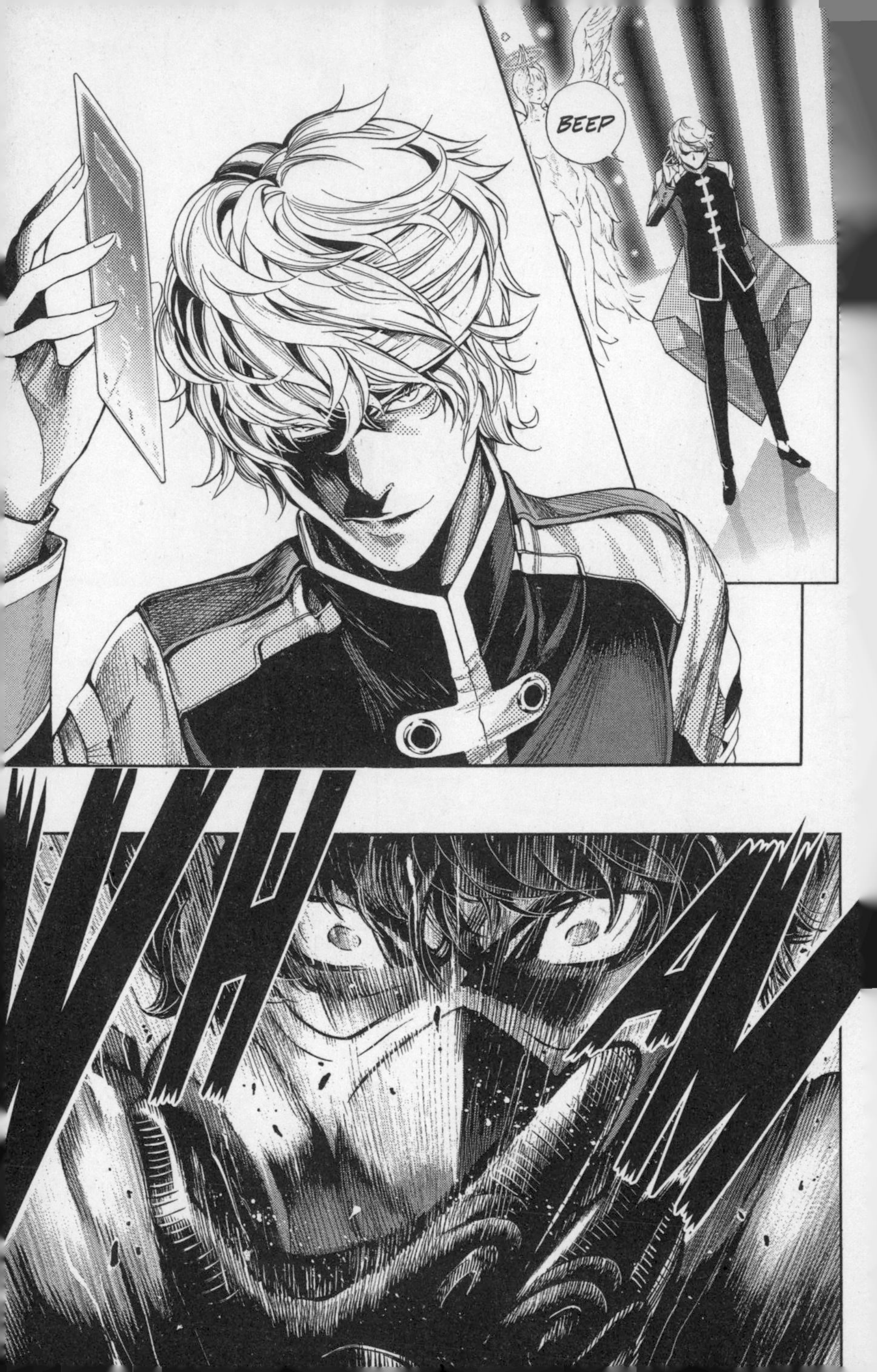
BEEP

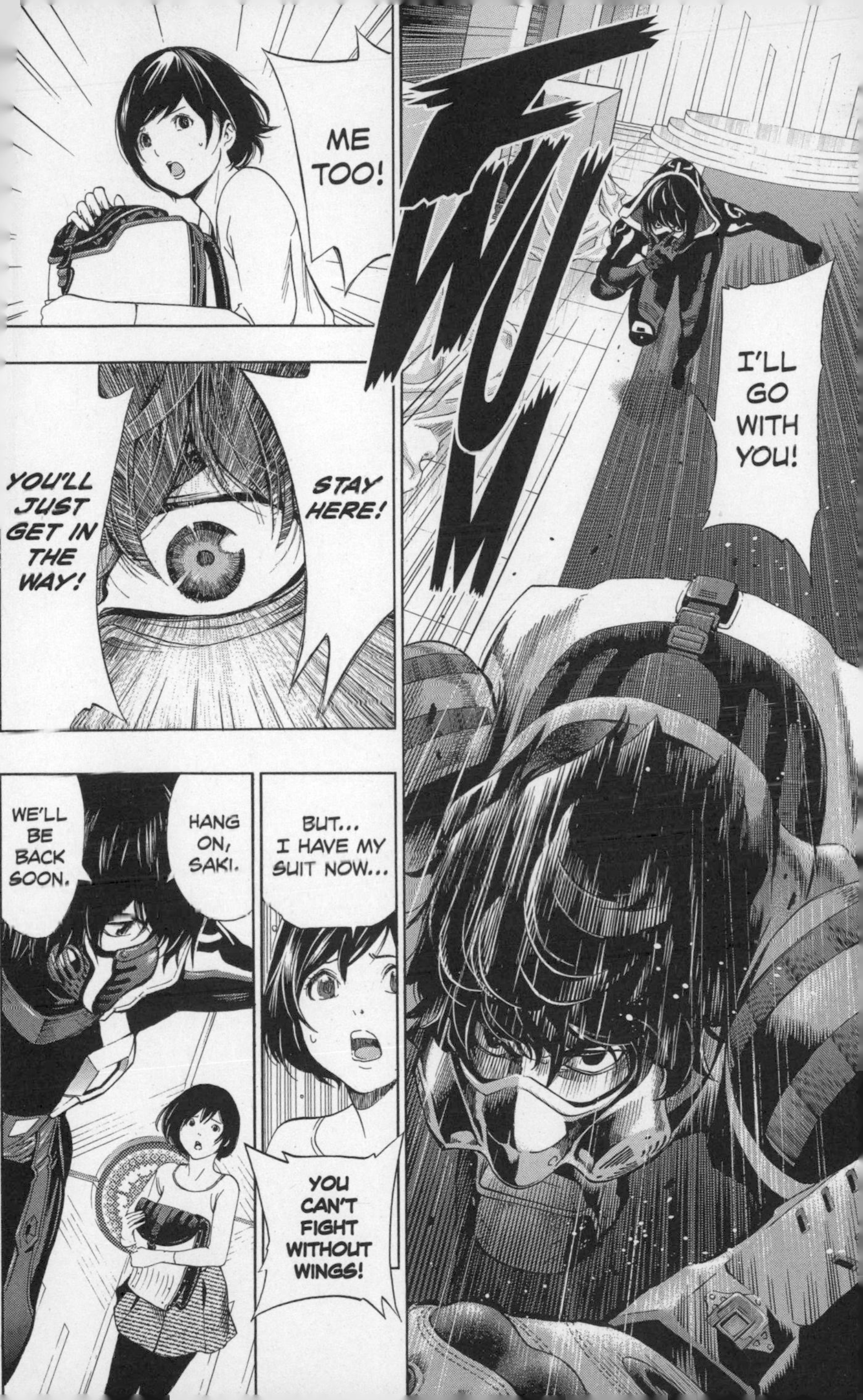
I'LL GO WITH YOU!
ME TOO!
STAY HERE!
YOU'LL JUST GET IN THE WAY!
BUT... I HAVE MY SUIT NOW...
YOU CAN'T FIGHT WITHOUT WINGS!
HANG ON, SAKI.
WE'LL BE BACK SOON.

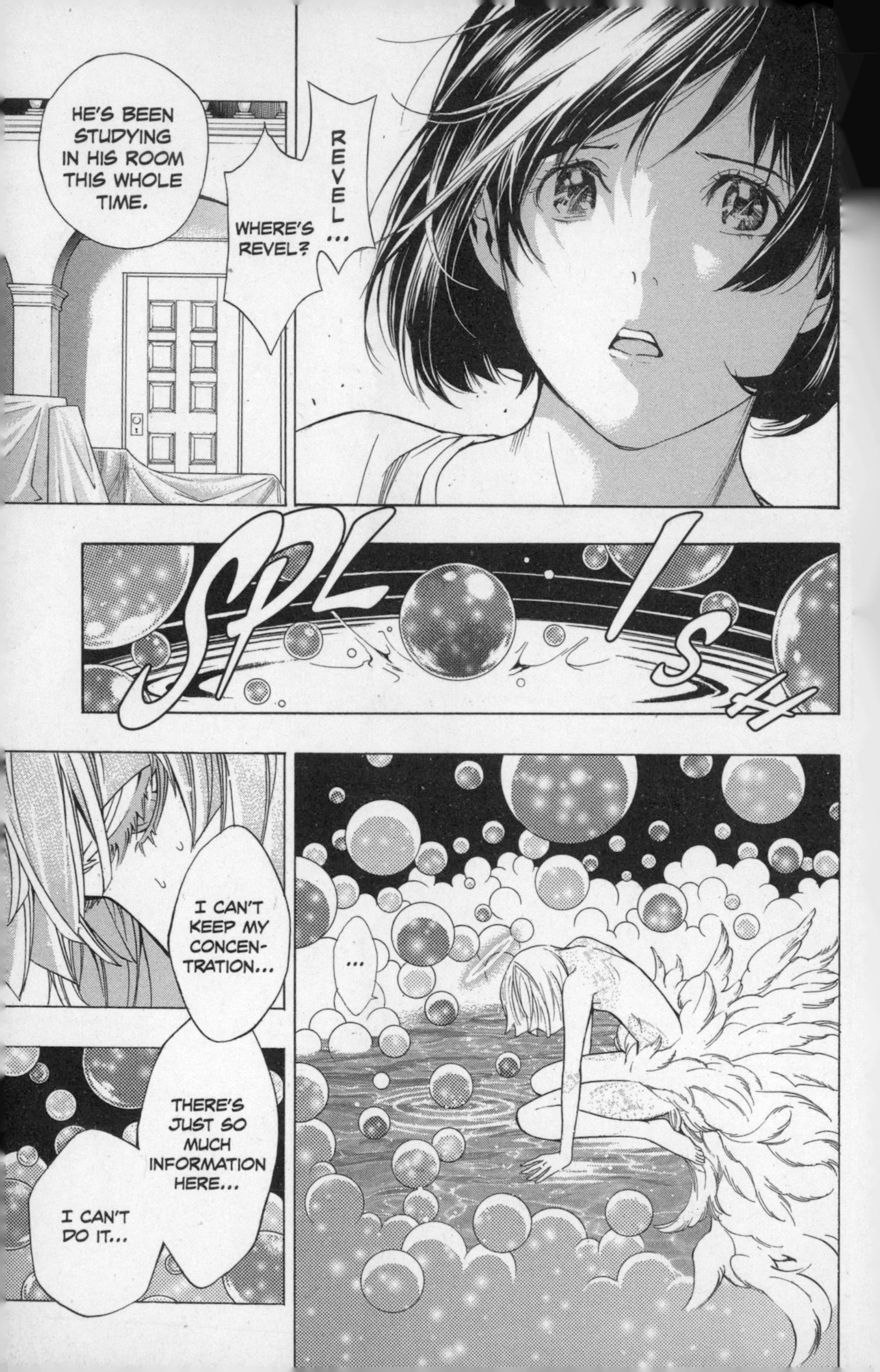
REVEL...
WHERE'S REVEL?
HE'S BEEN STUDYING IN HIS ROOM THIS WHOLE TIME.
SPLISH
...
I CAN'T KEEP MY CONCEN-TRATION...
THERE'S JUST SO MUCH INFORMATION HERE...
I CAN'T DO IT...

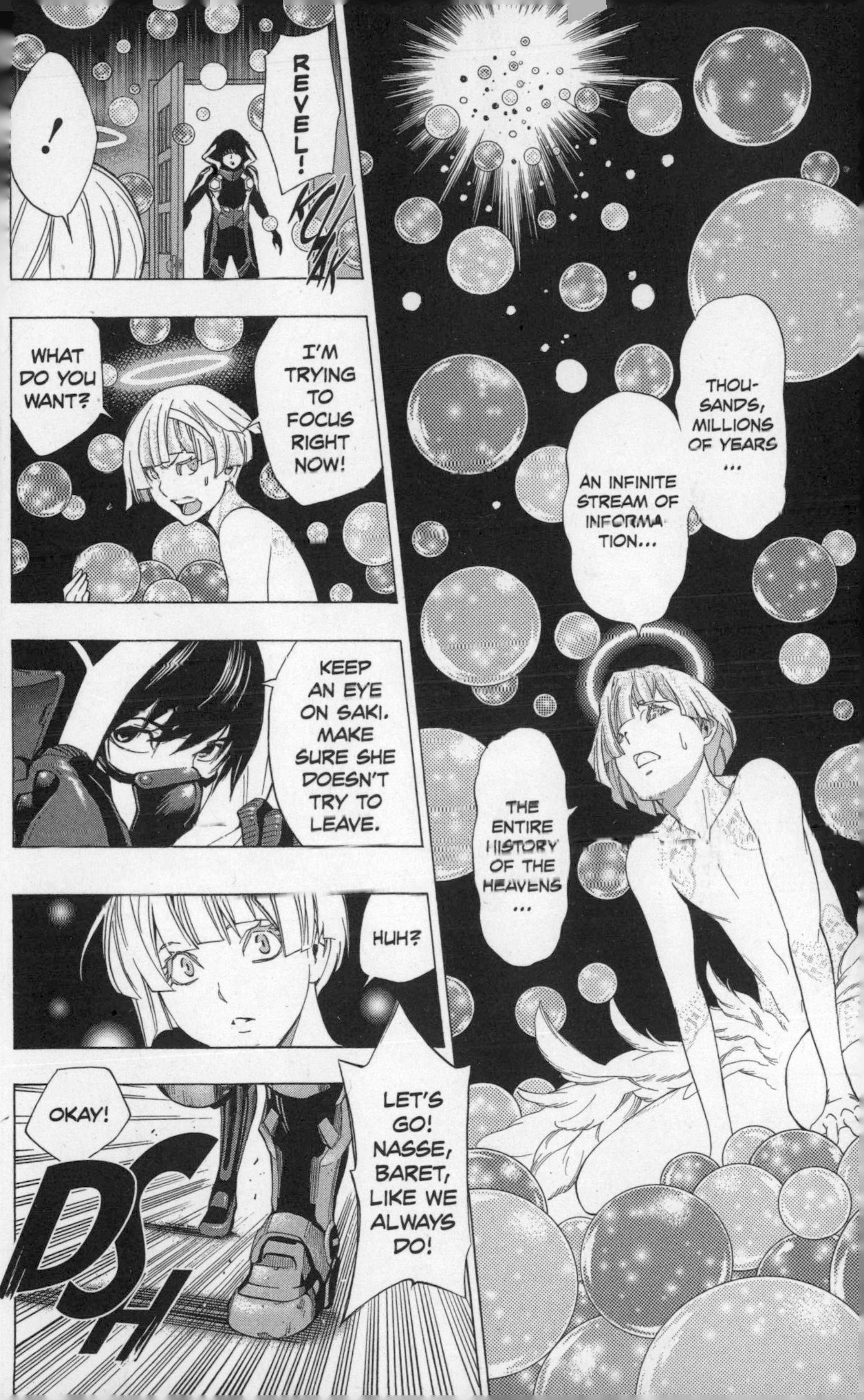
THOU-SANDS, MILLIONS OF YEARS ...
AN INFINITE STREAM OF INFORMA TION...
THE ENTIRE HISTORY OF THE HEAVENS ...
REVEL!
KCHAK
!
WHAT DO YOU WANT?
I'M TRYING TO FOCUS RIGHT NOW!
KEEP AN EYE ON SAKI. MAKE SURE SHE DOESN'T TRY TO LEAVE.
HUH?
LET'S GO! NASSE, BARET, LIKE WE ALWAYS DO!
OKAY!
DSH

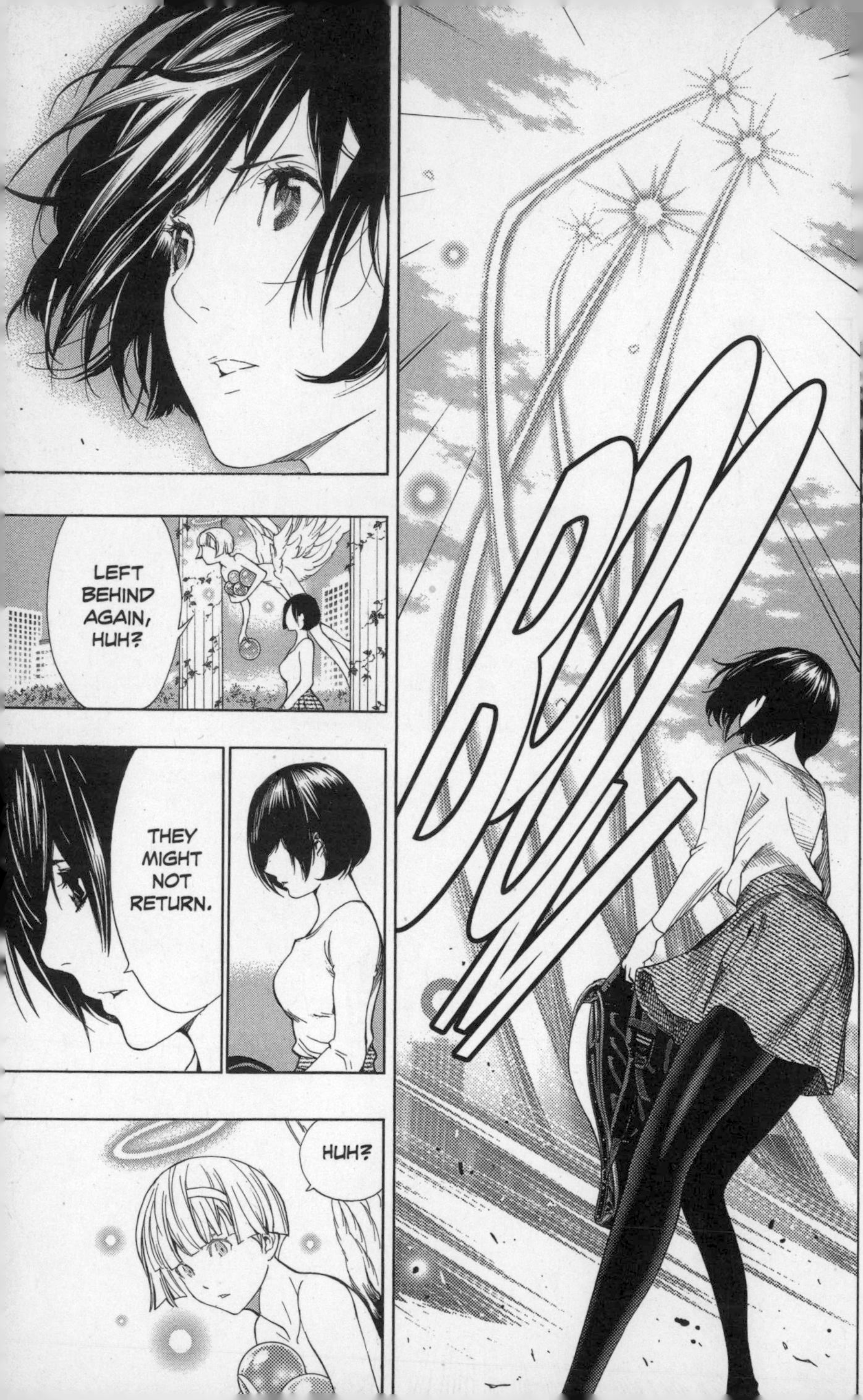
LEFT BEHIND AGAIN, HUH?
THEY MIGHT NOT RETURN.
HUH?

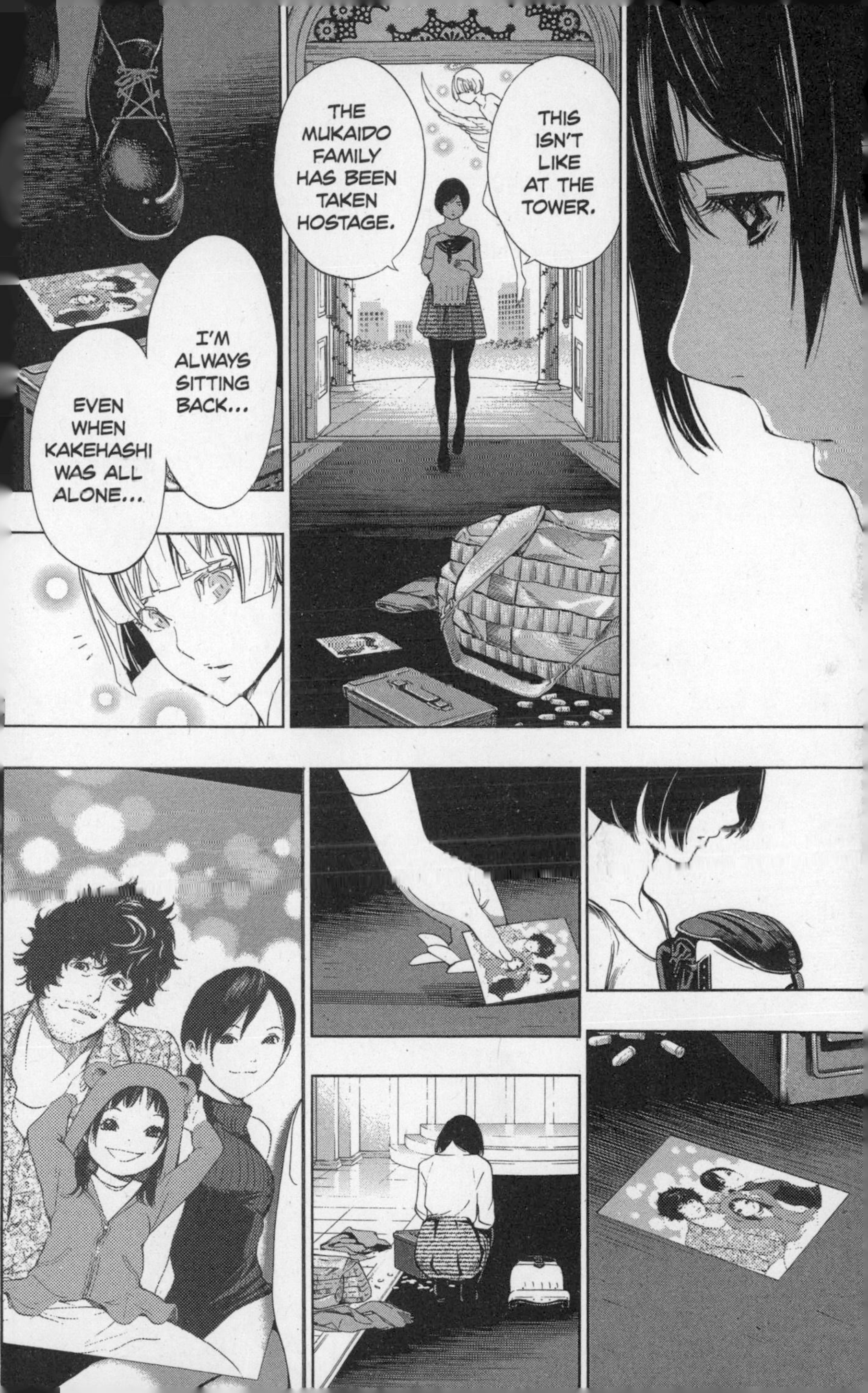
THIS ISN'T LIKE AT THE TOWER.
THE MUKAIDO FAMILY HAS BEEN TAKEN HOSTAGE.
I'M ALWAYS SITTING BACK...
EVEN WHEN KAKEHASHI WAS ALL ALONE...

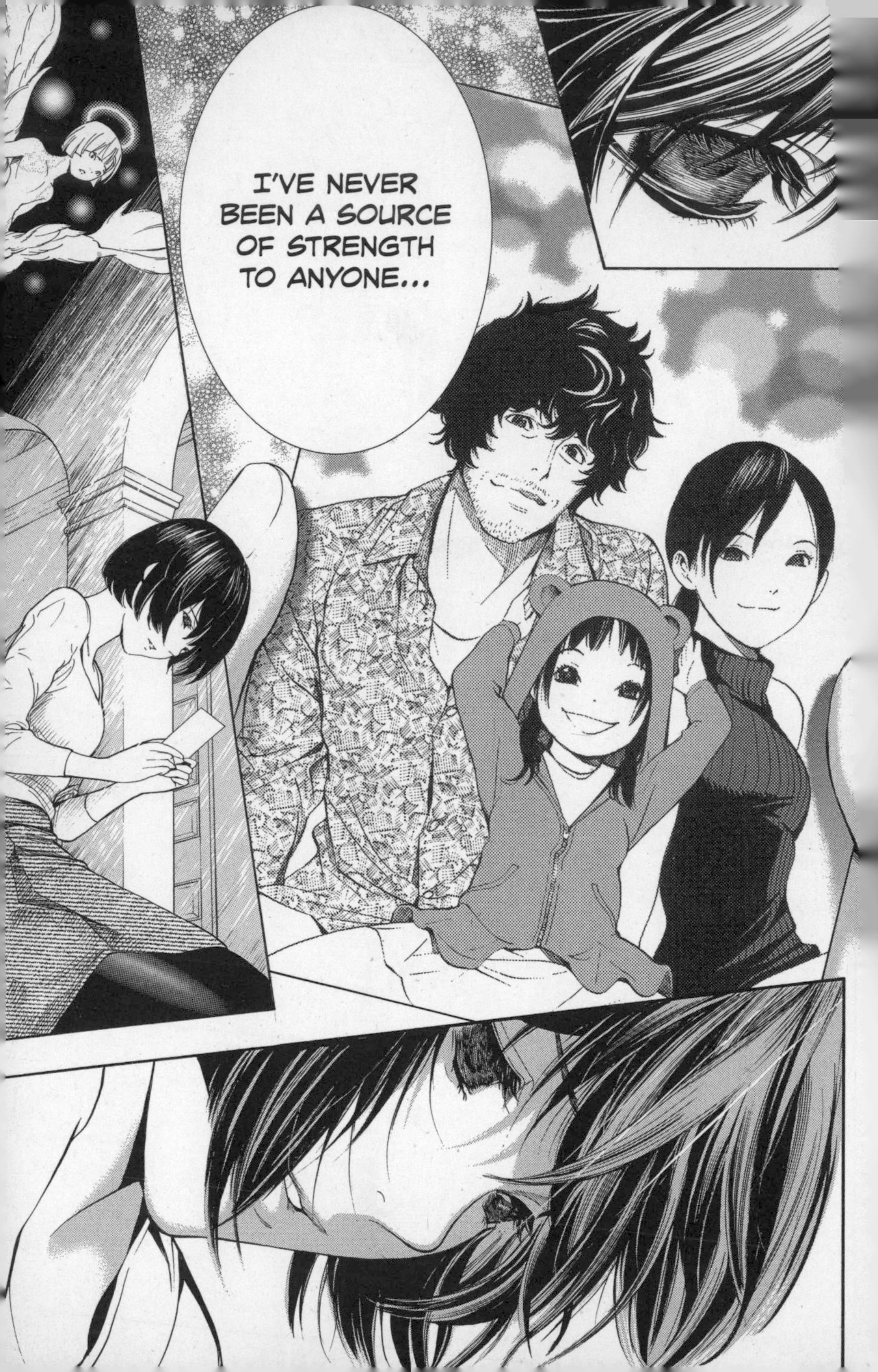
I'VE NEVER BEEN A SOURCE OF STRENGTH TO ANYONE...

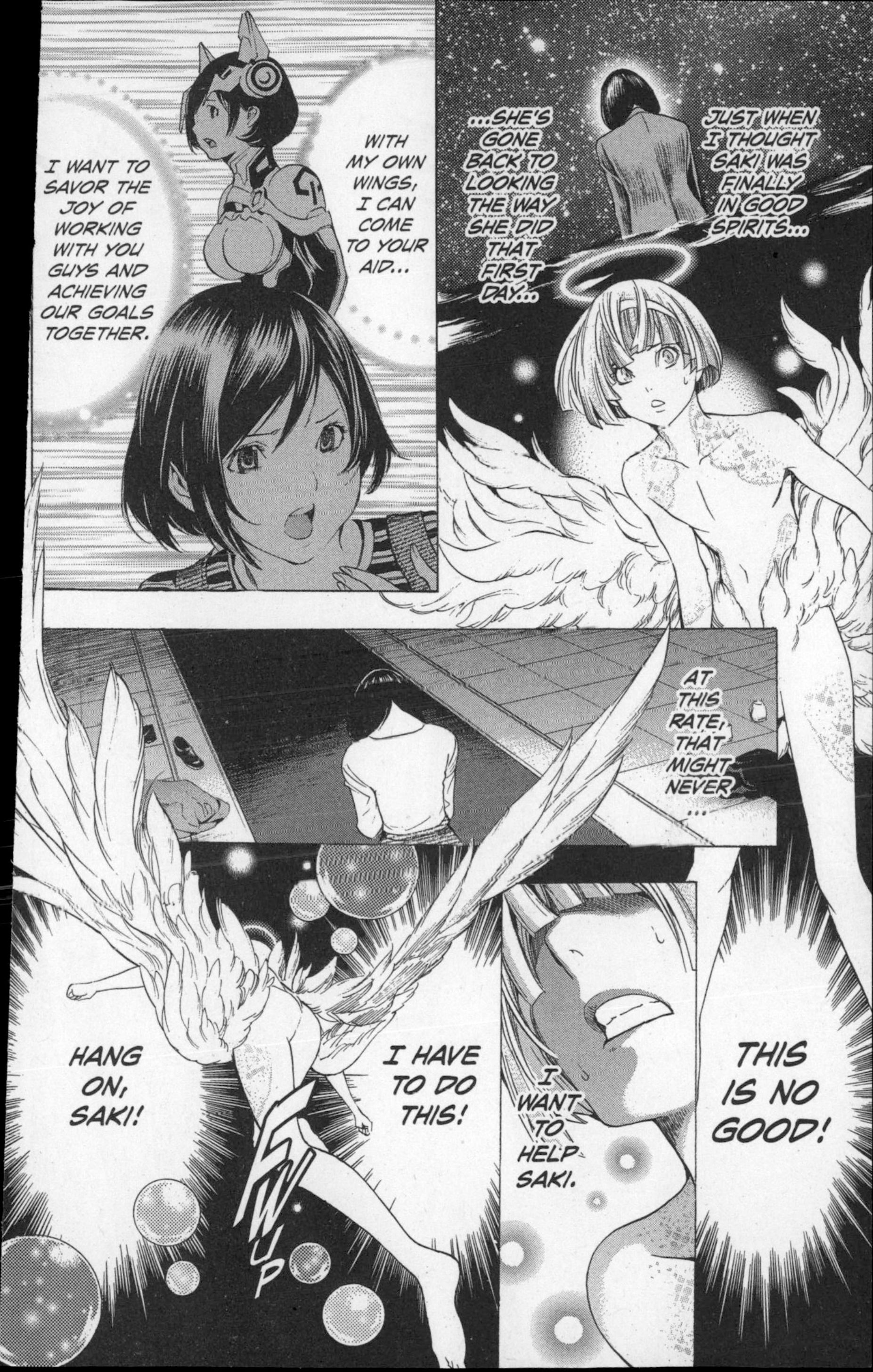
JUST WHEN I THOUGHT SAKI WAS FINALLY IN GOOD SPIRITS...
...SHE'S GONE BACK TO LOOKING THE WAY SHE DID THAT FIRST DAY...
WITH MY OWN WINGS, I CAN COME TO YOUR AID...
I WANT TO SAVOR THE JOY OF WORKING WITH YOU GUYS AND ACHIEVING OUR GOALS TOGETHER.
AT THIS RATE, THAT MIGHT NEVER...
THIS IS NO GOOD!
I WANT TO HELP SAKI.
I HAVE TO DO THIS!
HANG ON, SAKI!
FWUP

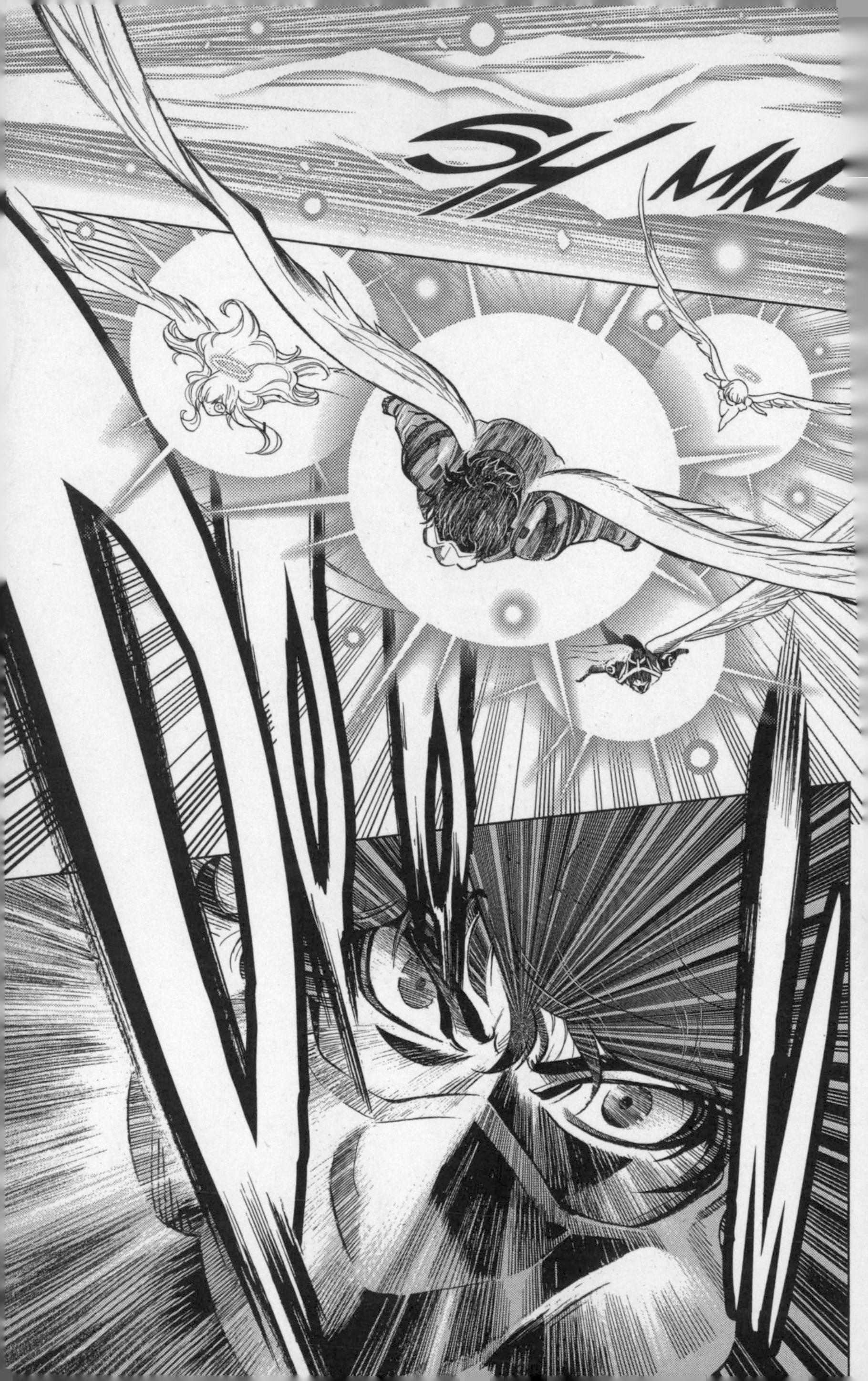
SHMM

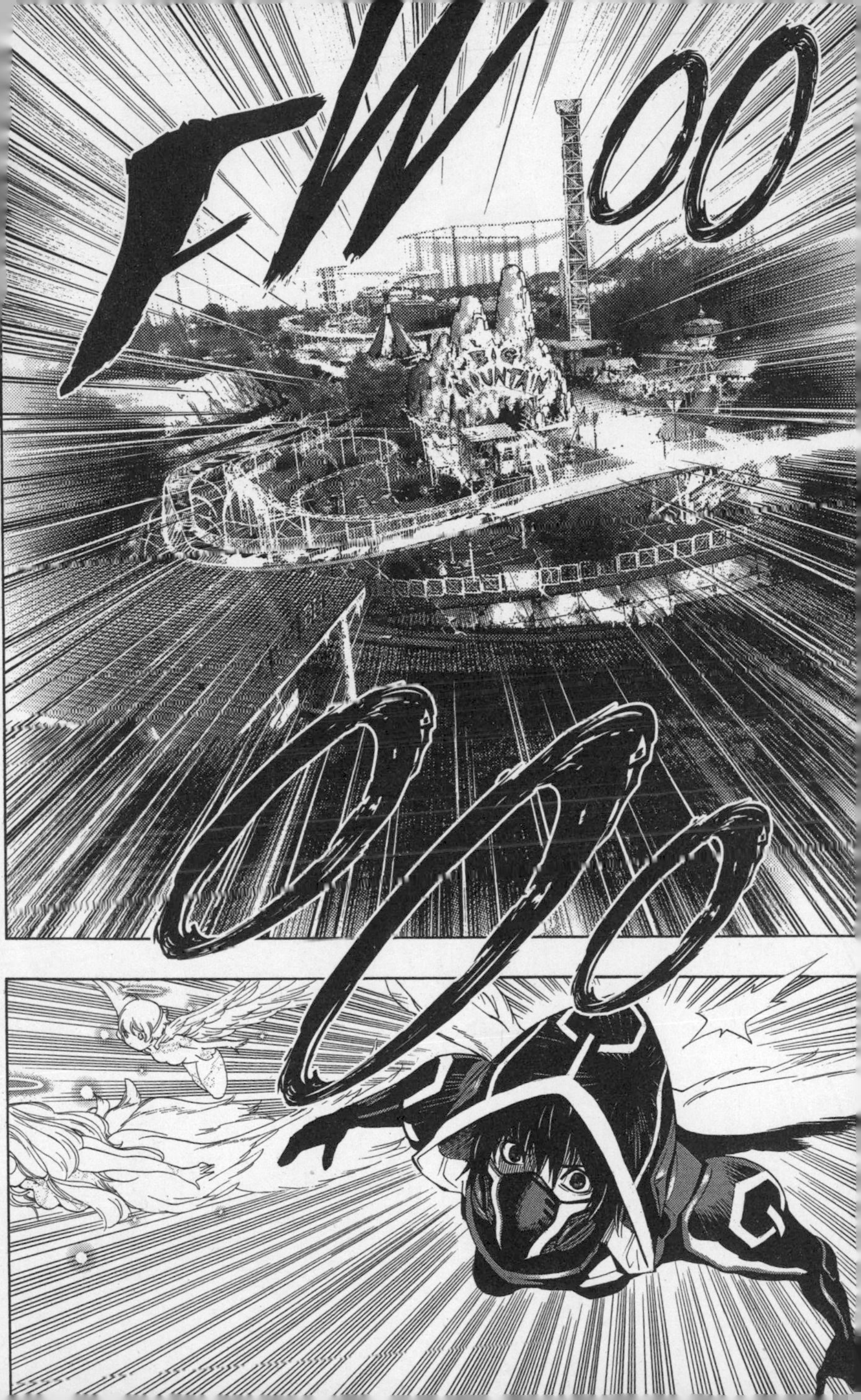
FWOOOOO
BIG MOUNTAIN

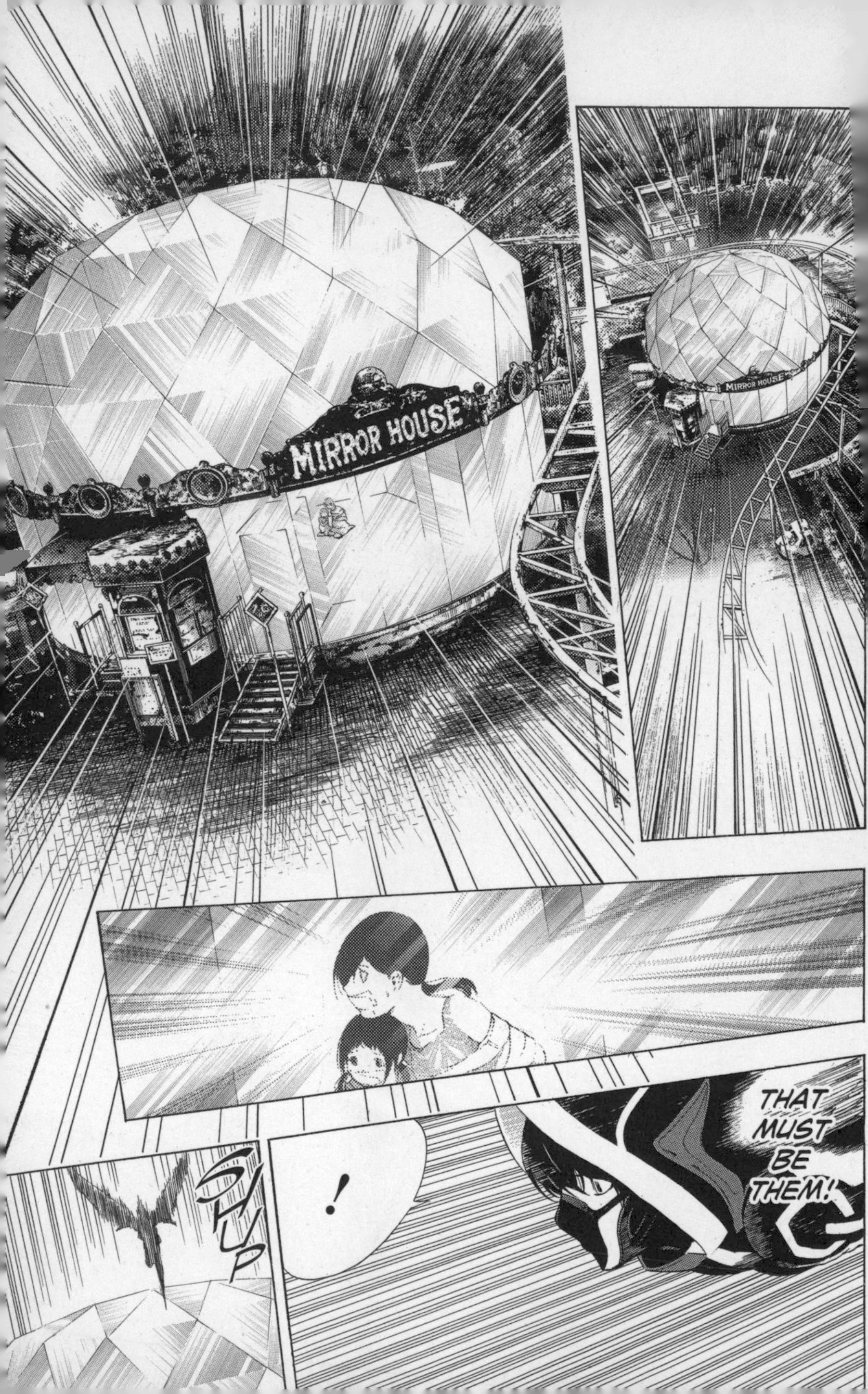
MIRROR HOUSE
MIRROR HOUSE
THAT MUST BE THEM!
!
SHUP

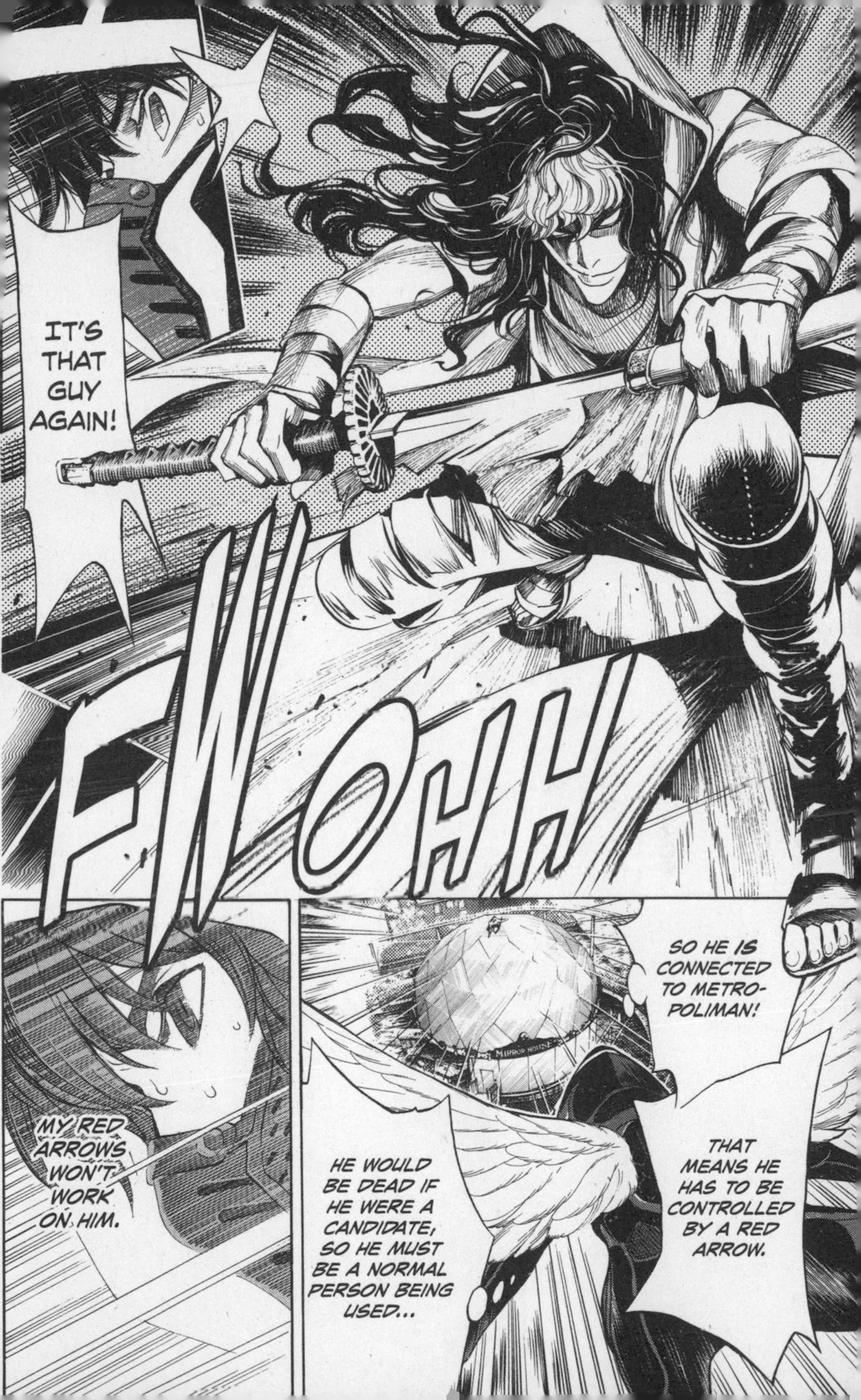
IT'S THAT GUY AGAIN!
FWOHH
SO HE IS CONNECTED TO METRO-POLIMAN!
MIRROR HOUSE
THAT MEANS HE HAS TO BE CONTROLLED BY A RED ARROW.
HE WOULD BE DEAD IF HE WERE A CANDIDATE, SO HE MUST BE A NORMAL PERSON BEING USED...
MY RED ARROWS WON'T WORK ON HIM.

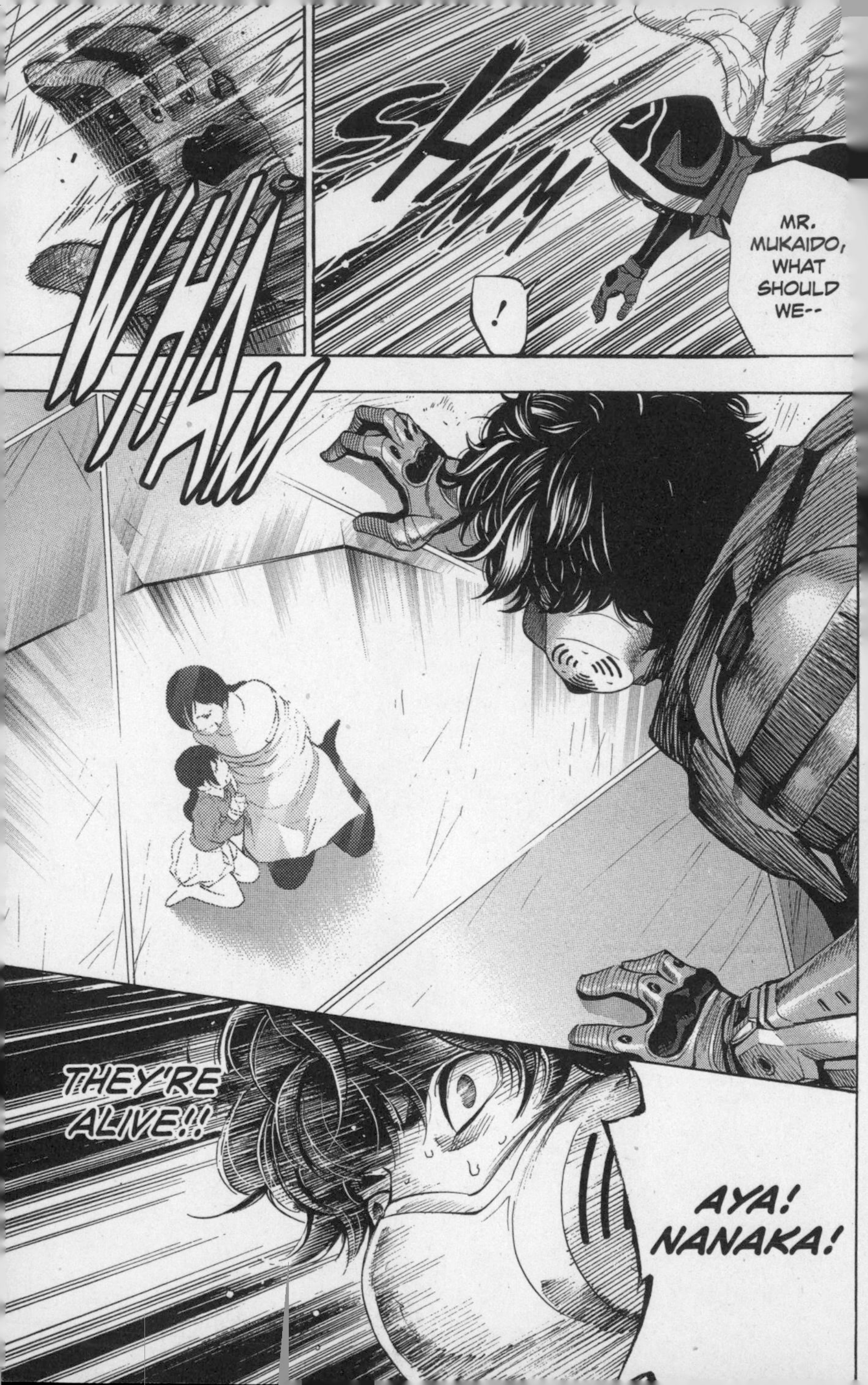
SHUM
MR. MUKAIDO, WHAT SHOULD WE--
!
WHAM
AYA! NANAKA!
THEY'RE ALIVE!!

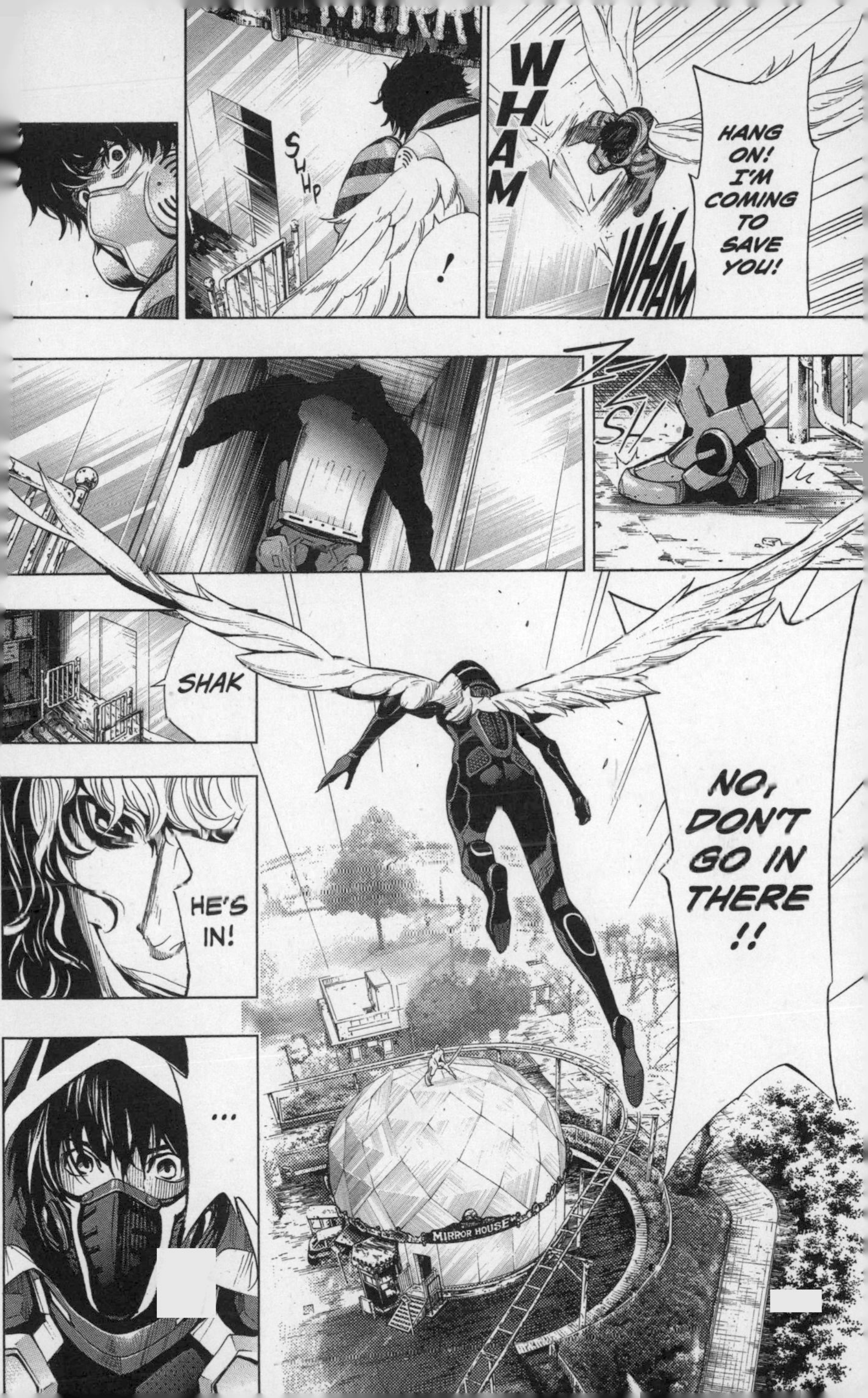
WHAM
HANG ON! I'M COMING TO SAVE YOU!
WHAM
SHHP
!
NO, DON'T GO IN THERE!!
MIRROR HOUSE
SHAK
HE'S IN!
...

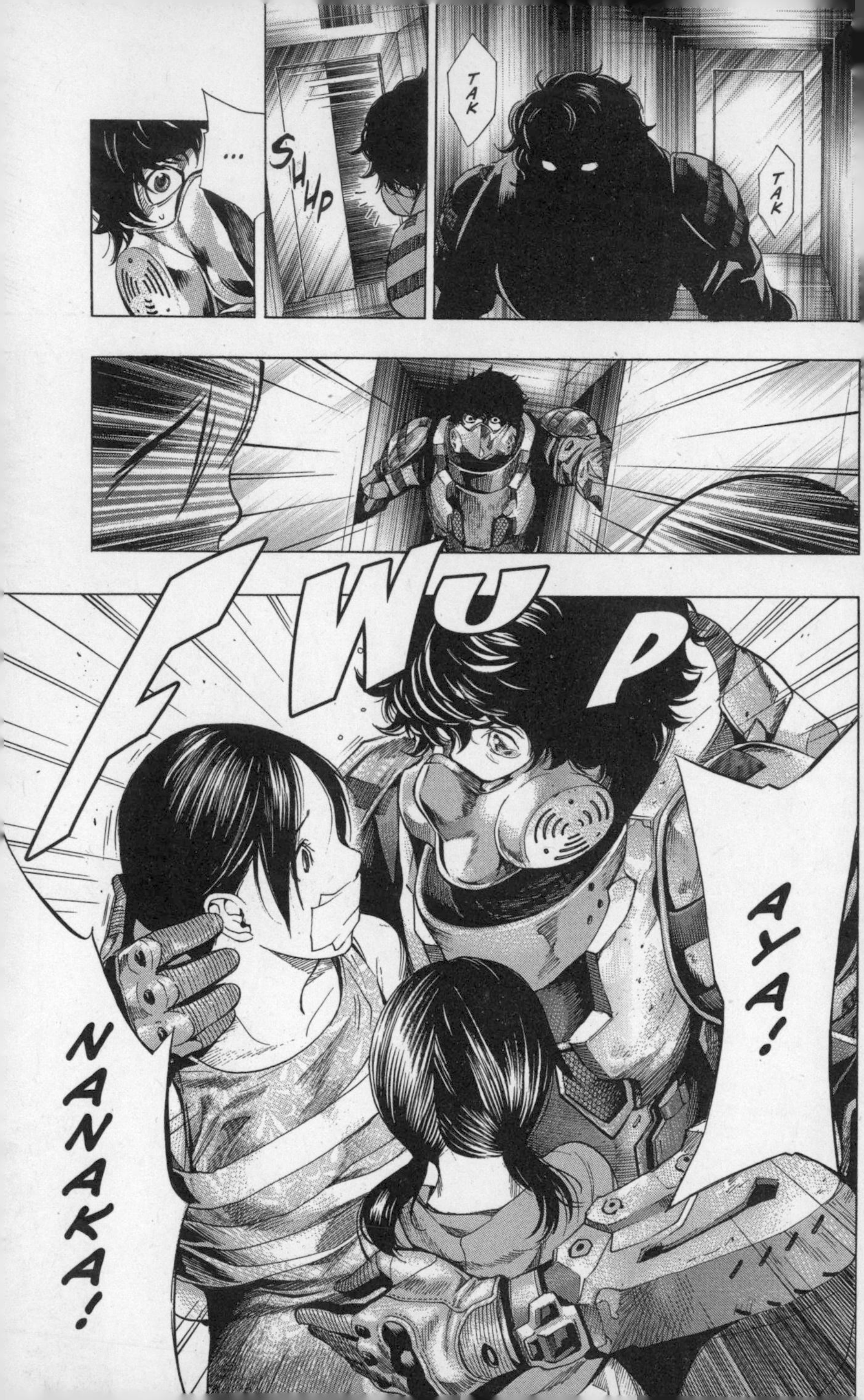
TAK
TAK
SHHP
...
FWUP
AYA!
NANAKA!

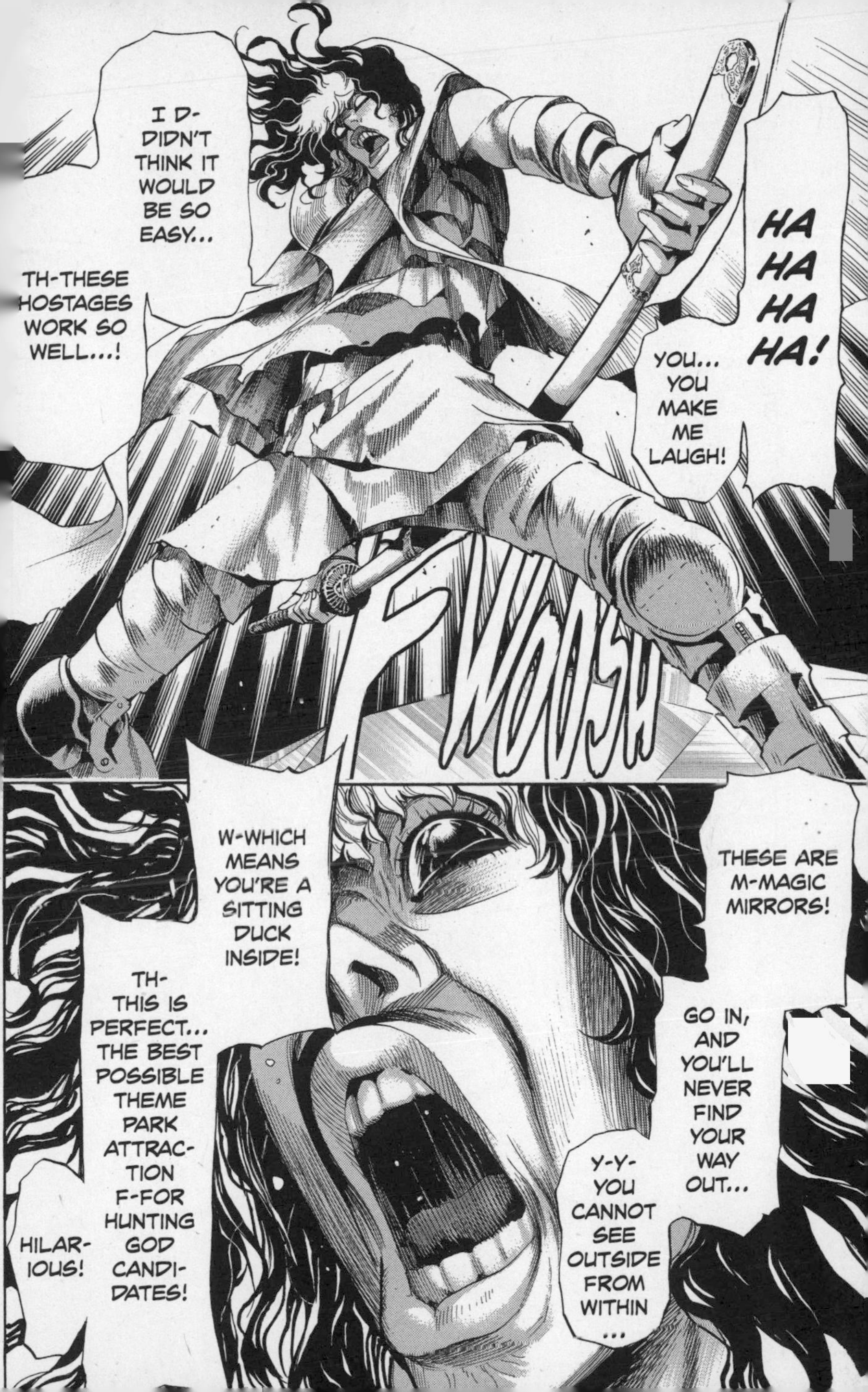
HA HA HA HA!
YOU... YOU MAKE ME LAUGH!
I D-DIDN'T THINK IT WOULD BE SO EASY...
TH-THESE HOSTAGES WORK SO WELL...!
WOOSH
THESE ARE M-MAGIC MIRRORS!
GO IN, AND YOU'LL NEVER FIND YOUR WAY OUT...
Y-Y-YOU CANNOT SEE OUTSIDE FROM WITHIN...
W-WHICH MEANS YOU'RE A SITTING DUCK INSIDE!
TH-THIS IS PERFECT... THE BEST POSSIBLE THEME PARK ATTRACTION F-FOR HUNTING GOD CANDIDATES!
HILARIOUS!

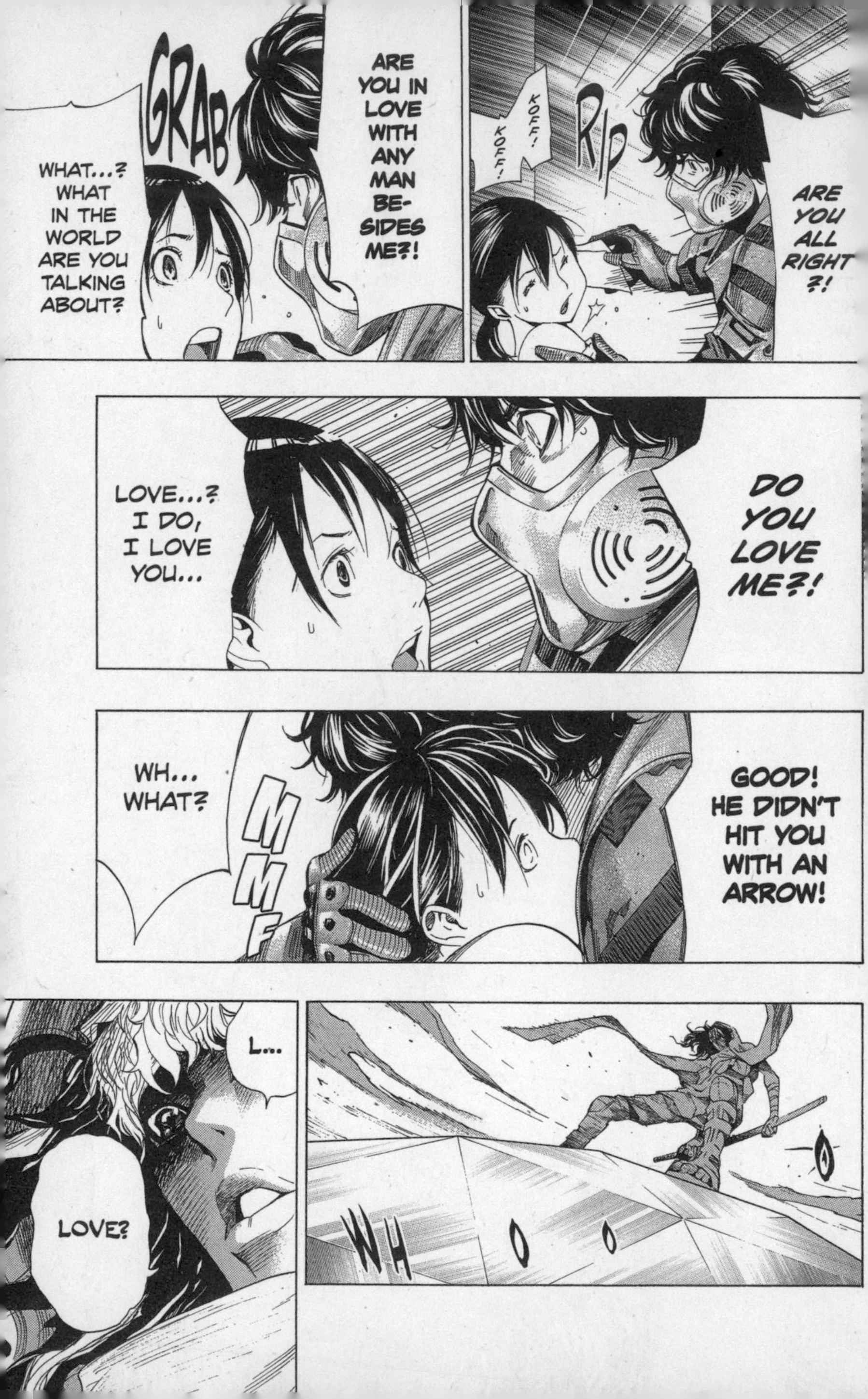

KOFF! KOFF!
RIP
ARE YOU ALL RIGHT?!
ARE YOU IN LOVE WITH ANY MAN BE-SIDES ME?!
GRAB
WHAT...? WHAT IN THE WORLD ARE YOU TALKING ABOUT?
DO YOU LOVE ME?!
LOVE...? I DO, I LOVE YOU...
GOOD! HE DIDN'T HIT YOU WITH AN ARROW!
MMMF
WH... WHAT?
WH
L...
LOVE?

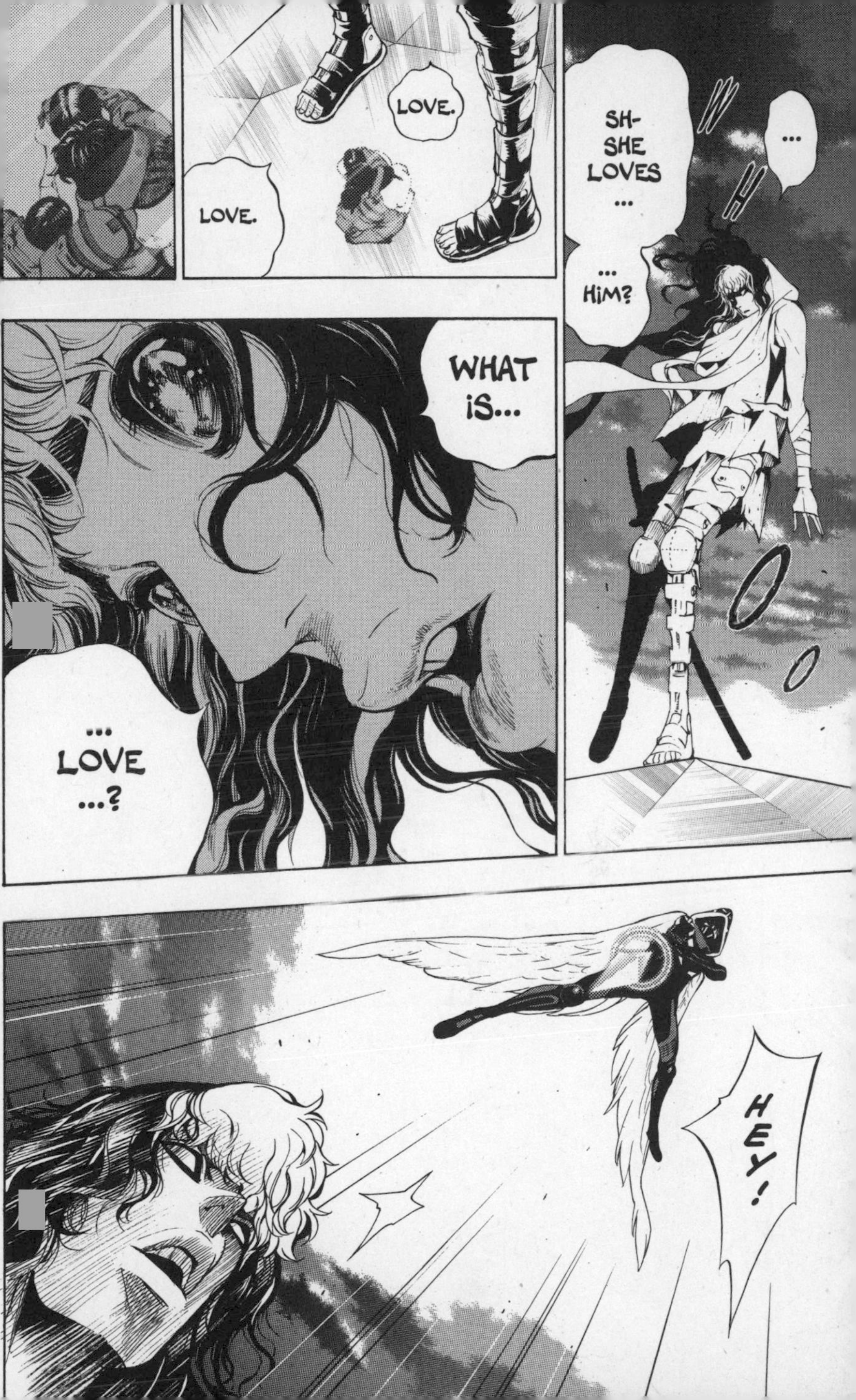
...
SH- SHE LOVES ...
... HIM?
LOVE.
LOVE.
WHAT IS...
... LOVE ...?
HEY!

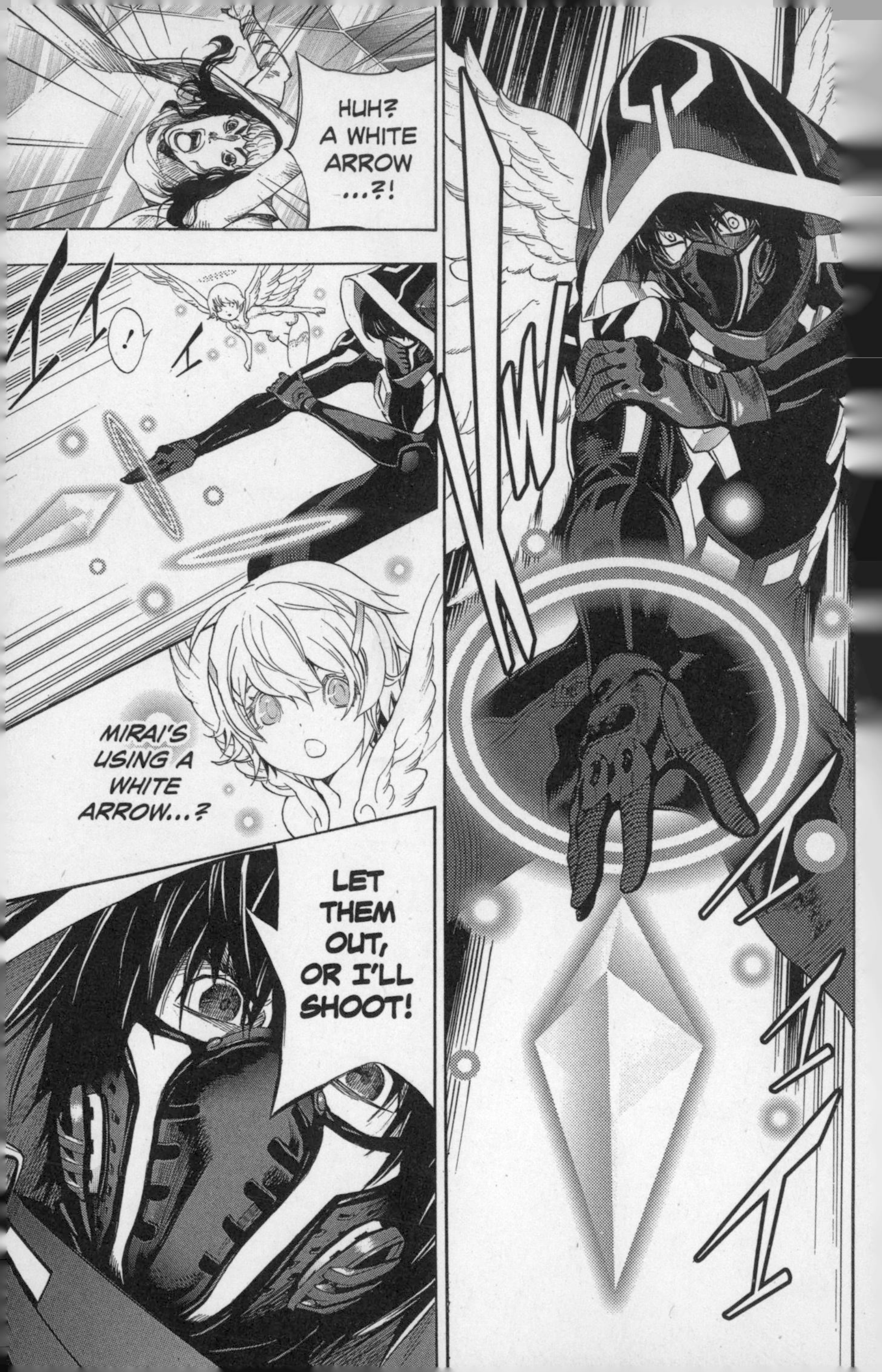
HUH? A WHITE ARROW ...?!
!
MIRAI'S USING A WHITE ARROW...?
LET THEM OUT, OR I'LL SHOOT!

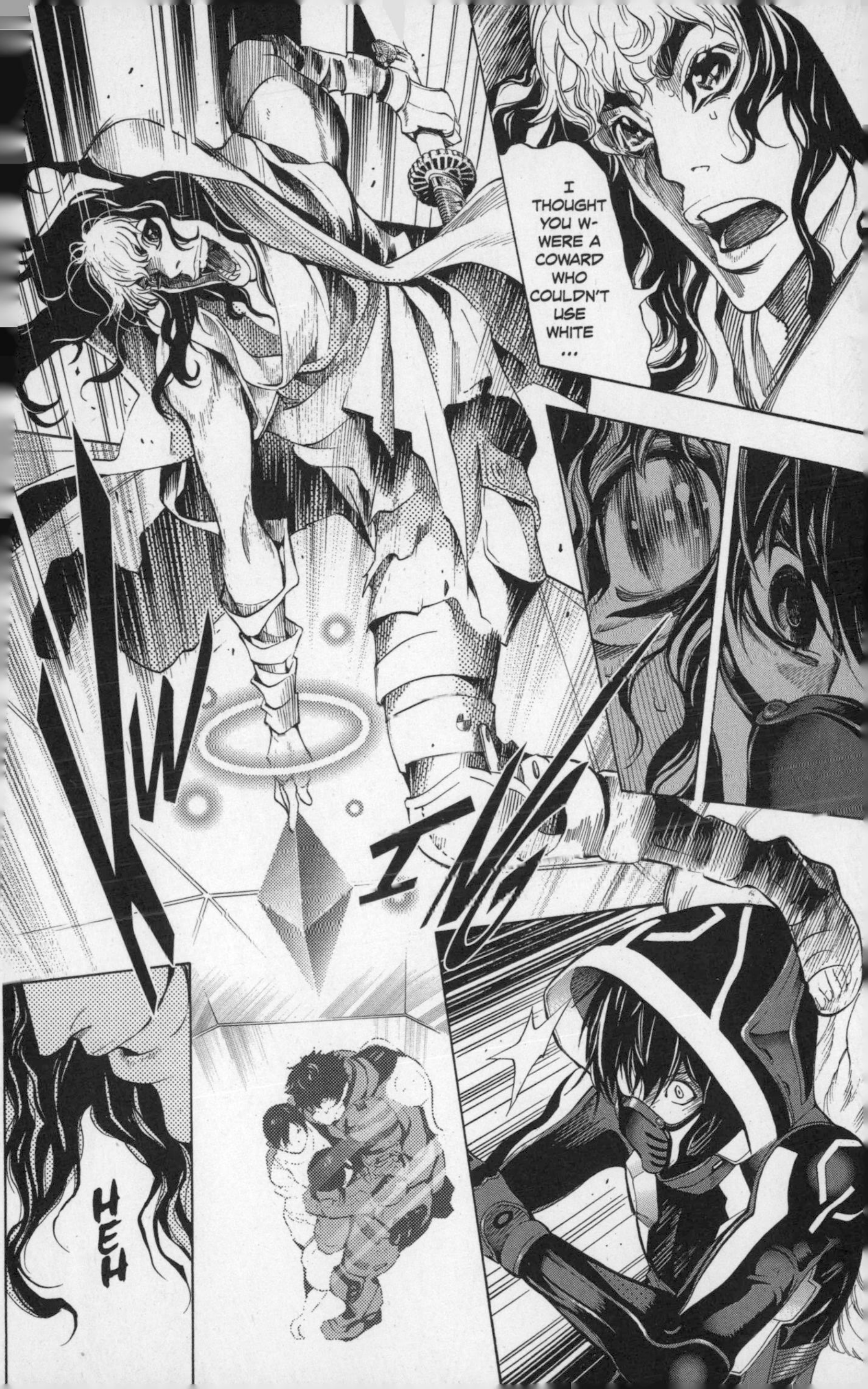
I THOUGHT YOU W-WERE A COWARD WHO COULDN'T USE WHITE ...
HEH

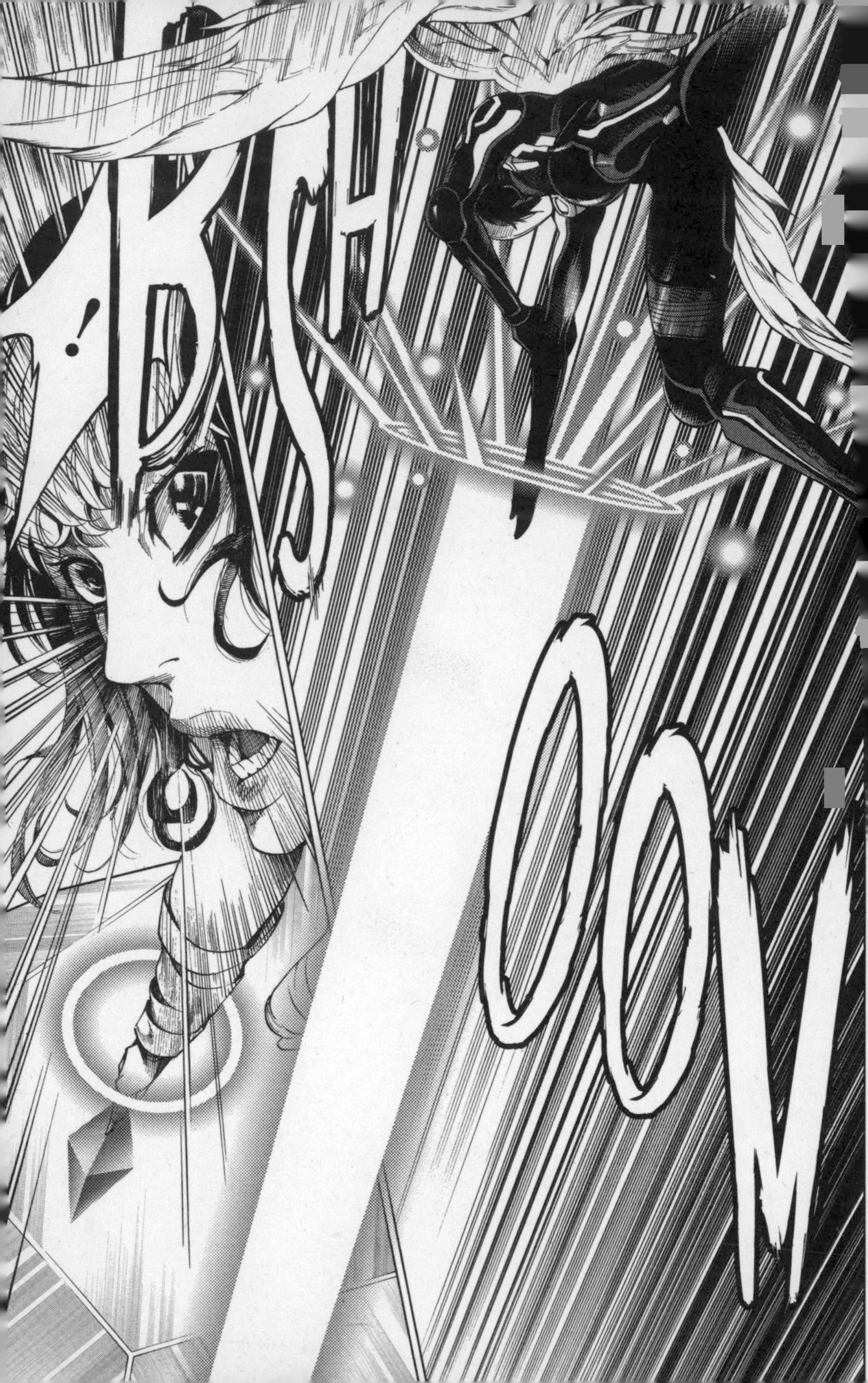
OOM

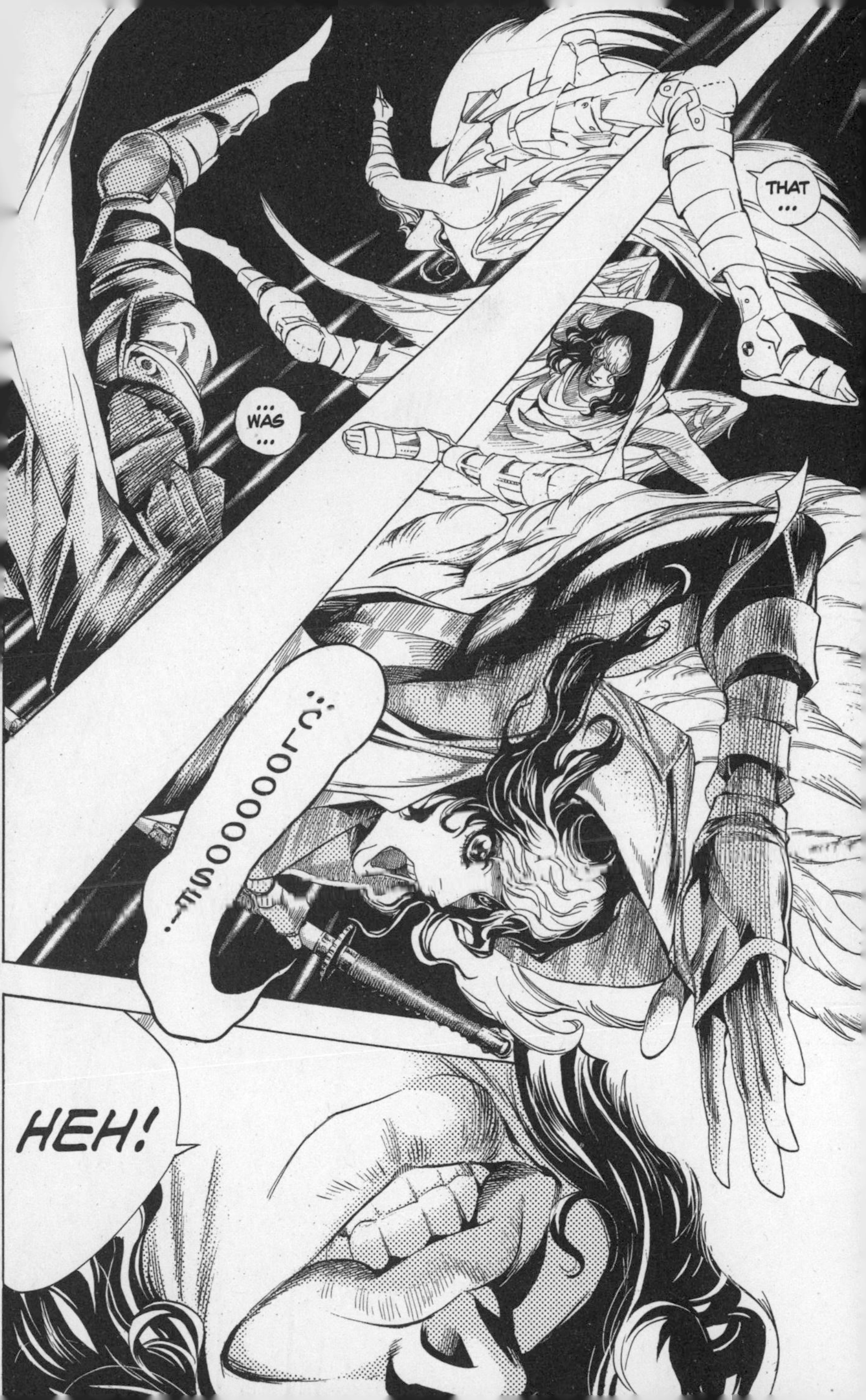
THAT ...
... WAS ...
...CLOOOOOSE-!
HEH!

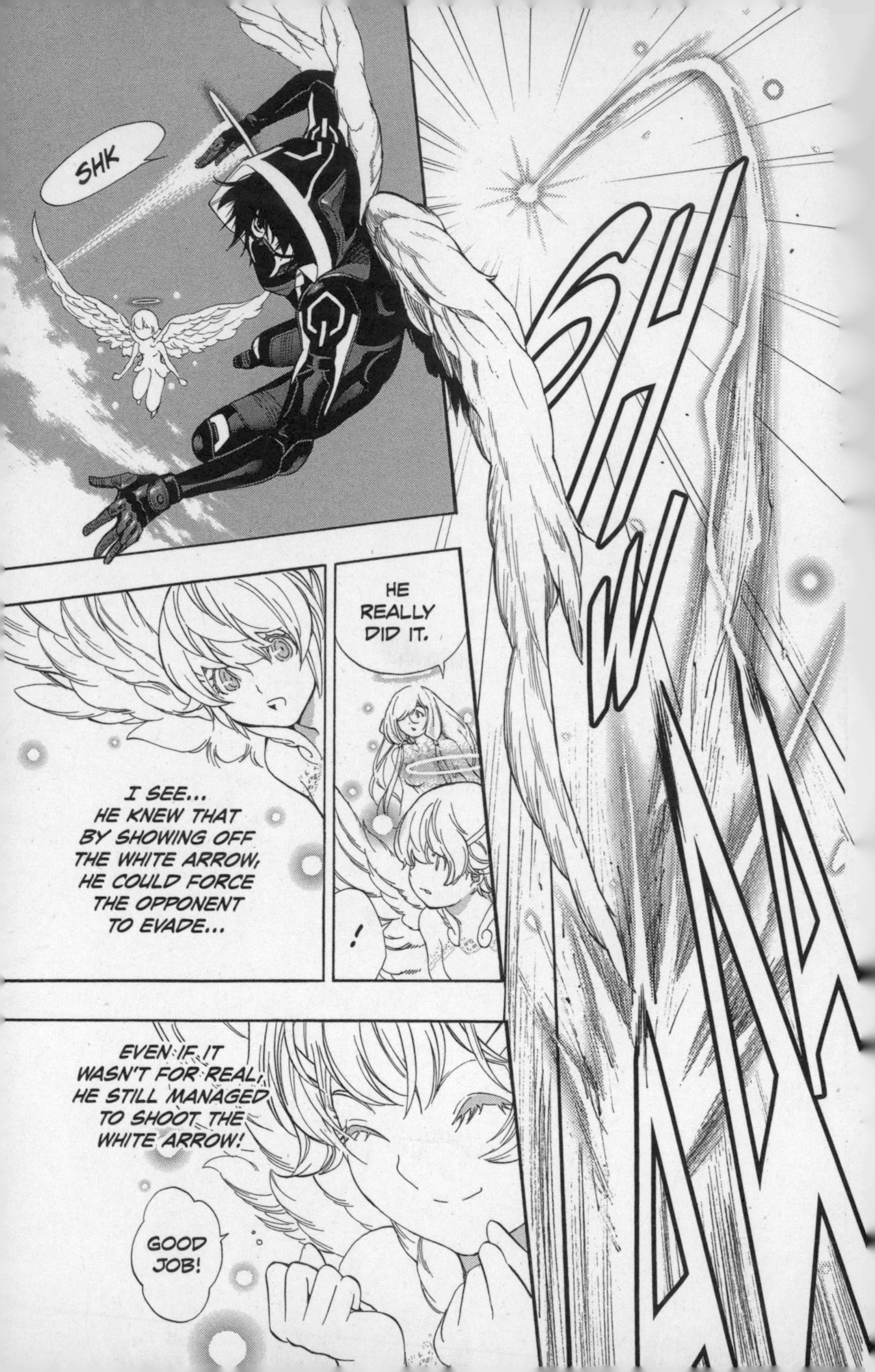
SHWAAA
SHK
HE REALLY DID IT.
!
I SEE... HE KNEW THAT BY SHOWING OFF THE WHITE ARROW, HE COULD FORCE THE OPPONENT TO EVADE...
EVEN IF IT WASN'T FOR REAL, HE STILL MANAGED TO SHOOT THE WHITE ARROW!
GOOD JOB!

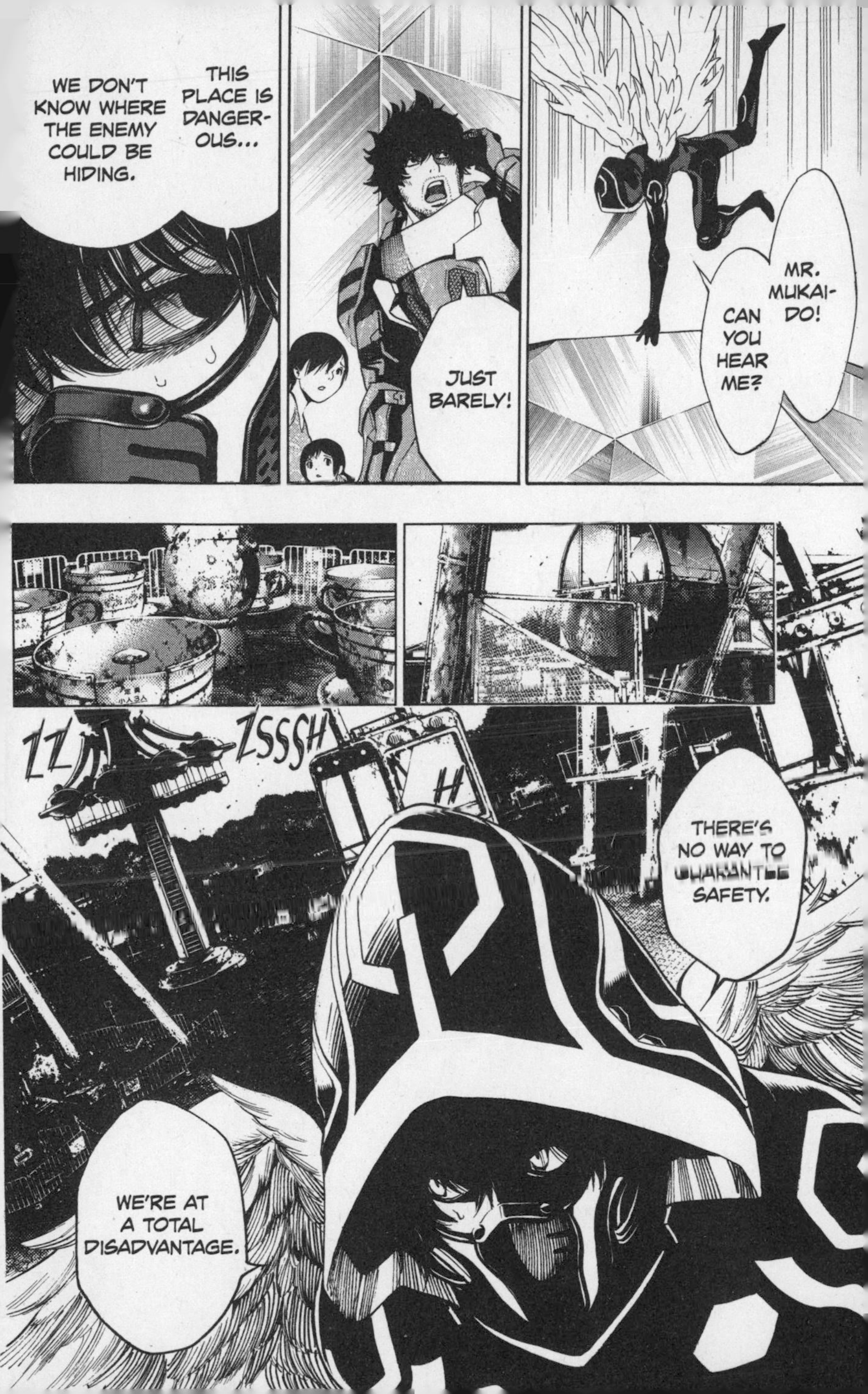
MR. MUKAI-DO!
CAN YOU HEAR ME?
JUST BARELY!
THIS PLACE IS DANGER-OUS...
WE DON'T KNOW WHERE THE ENEMY COULD BE HIDING.
ZZ ZSSSH H
THERE'S NO WAY TO GUARANTEE SAFETY.
WE'RE AT A TOTAL DISADVANTAGE.

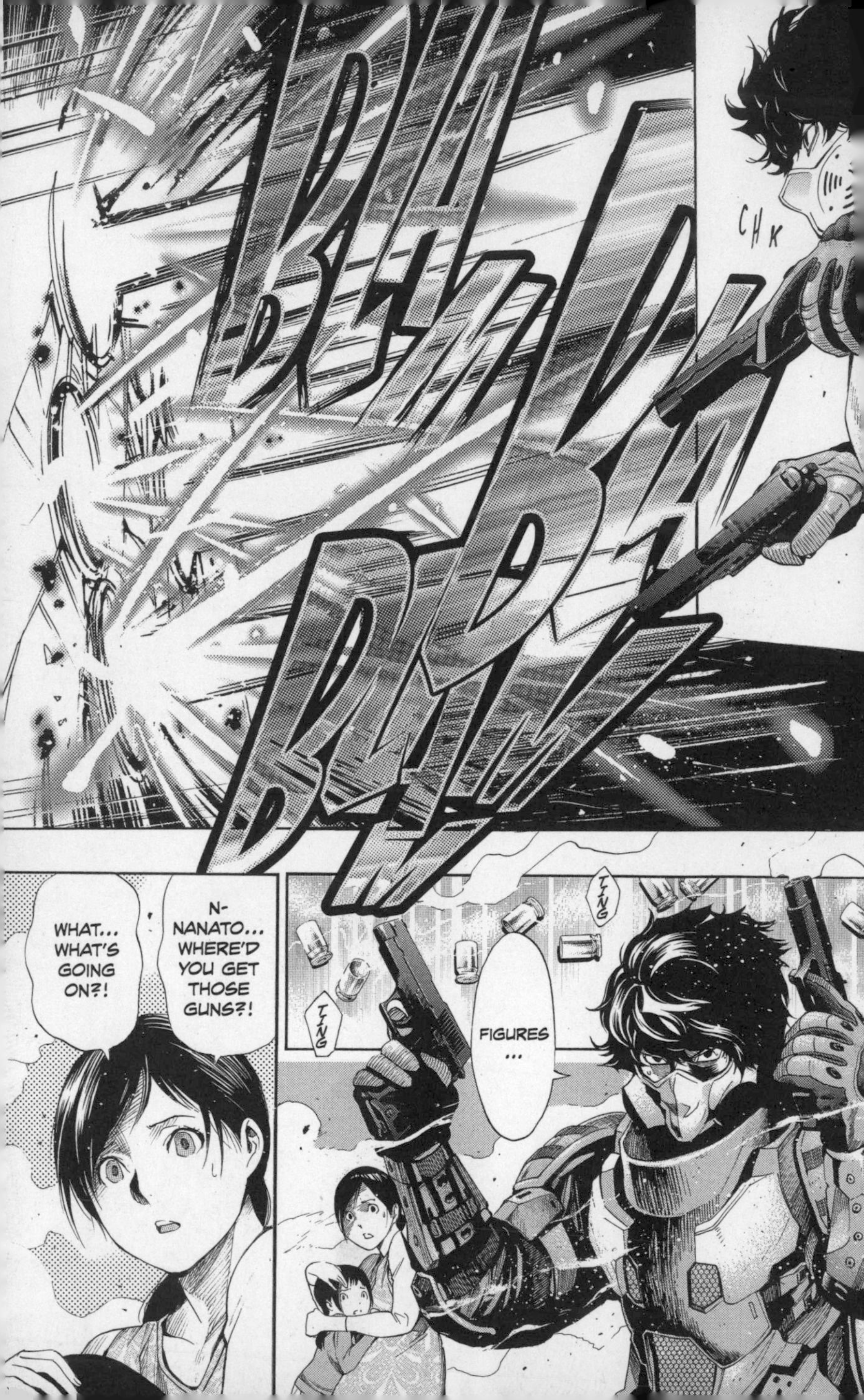
CHK
TING
TING
FIGURES...
N-NANATO... WHERE'D YOU GET THOSE GUNS?!
WHAT... WHAT'S GOING ON?!

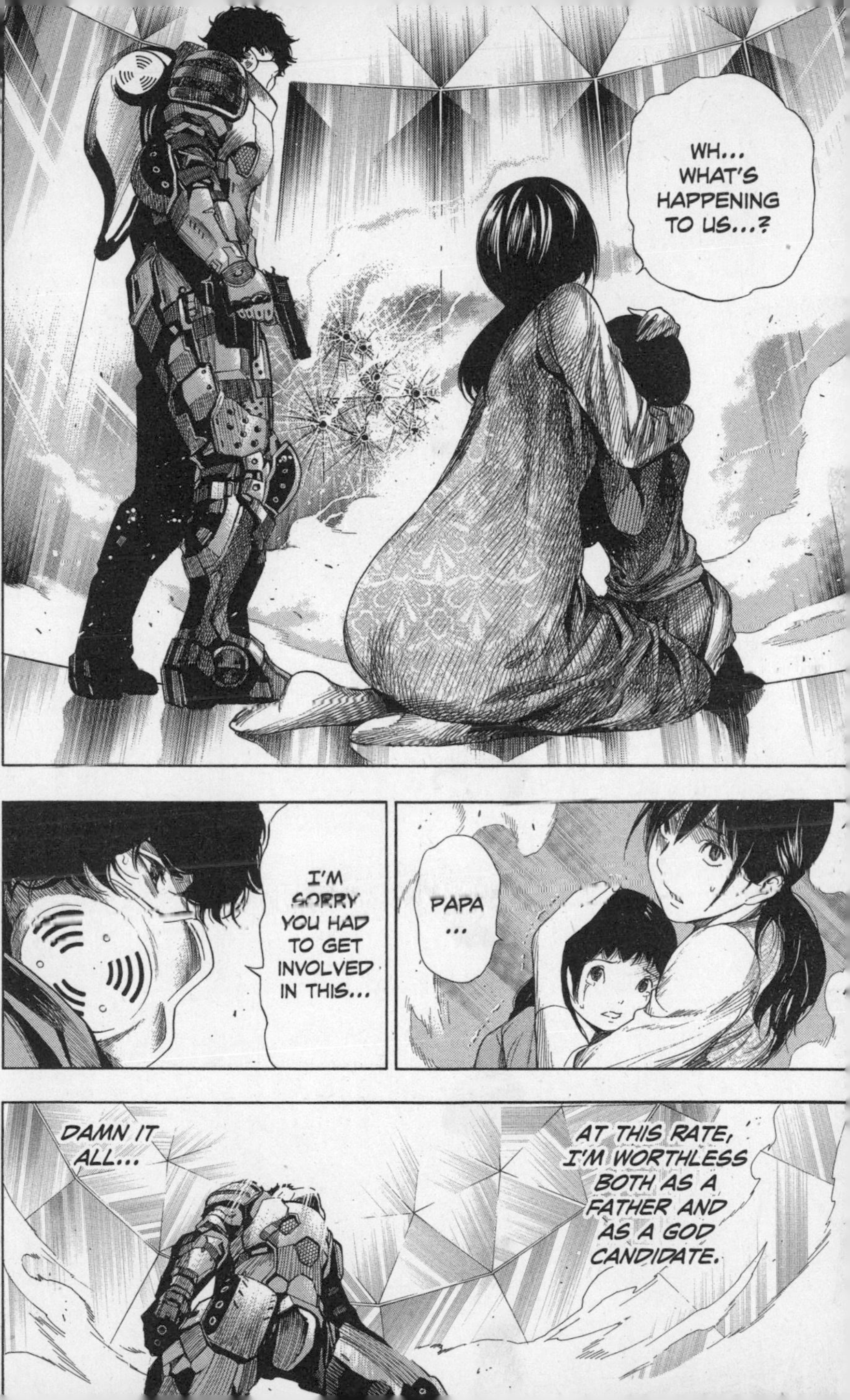
WH... WHAT'S HAPPENING TO US...?
PAPA ...
I'M SORRY YOU HAD TO GET INVOLVED IN THIS...
AT THIS RATE, I'M WORTHLESS BOTH AS A FATHER AND AS A GOD CANDIDATE.
DAMN IT ALL...

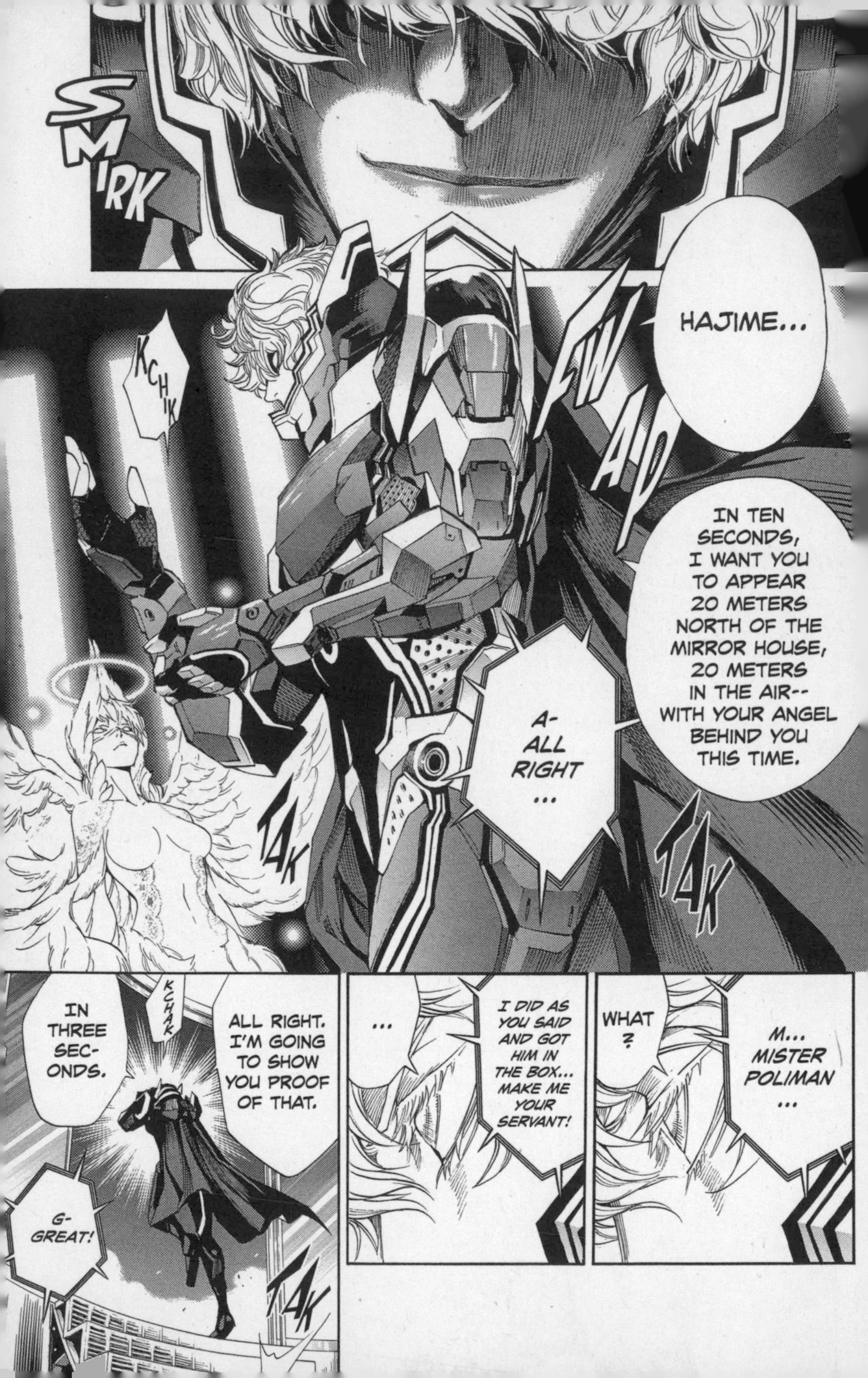
SMIRK
HAJIME...
FWAP
IN TEN SECONDS, I WANT YOU TO APPEAR 20 METERS NORTH OF THE MIRROR HOUSE, 20 METERS IN THE AIR-- WITH YOUR ANGEL BEHIND YOU THIS TIME.
A- ALL RIGHT ...
TAK
KCHIK
TAK
M... MISTER POLIMAN ...
WHAT ?
I DID AS YOU SAID AND GOT HIM IN THE BOX... MAKE ME YOUR SERVANT!
...
ALL RIGHT. I'M GOING TO SHOW YOU PROOF OF THAT.
KCHAK
IN THREE SEC-ONDS.
G- GREAT!
TAK

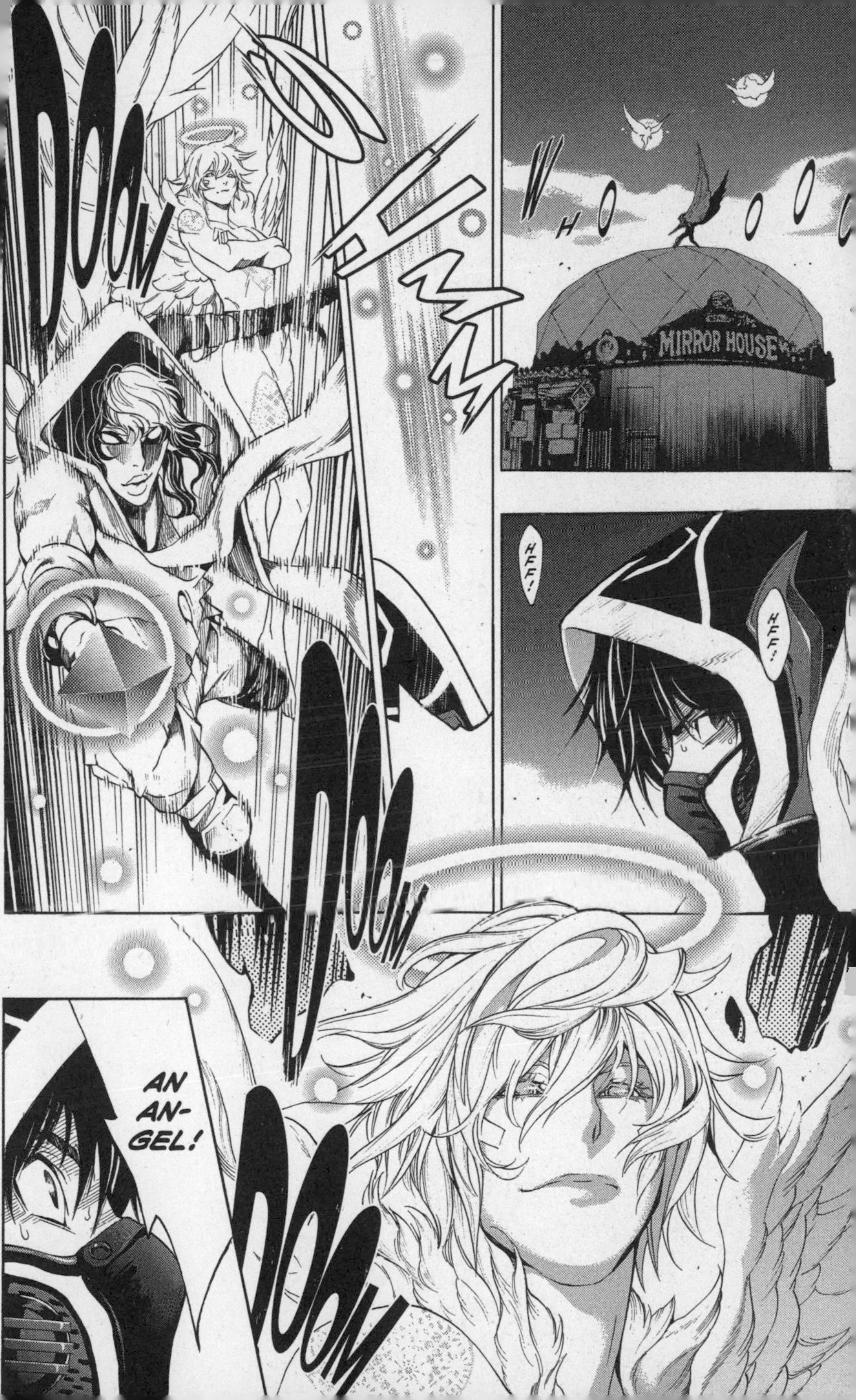
WHOOOO
MIRROR HOUSE
HFF!
HFF!
DOOM
WHMM
DOOM
DOOM
AN AN-GEL!

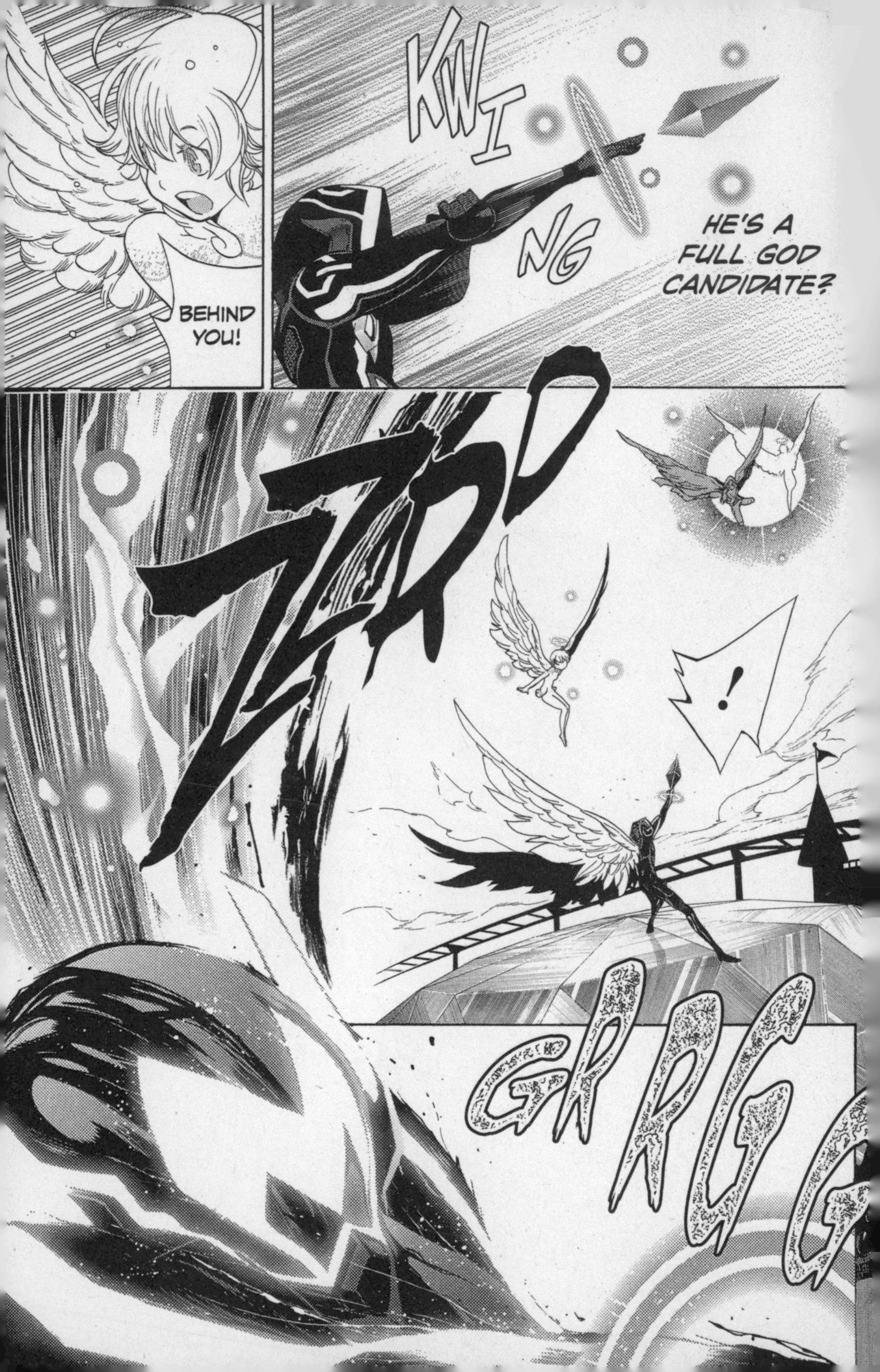
KWING
HE'S A FULL GOD CANDIDATE?
BEHIND YOU!
ZAP
!

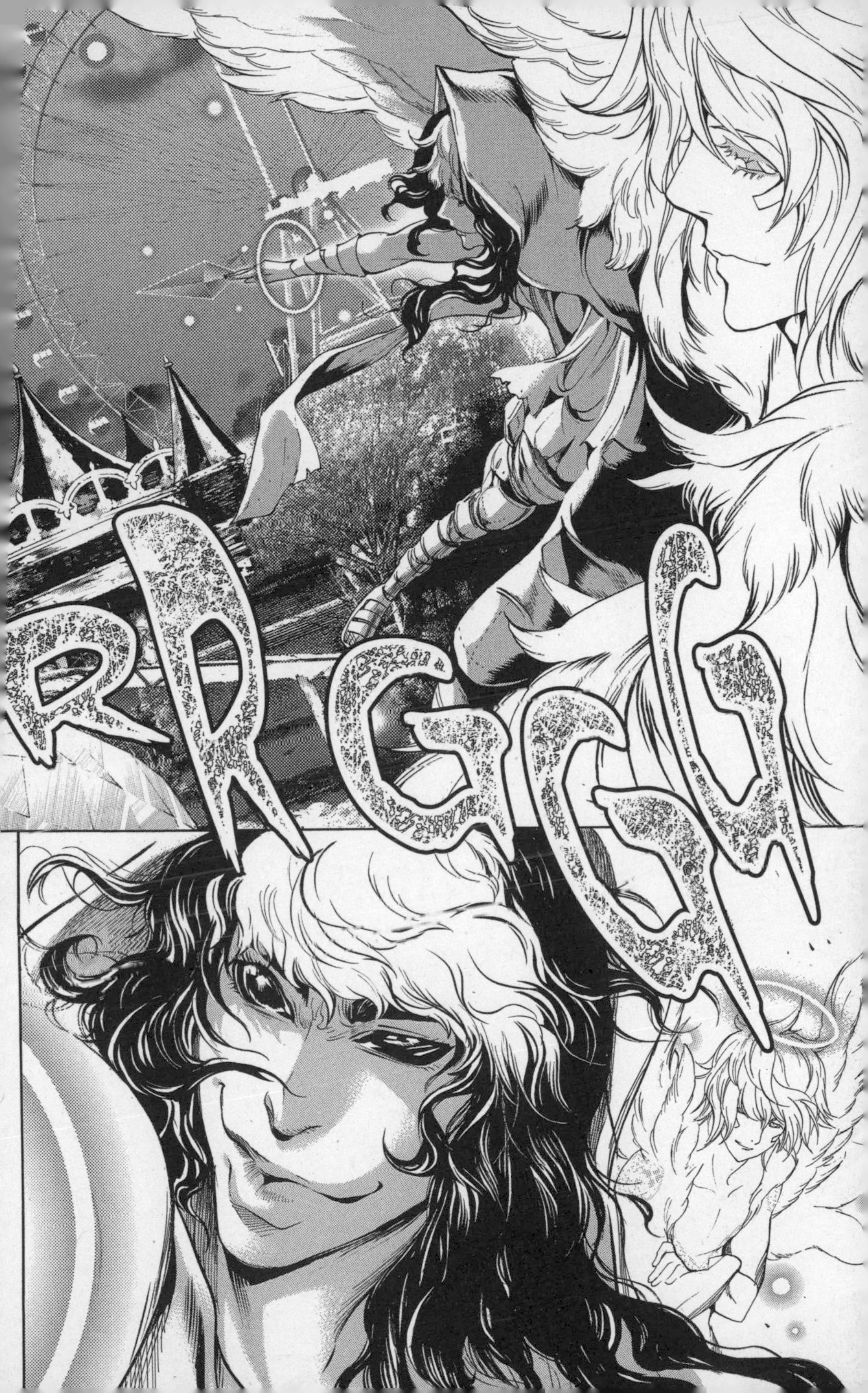
RRGGG

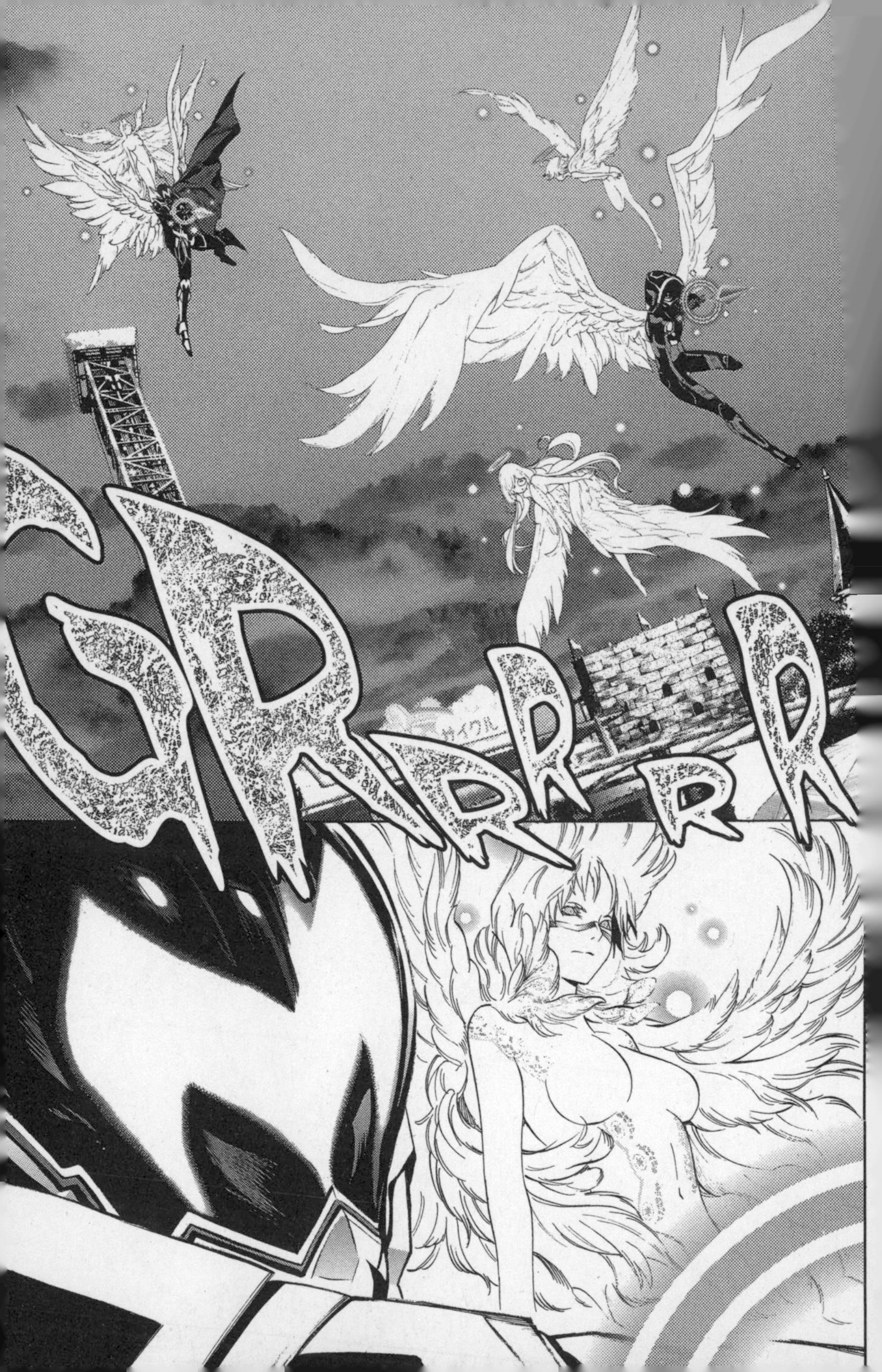
GRRRRR
サイクル

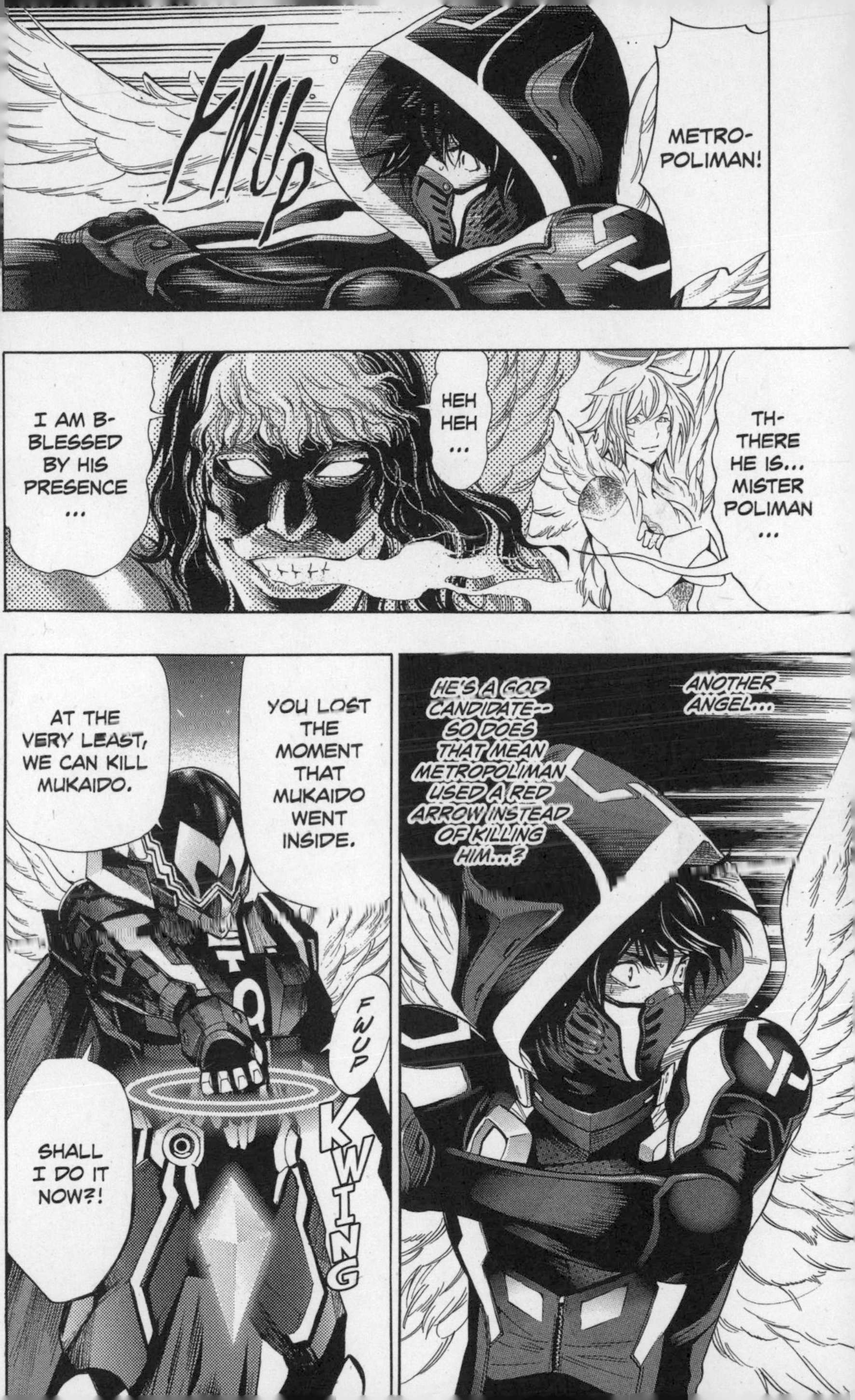
METRO-POLIMAN!
FWUP
TH-THERE HE IS... MISTER POLIMAN...
HEH HEH...
I AM B-BLESSED BY HIS PRESENCE...
ANOTHER ANGEL...
HE'S A GOD CANDIDATE--SO DOES THAT MEAN METROPOLIMAN USED A RED ARROW INSTEAD OF KILLING HIM...?
YOU LOST THE MOMENT THAT MUKAIDO WENT INSIDE.
AT THE VERY LEAST, WE CAN KILL MUKAIDO.
FWUP
KWING
SHALL I DO IT NOW?!

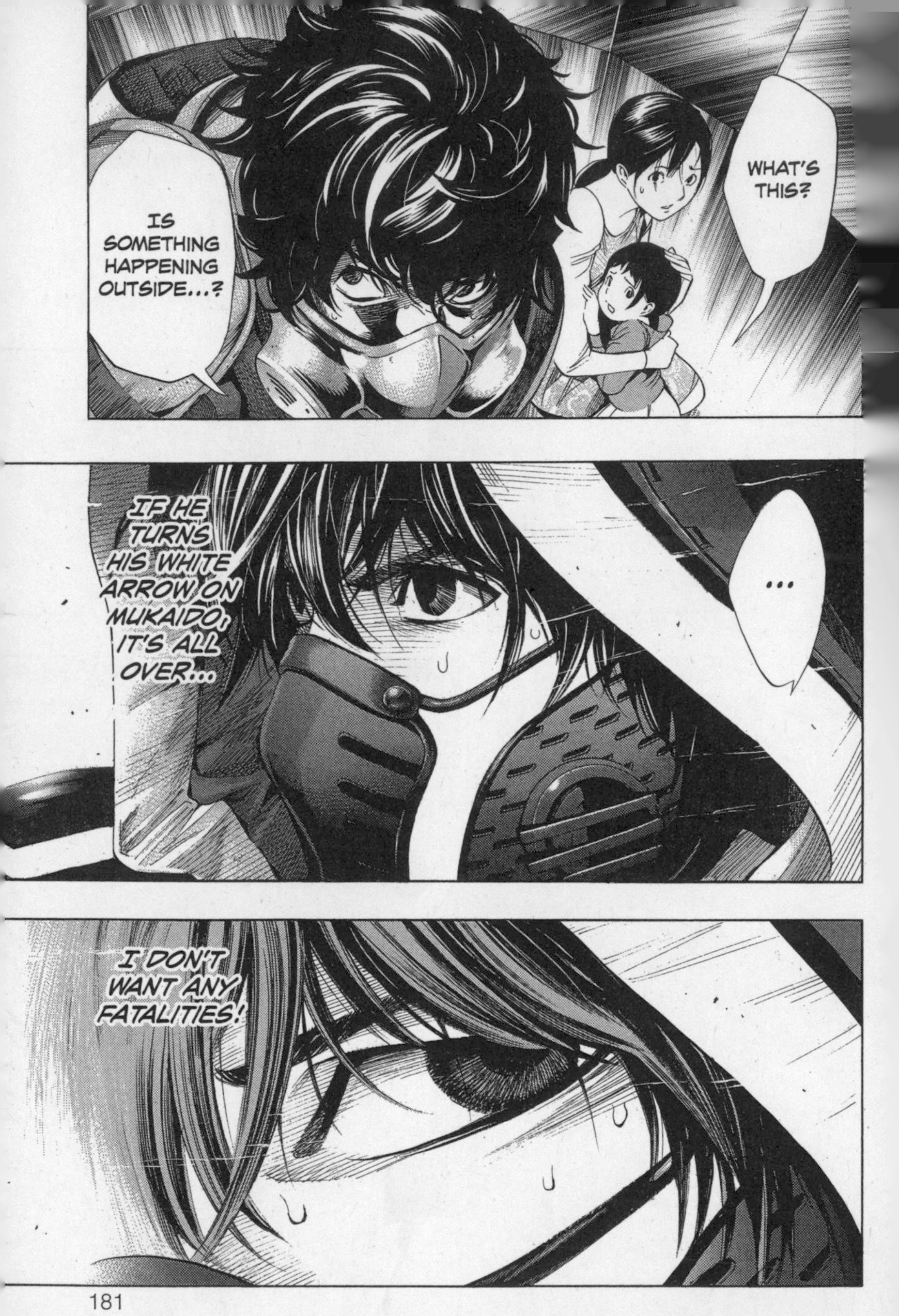
WHAT'S THIS?
IS SOMETHING HAPPENING OUTSIDE...?
...
IF HE TURNS HIS WHITE ARROW ON MUKAIDO, IT'S ALL OVER...
I DON'T WANT ANY FATALITIES!

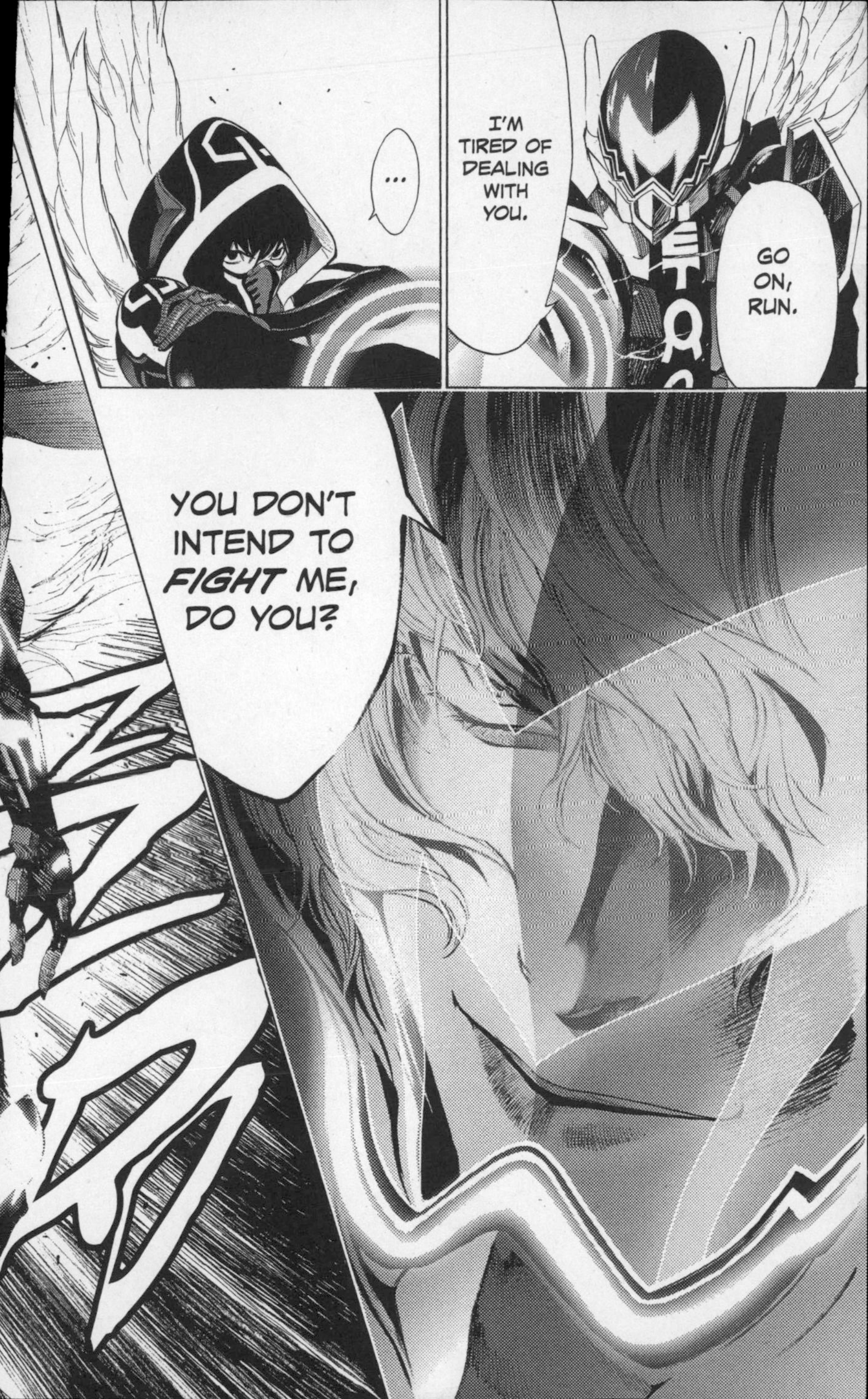
I'M TIRED OF DEALING WITH YOU.
GO ON, RUN.
...
YOU DON'T INTEND TO *FIGHT* ME, DO YOU?

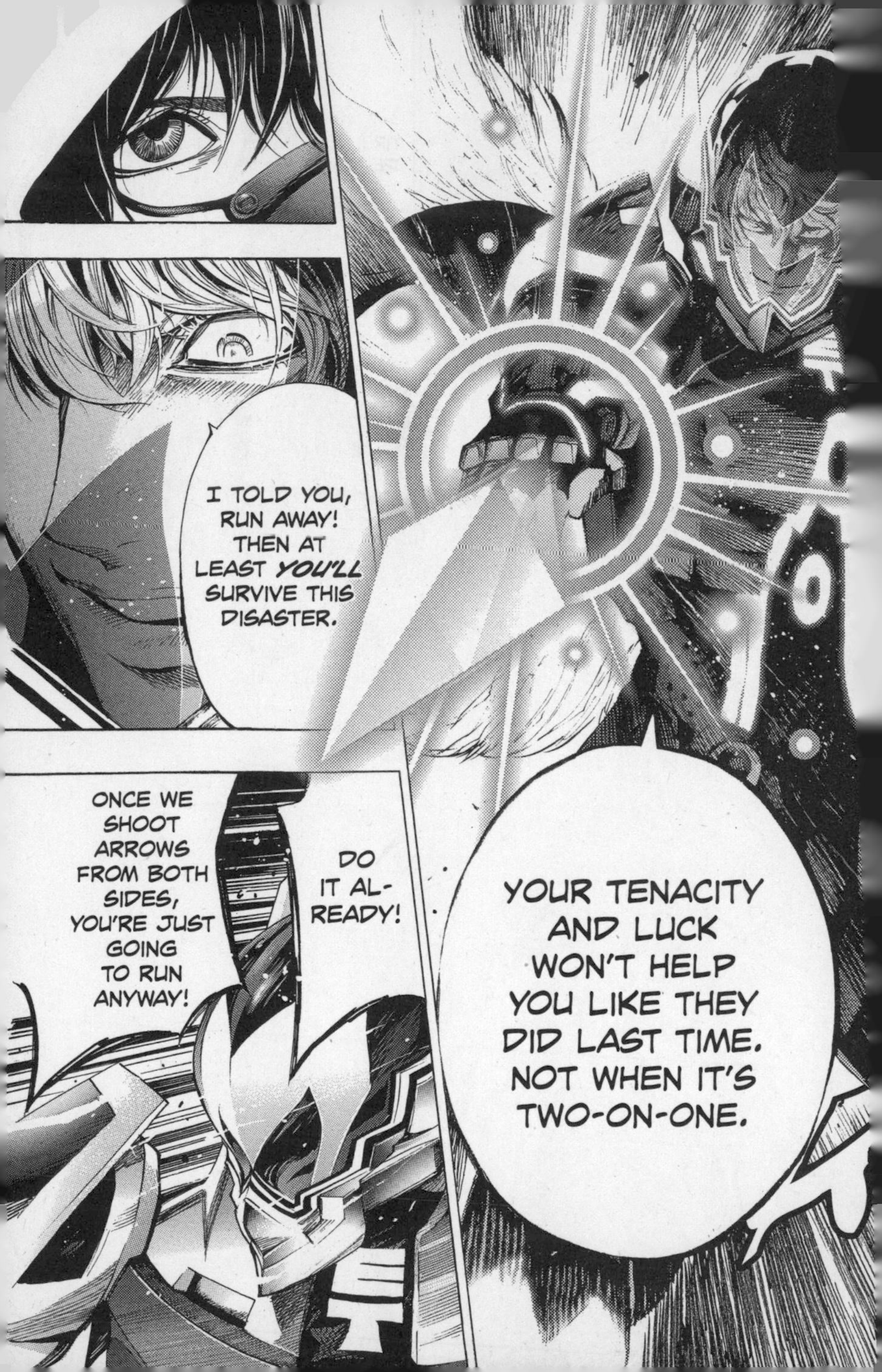
YOUR TENACITY AND LUCK WON'T HELP YOU LIKE THEY DID LAST TIME. NOT WHEN IT'S TWO-ON-ONE.
I TOLD YOU, RUN AWAY! THEN AT LEAST *YOU'LL* SURVIVE THIS DISASTER.
DO IT AL-READY!
ONCE WE SHOOT ARROWS FROM BOTH SIDES, YOU'RE JUST GOING TO RUN ANYWAY!

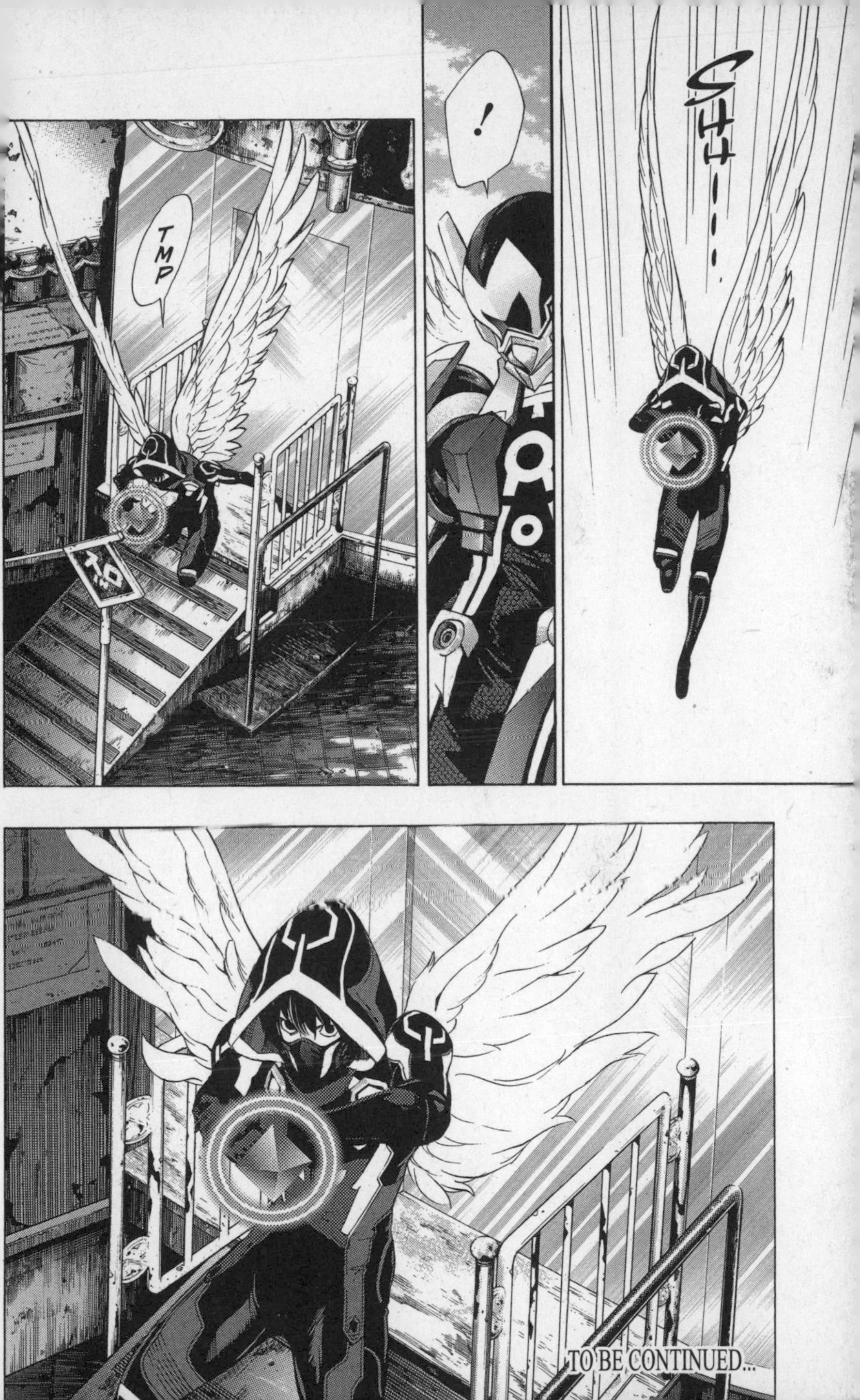
SHHH...
!
TMP
TO BE CONTINUED...

God candidates are chosen from among people who have lost their reason or will to live.

The tools an angel can give to a person depends on the angel's rank.
Special rank: Wings, red arrows, white arrows
First rank: Wings, red arrows
Second rank: Wings or red arrows

God is determined from among 13 human beings selected by 13 angels. The process shall take no more than 999 days.

Angels shall not use their own arrows and wings to directly affect god candidates.

The angel tools of deceased god candidates can be claimed and used by other candidates.

If angel tools are returned before a god is determined, the person who returned them shall die.

Angel tools from deceased god candidates can also be given to other human beings.

When a god is determined, the angel tools of the other candidates are forfeited.

Noncandidate human beings cannot see angel tools.

Angel wings can fly faster than the human eye can follow.

Wings can fly faster than arrows.

The speed of the wings is not affected by any amount of weight the user can carry unassisted. However, they cannot lift more than one extra person.

Angel arrows can strike any target with perfect accuracy, but only if the shooter can see the target.

Arrows cannot be fired while utilizing faster-than-sight wing flight.

Red arrows can pierce up to 14 people at one time.

Any person pierced by a red arrow will fall in love with the user for 33 days before the effect wears off.
The effect will only work on a specific person once.

When a person is under the effect of a red arrow, they cannot be pierced by other red arrows.

If the pierced person dies, that red arrow will be returned to its owner.

Any person pierced by a white arrow will die without fail.

Even a person under the effects of a red arrow may be unable to perform certain actions if lacking an adequate reason or intent to do them.

When a red arrow is used on another person possessing red arrows, they may be ordered to use those red arrows on the original shooter. In this case, the effect of the second arrow overrides the first.

T sugu mi **Oh** b **a**

Born in Tokyo, Tsugumi Ohba is the author of the hit series *Death Note* and *Bakuman。*.

Ta k e **s h** i Ob a **t**a

Takeshi Obata was born in 1969 in Niigata, Japan, and first achieved international recognition as the artist of the wildly popular *Shonen Jump* title *Hikaru no Go*, which won the 2003 Tezuka Osamu Cultural Prize: Shinsei "New Hope" Award and the 2000 Shogakukan Manga Award. He went on to illustrate the smash hit *Death Note* as well as the hugely successful manga *Bakuman。* and *All You Need Is Kill*.

PLATINVM END

VOLUME 5
SHONEN JUMP Manga Edition

o

STORY **Tsugumi Ohba**

ART **Takeshi Obata**

o

TRANSLATION Stephen Paul
TOUCH-UP ART & LETTERING James Gaubatz
DESIGN Shawn Carrico
EDITOR Alexis Kirsch

o

ORIGINAL COVER DESIGN Narumi Noriko

o

PLATINUM END © 2015 by Tsugumi Ohba, Takeshi Obata
All rights reserved.
First published in Japan in 2015 by SHUEISHA Inc., Tokyo.
English translation rights arranged by SHUEISHA Inc.

o

The stories, characters and incidents mentioned in this
publication are entirely fictional.

o

o

Printed in the U.S.A.

o

Published by VIZ Media, LLC
P.O. Box 77010
San Francisco, CA 94107

o

10 9 8 7 6 5 4 3 2 1
First printing, April 2018

www.viz.com   www.shonenjump.com

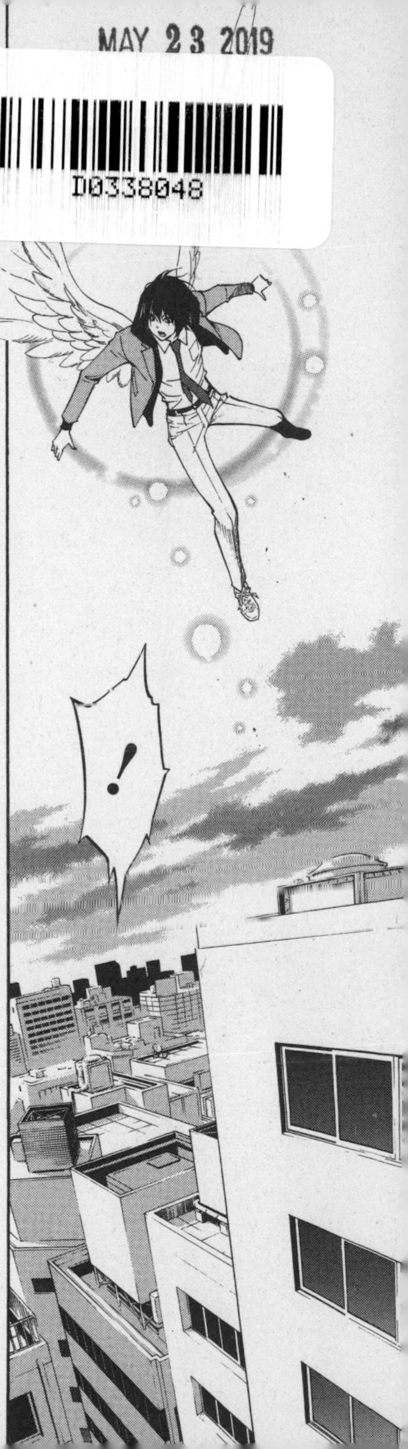
!

YOU'RE READING THE **WRONG WAY!**

PLATINUM END reads from right to left, starting in the upper-right corner. Japanese is read from right to left, meaning that action, sound effects and word-balloon order are completely reversed from English order.

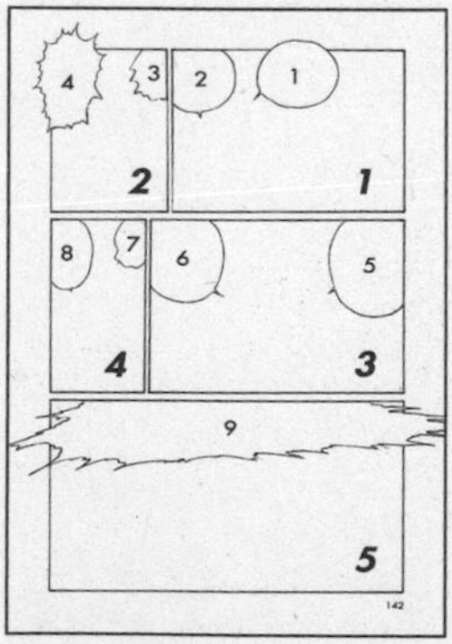
1
2
3
4
1
2
5
6
7
8
3
4
9
5